ONE SIGNAL
PUBLISHERS

ATRIA

Also by Jasper Craven

Our Veterans

God Forgives, Brothers Don't

The Long March of Military Education and the Making of American Manhood

Jasper Craven

ONE SIGNAL PUBLISHERS

ATRIA

New York   Amsterdam/Antwerp   London
Toronto   Sydney/Melbourne   New Delhi

ONE SIGNAL
PUBLISHERS

ATRIA

An Imprint of Simon & Schuster, LLC
1230 Avenue of the Americas
New York, NY 10020

First One Signal Publishers/Atria Books hardcover edition May 2026

ONE SIGNAL PUBLISHERS/ATRIA BOOKS and colophon are registered trademarks of Simon & Schuster, LLC

Simon & Schuster strongly believes in freedom of expression and stands against censorship in all its forms. For more information, visit BooksBelong.com.

For information about special discounts for bulk purchases, please contact Simon & Schuster Special Sales at 1-866-506-1949 or business@simonandschuster.com.

The Simon & Schuster Speakers Bureau can bring authors to your live event. For more information or to book an event, contact the Simon & Schuster Speakers Bureau at 1-866-248-3049 or visit our website at www.simonspeakers.com.

Interior design by Janet Evans-Scanlon

Manufactured in the United States of America

1 3 5 7 9 10 8 6 4 2

Library of Congress Control Number: 2026933579

ISBN 978-1-6680-8719-0
ISBN 978-1-6680-8721-3 (ebook)

Scan here to get book recommendations, exclusive offers, and more delivered to your inbox.

To my dad, who taught me how to wage peace

[God's] most dreaded instrument,
In working out a pure intent,
Is Man, arrayed for mutual slaughter,
Yea, Carnage is his daughter!

—William Wordsworth

Contents

Introduction

Illiberal Arts

In September 2025, I received word from a trusted source that Valley Forge Military Academy was closing after ninety-eight years. The place had been founded by a lieutenant general on an old-school promise, but one with seemingly endless appeal: "Send us your boy and we will return to you a man."

Since the dawn of America, the military has articulated some version of this pledge, solidly staking its claim on the monumental work of building the American man. While the military's masculine archetype was formed inside the wire, it went mainstream long ago, evident by a dizzying array of cultural tokens, from war movies and toy soldiers to cargo pants, Boy Scouts, bodybuilding, and the Hummer. Military principles have infused countless parenting books and informed self-help gurus across the political spectrum. Conservative Missouri senator Josh Hawley's 2023 book, *Manhood: The Masculine Values America Needs*, explicitly romanticizes the warrior archetype, arguing that "men are part of God's solution to danger in the world." Liberal alpha-bro podcaster Scott Galloway similarly argues in his 2025 book *Notes on Being a Man* that proper masculinity involves "acting as if you are wearing military fatigues, recognizing that a core reason you are here is to protect yourself, your partner, your family, and your country."

America is today in general agreement around certain precepts that all men should aspire to, among them strength, discipline, and self-sacrifice. On close inspection, however, it becomes abundantly clear that these traits are calibrated to enhance the aims of the military state, not the man. In truth, each tenet has nuggets worth living by. But as broadly interpreted today, these characteristics fuel stoicism, self-destructiveness, and nihilism, forming an outlook that is beneficial for cold battlefield environments but not at all equipped to handle the emotional complexities of civilian life. John Wheeler, a 1966 West Point graduate, aptly articulated this corrosive worldview, explaining that his commitment to the Army revolved around his belief that there are "things worth dying for." This distinctly masculine outlook, Wheeler reasoned, inverts a more optimistic, feminine-coded belief that "there are things worth living for."

I first heard about "the Forge," as insiders call it, in late 2020, when a group of concerned parents reached out and told me the place was falling apart. "We, the parents, paid for a product, we were promised a product," Scott Newell, a former parent and alumnus, told me back then. "And then they switched the product out and turned it into bullshit."

For much of its history, the Forge resembled a patriotic paradise. Cadets ranging in age from twelve to twenty-one aimed to build their bodies and sharpen their minds on a verdant, hundred-acre campus located on the outskirts of Philadelphia. Now, in Newell's eyes, the school was enabling the kind of masculine dysfunction it promised to prevent. "We have an entire generation in this country that has failed miserably at character and leadership and honor and integrity. And now I'm going to get choked up and cry," he said, not a lick of emotion tingeing his voice, "because that's all the stuff you learn at military academies like Valley Forge."

When I first dug into the Forge, I discovered an acrid strain of masculinity that was raw, violent, fiercely hierarchical, and quickly mutating out of control. I uncovered stories of vicious beatings, brutal rapes, predatory grooming, and widespread racism and misogyny. I was told about incidents of waterboarding, whippings, brandings with scalding forks, forced piercings, even horse abuse. These boys of the Forge were hurting, but had only learned how to hurt.

During the previous four academic years, local police had responded more than three hundred times to incidents on campus, including for cadets as young as thirteen experiencing psychiatric crises and demonstrating suicidal behavior. In the spring of 2016, a promising eighteen-year-old cadet named Carey Lecamp killed himself in his dorm room.

Most shocking, perhaps, was the behavior of the men in charge, who showed not only willful ignorance of this culture, but active complicity in it. They retaliated against boys who spoke out, fixed grades to burnish the school's reputation, and padded their own pockets. Some were also violent.

In 2023, not long after my investigation into the Forge was published in *Mother Jones*, its Board of Trustees voted to funnel their dwindling resources and institutional energy not into addressing cadet abuse, but instead to build "Crossed Sabres," a palatial farmhouse-style residence worth $1.7 million for academy president colonel Stuart B. Helgeson and his wife, Stephanie, to use, free of charge. The board also hired Mrs. Helgeson, a former insurance representative, as the school's chief development officer. As a flurry of former cadets filed lawsuits alleging long-lasting trauma from their time at the Forge, Helgeson took aim at the school's public critics, whom, he alleged, were "weakening the brand."

While the military's conception of masculinity has thoroughly leaked into America's cultural groundwater, it initially appeared to me that well would soon run dry. In recent years, a slew of military schools have shut their doors, including Howe Military Academy, in Indiana, which closed in 2019 after 135 years due to budget shortfalls and dwindling enrollment. A few years later, a Georgia military academy closed suddenly following a series of massive, gang-related brawls among cadets, where numerous shanks and improvised weapons were found. Then another academy, this one in Wyoming, went dark without notice.

In 2010, the New York Military Academy nearly closed. A band of school officials traveled to Manhattan to plead for a bailout from the academy's most famous alumnus, Donald J. Trump. According to two attendees of the meeting, Trump became visibly irritated after a rogue parent pitched an ambitious $50 million plan to build a hotel at the academy, along with a junior college. Then an alumnus spilled a Diet Coke on Trump's flashy carpet. "[Trump] was quite pissed off," one of the attendees recalled. "And then Miss America came into the meeting and distracted everybody. And that was the end of the meeting." While it looked for a moment as if Trump's alma mater might shutter forever, it was purchased by figures allegedly connected to the Chinese Communist Party for a cool $16 million. They run the school to this day.

The Forge's military high school closed, but its junior college remains open, as of this writing, and officials have announced plans to spin off the old high school into a charter. The Forge has further fortified its future through a training partnership with the Pennsylvania National Guard, plus an NSA-certified cybersecurity program and a gestating drone-pilot initiative. In October 2025, the Forge became the first signatory to President

Trump's "Compact for Higher Education Excellence," which demands, among other things, that participants ban affirmative action and crack down on programs that "punish, belittle" or "spark violence against conservative ideas." Three months later, in January 2026, the feds issued a $1 million grant to the Forge. It tasked the troubled academy with developing accreditation standards for military schools across America.

The Forge has also exported its brand overseas through a satellite campus in Qatar that imposes its punitive practices on an even younger cohort—elementary school kids—a sign that, even after perilous battlefield defeats in the Middle East, the image of the upstanding American military officer remains attractive on the world stage.

The deeper I have looked, the more evidence I have discovered that military education is not a dying, outmoded brand, but a generously resourced, always-and-forever force in shaping the American man. Its resilient influence is evident by the dozens of military schools dotting the American landscape and by the powerful institutions that alumni control. Four U.S. presidents, including Trump, have attended military schools, as have a handful of Fortune 500 CEOs, dozens of lawmakers, and top figures in the Defense Department, America's largest employer.

AMERICAN MASCULINITY IS PREDICATED on the wobbly assumption that man is violent by nature. In a 2025 speech before every senior American defense official, Trump's self-styled "Secretary of War" Pete Hegseth passionately defended this premise and derided pacifism as "naive and dangerous."

"It ignores human nature and it ignores human history," Hegseth argued. "Either you protect your people and your sovereignty, or you will be subservient to something or someone. It's a truth as old as time."

Hegseth has some history in his back pocket, but not much science. Men have fought many wars, that is true, but those leading them have never relied on innate aggression to naturally show itself. Rather, they have cultivated violence, often in closed and highly controlled educational environments. And often for years.

Since America's founding, military brass have painstakingly developed and refined a military curriculum that breeds loyalty, teaches obedience, and constructs violence, all the while convincing the public that conflict is a hardwired male instinct. One early West Point superintendent briefly let this assertion slip when he acknowledged that a cadet's "cruel" and "brutal" behavior is not "inbred," and, in fact, could be "absolutely eradicated." But it never has been.

Instead, the military's muscular masculine archetype has become one of America's most coveted assets. Like warfare itself, it is ever evolving. A diluted form of military manliness can be replicated in the civilian world, though it is always a clear knockoff. It lacks the high-and-tight haircut, the posture, the gaze, the mythic war stories of conquest, destruction, and dominance. Those who secure the genuine article make a devil's bargain. As sociologist Ramon Hinojosa writes, "the irony is that by accessing the resources of the military to construct a hegemonic masculinity, [men] will be subordinated and/or marginalized." The male military identity is ultimately false, and fleeting, for it is meted out in small doses by men in power, who, for institutional purposes, always withhold unconditional acceptance. Military masculinity is unsustainable. Real self-actualization is never achieved.

Many men nonetheless fight their way to the top of the military hierarchy. Some do so by toeing the line. Others become intoxicated by the obligatory respect and conditional salvation that their status confers. Some live with shame about the things they had to do to get there. Many in this latter group come to see the tragic fact at the heart of the military system: the military does not make them stronger; it alters and degrades them, sometimes forever.

Far before they see the front lines of battle, many cadets are diagnosed with PTSD, a condition that represents a powerful rejoinder to the assertion that violence is natural. If the human propensity for violence is innate, then it wouldn't create such persistent pain and mental turmoil in its wake. The mother of one cadet I met saw her boy transform from a warm and idealistic schoolboy into a withdrawn adult who drinks to excess and sleeps with a hunting knife under his pillow. Other cadets told me they go to bed with weapons in close proximity, or, decades after graduation, remain wracked by nightmares and anxiety stemming from their time on campus. During one recent "Hell Week" initiation for first-years at Virginia Military Institute, a lonely so-called "rat" in the mess hall responded to a superior's verbal lashing by smashing his face repeatedly on a table, a bloody mental break that got him sent home. "It took a football player to stop him," one of his classmates told me. "It was pretty gruesome." Another cadet sued the Missouri Military Academy in 2022 after allegedly facing weekly beatings so bad he attempted suicide while on break in hopes of forever forestalling his return.

Military academies long welcomed only white males. Today, this is no longer the case. The outsiders who integrated this system powerfully challenged the military's established masculine order. They experienced additional layers of hell. Kris Fuhr, one of West Point's early female cadets, has screamed bloody murder in her sleep every night since facing a slew of grotesque abuse as a seventeen-year-old plebe nearly five decades ago. "You can't be tortured for a whole fucking year and go through what we went through and not have that," she told me.

While the military does not publicly track suicides at its schools, many youngsters have been ground down to the point of seeking self-annihilation. During the summer of 1976, one West Point colonel cavalierly acknowledged to parents the brutality of these conditions. "Your kids are going to get depressed," he announced. "We usually get eight or nine suicide attempts the first year—cadets drink rifle oil, eat too many aspirins. So, it's critical for the new cadets to feel that they're doing well." How the colonel's directive squared with the steady parade of insults and devaluation these first-year "plebes" were about to endure was not entirely clear, though it seems the colonel assumed that families would shoulder the emotional load.

THE PENTAGON HAS ALWAYS UNDERSTOOD the profound impact of schooling on shaping society. Our learning system affects politics, influences the economy, interprets history, commissions research, and, most broadly, facilitates growth, from child to adult. Understanding this, the military has secured a prominent place for itself in academia—establishing five service academies, like West Point, plus various war colleges, a combat studies institute, a defense university, and a national intelligence university. These institutions have, in turn, seeded scientific journals, publishing houses, and academic awards. The military also oversees 5,200 ROTC programs in public colleges and high schools, and supports state-run, religiously chartered, and private military schools, like the Forge. These schools rear the elite military officer class; though lower down the ranks, enlisted troops are exposed to an abridged military education, too, via boot camp, which provides its own kind of schooling. That's why basic training concludes with a commencement ceremony of sorts, wherein friends and family members show up, beaming in their Sunday best and snapping congratulatory photos to celebrate the making of a boy into a troop.

The Pentagon's reach extends to even younger populations, too, in programs that appear innocuous, like the Boy Scouts or the Young Marines, and into civilian colleges and universities by way of hefty research grants. Between 2014 and 2024, Johns Hopkins University, as one example, received more than twice as much money from the Defense Department as it did in tuition.

Most American men receive some form of military conditioning, even if it isn't through official channels. Often it is inculcated through cultural osmosis—via fashion, literature, film—or passed intergenerationally through blood. While only a small slice of American men today have served in the armed forces, many have at least one relative in their family tree with a service record, and, perhaps, some psychic scars to show for it. Up until very recently, warfare has been man's defining vocation, with nearly 30 percent of all American men fighting for Uncle Sam during World War II. These sweeping levels of participation, calculated alongside service rates in other American conflicts, suggests that the military has altered the American man on a genomic level.

THE PENTAGON LIKES TO FRAME its training methods as peer-reviewed and pedagogical, a claim bolstered by its well-appointed military schools and their trappings, from grassy quads and student centers, to grades, academic robes, and degrees. All this has elevated, distinguished, and validated the world's most brutal profession, making bloodshed scientific and deriving an "art" of war.

But there is not much real art on these campuses, only black-and-white binaries. The creative ambiguities in the humanities get short shrift, in favor of math, science, and engineering—a trend now truer than ever as the service academies purge civilian professors and gut their already meek liberal arts offerings. This campaign is motivated by a new brashness among the brass to dispense with the pomp and circumstance of military society and noblesse oblige in favor of a brutal admission: that after all is said and done, the generals need bodies, not souls, pliant soldiers not creative minds or questioning individuals.

Just as the gauntlet of Greek Life at civilian colleges and universities rewards pledges through its chummy alumni networks of money men and corporate executives, military schools provide entrée to exclusive government corridors. There may be no immediate financial payoff within this world, but members gain access to something just as intoxicating: power.

Power is the true nucleus of these military environments, an indoctrination tool serving as both reward and punishment. Force and control are dangerous, cadets are told, but they can be channeled for noble aims. Many of the cadets I spoke to didn't enter these schools seeking power. Many had previously faced bullying, family strife, economic insecurity, or other antagonistic conditions. What they truly sought was armor, not weapons.

Once they enter the system, however, these young aspirants are cultivated to want power. That is because they find themselves in an atmosphere of insecurity that is most easily remedied through force. The best way to secure a modicum of peace is by climbing to the top of the hierarchy within the corps of cadets. At West Point and other military schools, the first year cadets at the bottom are called "plebes," or commoners. At the Air Force Academy, they're known as "doolies," which apparently stems from the Greek word *doulos*, meaning slave. At the Virginia Military Institute, they're labeled "rats." The only way to move up is by following the rules and targeting the weakest links. This structure is clarifying, for it suggests that the military does not tease out latent aggression—it breeds it.

MANY SERVICE MEMBERS RESIST THE MILITARY'S EFFORTS to capture their minds. Some snap out of it early, rebel against it late, or never believe to begin with. But there are also men who lose themselves entirely. Those who become reflexively pro-military should not be seen as weak or gullible. Many entered the field with a child's mind: malleable, optimistic, and a bit reckless.

It is no mistake that the troops serving on the front lines are called the *infant*-ry, or that the military school rank of "cadet" translates in French to "youngest child." War may be commonly described as a man's game, but it's boys who have long fed and fueled the whole enterprise. George Washington's Continental Army featured troops as young as fourteen, while the Civil War had more than 200,000 soldiers under eighteen. In its earliest form, West Point trained cadets as young as ten.

The military seeks young people not because they are the most physically adept, but because they are the most emotionally vulnerable. One study found that military cadets are often characterized by their sharp sensitivity, strong impressionability, and increased emotionality. For these young people, "each success provokes great delight, and a mistake or failure—deep concern and self-dissatisfaction." Another 1975 paper showed how the military reshapes boys through three interlocking components: "the acceptance of psychological control, the equation of masculine identity with military performance, and the infusion of raw aggression into the entire military mission."

Modern enlistment age in America was initially set at twenty-one, then pushed down to eighteen, then seventeen with a parent's permission, where it stands today. The average enlistment age today is nineteen. These are adults in the government's eyes, but many remain fundamentally innocent, years away from fully developed brains. Many are dreamers, some are virgins. Few have had a real job or lived outside of their parents' house. The few who harbor violent tendencies at this age generally have a history that's led to it.

Many boys who join share a tragic and misguided rejection of their youth and are impatient to become men—a transformation the military is happy to facilitate. It hastens their growth through heavy doses of pain and stress, often frontloaded in the early days of training, or in the first academic year. Some who make it through proudly refer to themselves, and each other, as "old men." Military schooling, or training, precludes natural, more complex versions of manhood from sprouting. What forms in its place is something strange and uncanny: a child's face extinguished of youth and its accompanying traits, like sweetness, empathy, imagination, and whimsy.

Beyond the military's promise of manhood is the interrelated assurance of bringing meaning to life. The military understands children's dreams, aspirations, and anxieties, and it promises to give them what they need, whether it's status, money, schooling, family, or just a place to escape. It pledges to wipe away an existing identity, and that's often exactly what people want—the chance to reinvent themselves in a new world. Marine general Charles Krulak once testified proudly to the transformative potential of the service via one of his economically disadvantaged recruits, who, after emerging victorious from the crucible of training, cried out "I am somebody!"

Many are looking for direction, community, or the chance to give back. The military provides synthetic versions of these things, ones formed through classical tools of indoctrination. What materializes is not an enlivening mission, but a dehumanizing one, a bait and switch perfectly articulated through the Freudian slip of a recent West Point graduate who told me he applied to the academy because, "I've always been interested in servitude."

Cadets and recruits alike are placed in environments of isolation, exhaustion, friction, and hierarchy. They are cut off from friends, family, and lovers, and told to make new ones. They are given new haircuts, new diets, new clothes. They are also exposed to new ideas, which are literally drilled into them.

Much like war itself, their training experiences are marked by sharp contrasts, highs and lows, hate and love, comedy and tragedy. Some cadets benefit from order, and through the academies' call to shared sacrifice, they develop a powerful sense of belonging. Others graduate broken or feeling ostracized. Some try to escape. Others die. Many find father figures or make lifelong friendships, including, at times, with kids who have hurt them. There is intense and intentional trauma bonding at these places, part of the military's drive to build friendship and loyalty via shared moments of intense agitation. All of this serves to ensure that soldiers disgorged onto the barren fields of combat stay dependable and connected—through their commitment to each other more than to any politics motivating the conflict.

All who survive training, or make it through military school, are held up as paragons of their communities. They are celebrated in school assemblies and American Legion events, their names and faces plastered across pages of the local paper. (Today, they can also board commercial airplanes early.) In many cases, the military will dictate how they live the rest of their lives. Faceless leaders will send troops out on foreign deployments and assign them new communities. This will influence whom they marry, how they vote, when they die. Etched on many of their gravestones will be little else than their name and service record.

The military's air of honor and exclusivity is held up through savvy PR and sloganeering—"the few, the proud"—plus the service academy system, which bills itself as the blood brother of the Ivy League. This elitism is also upheld through intolerance. The military was, and is, a bastion of white male conservatism, largely populated by people who covet the bestowal of a masculinity that does not countenance female strength, nor queer peers or those of color.

While the list of military school alumni boasts some of the world's most powerful people, the brass always needs bodies. They have, as such, turned to less-than-reputable sources, including military-style reform schools packed with troubled teens. The resulting class of men and women leading enlisted troops into battle includes Rhodes Scholars and former juvenile defendants.

This wide spectrum clarifies the historical dearth of options for American men, and also the failure of the American educational system to provide for those in need. The military schooling system is, in addition to everything else, a catch-all system for kids with unaddressed emotional needs and learning problems. In 1916, when the military lobbied hard to create compulsory military education, a New York City public school official named James Mackenzie powerfully asserted that the military simply isn't the answer to every child's problems. "If American boys lack discipline, by all means, let us supply it," he told *The New York Times*. "But not through training whose avowed aim is human slaughter."

Many embrace alternative paths when they are offered. Countless civilian students find interests and vocations they love in school, and some manage to pursue them, especially if they have mentorship and, increasingly, means. But there are few and dwindling paths into other forms of public service, few purely peaceful avenues to defend the nation or show strength.

When an anti-war movement sprouted during Vietnam, millions rushed to the cause, providing not only a direct threat to the Pentagon's immediate aims, but also an alternative path to meaning. Oddly enough, my own father, anxious to escape his turbulent family life, flirted with ROTC and, before that, military school as a youth—Valley Forge, in fact. But after attending a pacifist Quaker school, and finding a father figure at Boston University in Howard Zinn, he ended up a leader in the anti-war movement during Vietnam. My dad could just have easily become a hard-boiled colonel, but there was another option available to him, and he took it.

The peace movement my dad joined offered an alternative model for manhood. This helps explain the verve with which the military moved to violently shut it down. Since Vietnam, the military has continued to work to maintain its grasp on our perceptions and practices of manhood and to cast any countercultural forces as weak and effeminate. Over this same period, American society has mentored and championed girls in ways that have created new and transformational opportunities that redefine what it means to emerge into womanhood.

In the absence of fresh meanings and directions for men, our military's violence-affirming ideologies powerfully persist, animating unnecessary conflicts and overtaking America's masculine ideas. This is now spawning radical, revanchist, and vengeful undercurrents among soldiers and civilians alike.

Yet despite mounting evidence, Pentagon officials and other government leaders have failed to step in, and in some cases are actively obscuring problems, sometimes even feeding them. Today, the facts are clearer than ever: military schooling is an increasingly dubious and, when poorly overseen, potentially dangerous form of teaching, one that has spawned polarization, male isolation and frustration, and a child abuse crisis hiding in plain sight. It's also utterly ineffective at winning wars. And yet it nonetheless continues to be broadly and blindly declared as essential, even as credible voices raise alarms.

THIS BOOK FOLLOWS THE FOUNDATION, development, and dysfunction of the military education system through the voices of people who have lived through it. The reason to focus here is not simply due to the unique role of military schools in grooming the top talent that fights America's wars—though that is important and helps explain the last half century of military failures. Rather, these schools offer the clearest view into the stubborn influence and overall emptiness of military ideology, the cruelty of military training and masculinity, and the entire institution's reliance on schoolchildren. By tracing cadets' hopes and dreams, their wounds and regrets, and, in some cases, their grotesque transformations, one can see how the military's coercive, even cultish, curriculum takes hold—and, hopefully, how to provide America's children with an alternative path toward peace, and a natural, more tender form of masculinity.

The Founding Father

Many big ideas animated the American Revolution, but the rebellion itself was sparked by the indignities of life in a militarized state. In the fall of 1768, as the British crown imposed new laws and taxes on the American colonies, King George III called on an increasing number of troops, sailors, and spies to enforce his dictates and suppress any objections from his subjects.

The largest contingent of redcoats—a force numbering roughly one thousand—was deployed to the particularly nettlesome city of Boston. Colonists there retaliated against their military occupiers by stalking them, hissing at them, and dressing them down as "bloody-back thieving dogs" and "damned rascally scoundrel lobster sons of bitches." Some pelted troops with whatever was close at hand: stones, mud, oyster shell fragments, snowballs, even pieces of brick.

Others articulated their grievances in "The Journal of Occurrences," an anonymous, syndicated news column that chronicled a slew of alleged redcoat misdeeds against Bostonians. The first dispatch, from December 1768, tells of troops who seized a doctor "by the collar" and aggressively questioned him, as well as a woman they treated "with great rudeness." The column also alleged more disturbing behavior, including rape and assault. Tensions reached a boiling point in 1770 with the "Boston Massacre," in which nine British soldiers shot indiscriminately into a large crowd that was harassing them, killing five. Many subsequently came to view standing armies as intrinsically corrupt and irredeemable, "nurseries of vice," they alleged, and "the grand engine of despotism."

The Founding Fathers similarly viewed troops as the crucial predicate for government oppression. John Hancock, then a lawmaker in Massachusetts, inveighed against the "vile assassins" the Crown had sent to Boston, while Samuel Adams argued in a newspaper column that "no man can pretend to say that peace and good order of the community is so secure with soldiers quartered in the body of a city as without them." As fragments of a new government framework started to materialize, James Madison argued that "oppressors can tyrannize only when they achieve a standing army, an enslaved press, and a disarmed populace."

While George Washington had technically served under the Crown as a young major in the Virginia militia during the French and Indian War, he found the experience thoroughly emasculating. He once vented privately about his second-class status, in which bona fide British officers with a lower rank than him were still able to boss him around. Washington also alleged that British troops were paid nearly twice as much as colonial ones, even though, he dramatically insisted, "we must undergo double their hardship."

The Declaration of Independence, which formally launched the American Revolutionary War, lists among its major objections the Crown's attempts to create a military "independent of and superior to civil power." It further offered a bold vision for a new country, one marked by peace, equality, and happiness, where civilians always had the upper hand.

The insurrection that would create the American state was launched from this high moral ground, which, as quickly became clear, was not a particularly tactical one. The Continental Army was ad hoc and clumsy, composed of citizen soldiers up against an empire stocked with thousands of well-trained troops, sailors, and mercenaries. Their martial inadequacies quickly led to a series of stinging setbacks. These losses, and the ragged forces who lost them, would come to haunt the American psyche, and incite a great paradox: a country born with a bone-deep distrust of standing armies would transform itself into the most militarized empire in the world.

THE SEEDS OF THE AMERICAN MILITARY INDUSTRIAL COMPLEX first took root in the fine glacial soil of Upstate New York, specifically in a place Washington had deemed America's most strategically important military fort: West Point. The post was built on a windy bluff high above the Hudson River, a body of water that was at once a key asset and major vulnerability. The river provided a vital channel for transporting troops, supplies, and intelligence among colonial territories on its east and west banks. But the crown controlled the river's mouth—New York Harbor—and British forces repeatedly tried to stake their claim higher up the Hudson.

West Point stands sixty miles north of Manhattan, at a perfect defensive attack point. Currents here are strong and the river becomes perilously narrow, forming a rough "S" that forces big ships to steer carefully, and slow down. Stationed above the drink during the war were colonial soldiers and a long line of cannons. West Point also featured a thick iron-link chain that could be stretched from bank to bank as a final foolproof buffer.

One military historian grandly summed up the bucolic complex as one where "death and beauty intermingle" to form an atmosphere where cadets can't help but "fall into romantic communion with the ideals of self-sacrifice and love of country." One alumnus from the post-9/11 era described it more cynically as a "place constantly at war with the serenity of its natural surroundings," less a castle of integrity and more "Imperial Death Star from *Star Wars* after a public relations makeover." West Point is brimming with paradox and endlessly tense over its conflicting ideals, chief of which is its self-conceived identity as both a rigorous military training post and an elite liberal arts college. These opposing descriptions led one pair of former professors to deem the place a "schizophrenic institution."

In West Point's infancy, America aimed to keep the post small lest it bloom into an unaccountable military tool of the state. General Washington, the physical embodiment of the colonies' war for independence, similarly aimed to curb his own influence and image lest the citizenry come to view him as a monarch. These twin efforts were easier said than done. From the beginning, Washington was romantically mythologized by loyal scribes and historians as a brutal and unyielding warrior, the "political saviour of our nation" who bravely "conducted the Americans' thro seas of blood." The figure he allegedly cut, and the triumphant war he allegedly waged, helped form America's foundational warrior archetype, and its closely related, ever-evolving masculine mold.

In his book *First Among Men*, Maurizio Valsania contrasts the nuances of Washington's masculinity with the reductive warrior archetype formed in its place. Among other things, Washington was hailed as "physically majestic" and "virile," with "nice quads" and "well developed thighs." Legend insists that he easily bested a champion wrestler thanks to his "lion-like" grasp, and that, from his home at Mount Vernon, he could hurl a silver dollar across the Potomac River.

In his vainer moments, Washington nourished this image, proudly declaring in one 1799 letter to the Delaware nation "I am a warrior." He further cast himself as preternaturally cool during combat in the French and Indian wars. "I heard bulletts [*sic*] whistle," he bragged in a letter to his brother, "and believe me there was something charming in the sound."

The truth was that Washington was a weak, strange-looking fellow, born with a small head and sunken eyes. His arms were thin, his chest was indented, and he had a belly. Tuberculosis had weakened his lungs, and, when the war commenced, he had lingering smallpox scars. The legend of the silver dollar was particularly implausible, as the width of the river at Mount Vernon runs nearly a mile. Plus, the silver dollar didn't even exist until a few years before Washington's death.

Certainly, Washington was capable of barbarism and violent dominance, having become a slaveowner at eleven, after his father died. He ordered lashes for traitors and sometimes killed dogs who followed his troops. But he was also prone to emotion, loved dancing and fashion, avoided red meat, and mostly ate vegetables. In addition, Washington respected peace. After pacifist Quakers were conscripted against their will into his army, with some having rifles tied tightly on their backs, Washington intervened, allowing the men to follow their principles and return home. This intervention helped lay the groundwork for the American military's recognition of conscientious objectors. At the same time, though, Washington's virile demeanor proved highly influential, inducing countless generations of young American men to exaggerate their strength and ridicule the weaknesses of others.

Washington's mythical military manliness was most obviously undercut by his mixed record on the battlefield. Ahead of his appointment as commander of colonial forces, Washington had read a few military books, including Julius Caesar's *Commentaries*, a firsthand account of the Roman general's remarkable service in the Gallic Wars. But a year into his role, Washington admitted to lawmakers that he struggled with "limited and contracted knowledge" in the art of war. What his troops lacked in training, Washington hoped to make up in passion. To this end, he ordered they read *Common Sense*, Thomas Paine's impassioned plea for American independence.

But big ideas didn't protect against bullets, and Washington ultimately lost more battles than he won. Perhaps his most embarrassing defeat came in the fall of 1777, when he and his soldiers surrendered America's birthplace, Philadelphia, at the Battles of Brandywine and Germantown. These campaigns exposed the Army as the collection of community militias they were. Officers misinterpreted British movements, scouted battlefields poorly, and struggled to execute large-scale troop movements, including a famously chaotic retreat.

As winter set in, Washington and eleven thousand of his men fled twenty miles north to Valley Forge, a tactically sound, densely wooded plateau. There they built a sprawling encampment with fifteen hundred small log cabins and spent the snowy months licking their wounds. These soldiers were bruised, battered, and unsure of their next tactical moves. Some were suffering from hunger and disease. One wrote of subsisting off "a leg of nothing." Ultimately around two thousand died from disease. This embarrassing, emasculating chapter was later recast as a mythic turning point in the war, with Washington taking to the woods, kneeling in the snow, and providing the prayer that saved America.

GENERAL HENRY KNOX UNDERSTOOD THE VALUE of myth and symbolism but also knew their limits. He had helped organize the Boston Tea Party, a theatrical and emblematic rejection of British taxation and tyranny, and feverishly studied military science. Knox was a voracious reader, having landed his first job as a bookstore clerk at age nine, where he devoured texts on Greek and Roman military campaigns. At the age of twenty-one, he established the London Bookstore, in Boston, where he imported and sold European texts, including military books that were then populating Europe's nascent network of military academies. His rich self-education, mixed with his penchant for brawling in a local militia, primed him to become one of Washington's most reliable advisers.

As the cold winter of 1777 set in, Washington and his men were humiliated and cast out of Philadelphia. In response, Knox launched an early officer training program. He also designed Valley Forge's effective artillery park, a defensive matrix of cannons, dirt mounds, and troops. During the war, Knox oversaw arms production and organized logistics for the crossing of the Delaware. His collective contributions were later honored through the naming of Fort Knox, an impervious Army outpost and America's major repository of gold bullion.

As the war dragged on, Knox became increasingly jealous of England's weapons proficiency, much of which had been gleaned through courses offered at the Royal Military Academy. "We are fighting against a people well acquainted with the theory and practice of war, brave by discipline and habit," he wrote in 1776 to John Adams, who then headed the Continental Congress's Board of War. He had a far dimmer view of the Continental Army, which he described as a "receptacle for ragamuffins."

Most colonial officers had gained their skills through improvised trainings or real-world experience. Many were corrupt. According to a frank assessment by the Continental Congress, Washington's Army was shoddily built and "badly officered," with leaders frequently enlisting the lower ranks "to plunder and commit other offenses."

Knox believed that America needed to immediately establish military schools to remedy these problems and, in turn, win the war. "Officers can never act with confidence until they are masters of their profession," he argued. In response to his pleas, the Continental Congress established a committee to concoct plans for America's first Army school. A bona fide institution wouldn't materialize for decades, but in June 1777 Congress allocated funds for an officers' course, or so-called Corps of Invalids, first organized in Philadelphia before moving to West Point. It adopted a French model in which older, often wounded veterans served in light guard duties and taught younger officers.

It would take significant time, and many more resources, to establish a well-educated officer class. In the meantime, Washington turned to France, home to one of the world's oldest and most respected military schools, the École Militaire, which reared the brilliant and madly mercurial general Napoleon Bonaparte. It was at Valley Forge where Washington got word that the French had agreed to an alliance, and, correspondingly, would provide a vital injection of French military talent. Washington was then already relying on the assistance of various foreigners, including Friedrich Wilhelm Baron Von Steuben, a German-born officer who had served as the Prussian monarch Frederick the Great's aide-de-camp in the Seven Years' War. At Valley Forge, Von Steuben launched what's considered America's first bout of basic training. He broke down troops into regiments and taught them tactics and marching. Von Steuben had success, though he found American troops less pliant than what he was used to: "You say to your soldier [in Europe], 'Do this' and he doeth it. But [at Valley Forge] I am obliged to say, 'This is the reason why you ought to do that,' and then he does it."

ONCE THE WAR BECAME A BOUT OF EQUALS, it dragged on for another six punishing years. It was a perpetually brutal conflict, one in which roughly

25,000 American men, or roughly two percent of all men in the thirteen colonies, died from battle or disease. The deeply scarred country that emerged from the ashes was even more hardened in its skepticism of war, and those who waged it.

A majority of the men who went on to frame the U.S. Constitution were Revolutionary War veterans, including Alexander Hamilton. He worried that any new nation's intrinsic anxieties around conquest and imperialism "enhances the importance of the soldier, and proportionably degrades the condition of the citizen." This, Hamilton concluded, could easily inculcate conditions where "the people are brought to consider the soldiery not only as their protectors, but as their superiors." The Constitution did little to address these concerns, but the Bill of Rights was largely written to protect against another accumulation of blunt military power. The Third Amendment empowered citizens to reject quartering soldiers in their homes, while the Second Amendment granted them arms should they need to curtail state power. An early draft of the Second Amendment had also granted certain citizens the right to abstain from violence, providing that "no person religiously scrupulous of bearing arms, shall be compelled to render military service in person."

While the American public viewed the military skeptically, they were also deeply grateful to the men who had wrested their freedom from English tyranny. They were especially reverent, even pious, toward Washington, the man who had led troops for eight long years. In 1789, Washington was unanimously elected America's first president by a small group of "gentleman" electors. He, in turn, appointed Knox as secretary of war. It was in these roles where both men lobbied to establish a military academy, arguing it was key to maintaining independence. They faced stiff headwinds, including from lawmakers, who fretted about a "professional military," and Secretary of State Thomas Jefferson, who argued that the Constitution specified no powers to create a federal military academy. He argued, instead, for military power to be organized diffusely at the state level.

Around 1784, Congress effectively disbanded the standing Army, declaring that it was "inconsistent with the principles of republican government, dangerous to the liberties of a free people, and generally converted into destructive engines for establishing despotism." And yet a small cell of about eighty men survived this drastic drawdown, the majority of whom were stationed at West Point. They comprised the resilient germ from which America's military industrial complex would grow.

About a decade after the war, Congress first inched toward expanding West Point from a post into a school, allocating a small budget to support station engineers and artillerists there and create a fledgling cadet training program.

Five years later, in 1799, as Washington laid on his deathbed, he wrote to Hamilton, arguing that a military academy was an "object of primary importance to this country." Hamilton drafted plans for such an institution but couldn't get anything passed before his old friend died. While Washington had expressly wished for a low-key, private funeral at Mount Vernon, Americans sent him to the afterlife with two events befitting a king. They also symbolized his strong belief, at least relative to many fellow Founding Fathers, that the military was an institution worth sanctifying.

The first, more modest pageant at Mount Vernon included four sermons, eleven pieces of artillery, and a single riderless horse—an honor for great military men dating back to Genghis Khan. The second, far larger funeral, in Philadelphia, featured cavalry and a procession of soldiers, who fired their minute guns in memorial for an hour.

A few years later, in 1802, Jefferson, now president, reversed himself on the constitutionality of a military school. This was part posthumous favor to Washington, part practical response to acute military challenges involving a series of frontier skirmishes with indigenous fighters and imperial forces who then still claimed a swath of North America. Jefferson also believed strongly in the idea of a national scientific university. That March, he ratified legislation that formally organized West Point as a military academy with a strong scientific grounding. The law was monumental for what it signaled about the future. West Point was America's first experiment in national education, and it was focused exclusively on building soldiers. More specifically, it sought to produce soldiers who resembled George Washington.

Chapter 2

The Thayer Method

West Point was formed around an impossible mission: to create a military leadership class that was deeply ethical, unfailingly adept, well-coiffed, and strong. Officers, in other words, who were also gentlemen. Make no mistake—some cadets hewed to this standard, but many others became seized by elitism, jealousy, and violence, and were flawed in their battle-thinking, leading one senior military official to compare the academy to a "punky, rickety child."

At first there were just a dozen male cadets, an all-white, generally privileged bunch who ranged in age from ten to thirty-four. Courses lacked rigor, and sometimes textbooks. Many cadets graduated in just one year. Funding was anemic, meals were thin, and adult supervision was sparse. This meager environment nonetheless produced some impressive graduates, including a trio of brilliant engineers who served as consequential superintendents. One was West Point's first graduate, Joseph Swift, who designed defense batteries along the Atlantic coast. Another was Alden Partridge, who specialized in math and cartography. Then there was Partridge's archenemy, Sylvanus Thayer, an expert in fort building who worshipped at the altar of Napoleon Bonaparte. Like his idol, Thayer was not just smart, but cunning. He ultimately deposed Partridge in an academic coup d'état that led him to be crowned West Point's true father. His imprint would remain on West Point for centuries to come.

Thayer's early years lacked warmth and parental attention. A middle child of twelve, Thayer was born in Braintree, Massachusetts, on June 9, 1785. Like countless towns in the Commonwealth back then, Braintree was badly bruised, its residents still reeling from the aftershocks of the Revolutionary War and earlier skirmishes with indigenous and colonial fighters.

During these crazed conflicts, fathers called to the front lines routinely armed their boys, some as young as ten, with muskets and ordered them to defend the household.

Thayer's father, Nathaniel, had fought in the Revolution, though Sylvanus wasn't born until two years after the hostilities ended. Little is known about the relationship between father and son, or, for that matter, many other intimate details of Thayer's life. Like Washington, he was keen to the power of legend and legacy, and reportedly ordered one of his sisters to burn many of his papers following his death. What's left are scattershot details, many of them laudatory and most strictly involving his career.

What's clear is that Thayer always wanted to impress his father, a stoic man likely traumatized by his service who often withheld approval, according to Thayer biographer George Eliot. When, for instance, Thayer enthusiastically informed his father that he had been personally appointed West Point's superintendent by President James Monroe, Nathaniel was "noncommittal as usual," though Thayer "knew he was proud."

Thayer came from a long line of Puritans, the fervently strict, uncommonly harsh sect that settled the Massachusetts Bay Colony during the early seventeenth century. Puritans predicted a coming Judgment Day, and punished even minor doctrinal lapses like smoking, fornication, or blasphemy with whippings, brandings, and other maiming. Famously, leaders also disciplined guilty citizens with scarlet letters sewn to their garments. "B" was stitched for blasphemy, "D" for drunkenness, and so on.

In 1630, John Winthrop, a Puritan and the first governor of the Massachusetts Bay Colony, gave his famous "City on a Hill" sermon, which articulated a divine and questionable theory of American exceptionalism that has since been invoked on countless occasions to propel America into battle.

War stories communicated to young Thayer were surely sanded down and shot through with these sentiments, forming in him a sensational understanding of war and American independence. Many of the heroes in Thayer's life were veterans, including Washington, who died when Thayer was just fourteen. Funerary reports on the Founding Father were fawning and far-reaching, with some quoting a stirring speech from Washington's loyal aide Henry Lee, who described America's early leader as "first in war, first in peace, and first in the hearts of his countrymen." Ironically, Henry Lee's boy, Robert E., would one day study under Thayer at West Point, then set out to destroy the democratic republic his father had helped establish.

WHEN THAYER WAS JUST EIGHT, his father sent him to live with his aunt and uncle in New Hampshire. He was the only one of his siblings to be fostered out of the house, though it's unclear why. It was at his new home, in a town fittingly named Washington, where Thayer's thirst for martial glory arose. Thayer's uncle Azariah Faxon was, like the boy's father, a Revolutionary War veteran. After the war, Faxon ran a local general store in Washington frequented by another veteran of the conflict, Major Benjamin Pierce, who would go on to become New Hampshire's eleventh governor.

On a warm summer day in 1797, Pierce arrived at Azariah's store on horseback, waving a newspaper and roaring about the savvy tactics of France's wunderkind warrior, Napoleon Bonaparte, who was then running the Austrians out of northern Italy. Thayer, just twelve at the time, had grown obsessed with Bonaparte. "It stirs me all up to read how a young man, only twenty-eight, can beat all those Austrian generals with so much more experience," he gushed to Pierce. "Seems as though there must be some big reason for it."

"He studied the art of war," Pierce explained. "And had brains enough to apply what he'd learned to actual warfare." The major added wistfully that, without their own military schools, colonial fighters had to secure their expertise "at the price of blood."

West Point hadn't yet been established, but Pierce drew a vivid picture in Thayer's imagination of what it might look like: not simply a fight club but a temple of knowledge, a place to teach science, engineering, and other skills to "aid us in the works of peace as well as those of war."

Thayer was bowled over by the idea of this imaginary place. According to Eliot, his biographer, Thayer ventured later that day to a nearby creek to go fishing. It was one of his favorite hobbies, but he found himself distracted that afternoon, caught up in the awesome idea of becoming a warrior. Pierce's sweeping speech had Thayer feeling restless and self-aware. He wanted a life of consequence, and suddenly felt that the military could imbue it with meaning. From then on, Thayer's dreams were often marked by visions of him marching proudly in a military uniform, an American flag waving starkly against the sky. Thayer, like countless other American boys, had become hooked on the idea of being a hero.

In the fall of 1803, Thayer matriculated at Dartmouth, located forty miles north of Washington, New Hampshire, on the banks of the Connecticut River. The still-young Ivy was then overseen by yet another Revolutionary War veteran, John Wheelock. Thayer later borrowed elements of Dartmouth's culture, and Wheelock's paternalistic, autocratic leadership style, to run West Point. They included the school's recitation model of learning, and Wheelock's grave and distant demeanor toward his students. Dartmouth's student body was small back then, and yet still one student remarked that, despite spending considerable time with Wheelock over his four years, "I never felt the smallest degree of familiarity with him, nor do I believe that any of the students or young men did."

Outside of class, Thayer studied Bonaparte's campaigns endlessly, earning the distinction as the only Dartmouth student subscribed to the *National Intelligencer,* a newspaper focused on foreign affairs. He also joined the United Fraternity. One of his brothers was Alden Partridge, his future rival. Fraternal activities back then seemed to consist mostly of genteel discussions, but there were also secret ceremonies and evidence of transgressive behavior. Eliot notes that Thayer "held his own in the debates, and in the free-for-all fights" that sometimes broke out between rival frats. Patriarchal authority suffused the tight-lipped society, with one discussion during Thayer's day revolving around whether women should be excluded from succession to the British throne. A consensus quickly emerged among the brothers that, indeed, they should be.

Throughout his time at Dartmouth, Thayer sought updates about West Point from Major Pierce. He was anxious about another big war with the British and urged bright young men like Thayer to rid the Army's officer class of "worn-out old men" and "rotten scoundrels" with their "dead ideas." Thayer followed Pierce's advice and, in March 1807, received an official commission to West Point via a crisp letter hand-signed by President Jefferson. Thayer was so ecstatic by the news that he skipped graduation and traveled to West Point, even though he was the Dartmouth class valedictorian and set to deliver remarks.

WHEN THAYER ARRIVED ON THE HUDSON, the school was convulsed by a lack of discipline, a weak curriculum, and unclear lines of authority. The only thing the academy seemed to have figured out was how to inflict pain.

Thayer made his Dartmouth lineage loudly and proudly known, boasting about his wits, and insulting West Point's rigor, including by taking potshots at the academy's math department, to which Partridge then belonged. Once Partridge caught wind of Thayer's pomposity, he drilled him mercilessly for days, ordering Thayer into silence before having him march and snap perfectly into a salute time and again. From then on, Thayer largely silenced his inner resentments and expertly navigated his courses. Within a year, he had completed his studies and was commissioned as a lieutenant. Then, in what surely felt like a delicious dig at Partridge, he was employed by West Point to teach math.

Thayer was sometimes deployed to unfinished military forts, too, where he drafted structural and tactical improvement plans. Some of this work was overseen by West Point's first graduate, Joseph Swift, who confided in Thayer that the academy's mission to professionalize the military was moving at a glacial pace. Swift also expressed concern about another big war with the British and wanted the Army to quickly rid itself of dead wood.

The British had continued to bedevil the new nation, in particular with increasingly antagonistic actions toward American shipping vessels. Shortly before President Madison formally commenced the War of 1812 as a response to this enmity, Congress partially reorganized West Point, creating new professorships, solidifying graduation requirements, and expanding the number of commissioned cadets, from a few dozen to 250. Cadets were now required to be at least fourteen, but manpower needs were acute and, as such, children as young as twelve would sometimes be brought to campus.

As the war ramped up, Swift, Thayer, and other school officials were called away from West Point to fight, and Partridge was promoted to acting superintendent. He instituted more academic offerings, though not particularly rigorous ones. One cadet surmised that even "the most common genius" could complete a West Point engineering course in a week. Partridge also instituted new disciplinary practices, some quite draconian. Cadets found guilty of severe offenses, like fighting, could be confined to an underground cave on campus known as the "Black Hole." Still, Partridge harbored empathy for his cadets, seeing them "almost as my own children" and pledging to "treat them accordingly." He was prone to bend the rules and never left cadets in the hole for more than thirty minutes. In some cases, he didn't punish them at all.

Some faculty grumbled that Partridge's paternal instincts leaned especially toward cadets from affluent or political backgrounds, or among those who had demonstrated loyalty. One math professor charged that he "graduates his pets without regard to their qualifications and abuses those who do not curry his favor."

WHILE PARTRIDGE REIGNED ON THE HUDSON, Thayer was promoted to captain and thrust into America's unresolved territorial disputes. He and other West Pointers in the War of 1812 generally demonstrated bravery and decent battlefield knowledge. But American soldiers couldn't hold a candle to Europe's finest, in large part because, as Thayer saw it, the Army lacked knowledge and discipline. One senior commander for America's Niagara Army had, for instance, devised a major campaign from a single dog-eared book of French drill tactics. Men in Thayer's unit, and others, were also known to disobey orders, or desert altogether.

Thayer's first and only real brush with combat came during the disastrous 1813 Battle of Châteauguay. One officer who participated in the campaign later said that no soldier with "any regard for his reputation would voluntarily acknowledge himself as having been engaged in it." It was an early and audacious—some might even say delusional—example of misguided American exceptionalism, one in which a few thousand American troops foolishly attempted a two-front campaign to penetrate lower Canada and capture Montreal.

During the battle, Thayer was stationed at the banks of the Saint Lawrence River, a borderline in upstate New York between America and Canada. Here, amid hardwood forests of oak, birch, and sugar maple, Thayer and his men navigated confused routes, demonstrated poor communication, showed no real combat prowess, and were ultimately defeated by a far smaller force of Canadian and indigenous fighters.

At one point, an officer alerted Thayer that a confused band of "half-trained idiots" was mistakenly attacking a pack of fellow militiamen. Thayer jumped on his horse and raced toward the action, hoping to quell the friendly fire. Before long, he confronted an indigenous warrior and clumsily tried to swat the fighter away with his saber, only to hit "something hard." Based on Thayer's immediate surroundings, chances are high that it was a tree. Amid this failed melee, Thayer's stallion became spooked and reversed course. According to Eliot, Thayer failed to stop the infighting, galloping back to camp deeply embarrassed, "the torment of failure eating at his heart."

As military mistakes mounted, Swift reiterated his belief to Thayer that the Army needed to solidify and professionalize, forming "a professional officer corps grown from selected seed and carefully nourished through the years of peace." Thayer insisted that West Point was "the garden in which that goodly seed must be planted," and Swift agreed, adding coyly, "I mean to see that the right gardener is chosen to bring forth a goodly crop."

This conversation was followed by the conflict's most devastating example of American military incompetence. In August 1814, thousands of British red coats sailed up the Potomac, besieged Washington, D.C., and set fire to the White House and the Capitol. It was a symbolic wound on a par with Washington's loss of Philadelphia and subsequent retreat to Valley Forge. The attack significantly inflamed public disaffection with the war, and the military. Rumors even spread that New England might dispense with the economic pain wrought by British seafarers and sign its own peace accord with the monarchy.

Not long after D.C. burned, Thayer drafted a letter to Swift making the case to be West Point's master gardener. "I have improved the quality of the forts," he argued. "I am not permitted to try to improve the quality of the men." In Thayer's view, Partridge had made West Point too kind and forgiving. One professor, he claimed, felt that, thanks to Partridge's light touch, West Point had "gone to the dogs." What the place needed, Thayer argued, was an emphasis on "discipline and subordination." Fundamentally, he believed that West Point needed to fit an authoritarian mold should it hope to fortify democracy. It was a risky bet, but Swift and other powerful military leaders quickly bought in. They decided that Thayer was worthy and capable of running West Point.

SHORTLY BEFORE BECOMING WEST POINT SUPERINTENDENT, Thayer had his boyhood wish come true. Once the War of 1812 ended in a messy draw, Thayer embarked on a boat called the *Congress* with a fellow officer named William McRee. The pair sailed for Europe, where they would acquire texts to drive Thayer's academic transformation on the Hudson. The adventure would also offer Thayer an opportunity to tap into his longstanding obsession with his idol, Napoleon Bonaparte, who remained a significant albeit diminishing martial force in Europe.

Thayer departed on June 10, 1815, the day after his thirtieth birthday. He and McRee arrived in Paris that July and stayed in Europe for the better part of two years. The length of their trip was largely owed to the long denouement of the Napoleonic Wars, which transformed the military schools Thayer planned to visit into active posts. France had once again pinned its hopes on Bonaparte, with Parisians taking to the streets each night and crying out "*Vive l'empereur*." The conflict, however, ended in failure, with Napoleon's embarrassing defeat at Waterloo, followed by his permanent exile.

During his travels, Thayer visited Bonaparte's alma mater. He dropped in on other French military schools, too, then set sail on a boat bound for New York Harbor. Stowed on the ship was a treasure trove of military knowledge, including one thousand military books Thayer had stamped in gold with West Point's seal. He was now confident he had the necessary texts to build an Army that was invincible. The only barrier that still lay before him was his former fraternity brother, Alden Partridge.

After returning stateside, Thayer sailed to West Point armed with a decree, co-signed by President James Monroe, declaring him as Partridge's rightful replacement: the new master gardener. Swift had warned Thayer ahead of time that removing Partridge would prove difficult, for he was "literally wedded to the academy." McRee, Thayer's European compatriot, urged his friend to seize power like a broom. "See that you sweep clean," he advised. "And fast."

As he marched from the water up West Point's steep bluff, Thayer saw that the school had changed since his time as a cadet. There were new buildings on campus, and the blue uniform he had worn was now gray, a reflection of the military's wartime inabilities to use the sea to source blue cloth.

Thayer arrived at his alma mater on a yellowy summer evening, passing through campus before arriving at the superintendent's dark, damp quarters. There, he nervously confronted Partridge, a man described as having "basilisk eyes."

Partridge was visibly overwhelmed by his duties. He appeared pale, beleaguered, and was shedding stress. But he wouldn't go down without a fight. While Thayer had always projected an air of supremacy, Partridge had always derived a certain power from his superior rank and age, even if he was only four months Thayer's senior. For Partridge to now be usurped by his younger, lower-ranking foe would open a wound that never fully healed.

Following a few tense moments, Thayer explained curtly that he was to be West Point's new man in charge, a declaration that caused Partridge to storm out of his quarters. The incumbent skipped town early the next morning, leaving Thayer technically in charge but without a formal change of command ceremony, something Thayer viewed as vital to securing the respect of Partridge loyalists.

A few weeks later, Thayer was munching in the mess hall when he heard a band of cadets yell "Hooray for old Pewt!" This was Partridge's nickname, but Thayer paid the exclamation no mind, assuming it was simply the work of a few disgruntled cadets pining for their less severe father figure. The next day, however, he heard the same energetic cheer, peered out from his office window, and went white. Partridge had returned.

Minutes later, Partridge stormed into Thayer's office and verbally reasserted his authority as superintendent, citing regulations that deemed the school's most senior engineer its rightful leader. He had effectively replicated Thayer's coup, but in reverse. It was convincing enough that, early the next morning, Thayer packed a small bag, skulked down to the boat landing, and left campus. What he wanted was clarity from the War Department. To his great relief, Swift strongly reinforced his standing, sending, as evidence of his support, his personal aide back to West Point with Thayer. Thayer once again confronted Partridge, demanding his superior's ceremonial saber and ultimately placing him under arrest. Partridge was ultimately convicted of insubordination and given a path to resign, at which point he became West Point's most biting public critic.

NOW FULLY EMPOWERED, Thayer peeled back the school's layers and discovered significant rot. Professors testified that Partridge had engaged in favoritism and failed to uphold order. Some cadets came and went from campus as they pleased, including one who had been on the rolls for eight years despite living permanently in Orange County, California. Legend also tells of a forty-year-old with a family, and another who only had one arm.

Early on, Thayer compiled a forty-three-person list of "deadwood—a tally of the overage, the physically infirm, the mentally incapable, and the confirmed troublemakers." Then he dismissed them. The rest were churned through his Puritanical gauntlet, which aimed to form what Thayer described as a "soul worthy of inhibiting a body which is to wear an officer's uniform."

Thayer spent weeks brainstorming a new school structure before landing on a simple concept, one that has since populated corporate office presentations ad nauseum: the leadership triangle. Each of its three sides denotes a core West Point value: education, honor, and discipline. Thayer placed honor at the base of the triangle because he saw it as the school's foundation. From there sprang a series of strict rules and regulations meant to fortify the triangle and tame what he viewed as the "unmilitary, lax, and rebellious" corps of cadets. He described the triangle as an explicitly authoritarian structure, one where "gentlemen must learn it is only their province to listen and obey."

Thayer's triangle was upheld through a grueling fifteen-hour school day, one that prohibited idle time, and, by extension, the imagination and independence that such time allows. All cadets were to awaken at dawn to the loud beat of a drum. There would follow two hours of drills before breakfast, then a day packed full of classwork and physical conditioning. Thayer also restricted cadets' ability to leave campus and abolished vacations. "There was no more leave," Eliot writes. "There was no more anything that made life worth living, it seemed." Thayer also banned certain signature ingredients of youthful hijinks, like alcohol and games, plus romance novels and plays, contributing to an atmosphere of deadening uniformity. Cadets wore the same outfits, used the same shorthand, and lived in identical bedrooms, forming what *Harper's Magazine* once described as a student body of "little tin soldiers all stamped from the same base metal."

Thayer also deployed a set of austere academic policies, many of them intensified Dartmouth practices, which collectively came to be known as "The Thayer Method." Thayer restricted lecturing and made cadets largely responsible for their own learning, laying down the expectation that they master concepts through intense at-home studying and come to class prepared to put them into practice. This style proved largely successful in teaching science and math courses, but was at odds with the humanities, which require room for debate and discussion. Absent these traditions, cadets read books for facts, not meaning, leading one officer to acknowledge that his peers "can't write because they can't think."

Thayer was dogmatically focused on math and science, discarding Latin and the classics and packing other core liberal arts courses—including history, grammar, and geography—into a single course that many felt was deeply reductive. Some said it basically rehashed lessons they had learned in grade school. None of this seemed to bother Thayer's overseers at the War Department, who often called cadets into service once they had taken a few basic military courses. West Point's antagonism toward the humanities has powerfully endured, summed up appropriately by an on-campus parking sign that popped up during the Cold War. It read: "Reserved—Professer [*sic*] of English."

As Thayer scrapped the humanities, he gave the human body academic standing. West Point was the first American college or university to hire a physical education instructor, seeding a program from which emerged many fine athletes. Also, the jumping jack, plus, some claim, the man who invented America's pastime: baseball.

Thayer introduced numerical grades to American education, supplanting a tiered, Latin-based criteria with a new hyper-precise system of assessment. He had picked up this idea from École Polytechnique, which had itself cribbed the practice from Cambridge. Thayer was characteristically intense about grading, posting daily assessments on public bulletin boards, and resectioning cadets frequently to account for their standing. (Once technology allowed for it, West Point recomputed cadet grades to the third decimal point, daily.) This approach not only fueled intense competitiveness among cadets, but the frequent shuffling of courses also precluded the cerebral experience of settling into a classroom and bonding with a teacher. In his 1992 book *Technopoly*, Neil Postman argues that Thayer's grading system planted the seeds for a managerial class policy in America, forming what French philosopher Michel Foucault described as the "calculable person."

Thayer's other major innovation was his punishing student hierarchy, organized formally as the Fourth-Class System, where first-year students were ranked at the bottom and expected to always defer to upperclassmen, speak only when spoken to (in many contexts), perform menial tasks, and accept constant corrections of posture, speech, gait, and attitude. It was designed to indoctrinate new cadets, or "plebes," around a shared military mission—and to engender in them absolute submission. This was a largely cadet-led system, one that also served as a second, unofficial layer of the admission process, in which older cadets test the pliability of plebes and run out the ones who aren't deemed up to snuff.

Thayer's system commenced with Beast Barracks, a summer of miserable conditioning exercises and induction rites overseen by upperclassmen, followed by a year of constant subjugation, much of which revolves around servitude to the seniors. It has become an especially rank example of hypocrisy at the service academies, where savage, power-drunk seniors are held up as ethical paragons to be unleashed on packs of younger, largely helpless and putatively untamed "beasts" in desperate need of "breaking in." One cadet described this initiation as a terrible rebirth: "I began to think I was someone else. I felt as if I must have died and that this was my second tour on earth, a punishment for a wicked first life."

Thayer's student hierarchy was organized not only through age and academic standing, but also height. Low-scoring "goats" sat at the back of the classroom, while the so-called engineers were given plum seats up front and special privileges. This system made it feel as if everyone in the student body were members of the same fraternity, with Thayer its chapter president, a leader, described by one cadet, who gave the impression that "his eye was ever on them."

In ideal conditions, Thayer's hierarchy led ethical senior cadets to hold junior ones accountable for legitimate violations of core military precepts. In reality, it has always favored the most imposing and power-hungry cadets, while endangering the vulnerable ones. This system also formed a separate and volatile channel of power and punishment outside adult supervision. Thayer's assumption that cadets would step up and act responsibly belies the reality that he was essentially handing his reins over to children, a population that often permits emotion to overcome common sense.

Thayer's tutelage of America's fledgling officer class was generally greeted with approval from the powers that be, though some felt he overcorrected from Partridge's laissez-faire approach. Early in Thayer's tenure, a professor hailed his system as a pure meritocracy, one befitting "the son of a beggar, or a king." Two years later, however, this booster had come to see the place as oppressive. "We need less military and more civilian influence here," he said. Following his own visit, Charles Dickens wrote of West Point's lush, sweeping campus before noting that its "course of education is severe, but well devised."

Even Thayer's close friend McRee blanched at the cadets' austere conditions. "Goodness, Syl," he wrote, "the lads are regulated every minute of every day. The pressure never lets up. Your system has no safety valve." He suggested that his friend put "a little human warmth into the old girl somehow, if you want boys to adore her."

Thayer was irritated by McRee's criticism, though he ultimately came to embrace some of it, albeit in his own limited way. His major remedy, ironically enough, consisted of an order: that all cadets seeking permission for acts not stipulated by regulation run them by Thayer during his office hours. This brought cadets in proximity to West Point's father, which some viewed as a form of harassment, though others nurtured bonds. It was Thayer's small attempt to be more paternal and less paternalistic toward West Point cadets—the only sons he would ever have.

Thayer's other major realization was that Christianity could serve as a powerful binding agent for his military project, an easily imported belief system that would at once form resilience and motivation in his boys and help them elide the major moral questions at the heart of the burgeoning imperial project to which they belonged. The military state's warm relationship with the church continuously intensified, perhaps most flagrantly during the Vietnam War, when megachurch pastor Billy Graham served as a close aide to President Richard Nixon. Graham's blessing of the war machine was graciously recognized in 1972, when he was presented with the Sylvanus Thayer Award at West Point. During the ceremony, Graham asserted that Thayer's vision needed to be "rekindled and revived" to "guide our nation through this perilous period."

In 1825, Thayer appointed Chaplain Charles McIlvaine to charter West Point's religious culture. Soon, all cadets were mandated to attend his fiery Sunday sermons. Like Graham, McIlvaine wielded words with powerful emotion, swaying hearts and minds through services, school lessons, and intense interpersonal counsel. As word of his zealotry spread beyond West Point's walls, one major in the New York militia complained that Thayer was "turning a military academy into a theological seminary." Around this time, a group of professors objected to the academy's chapel requirements. Most of them were swiftly reassigned to unpopular posts, often solitary forts on the frontier, and replaced with faculty who were religiously minded. By the mid-1800s, an estimated 90 percent of professors and their families were true believers.

Pastor McIlvaine was followed by John French, a chaplain who wrote a West Point textbook called *Practical Ethics* that was taught for decades. It featured Bible verses and flow charts that placed America and God as the highest points of cadet authority, and justified violence meted out in service of these masters.

In 1858, a cadet named Tully McCrea wrote a letter home arguing that Chaplain French had acted blasphemously, teaching the Bible's famous "Thou shalt not kill" passage in a way that, according to McCrea, "twisted it" to justify bloodshed. While the young cadet initially deemed French no more qualified to preach than "the man in the moon," French had, by Mc-Crea's graduation, meaningfully swayed him. At this point, McCrea remarked that French's sermons were "eloquent and affecting," containing a "great many realized truths." Just as Thayer had hoped, McCrea was born again as a soldier.

THE MAN WHO ENFORCED THAYER'S SPARTAN DICTATES at West Point was his commandant, Captain John Bliss, whose last name betrayed his violent temper. Bliss oversaw the Department of Tactics, a unit chiefly responsible for teaching military skills and doling out punishments. Much of this work was undertaken by so-called TAC officers, an acronym that sounds imposing but technically stands for "Teach, Advise, and Counsel." Some in the role earnestly embody their remit. Others are angry, harsh, and bruising.

Bliss was the brutal type. Like a gun, he was cold, hard, and easily triggered. On a chilly evening in November 1818, Bliss lost his temper and assaulted a cadet. The morning after, five cadets confronted Thayer in his office and demanded that their commandant be removed. The protesters' leader was Thomas Ragland, whom Thayer judged to be a Partridge loyalist and, consequently, viewed skeptically. Ragland, for his part, contended that Bliss's violence was completely unjustified—a response to a "fancied fault" that was directly at odds with West Point's conception of the gentleman officer. He furnished Thayer with a petition against Bliss signed and supported by nearly two hundred cadets in total agreement.

While Partridge had encouraged cadets to air their grievances, Thayer viewed Ragland's uprising as a threat to his supremacy and good military order. He refused to take possession of the petition, then ordered Ragland and his compatriots out of his office. A larger contingent returned the next day, armed with a longer list of allegations against Bliss, including that "without the shadow of provocation," he had barked at cadets, thrown stones at them, even pushed one off a railing.

"I told you yesterday that collective action of this kind will not be tolerated," Thayer warned Ragland. "We will not suffer this constant abuse, sir," Ragland countered.

From there, Thayer moved to ensure that, indeed, they would. He ordered the petition's organizers to be suspended from duty and told them to all leave campus within six hours. He then sought to charge them under a military court-martial. Ragland and his boys begrudgingly left campus, but not before arguing that West Point cadets didn't explicitly fall under military law. In the weeks that followed, Thayer motivated the War Department to formally declare that cadets qualified as active-duty troops, placing them under the authority of the undemocratic and punitive military justice system, which is vulnerable to command influence and focused on maintaining order above all else. Secretary of War John Calhoun also heartily endorsed Thayer's dismissal of the miscreants, calling their actions "highly reprehensible." While Bliss eventually left West Point, he stayed in the Army and was put in charge of a regiment.

Thayer used his expanded authority to further consolidate power and professionalize school operations. Cadet intransigence mostly subsided, save for a few outbursts against his harsh hand. Legend has it that one pack of cadets grew so angry with their godfather that they pointed a loaded cannon at his living quarters and lit the fuse. Thankfully for Thayer, it failed to fire.

CADETS ALSO STAGED A HIGHLY INEBRIATED INSURRECTION during West Point's Christmas party in 1826. Ahead of the gathering, a crew of cadets smuggled whiskey on campus from nearby taverns. This pack included future Confederate president Jefferson Davis—who had developed a mean drinking habit at the academy, having once gotten so blitzed that he fell down a sixty-foot ravine.

When the holiday party started, Davis and others spiked their favorite holiday drink and became rip-roaringly drunk. This precipitated what's now known as the Eggnog Riot, a reckless rebellion during which dozens of cadets smashed windows, broke furniture, and, in a few cases, attacked administrators. One official was hit in the head with a board. Another was shot at with a pistol.

The riot came at a highly inopportune time for Thayer, who was then facing sharp public dissent. Newspaper headlines blared that West Point was a useless expense, a "hot bed of aristocratic tyranny," even a "military prison for our youth." Numerous lawmakers introduced bills to abolish the school, including famed frontiersman and former militia officer Davy Crockett, who, in a floor speech, argued that the school was dangerously elitist, promoting military officers as society's supreme citizens. Crockett further charged that these elite cadets were "effeminate and pedantic," learning unnecessary lessons while being spared from gritty conditions that could "injure their beauty." Crocket's indictment stuck in Thayer's craw, and in the public imagination. Over the next two decades, Tennessee, Ohio, Connecticut, Maine, and New Hampshire all passed resolutions endorsing West Point's abolition. Various federal factions embarked on their own periodic termination campaigns, the last of which apparently occurred on the eve of the Mexican American War, when lawmakers came within a single vote of abolishing the academy entirely.

Public opposition was fueled further by Alden Partridge, who, in 1830, published a lacerating pamphlet called *The Military Academy at West Point, Unmasked*. Authored under the pseudonym "Americanus," Partridge charged, like Crockett, that the school promoted a "military aristocracy," and that "mercenary" administrators subjected cadets to "degrading punishments" that forced them into "gaudy slavery." Partridge specifically alleged that one cadet had received three hundred lashings. He also charged that, amid the Bliss affair, Thayer had forced Ragland and his crew to flee campus on a rowboat in freezing November weather, conditions that "hastened, if not occasioned," one of the cadet's deaths. "Suppose this mode of punishment were adopted at our colleges and universities, would it be submitted to?" Partridge asked. "No."

Thayer tried to tamp down criticism through his creation of the Board of Visitors, a PR creation that offered the patina of oversight but lacked the traditional powers of school trustees. The board was to be composed of "five gentlemen versed in military science," and chaired by Thayer. Virtually all their reports were favorable, and most recommendations echoed school priorities. In 1826, for instance, the board advocated for the abolition of liberal arts courses—including rhetoric, law, and ethics—arguing they were inessential to the mission of rearing soldiers.

Thayer's board placated some critics, but not President Andrew Jackson. A hardcore populist and proud anti-intellectualist, Jackson agreed with his friend Crockett, a fellow self-taught militiaman, that West Point concentrated too much power among the elite and entitled officer class. Jackson labeled Thayer "a tyrant" and moved to dilute his power, floating laissez-faire reforms and deploying a pack of loyal officers to oversee operations. Jackson also reinstated cadets Thayer had dismissed for academic or disciplinary issues, and unilaterally granted others extended periods of leave. Among the cadets he reinstated was a bunch of well-connected boys who had set fire to West Point's guardhouse.

Back on his heels, Thayer defended his methods while aiming to placate Jackson. He noted, among other things, that fourteen reports in a row from the Board of Visitors had found nothing to complain about, and that the board itself included many strong allies of the president. It wasn't enough to soothe Jackson's crusade, leading Thayer to ultimately retire. Shortly before his fiftieth birthday, in the early summer of 1833, he quietly boarded a boat on the Hudson and returned to Braintree. He never graced the campus again, mostly out of a respect for authority, a deference first inculcated in him as a West Point cadet and later fortified through his fight with Partridge.

Two years later, Jackson issued a memo expressing qualified contrition for the "lenient system" he had imposed at West Point. He further pledged to reinstate a sense of Thayer-ian order. Jackson's pivot came in response to various forces, including a series of high-profile resignations from West Point professors and TAC officers loyal to the Thayer Method, plus a congressional report vindicating West Point for all it had done to elevate the "character of the military establishment" in the public consciousness, owed largely to the ambitious public works projects that Army engineers were spearheading across the country.

West Point's godfather spent the rest of his career designing forts, mostly in and around Boston. After his death, Thayer's body was interred at West Point. Today, honored members of West Point lay a wreath at his grave as part of the school's graduation ceremony. The academy also honored its father through the construction of Thayer Hall, a cold, austere academic building made of stone that seemed a perfect tribute to its namesake's flinty nature. Janitorial staff have since joked that, thanks to West Point's exacting expectations over cadet behavior, it is the easiest classroom building in the world to clean.

AT THE TIME OF THAYER'S RETIREMENT, his concept of military education had yet to be adopted by America's other major military branch: the U.S. Navy. Aspiring naval officers were then undergoing on-the-job training on the high seas—that is, until 1842, which saw a controversial trio of killings of young midshipmen by officers on a training mission of the USS *Somers*. Ninety of the ship's 120 sailors onboard were juvenile trainees, some as young as fourteen. This bunch frequently irritated the older sailors, who scolded the boys, among other things, for being disorderly and unkempt, and for frequently masturbating.

One of these youngsters was nineteen-year-old Philip Spencer, a known miscreant, but also precious cargo. He was the son of President John Tyler's secretary of war, John C. Spencer. Once out on the water, Philip vocally romanticized the idea of turning the USS *Somers* into a pirate ship. At some point, his claims reached a crescendo and the ship's paranoid commander came to believe him, charging Spencer and two other young seafarers with planning a mutiny, then executing all three by hanging them from the yard-arm—without the benefit of due process. After the *Somers* returned to Brookyln, the incident quickly spiraled into a national scandal, rocking the Navy, which, in 1845, embraced the Thayer Method and formed the U.S. Naval Academy.

Thayer's values were then spreading to other schools, too. For the first twenty-six years of its existence, West Point was effectively the only institution in America teaching civil engineering, leading many early graduates to spearhead similar programs at other institutions, including Harvard, Yale, Dartmouth, the University of Michigan, Columbia, and Brooklyn Polytechnic. When West Point still stood alone in this field, President John Quincy Adams had empowered Thayer with great influence over the future of American infrastructure, granting him with the mission and authority to design roads, trains, bridges, and canal systems across America.

Early West Point graduates helped build many things, including much of New York City. They played crucial engineering roles in the development of Riverside Drive, Central Park, the Croton aqueduct, and the city's grandest achievement, the Brooklyn Bridge, at the time the world's longest suspension bridge, whose mammoth stone archways became iconic across the world.

Other West Pointers served as early leaders in Gotham's police force, its public works agency, and its dock and street departments. Additional engineering marvels outside the five boroughs, from the Panama Canal to the Washington Monument, led Brown University president Francis Wayland to declare in 1850 that of America's 120 or so institutions of higher learning, West Point had "done more to build up the system of internal improvements in our country than all the colleges combined."

While some West Pointers pioneered early public works, others became foundational figures in what became the military industrial complex. At the head of this pack was Henry du Pont, who managed his family's lucrative chemical company, which came to manufacture much of America's gunpowder. Joseph Swift was among a group of grauduates who formed the Cold Springs Foundry, located just up the river from West Point, which produced war engines and armaments. In the centuries since, countless other alumni have taken prominent roles at major weapons companies, including Rolls-Royce, Lockheed Martin, and Boeing.

THAYER'S WEST POINT CREATED MEN that were skilled at building things, but also, as history would soon show, at tearing the country to shreds. This was no surprise—after all, the academy was both an unrivaled engineering school and one that specialized in killing. These dark arts were taught in military drills, motivated through brutal hazing, workshopped in schoolyard rebellions like the Eggnog Riot, then put into practice when the scent of war filled the air. This was an intense, fast-developing educational system whose volatility wasn't fully clear to the American people until the onset of the Civil War.

If slavery was the conflict's powder keg, West Point was the match that sparked the rebellion. This history confirms the fact that when a country invests inordinate public resources to train men and build bombs, it also creates economic and societal pressures that can easily tip into violence.

At the outbreak of the Civil War, a staggering three-quarters of all military officers hailed from West Point. Their high rate of participation was evident from the fact that each side adopted one of West Point's first two uniform colors: blue for the union, and gray for the confederacy. In total, the school contributed 294 officers to the Union and 141 to the Confederacy. This led to fifty-five of the war's sixty major battles being led on one or both sides by graduates, all of whom were drawing from the exact same base of knowledge and training. This created surreal internecine dynamics, an intraschool rivalry in which West Point technically lost many of the battles that it won.

The Civil War's stark geographical divides were intimately familiar to West Point graduates. In the decades leading up to hostilities, they had been inexplicably divided into northern and southern companies. West Point's defenders argued, somewhat credibly, that the school experience, taken in its entirety, formed a strong sense of national unity. Seventy-six percent of southern cadets from the class of 1861, for instance, remained loyal to the union. Still, that very same year, the school briefly elevated P.G.T. Beauregard, an avowed secessionist, to the position of superintendent, legitimizing him and his lost cause. Nine years before that, Robert E. Lee had been elevated to superintendent, a position he held for three years. Lee was a popular leader, with one cadet testifying that his "manly and consistent conduct" engendered the "respect and esteem of every Cadet in the Corps."

After the Civil War, Lee also served as president of what's now called Washington and Lee University, in Lexington, Virginia. During his influential tenure, Lee was deemed the spiritual founder of Kappa Alpha, a military-style fraternity with especially sadistic hazing rituals that long harbored strong ties to white supremacist figures and the Ku Klux Klan.

Another West Pointer, Jefferson Davis, was appointed America's secretary of war before becoming the first and only president of the Confederate States of America. Thayer was especially fond of both cadets Lee and Davis, declining to court-martial the latter as a cadet after the Eggnog Riot while throwing the book at twenty others. Curiously enough, the most famous West Pointer who fought for the union, Ulysses Grant, generally disliked his time at the academy, due mostly to its relentless focus on discipline. In his memoirs, he called West Point's culture "wearisome" and its academics "uninteresting."

Cadets who hailed from the North were more likely to be skeptical of the military establishment, an attitude owing mostly to the region's lingering memories of British military rule. Southerners, meanwhile, embraced what famed political scientist Samuel Huntington described as a "cult of romantic chivalry" around service. This affection mostly accrued from frequent and well-coordinated uprisings by the people the southerners had enslaved. During the years leading up to the Civil War, the South undertook an unprecedented buildup of military schools, including the Citadel, in Charleston, South Carolina, which was initially founded as an arsenal after local law enforcement discovered and foiled an insurrection plot by a former slave named Denmark Vesey. A cadre of the Citadel's fresh-faced cadets also technically launched the Civil War, firing the war's first cannon shots from an artillery battery on Morris Island, South Carolina. Soon after, dozens of West Point graduates resigned their commissions and defected to the South.

The Virginia Military Institute, or VMI, America's first state-chartered military school, was founded in 1839 amid lingering fear over Nat Turner's slave rebellion. Years later, in 1859, nearly one hundred VMI cadets stood guard on the execution day of another famed abolitionist rebel, John Brown.

During its early years, VMI recruited a bunch of West Point alumni and faculty to shape the place, including its inaugural superintendent. It also recruited West Point's famed French engineering professor Claude Crozet, who had previously served under Bonaparte, including during the Frenchman's massive invasion of Russia. Once in the American South, Crozet designed a 4,273-foot-long tunnel that runs under one of the Blue Ridge mountains. It proved crucial to the Confederacy during the war, helping them safely move soldiers and supplies between the foggy Shenandoah Valley and the city of Richmond. The Citadel and VMI funneled many officers into the Confederate ranks, including General Thomas "Stonewall" Jackson, who taught physics at VMI, leading the school to memorialize Jackson in 1912 with a bronze statue that, for more than a century, all passing cadets, Black and white alike, were expected to salute.

As America became riven by the Civil War, Thayer, the influential godfather to the men barking orders on both sides, receded to the background, occasionally giving military advice to Union officers but generally looking, it seems, to minimize any negative attention. The only real sign of his presence came indirectly through "Fort Thayer," an earthwork redoubt that sat above a ravine on the outskirts of Washington, D.C.

AS THE CONFEDERACY'S WAR DEPARTMENT and battle tactics took shape, Congress became incensed that West Point had reared so many turncoats. Some renewed their push for the school to be abolished, including Zach Chandler, a noted abolitionist from Michigan and Republican Party co-founder, who charged that West Point had, within the last half century, produced more traitors than "all the institutions of learning and education that have existed since Judas Iscariot's time." Senator James H. Lane of Kansas similarly insisted that, should the North fall, an appropriate epitaph would read: "Died of West Point Pro-Slaveryism."

In an 1861 report, Lincoln's secretary of war Simon Cameron bemoaned the "extraordinary treachery" of the school's confederate alumni, warning that the place was plagued by "a radical defect." He specifically faulted the school's shallow focus on morality, in which rules and regulations dictate actions, but not thought. This formed a system, Cameron argued, that substitutes "habit for conscience."

It's nearly impossible to curb military power when the bullets are flying, and, indeed, any clear-eyed warnings about West Point's failings were overwhelmed by a panicky desire for more union soldiers. A salve was inserted into America's landmark education bill, the Morrill Act, which granted thirty thousand acres for each member of Congress a given state had for the purpose of building public universities that would teach agriculture, engineering, and classical studies. States could sell the land and use the proceeds to establish and endow the colleges—or they could use all or part of the lands for the colleges, themselves. On July 2, 1862, President Abraham Lincoln signed the legislation, so named for its author, Vermont congressman Justin Morrill. In part as a favor to Lincoln, Morrill had quietly inserted a War Department carve-out requiring all these new land grant colleges to establish military programs, a statute that would ultimately evolve into the Pentagon's Reserve Officers' Training Course, or ROTC.

Morrill's bill served as early evidence of a profound American shift away from traditional isolationism to a more aggressive posture of military "preparedness." In arguing for the bill's passage on the House floor, Morrill stoked nebulous fears of a coming invasion, arguing that military "unpreparedness" offers "too many temptations, even to a foe otherwise weak." As he saw it, "the national school at West Point may suffice for the regular Army in ordinary years of peace, but it is wholly inadequate when a large army is to be suddenly put into service."

Morrill's military carve-out was not included in an earlier draft of his bill. He inserted it only after being swayed by his close friend and neighbor, Alden Partridge, who argued truthfully, though somewhat cynically, that West Point's monopoly on army commissions was dangerous and monarchical. Rather than concentrate military power in one fortress on a hill, the bill would purportedly decentralize it. Morrill also hoped that the act of filtering cadets into traditional liberal arts environments would challenge and expand narrow military thinking.

Key parts of his thesis were correct. Elitism permeated West Point to its core, cleaving deep divides, not only among citizens but also with the many officers who began to emerge from ROTC and other alternative officer-training environments. West Point graduates have always considered their alma mater as a semi-secretive club, one that came to be known colloquially as the "West Point Protective Association," or less charitably, SHIT: the "South Hudson Institute of Technology." Graduates are known today as "ring knockers," a testament to the blinding glint of their class rings, and to their outsized grasp on military power. "West Point influence is like a drop of blue ink in a glass of water," one general who hailed from ROTC once explained. "It isn't much in volume, but it influences the coloring of the whole glass."

Many officers reared in ROTC would come to ensure a healthy check on West Point's blinkered instincts, much to ring knockers' chagrin. In one prototypical gripe, much like Von Steuben had experienced during the American Revolution, a West Pointer grumbled that when he gives ROTC officers orders, they are "inclined to ask 'Why?'" However, Morrill's belief that military programs would remain peripheral to land grant universities' larger agenda proved sorely mistaken. Military brass used the campus foothold Morrill gave them to eventually expand and entrench their power in schools across all fifty states.

Morrill's military training mandate lacked concrete guidance and, in its early years, was unevenly applied. Some schools neglected the requirement entirely while others established muscular programs. The year after the Civil War ended, in 1866, Congress passed toothy new legislation to better enforce the Morrill dictates, instructing active-duty officers to deploy to all land grant schools with 150 male students or more. Weaponry also flooded schools across the country, forming, in some schools, an inescapable aura of military life. At the University of Illinois, for instance, the military salute became the standard form of recognition between professor and pupil.

At the same time, Boston and several other cities mandated "military gymnastics" in all public high schools. Congress also bolstered the U.S. Naval Academy, and, in 1876, established the U.S. Coast Guard Academy. That same year, Ohio State created a robust military sciences department and opened a school of Mechanical Trades and Munitions that carried out weapons development during World War II. In 1898, almost every man in Ohio State's senior class abandoned their courses to fight in the Spanish American Civil War.

A particularly intense military apparatus grew at Iowa Agricultural College, where all able-bodied males were mandated to drill and wear uniforms. The program's leader, general James Geddes, was, for a time, the highest paid professor on campus. He also served in important administrative roles, including, in 1882, as president. Archival documents list an impressive catalogue of weapons secured for the Iowa program, including muskets, rifles, and sabers. One report at the time claimed the college was as well armed as any unit of the Iowa National Guard.

For a dozen years after the war, the U.S. Army also occupied the South as part of reconstruction, a policy that inflamed southern resentments and helped birth a racist countervailing militia force called the Ku Klux Klan. Over this same period, southerners were temporarily banned from West Point's campus, while a contingent of Union veterans, many of them West Pointers who were wounded or traumatized, were called back to campus to teach the warriors of tomorrow.

This cycle, of West Point effectively teaching itself, has remained unbroken, solidifying its insular, elitist culture, and complicating the school's ability to objectively look back and critically assess its role in promulgating American war policy and battle tactics. Appointing battle-hardened officers to teaching environments has also led young cadets to undergo a hefty program of toughening. This is a tragic act of love and misdirected care, born from a protective instinct but deeply damaging nevertheless. While Grant had bristled at discipline as a cadet, he shifted his thinking after surviving the war and becoming commander in chief. After a cadet had been dismissed for brawling, Grant reinstated him, believing that cadets must know how to fight.

Some who had experienced war hoped to instill new lessons, or even prevent conflict altogether. Try as they might, however, the academy was permanently bent toward conflict. In the wake of the Civil War, it seemed that perhaps the country was, too. Still, West Point realized it needed to project a more aspirational identity, focused on a set of pure, positive principles. In 1898, the school enshrined its mission with a simple three-word credo: "Duty, Honor, Country."

THE SAME YEAR AS WEST POINT ADOPTED ITS NEW MOTTO, it welcomed a nineteen-year-old plebe to campus, Oscar Booz. He had all the mental signatures of a perfect military officer, smart and morally upstanding, but was relatively small for his age. A medical examiner noted in Booz's application materials that, while he was a generally excellent candidate, his "chest muscles are not as well developed as could be desired."

Oscar strictly adhered to West Point's core tenets while evincing skepticism toward its despotic hierarchy. He bristled vocally when upperclassmen yelled at him, outbursts that resulted in more abuse. Upperclassmen labeled him weak, cowardly, and sacrilegious, with some baselessly charging that he had feigned reading his Bible in chapel, stuffing instead a secular text within its pages. In fact, Oscar was highly devout, with other cadets calling him a "deadbeat" for his commitment to Christian tenets. When their anger with Oscar reached a fever pitch, cadets forced him into West Point's underground fight club, which appeared to be sanctioned by administrators, even as bare-knuckle boxing was then illegal. Clear signs of the club were everywhere, from piles of bloody towels in laundry baskets to black eyes and loose teeth.

At the beginning of Oscar's brawl, he and another cadet, Frank Keller, were encircled by cadets, stripped to the waist, and egged on. Within seconds, Keller jabbed Booz in the eye. Booz started to bleed, then started to cry. "The upper classmen are brutes and bullies," he later wrote home. "They have an eager desire to injure."

Oscar was also ordered to chug Tabasco sauce. He complained to his bunk mate that the sauce made him dizzy, and his face started to lose its complexion. Several weeks later, he left the academy and returned home. He had been at West Point for just a few months, and yet it had already left him in failing health. A family doctor discovered bruises across his body and observed that his throat was badly swollen, likely from the hot sauce. He diagnosed him with a rare form of tuberculosis in his larynx. As winter set in, Oscar became bedridden and delirious. Sometimes he hallucinated that he was back on campus. "Here comes the inspector," he once exclaimed. "Is everything all right?" Days later, on December 3, 1900, Oscar Booz died. He was nineteen.

His death spurred fevered press coverage and the first major congressional scrutiny of the military educational model. First, the War Department launched an internal inquiry, which brass and their congressional allies pledged would be impartial. Unsurprisingly, it wasn't, asserting forcefully, but absent any fact, that Oscar had not been hazed, a finding pugnaciously echoed by West Point Superintendent A.L. Mills, who described the inquiry as an "unjust attack" on the academy's "manly body of cadets." Congress followed up with its own special inquiry, which, in February 1901, produced a shocking 630-page report detailing frequent child abuse within the corps of cadets.

Lawmakers found that upperclassmen had developed more than one hundred distinct methods for making a plebe feel like an "unknown, a stranger, and an inferior." First years were deprived of simple joys, like laughing or smiling, and underwent intense physical gauntlets, ordered routinely, for instance, to undertake high-stakes wall-sits, in which a bayonet was pointed up toward their asses. In 1897, George Marshall, later to become a famed soldier and statesman but then a "rat" at Virginia Military Institute, slipped while undergoing this rite, leading the saber to tear his buttocks, nearly causing permanent injury.

Plebes were forced to ingest lots of foods, including tabasco, which was known as "hell sauce." One plebe was reportedly forced to consume 130 prunes in one sitting. These and other forms of light torture—which made plebes puke, faint, or even convulse uncontrollably—were deemed crucial in breaking down a cadet's civilian identity and constructing a military one, built around collective pain and the masculine pride of suffering. Then there was the fight club. According to witnesses, brawls generally lasted until a participant was "knocked insensible." Investigators identified more than forty fights in those years, virtually all of which had led to at least one participant being hospitalized. One bout lasted a staggering fifty-eight rounds.

The congressional inquiry uncovered evidence that another boy, John Edward Breth, had died a year before Oscar due to his own severe hazing, and that upperclassmen had driven out another plebe because he was Jewish. One of the purported masterminds of cadet hazing in Oscar's day was William Augustus Mitchell, who had previously served in a senior leadership position at Alabama Polytechnic Institute's chapter of Sigma Alpha Epsilon, another early and illuminating example of the long-standing interplay between military and civilian frat life.

At the investigation's conclusion, Representative Edmund Driggs of New York pronounced West Point's hazing culture to be "detestable, disgraceful, dishonourable, [and] disreputable." He also charged that such treatment was "unmanly." And yet Driggs and other lawmakers foolishly failed to identify a reason for this behavior, writing in their report that "something" had "benumbed the consciences of most of these otherwise creditable young men." Never did they reason that it was the school's vicious cycle of hazing that had itself degraded the ethical sensibilities of these cadets.

Hazing was one of Thayer's most well-devised ingredients in making a military man, something that scrubbed away individual identity, crafted institutional loyalty, and established generalized, easily directable strains of anger. The military needed soldiers with conditional morality and violent urges, instincts that hazing inculcated. Before they arrived on the battle-field, these boys had nowhere to direct their urges other than inwards, or at each other. One cadet vividly compared this experience to "a bucket of testosterone inside a pressure cooker."

In the case of the Booz investigation, Thayer's program—which stressed the masculine virtue of suffering in silence—proved protective of the institution he helped birth. Many cadets hauled before Congress to testify fiercely defended hazing. One said it produced "prompt and unquestioned obedience," while also eliminating weakness and purging arrogance—Thayerian prerequisites, they claimed, for a man of war. In their eyes, Oscar's treatment was justified in service of making him battle ready. They claimed that he entered the academy as a "coward" and a liar—"not a strong man," though the real reason they had targeted him wasn't that he was incapable of joining the officer class. It was that he had challenged their social hierarchy.

Even so, Oscar had internalized at least one vital West Point virtue: silence. Shortly before his death, his father pressed him repeatedly for the names of the cadets who had hazed him. Each time he refused, just as he had declined to file a hazing complaint when he was at West Point. In Oscar's eyes, it "would not be manly to do that."

IN 1901, AS PART OF THEIR INVESTIGATION, Congress questioned a model West Point cadet named Douglas MacArthur. In addition to the punishing day-to-day pressures he faced at the academy, MacArthur was then also being closely watched by his mother, Mary, who, according to school lore, stayed in West Point's on-site lodgings, known today as the Hotel Thayer, for the entirety of his tenure. Mary was not simply in close proximity to her young Douglas, but had secured a room with "a view of her son's dorm window, so she could check on whether he was studying at night."

The future general was a person of interest in the Booz investigation because he had overseen West Point's unofficial "Plebe Fight Commission." MacArthur's biographer, William Manchester, recounts in *American Caesar* that, as a plebe, MacArthur himself had been laid unconscious and sent into convulsions after three separate groups of upperclassmen forced him to perform deep knee bends over broken glass, known internally as

"Eagles." When it came time to testify, MacArthur acknowledged that he viewed his hazing as unnecessary and cruel, but he minimized his abuse, deeming the intensity of his hazing as "greatly exaggerated," the claims of his convulsions "erroneous." "I had what you might call aggravated cramps," MacArthur insisted.

The investigation ultimately found that Oscar and other fallen cadets "were never well after they left the Academy, but we cannot affirmatively find that their death was caused by their treatment." Still, lawmakers proposed ambitious measures to suppress hazing, including one that would create a federal definition for such practices, banning specific behaviors and mandating expulsion for all cadets found guilty of them. They were to be given no chance at return, either to West Point or the military writ large. Archival news clips indicate that the bill passed in the House, then, in the Senate, was deemed "more cruel than any form of hazing the cadets had indulged in."

A toothless compromise delegated accountability to West Point and the War Department. It also allowed cadets found guilty of hazing to return to campus two years after their expulsion. Many later did. These regulations were as weak as they were unevenly applied. A few years after their passage, they were usurped by new dictates empowering upperclassmen with more authority over plebes, a quiet concession to the belief that abuse is elemental to the alchemy of military education.

From then on, West Point's violent nucleus was free to thrash and thrive. America was then hardly a hundred years old, and yet warfare had become an elemental, inescapable part of life, one that the country's leader felt was easier to romanticize than to remediate. Early evidence of this phenomenon emerged two years after Oscar's death, when Harrie Irving Hancock, a prominent writer of books for boys, proclaimed that West Point "turns out the finest physical specimen of manhood to be found in the world."

Subsequent attempts to outlaw hazing only hardened the military's resolve to defend it. In a 1908 article in *The New York Times*, numerous academy graduates insisted that hazing "benefits character" and brings "a mother's darling . . . down to earth." One wished that academics be cut, and the beatings continue. Another recounted the mythical tale of a cadet who arrived spoiled and arrogant. After experiencing a high dose of hazing, the boy purportedly became humble, accountable, even lovable. "He became humanized," the officer argued. "Hazing saved him."

Chapter 3

The Sons of Mars

While France inspired Thayer's design for a military university, it was England that pioneered the program perfectly designed to arm and excite younger lads.

The genesis of the idea came from a highly decorated British cavalry officer named Robert Baden-Powell, who commanded regiments in the Second Boer War, a particularly destructive imperial conflict in southern Africa that bridged the nineteenth and twentieth centuries. Baden-Powell penned an unorthodox military training manual he called *Aids to Scouting*. Peppered within the typically dry pages on tactics were fun games focused on building skills, like tracking, observation, first aid—plus thrilling yarns detailing Baden-Powell's military exploits.

The manual, published in 1899, caught the eye of English teachers and youth groups looking to compel their pupils to go outside. In response, Baden-Powell adapted the text to broaden its appeal and rechristened it *Scouting for Boys*. It went on to sell 150 million copies, making Baden-Powell filthy rich and serving as the springboard for the creation of the Boy Scouts, a venture that revolutionized military recruiting in the Western world.

Baden-Powell long insisted that his program was exclusively focused on "citizenship training," though many began to call the Scouts "embryonic soldiers." By the onset of World War I, Baden-Powell had mobilized an army of roughly 200,000 Cub and Boy Scouts, half of whom were employed in official wartime duties. He coordinated their responsibilities directly with the British War Office and bragged publicly that he had more than a thousand Scouts in every British county. Among other duties, the boys transmitted intelligence, supported relief and first aid missions, and organized patriotic parades that ended at local recruiting stations. Some guarded bridges and rail lines. Others looked after local water supplies, worried that Germans might poison the water. They were also alert to the sounds and behaviors of birds, which, they were instructed, could indicate an enemy intrusion. In service to these duties, young Scouts sometimes identified innocent foreigners, fueling a military dragnet that led to unjust detentions.

Scouts who put in at least fifty days of military work earned the organization's coveted "War Service" badge. These light duties and faux decorations had an acute effect on the psyche of British juveniles, inciting a restlessness for real war service. In August 1914, one ten-year-old Scout wrote to his local newspaper requesting that the War Office send him a rifle and ammunition. "When the war is over," he calmly explained, "I will return the rifle and what ammunition I have left." Around the same time, a fourteen-year-old in Manchester attacked a fellow Scout with a knife. Many Scouts abandoned their studies altogether to contribute full-time to the war effort. More than eighty-four thousand former Scouts and Scoutmasters fought, and about eight thousand died.

The Scouting movement was exported to the United States in 1910, via a newspaperman and entrepreneur named W.D. Boyce. He had been impressed by the impeccable manners of a Scout he encountered during a trip to London.

The Boy Scouts of America initially included opposing naturalist and militaristic wings. For a time, the tree huggers seemed to dominate. This was evident by a decidedly anti-war illustration that ran in the November 1914 issue of the organization's in-house magazine, *Boy's Life*. It depicted a Scout guiding Lady Liberty away from the battlefield, toward "permanent peace." The organization's militarist flank, however, viewed peace as effeminate, and sought to activate their infrastructure for explicit wartime matters. Organization leaders recognized these competing influences and initially compromised by remaining neutral on the questionable and looming European war, a stance that angered President Theodore Roosevelt, an early, burly American he-man who coined his own nickname: Bull Moose. In a stern warning to Scout leaders, Roosevelt warned that any "effort to prevent boys of this country . . . from being trained to arms" amounted to "treason."

Colin Livingstone, the first national president of the American Boy Scouts, aligned the Scouts with Bull Moose, by explicitly promoting manliness and militarism. Under Livingstone's watch, the number of Scoutmasters with a military background doubled, while Scouts themselves were introduced to more service-adjacent activities, like shooting firearms. *Boy's Life* began to run advertisements for military schools and ran stories fusing naturalism and militarism in ways that eased a potential soldier's path into violence. Boy Scout leaders also pivoted away from Lady Liberty and another feminine symbol of American patriotism and virtue, Miss Columbia, and shifted their allegiance to the more masculine Uncle Sam.

By the time America entered World War I, Livingstone had mustered a force of 300,000 Scouts, whom he funneled seamlessly into the war effort. Troop leaders coordinated directly with the Committee on Public Information, handing out millions of propaganda pamphlets and posters to the public. Scouts sold tens of millions of dollars in war bonds, leading Treasury Secretary William McAdoo to marvel over these "unpaid helpers" seized by "patriotic fever." Scouts also organized a "Victory Garden" campaign, in which they planted crops as part of a national food effort. Its tagline read: "a Scout with a hoe may equal a man with a gun."

Over this same period, hundreds of private military schools opened their doors, and tens of thousands of students poured into them. These schools generally served younger populations, mostly students in middle and high school. Most of them established formal pipelines to the military, but subsequent service was generally optional, and school leaders presented their programs to parents as lowercase "m" military programs meant exclusively to "develop young gentlemen."

Most of these schools adopted the punishing culture and curriculum of the Thayer Method. Valley Forge Military Academy, located a stone's throw from George Washington's old encampment, was a virtual carbon copy of West Point. It initially adopted the same uniforms and crest as the academy, along with a tweaked version of Thayer's "triangle of success." The life of a young cadet there often resembled that of a West Pointer, or even an overseas G.I. In April 1930, for example, Forge cadets were called to the scene of a deadly explosion at a fireworks factory outside Philadelphia, where they instituted a security perimeter, directed traffic, and discouraged pilfering. Cadets clearing debris also discovered dead bodies. Some adopted adult coping mechanisms in response, sneaking cigarettes and downing alcohol. Others wrote forlorn letters to girls they left back home.

Valley Forge and dozens of other schools organized under the auspices of the Association of Military Colleges and Schools of the United States

(AMCSUS), which was formed in 1913. Another member is New York Military Academy, a high school founded by Union veteran Charles Jefferson Wright. Its list of notable alumni includes Gambino family crime boss John Gotti and two-term U.S. president Donald J. Trump. The U.S. military frequently consorted with AMCSUS, guiding curricula and paving a reliable cadet pipeline to the service academies. The government provided weapons for member schools through its ready supply of surplus military gear—and Washington waived certain cumbersome regulations for the schools, including asbestos removal requirements.

The inaugural meeting of the Association of Military Colleges and Schools featured remarks from Secretary of War Lindley Garrison, who fussed that "America was the most warlike nation on earth, and yet the most unmilitary." Military bigwigs and their attachés attended virtually every subsequent meeting, including one in which military school leaders schemed to find teachers, psychologists, and neurologists who would protect the prophylactic benefits of their programs from the "pacifist onslaught."

THE MAIN TOOL USED BY THE MILITARY and its civilian allies to steel against pacifism was panic. In the run-up to the First World War, a coalition composed of military leaders, public school administrators, PE teachers, politicians, and powerful titans of industry organized under the umbrella of what they called the "Preparedness Movement."

This was an alarmist, astroturfing campaign aimed to whip up public worry about percolating foreign threats. Their goal was to expand domestic military power and civilian acceptance of it, chiefly through the promotion of compulsory military education. Preparedness advocates also built substantial momentum toward the establishment of the National Defense Act of 1916, which expanded the regular Army and National Guard—and created mechanisms that were later used to draft men into World War I—a move that triggered a substantial antidraft movement.

The roots of the Preparedness Movement date back to 1913. That's when, 260 miles due north of West Point, Douglas MacArthur, then an Army captain, launched the first in a slew of Boy Scout–style military summer camps geared toward kingpins of industry and politics. Thirteen thousand influential Americans, many of them key businessmen, went camping in a bizarre military charm offensive. It came to be called the "Plattsburgh

Movement," so named for the location of an early gathering that featured a particularly powerful set of campers, among them New York City mayor John Mitchel, *New York Times* scion Julius Ochs Adler, and Teddy Roosevelt Jr., the eldest son of the former president. In his 1899 speech "The Strenuous Life," the elder Roosevelt had described an increasingly cooped-up "hypercivilized man of the great industrial centers," who avoids "contact with the rough world of actual life."

As an antidote, Roosevelt vocally championed preparedness and compulsory military training. "The military tent, where boys sleep side by side," he predicted, "will rank next to the public school among the great agents of democracy."

The military had clear-cut reasons for supporting the preparedness movement: they needed men. In 1915, shortly after the European conflict commenced, military brass authored a staff report warning that the department had a grossly insufficient number of ground troops were it to confront an American land invasion. Schoolchildren, they reasoned, were the critical untapped resource.

Early-twentieth-century businessmen worked with a different set of incentives compared to the military brass. They viewed martial training as helpful to creating a compliant society to preserve the social order from which the wealthy and powerful benefited. During the decades before the war, business leaders tested numerous experiments to foment these conditions, including a youth organization called the "Junior Police," a juvenile street cleaning league, and various reformatories out of which ultimately spawned the troubled teen industry.

American business was facing domestic worries that included class conflict, which grew out of strikes and the labor movement. A substantial American left similarly blossomed, especially in cities, immigrant communities, and the agrarian west and midwest, elevating hundreds of reform-minded socialists and populists into elected office, as mayors, congressmen, state legislators, and more. Industrialists responded by issuing injunctions, hiring strikebreakers, making selective reforms, and ramping up their support for compulsory military education, feeling it would create "productive" and "obedient" workers. Many were happy to pony up taxes for these often harsh and stifling public school programs, a cost of doing business they personally avoided by paying to send their children to private schools.

THE PREPAREDNESS MOVEMENT'S NAME REFLECTED its most glaring vulnerability, namely that Americans then lived in a brief pocket of peace. Since no immediate threats imperiled to the homeland, preparedness leaders tried to concoct them, raising the specter of a land invasion and saber-rattling about rulers an ocean away. At the same time, a ragtag but powerful peace coalition formed and entered the fray, one composed of socialists, trade unionists, and faith leaders, plus suffragettes and (especially) female educators, who fought at the front of the pack.

The peace movement's most powerful and well-funded foe was the National Security League. It was founded on December 1, 1914, at the Hotel Belmont in New York City by 150 well-heeled titans of the Gilded Age. This impeccably dressed pack included Cornelius Vanderbilt, Henry C. Frick, Andrew Carnegie, and Simon Guggenheim. Their charter was to investigate the state of armed preparedness in America, as well as promote universal military service and "patriotic education." They backed their mission with more than $600,000, or roughly $20 million in today's terms, fueling powerful propaganda efforts, including the printing and distribution of more than a million alarmist placards reading: "We Are Unprepared." The league also held countless patriotism events, some including legions of Boy Scouts. They lobbied for legislation to increase military school training, and fostered allies in and out of the classroom.

The league easily enticed physical education teachers, then represented by the Playground Association of America, which was eager to grow and legitimize the profession. Prior to 1915, just three states—Ohio, Idaho, and North Dakota—had a mandated physical education curriculum. The association launched a vigorous campaign around war and American weakness to benefit their nascent industry.

The Security League had its own business interests at heart. During the 1918 midterm elections, they created scorecards that gave high patriotic marks to candidates supportive of armed conflict and the military. They made "loyalty" a defining issue of the campaign season and launched a well-funded campaign against more than a hundred isolationist lawmakers, many of whom lost their elections. But eventually, the league's mask slipped, revealing its true aims, which included members' domestic business interests. During one closed-door policy meeting, league officials exclusively asked Edward King, an Illinois Republican, about domestic matters, including his positions on unions, the nationalization of the railroad industry, and J.P. Morgan.

One of the slogans concocted at the Plattsburgh business camp was "Prepare the Eagle to Protect the Dove." In truth, the Security League and its allies were bitter and hostile toward pacifist leaders, many of whom were women. Contemporary feminist scholar Susan Zeiger argues that the preparedness movement's struggle was not just over the future of the military's size and scope, nor the future of business power. It was also, she asserts, a crucial fight over America's "shared vision of manhood."

Time and again, the League and its allies raised panic over the "feminization of teaching," a noxious trend in which boys were coddled and softened, rather than instilled with the lessons of hardship and propelled toward Machiavellian self-interest. One preparedness advocate complained that "the boy in America is not being brought up to punch another boy's head or to stand having his own punched in a healthy and proper manner."

The activist core of female teachers who agitated against the militarization of their classrooms generally didn't shy away from the movement's gendered framing. Many cast their cause as an explicit fight against "the sons of Mars," an explicit reference to the Roman god of war. These so-called Martians included people like Army lieutenant Edgar Steever, who pledged that military drills would "put a little stiffening into the American boy and make him more manly, and make him better material to work on educationally." Admiral F.E. Chadwick, an early instructor at the Naval Academy, warned that to put a boy under "woman tutelage is to do violence to that most precious possession, his masculine nature."

"He will never recover," Chadwick concluded. "He goes through life a maimed man."

The military's convenient remedy was expanded military education. As such, they proposed to secure unencumbered access to American youth, demanding, among other things, that public schools provide them with the names and addresses of all schoolboys eligible for service. Military leaders influenced public school curriculum through intense lobbying, priming students for nationalist grooming by weakening foreign language offerings and agitating for a social studies curriculum that emphasized and legitimized conflict. These forces also secured the mandatory recitation in public schools of the Pledge of Allegiance each morning. Some officers in

Minnesota paid local girls one dollar and a piece of clothing for every boy they directed to a military recruiting station. This latter piece of intelligence was gleaned by the American Peace League, the major antagonist to their security-obsessed brothers. They were one of a handful of scrappy but effective organizations that viewed the Preparedness Movement as a psychological operation meant to instill harmful tendencies in American boys. They had little money but still built a savvy national apparatus, founding chapters in forty-five states and territories across the country, including Michigan, Oregon, California, and Massachusetts. Many branches had hundreds of members.

These activists penned and promulgated their own competing curriculum, a four-hundred-page vision for grade school entitled "A Course in Citizenship." It recast citizenship as global, not national, and reoriented social studies to question and investigate conflicts in depth and shift the focus to notable civilian figures, not "wholesale murderers."

WHILE THE LION'S SHARE OF WOMEN in the peace movement stayed fully aligned to their cause, many of their male adherents prematurely defected. President Woodrow Wilson, who led his country into World War I, had been a member of the American Peace Society. He had once embraced the sage advice of President Washington, who, in his farewell address, warned America to never "entangle our peace and prosperity in the toils of European ambition, rivalship, interest, humor, or caprice." Wilson's secretary of state, William Jennings Bryan, had a similar pacifist streak, and in 1914 banned American financial institutions from doing work with any of the war's belligerents.

J.P. Morgan bristled against Bryan's dictate, having been appointed as the financial broker between English and French figures seeking American goods and armaments. Morgan successfully lobbied Bryan to lift his ban while other industrialists, eager to cash in on the war economy and protect their foreign investments, pushed Wilson, in April 1917, to enter the conflict. While most Americans fiercely opposed our involvement in the European war, Wall Street was, according to one dispatch, "bright with the Stars and Stripes floating from banks and brokerage houses."

Another defector from the peace movement was Henry Ford, who, in 1915, had funded the "Peace Ship," a vessel packed with pacifists that sailed to Europe hoping to end hostilities. The vessel was pilloried in the press as a "Ship of Fools." These optics only intensified when a bunch of passengers, including Ford, came down with a dastardly strain of influenza. Not long after Ford's ill-fated adventure at sea, he became one of the war's major motor suppliers.

In 1915, the Preparedness Movement saw its signature issues validated when Senator George Chamberlain of Oregon introduced legislation mandating military training for all American boys aged twelve to twenty-three. It was a near–carbon copy of a successful Australian effort, launched in 1909, to leverage xenophobic worries against Japanese expansionism to become the only English-speaking nation with compulsory military education for boys aged twelve and up.

Between 1911 and 1915, 34,000 Aussie boys had resisted this mandate, and 7,000 were jailed. Chamberlain's bill similarly proposed that boys who disobeyed orders be imprisoned for up to twenty days. While federal legislation in America faltered, the Security League seeded and supported dozens of other proposals in local and state bodies. Teachers defeated most of these efforts, but the Security League held special power in New York, which in 1916 passed a law mandating three hours a week of extracurricular military training for all high school–aged boys. A similar statute passed in neighboring New Jersey and a couple of other states.

That summer, the New York National Guard, on orders from the Security League, marshaled one thousand boys to Peekskill for an abridged training camp to test their new curriculum. The Guard also identified, trained, and deputized roughly three hundred school officials, many of them principals and PE teachers, to prepare and deploy the coming trainings. This curriculum had first taken shape in 1912, when military brass and sympathetic college administrators convened at the Army War College for a conference to establish a formal and replicable slate of military training standards.

Despite the mandate, attendance rates for school military trainings hovered around 50 percent across New York, with numbers in the five boroughs plunging to as low as 2 percent. A news article in 1917 chronicled a particularly vocal rebellion at a mostly Jewish school in Williamsburg. There, students covered the walls in posters opposing the trainings. When asked by a reporter for comment, one student simply replied, "War is hell."

Desperate to snuff out these pacifist sentiments, New York imposed teacher loyalty oaths, which, in turn, fueled the rise of teacher evaluations, which conservative administrators used as a cudgel. During this crackdown,

Columbia University's president, Nicholas Butler, formerly of the Carnegie Endowment for International Peace, became yet another man with fair-weather pacifism, purging a string of anti-war professors on baseless grounds. Butler's actions were fiercely opposed by famed progressive educator John Dewey, then a member of the faculty, who believed that students were the crucial engines of peace and coexistence. Out of Butler's crackdown emerged the American Association of University Professors, initially led by Dewey, which, over the intervening century or so, has organized effectively to secure academic freedom and other faculty protections.

Middle and high school teachers were fighting against the militarization of the classroom, too, but they lacked a college faculty's organizational heft. The American Federation of Unions was just getting started. They lacked sufficient membership or resources to flex real muscle. During its 1915 annual meeting, the National Education Association took a strong stand against military training. A year later, however, they capitulated, though not before inviting Major General Leonard Wood to promote his case at their conference, where he pledged that students forced to drill would develop "a better physique, a greater degree of self-control, habits of regularity, [and] promptness."

New York's public school teachers contended with a zealot in the form of retired general Thomas Wingate. He was a member of New York City's board of education who proclaimed that the pacifist teacher was "a thousand times more dangerous than the teacher who gets drunk and lies in the gutter." Wingate exerted intense administrative pressure on such teachers, investigating and firing scores of them for being insufficiently supportive of the war machine. He packed the classrooms with Krag rifles, furnished by the War Department on the condition that they be safely stored. Among his other harebrained schemes, Wingate also tried, and failed, to force the city's education board to issue high school diplomas to all boys who dropped out to serve.

Among the teachers Wingate targeted was a Quaker woman, Mary McDowell, who taught at the Manual Training High School, in Park Slope, Brooklyn. She refused to take his loyalty oath, declined to teach patriotism in class, and wouldn't urge her students to sell war bonds. In response, school officials charged her with "conduct unbecoming of a teacher."

Rather than accept her dismissal, McDowell fought it, for years, waging one of the first American battles over academic freedom. She won, and was the only teacher from this period who secured her reinstatement, forcing school officials to concede that her dismissal was "too severe" and made amid "great public hysteria."

McDowell had herself been a brilliant student, earning degrees from Swarthmore, Oxford, and Columbia before settling into her beloved public teaching role in Brooklyn. One teacher evaluation described her as "in every way the best." She could be humble and shy but was also prone to bone-deep expressions of her pacifism. Every year, she donated one-fifth of her teacher's salary to the Red Cross, and spent countless hours in the city streets, pamphleting for peace.

McDowell later spoke out against the military draft for World War II, arguing that it unfairly targeted working-class and immigrant men—and undermined democratic reforms by normalizing coercion. She also spearheaded the idea of war tax resistance, withholding, for many years, 60 percent of her federal taxes meant for the War Department and sending it instead to the American Friends Service Committee, a Quaker peace group. "In rain, in snow, and in the heat of summer she would always come," reflected celebrated peace and civil rights activist Bayard Rustin. McDowell's spirit—and her tax resistance—were later adopted by activists who opposed the war in Vietnam.

Chapter 4

Scabbard and Blade

Amid the runaway success of the Boy Scouts, the U.S. military looked for a novel approach to hook college kids. They landed on a proven structure for enticing young men: the fraternity. Their scheme dispensed with Greek letters for a cool cloak-and-dagger name: Scabbard and Blade.

The Blade, as I like to call it, was pitched as a fun extracurricular complement to the Reserve Officer Training Corps (ROTC), which trained officers on America's college campuses. Congress had formalized ROTC through the passage of its 1916 defense bill, but the program wasn't thoroughly up and running until after the 1918 armistice. The wartime military instead met its manpower needs in May 1917 with a draft law called the Selective Service Act.

While ROTC didn't meaningfully assist with World War I, a major at the time argued that the program's establishment had a substantial second-order impact: "training the popular mind to the necessity and needs of defense." A similarly calculated argument floated in the *Army and Navy Register* reasoned that ROTC would "keep the naturally pacific mind of America" from becoming so.

Days after World War I ended, the military announced sweeping plans to establish three hundred ROTC units across the country. It also launched the Junior Reserve Officer Training Corps, or JROTC, which began popping up in public high schools.

The military piloted the first chapter of their Scabbard and Blade fraternity at the University of Wisconsin, curious, it seems, about whether their boat would float in hostile territory. Wisconsin had seen intense student agitation after the War Department asserted, without merit, that the Morrill Act stipulated all ROTC units in land grant schools be compulsory. In

1923, the Wisconsin state legislature pushed back at this interpretation by passing a law strictly declaring ROTC an elective, a move that led many ROTC programs in the Badger State to wither.

Similar trends developed in other states, too. The War Department responded by casting ROTC as a fun, harmless elective. Campus military leaders hosted social gatherings, including roller-skating derbies and horse shows, staged mock battles, and offered students generous scholarships. At many schools, including Wisconsin, this more restrained recruitment approach proved wildly successful.

In the interregnum between the world wars, the military established successful Blade chapters at dozens of colleges and universities. They also published an official propaganda organ molded on *Boy's Life*, called *The Scabbard and Blade Journal*. It featured colorful tales about Bonaparte, articles on the merits of law enforcement and military service, and lessons on physical fitness. One typical piece declared that "America has grown soft." It cited a study claiming that 75 percent of schoolchildren had physical defects.

The Blade's founders had ties to powerful men's organizations, like the Masons and the Elks, and its national leader, T.S. Crockett, closely collaborated with the War Department. He and other Blade leaders also corresponded with key preparedness figures, including those from the National Security League, the Allied Military Defense Council, and the Reserve Officers Council. The fraternity also worked in tandem with the National Society of Pershing Rifles, an older military honor society and drill team named after its founder, John Pershing, the famous West Pointer and highly decorated World War I general. He had started the student group while teaching military science at the University of Nebraska.

Scabbard and Blade blended the trappings of secret societies and frat life to form an organization that lit up the male id. There were physical drills, shiny service badges, and the promise of women. Chapter leaders routinely threw glamorous parties, some of which the military previewed and publicized in local papers. Some of their postings listed the names and photos of pretty women who planned to attend. The Blade chapter at the University of Arizona once hosted a twelve-hour-long "Kissation" ceremony. The brothers later estimated that "some 250 girls were 'pledged.'"

Initiation rituals were closely held secrets, discussed euphemistically, though it was reported that pledges at one school had to walk around campus tied to a toy cannon dragging behind them. Brothers conducted flag-raising ceremonies at sports games and screened patriotic motion pictures on campus. The West Virginia chapter even created a college radio program called "The University's Part in National Defense." When they weren't promoting war, Blade chapters monitored anti-military protests, which had become frequent. In May 1925, for instance, hundreds of Howard University students went on strike from their coursework to protest the school's compulsory ROTC programs. They held picket signs with messages like "What is this going to be—an army or a university?" (Howard initially expelled the student strikers, before ultimately reinstating them, and making ROTC an elective.)

In 1931, Blade sources at the University of Michigan happily reported up the chain that there was "no pronounced pacifism on the campus." A year later, Crockett thanked another contact for providing a tip concerning an upcoming meeting of an anti-war student group. He said the meeting would be monitored by an unnamed agent who would "prepare a report."

Blade members at Wisconsin also produced and distributed a list of prominent scholars, teachers, and politicians deemed "dangerous and red." It included prominent pacifists, like John Dewey, as well as left-leaning college presidents at places like Vassar and Mount Holyoke—a strikingly similar campaign to the second Trump administration's attacks on academic freedom.

ONE OF THE FEW MEN FROM THE PEACE LEAGUE DAYS who stuck with the cause was Dewey. In 1925, he helped form a new group called "The Committee on Militarism in Education," or CME. Whereas the activism in the run-up to World War I had been largely driven by women and focused on protecting schoolchildren, this new, postwar outfit had a spiritual core and focused largely on resisting ROTC.

CME's chairman was George Albert Coe, an ordained minister and professor at Columbia's teacher college, who charged that using religion to justify war was satanic, taking special umbrage with the British military hymn "Onward, Christian Soldiers!"

The group was kickstarted with a $5,000 grant from Charles Garland, the wayward son of a New York banking scion who used his family fortune to support socialist causes. CME undertook a two-pronged mission: to abolish compulsory ROTC in college and prohibit it from seeping deep into high schools, and, more philosophically, to convince the American public that military force was not a natural inclination, but the result of relentless indoctrination.

Reverend Coe argued that war was a "state of mind," one derived through society's careful shaping of mental mechanisms and responses, including by exploiting childhood innocence rather than appreciating the beautiful ways in which students, unburdened by cynicism or assumption, see and think about the world. "If [educators] were granted a free hand," Coe wrote, "we could prevent war altogether, we could make it as obsolete as cannibalism." Dewey similarly criticized the military's brand of education as one that "trains children to docility and obedience," making them "suited to an autocratic society." This was fundamentally at odds with what Dewey argued education should be—a process of expanding thinking, not limiting it.

Clergymen then maintained significant cultural and educational influence, outnumbering college presidents and professors by about seven to one. So while Coe and his allies were ardently anti-war, others were acting out of more practical considerations, worried that the general might soon replace the pastor as the overriding influence on American youth.

Shortly after its founding, CME connected with Winthrop Lane, a progressive journalist who had previously uncovered abusive treatment of conscientious objectors at Fort Leavenworth, Kansas. They had been given lengthy sentences for their beliefs and had faced a perilous backlash for helping organize a prison strike against their conditions. Some, Lane found, were holed up in solitary confinement for three days and fed only bread and water.

The CME sicced Lane's investigative chops on ROTC, leading to a blistering report that undermined the college program's genteel demeanor. Lane's report pulled almost exclusively from official military materials, mostly ROTC course catalogues and training manuals, which included gruesome instructions on how to kill with a bayonet. His exposé also presciently warned that, through the injection of military influence, "a precedent is set whose possible consequences to academic freedom should be clearly foreseen."

The committee produced 150,000 copies of Lane's report and distributed them to a wide array of sources: clergy and civic clubs, plus every American governor and congressperson. Newspapers reprinted large swaths of the report, as did church publications and *The Nation* magazine.

The pamphlet was further championed by prominent civil rights leaders, including NAACP founder W.E.B. Du Bois, noted chaplain Henry Sloane Coffin, suffragette Jane Addams, and Zona Gale, a noted playwright and the first woman to win the Pulitzer Prize. Together they called for the abolition of military schooling. This spooked the War Department, which sent an official communiqué to its commanders reiterating their commitment to expand military education to "the greatest possible number of students." At the same time, Assistant Secretary of War Hanford MacNider tried to cheapen and minimize this pacifist tide, deriding opponents as "paid agitators [and] sentimental sob-sisters."

Nevertheless, CME's work stirred up public outrage and achieved impact. The War Department removed its student bayonet training regime and sixty-five colleges and high schools dropped out of ROTC entirely. Another dozen made the courses elective, not compulsory, while the generally conservative city of Cleveland, Ohio, voted to eliminate military training in its high schools, despite vocal lobbying from veterans' groups and war officials.

CME also secured a bipartisan federal bill to entirely abolish compulsory military school training, and hearings were held in April and June of 1926. Ahead of the hearings, CME activated hundreds of American educators to petition their representatives to vote for the bill. It was further cosigned by the American Federation of Labor, which called for an immediate intervention to prevent "military saber rattlers from making goose-steppers out of the schoolboys of America." In an unexpected twist, President Calvin Coolidge also expressed his opposition to compulsory military training during an off-the-cuff newspaper interview.

The War Department responded with its own lobbying blitz, casting the bill's supporters as "paid agitators" and "communist dupes." The Reserve Officers Association derided the bill as "defeatist," something concocted by the "sick minds of socialists and communists." The all-powerful American Legion leveled its own charges of subversion against the bill's supporters, mobilizing local ROTC support groups. Meanwhile, the *Blade* issued bulletins warning that the bill was the work of communist traitors seeking to create a "helpless state." According to the book *Breaking the War Habit*, agents from a private intelligence firm founded by former military brass spied on CME officials on at least two occasions. In the end, the military's covert activities, coupled with its public carpet-bombing, overwhelmed CME's mighty but comparatively modest campaign. Their bill died before ever receiving a vote in the House Committee on Military Affairs.

THE SENTIMENTS ON CAPITOL HILL DIVERGED SHARPLY from those on college campuses. In a 1932 poll, 81 percent of 25,000 surveyed students said they opposed compulsory ROTC. Two years later, 25,000 American students went on strike from their courses to advocate peace. By 1936, the strike had swelled to a half million. A Brooklyn reporter followed thousands of students as they marched to Borough Hall, with hand-scrawled signs reading "Schools not Battleships" and "Abolish the ROTC." Farther north, Harvard's strike committee handed out flyers reading: "Military drill is being used to prepare us to fight for the profits of big business."

That same spring, student journalists at Penn State uncovered "storm trooper sadism" within the local ROTC chapter. The student paper reported that at least two underperforming Penn State cadets were sent down a line of seventy-five brothers who whipped them hard with their pistol belts. One senior cadet who refused this order was, according to the report, "tongue-lashed" by an ROTC sergeant, who lectured him on the "inadvisability of being a slacker in the Army."

It was in this moment that CME mounted its final offense. Leaders demanded Penn State investigate its ROTC leadership and sought passage of a new bill to eliminate compulsory military education. Their renewed legislative push was strengthened by support from Catholic, Protestant, and Jewish groups, including the federal Council of Churches, plus the National Students Federation, a conglomeration representing more than a half million students from more than a hundred colleges and universities. Advocates also gained support from Guy Stanton Ford, then the president of the University of Minnesota. He testified that his decades witnessing ROTC drills had convinced him that the curriculum, a near–carbon copy of the Thayer Method, not only proved ineffective at improving students' moral standing, but also that it didn't seem to meaningfully contribute to national preparedness.

In correspondence from spring 1937, representatives from the Blade coordinated legislative oppositions with the Army and Navy Union, laying out their plans to "defeat" the bill and retain the number of federally funded active reserve officers at thirty thousand. It echoed earlier efforts from the fraternity to activate members in opposition to proposals weakening the Army budget. In the end, CME's second legislative push also failed, leading

ROTC units, both compulsory and voluntary, to keep sprouting up at colleges and universities.

In the wake of these failures, CME confronted the fact that it was financially overextended, falling behind on payments to staff before ultimately cutting them loose. Internecine struggles were also emerging over whether to remain hardened pacifists or become neutral, or even anti-Communist, in the face of a brewing World War II.

In May 1939, as Adolf Hitler prepared to invade Poland, CME acknowledged in an internal report that the storm clouds of conflict had pushed its finances to a "starvation point" while providing the space for ROTC to reach a "saturation point." CME officials picked a few last smaller battles, including against a proposed JROTC program at a high school in Queens, and won. But each canceled chapter or converted pacifist paled in comparison with the military's far larger maneuvers. In a quick two-year burst, the War Department had added more than a dozen JROTC units in Chicago high schools alone, a rapid expansion that brought with it 10,000 new junior cadets, many of them poor people of color. By 1940, the War Department had at its beck and call 100,000 cadets from a staggering 220 civilian colleges and universities.

That September, Congress passed, and President Franklin Delano Roosevelt ratified, the Burke-Wadsworth Act, the first peacetime conscription in U.S. history. It was the final blow for the committee, and the death knell of the larger campaign against compulsory military education. With the stroke of Roosevelt's pen, every American boy was obligated to the state should Lady Liberty—or rather, Uncle Sam—need them.

Chapter 5

Weakness Is a Crime

Beyond a war's major tactical goals—land, resources, and the like—lies an impalpable but equally motivating factor: the claim of superior national strength. The regions of Europe that were devastated by the First World War, and would come to incite the second one, were not only desperate for territorial conquest and economic revitalization, but also for societal vitality and retribution. From these deeply felt and easily articulated sentiments emerged leaders who promised prosperity, independence, identity—and raging domination.

On paper, America had substantially shared in the winning of this so-called Great War, entering the fray late but still emerging with enhanced economic, military, and political power. But, like the Europeans, Americans become intoxicated by the scent of strong men. One bombastic embodiment of America's increasingly burly and bellicose id was Bernarr MacFadden, a pioneering fitness guru and magazine magnate who also dabbled in alternative medicine, politics, and foreign policy. Desperate for fame and power, he ran unsuccessful campaigns for New York City mayor, U.S. Senate, and even the presidency.

MacFaddden was a hawk with pecs, a man who spent his formative years teaching in military schools, then chartered two of his own, hoping to impose his love of physical strength onto American children, the War Department, and the world. He was also mercurial, hypersexual, and conspiratorial—an uncanny progenitor, in many ways, of today's manosphere.

Many Americans were leery of another world war, a perspective MacFadden's media empire gave occasional voice to. One particularly pointed essay argued that the Great War was a downright deception, a bloody exercise in wealth production for the "DuPontcracy" recast as a noble fight for democracy. (As context: the giant chemical company, long overseen by

West Point graduate Henry du Pont, had dominated the gunpowder market since before the Civil War.)

But, despite a few pacifist flutters, MacFadden's media arsenal was largely aimed at instigating conflict through his advocacy of muscular, militarized masculinity that reinforced nationalist, supremacist, and authoritarian power. MacFadden personally saw war as the ultimate strength competition and felt that the prospect of a new one might finally whip America's youth into proper shape. A national fitness campaign would ensure victory, he reasoned, and solve many other personal and societal ills.

MacFadden expressed a maximalist view of the male form. "Men should be men," he wrote in one representative essay, "square-shouldered, bright-eyed, with the form of an Apollo or a Hercules and with the power of a giant in a muscular body." The best way to reach these goals, he reasoned, was militarized training. "We must prepare for war up to the hilt," he demanded, while simultaneously dismissing the "peace-at-any-price fanatics."

This kind of saber-rattling benefited the military brass and padded MacFadden's pockets. When, for instance, America first constructed a national military draft system in 1917, MacFadden shamelessly hocked his book, *Vitality Supreme*, as providing the formula for battlefield success. "Now that the Conscription Bill has been passed by Congress you don't know when you will be called upon to defend the lives of those you love—wife, mother, sister, or helpless kiddies," reads one ad. "Could you make good in this crisis, or would you crumple up like a mere shell? A bluff is no longer good. You will have to deliver or suffer the consequences." He later created and sold a cereal called Strengthfude.

MacFadden's magazines similarly promised the secrets to strength, with military service framed as the ultimate panacea. One cover in the run-up to the war featured a drastic diptych showing a man physically transformed by military training. Another endorsement came from Senator Ernest Lundeen, a Minnesota Republican. His headline read: "Why I Am Sending My Boy to Military School." It was an especially remarkable essay considering Lundeen's own strict opposition to American involvement in World War II, a position later explained, perhaps, by his covert ties to Nazi Germany.

Such rhetoric solidified the idea of the U.S. military as the ultimate personal trainer. One advert around this time for a military school in *National Geographic* pledged to build muscle on the "hollow-chested boy." A century later, in a 2010 sociological study, forty-three ROTC cadets and enlisted personnel hailed the benefits of a military body, including one who, during his interview, flexed his muscles and said "pah-pow."

MacFadden's love of brawn led him to lightly collaborate with some of the world's strongmen, though not Hitler, before ultimately retreating back into American trenches. There, he helped define and push forward America's impossible fitness and masculinity standards, which bedevil boys to this day. MacFadden forcefully asserted the primacy of the body over the mind, dismissing traditional education efforts as doing little more than filling children's brains with "a vast storehouse of knowledge, a larger part of which is never used."

He promoted his vision in his magazine pages and applied it at his own military schools: Castle Heights Military Academy, in Lebanon, Tennessee, which imposed a daily sports requirement and maintained an ROTC unit, and another, in Tarrytown, New York, which, an advert bragged, was staffed by a "young, energetic, well-liked ex-military man in charge of [students] at all times." MacFadden later turned his enticing ideology of corporeal excellence into a religion called Cosmotarianism, which promised that the man who cherished his body was destined for heaven. Few officially converted to his sect, and MacFadden's name has been all but lost to history. But countless boys today adhere to the ideology he helped establish, crunching away in the gym while quietly praying for a ripped rebirth out of the ashes of their own weakness. His legacy elevated the physical form as equally important, if not more so, to the day's prevailing masculine traits, like smarts, service, and manners—ransacking the psyches of countless boys by instilling in them insatiable and largely unrealistic beauty standards that, in turn, can breed unshakable self-consciousness, unchecked narcissism, and the destructive urge to show off one's muscles through aggressive action.

MACFADDEN'S OBSESSION WITH STRENGTH WAS BORN, as it so often is, out of his own perceived inadequacies. His given name was Bernard Mac-Fadden, though he tweaked it in his early twenties to "Bernarr," believing it sounded more powerful, like a lion's roar. As a boy, he was small, weak, and frequently sick. His home state of Missouri was, too. The Civil War had ravaged the state, leaving the land scarred from fighting, pillaging, and arson. Around Mill Spring, where MacFadden grew up, infrastructure was weak and poverty widespread, with desperate bands of guerrillas roaming the countryside.

His father, William, was a broad-shouldered, barrel-chested, Scotch-Irish Union veteran with a violent temper and a nasty drinking problem. He died when MacFadden was four. His mother, Mary, died a few years later from tuberculosis. Once orphaned, MacFadden landed on a farm in northern Illinois, where he chopped wood, fed livestock, and built structures. Soon, he started to see his health improve.

By the time he was a teenager, MacFadden was in good shape, but remained slight, weighing just over a hundred pounds soaking wet. He wanted to get stronger, and look it, too, so he picked up two dumbbells for fifty cents at a local store and started pumping. He complemented this weight-training regime by restricting his diet mostly to half-cooked vegetables. He also participated in intermittent fasting.

MacFadden grew up around German immigrants who had imported gymnastic practices from their motherland. He spent many hours at a local facility navigating the horizontal bars. He started to wrestle, too, then proclaimed himself a "teacher of higher physical culture." In his early twenties, he landed a job as an athletic trainer at Bunker Hill Military Academy, in Illinois, which was geared toward boys with academic issues. He arrived at Bunker Hill with only an elementary school education, and took English and history classes during his free time. He also started writing a pulpy romance novel that one publisher called "the crudest piece of junk I have ever read." MacFadden later filled a similar post at Marmaduke Military Academy, in Missouri, where, among other things, he impressively coached the football team to a tie with the University of Missouri's B squad. It was at Marmaduke that MacFadden honed his powers of influence with American boys and discovered their potential market value. He also miraculously published his first book, now titled *The Athlete's Conquest*, which he then sold to virtually every student.

Following his stints at these military schools, MacFadden branded himself as one of America's first personal trainers, complete with an unforgettable tagline: "Weakness is a crime; don't be a criminal." Military strength was MacFadden's specialty, and he endlessly studied the training regimes of English, German, French, and Egyptian soldiers. He subsequently developed and promoted his own theories for how the U.S. Army could transform itself into a "monumental physical culture school." His prescription included a new soldier's diet and severe lifestyle restrictions, including bans on whiskey, beer, and prostitutes.

In 1899, MacFadden founded America's first fitness magazine, *Physical Culture*. He subsequently launched other popular periodicals and wrote dozens of books, with titles like *Virile Powers of Superb Manhood*, *Woman's Sex Life*, and *The Miracle of Milk*. He believed that prescription drugs and vaccines poisoned the body and argued that every disease could be cured through physical exercise. He also published similarly kooky columnists, including a Spanish man who swore by the benefits of a grass diet. MacFadden himself hocked figs, dates, and fruits as miracle foods, while indicting white bread as "the greatest humbug ever foisted upon a civilized people."

Should anyone need proof of MacFadden's claims, they needn't look further than his own flawless skin, which he often showed off. Just inside the front jacket of his 1926 text *The Book of Health* is a big black-and-white photo of MacFadden, standing shirtless and stern. While many of his theories were unscientific, some had real merit. When, after World War II, Congress formed a committee to address the epidemic of disabilities wrought by the conflict, it endorsed several of his naturopathic beliefs around physical therapy, breathing exercises, and light, heat, and cold treatments.

At its height, MacFadden's publishing empire reached roughly 20 million people a week, making him a comparable publisher to Henry Luce, the man behind *Time*, or William Randolph Hearst. Countless Americans took his promotion of exercise to heart. This slotted conveniently into the military's own demands that American men prepare for the coming onslaught. At the start of World War II, only about a third of Americans exercised. By 1942, nearly 60 percent reported that they had developed a routine.

MACFADDEN'S IDEOLOGY OF CORPORAL EXCELLENCE often verged on soft eugenics. He articulated these beliefs himself, and published work by Albert Edward Wiggam, who advocated for selective breeding and forced sterilization. Other noted champions of American military training shared this ideology, including Johns Hopkins physician and preparedness leader Hugh Young, who, in 1917, opined in *The New York Times* that "military training would make us a new race."

Stanford University's founding president, David Starr Jordan, was the rare eugenicist whose beliefs steeled him against war. Starr argued that empires fell after warfare due to their most valiant being killed on the battlefield. "No nation can grow in strength," he contended, "when its bravest and best are each year devoured by the Army." One scholar summarized MacFadden's ideology as "nationalist principles infused with a fascist respect for authority and a stress laid on the muscular body." This overlapped with the worldviews of Adolf Hitler and Benito Mussolini, who used sports and physical pageantry to foment nationalism and showcase empowerment to their followers.

Mussolini was particularly obsessed with the human form, constructing what political writer John Ganz deemed the original "Jock-Douche" fascist archetype. Mussolini, like MacFadden, frequently appeared shirtless, including in 1937 on the cover of a French magazine that hailed him as the "sporting dictator."

Mussolini's favorite sport was soccer, and his favorite club was S.S. Lazio, which had been founded in 1900 by Italian Army officers who built a fascist fan culture that persists to this day. Il Duce built a stadium in Rome for them, then launched a successful campaign for Italy to host the second ever World Cup, in 1934. Three days after Italy's team beat Czechoslovakia to clinch the cup, Mussolini and Hitler met in Venice for the first time. The Third Reich subsequently constructed its own unrivaled Olympic team, which won the most medals of any country during the 1936 Olympic Games, in Berlin.

As the pair of fascists showcased their ideal men, they also sought to obscure symbols of Jewish strength. In 1938, Italy formally excluded Jews from most facets of Italian society, including sports. Among those affected was famed boxer Primo Lampronti, who was stripped of his title and forced to stop fighting.

Hitler similarly banned Jews from German sports clubs and recreational facilities, and froze many out of the Olympics and other world sporting events, including middleweight boxing champion Eric Seeling. Hitler's ideal Aryan was a man "of slender build, as agile as a greyhound, as tough as leather and as hard as Krupp steel." The Führer also expected young girls and women to be fit so that they could "provide the state and its people with healthy children." To meet Hitler's vision, schools imposed ten hours of physical education every week to compensate for what the government derided as a "purely intellectual" curriculum.

After Italy issued its own physical education mandates, MacFadden sought to shape them. In the early 1930s, he visited with Mussolini in Italy and took personal responsibility for the strength of forty Italian naval cadets. He then brought them to New York for six months, where they were trained hard, provided "pure" food, and introduced to American culture. All forty claimed a marked improvement in their musculature.

Soon after, MacFadden featured an interview with Mussolini in *Physical Culture*. It praised Italy as "a whole country organized for work," and noted the contrast to America's more sedentary, selfish culture.

MacFadden's highly publicized Italian experiment elicited an invitation from Portugal, then recently overtaken by its own strongman, António de Oliveira Salazar. He viewed his country's future not through arms but agriculture, and was desperate to rear a population strong enough to till the soil. In 1932, Salazar asked MacFadden to devise and implement a training regime for schoolchildren. MacFadden happily obliged, applying his unique calisthenic system by establishing an eponymous "Children's Colony." The reported effects were universally positive, transforming the faces of countless Portuguese boys from "dull and stupid" to "alert and interested," at least according to an issue of *Physical Culture*.

In addition to his extreme emphasis on the human body, MacFadden also admired the strongman's ability to dispose of his opponents. When, for instance, he publicly called for all enemies of "Americanism," namely Communists, to be punished, he suggested "deportation or concentration camps," musing that "Mussolini's Castor oil penalty might be desirable in some cases." MacFadden was referring to the common practice among Il Duce's fascist goons to force-feed dissidents oil to induce extreme diarrhea.

BY THE LATE 1930s, MacFadden had firmly replanted himself on American soil and rebranded himself an unwavering ally of democracy. He was severely critical of the Third Reich, though still insistent that the Germans had an upper hand to America's "race of weaklings." MacFadden's predictable answer to this problem was his patented routine of calisthenics and supplements, a campaign he dubbed "Vitamins for Victory."

The *Scabbard and Blade Journal* expressed its own tinges of jealousy about the strong, obedient youth that authoritarianism was cultivating. One contributor ascribed the "unquestioning obedience" of "the Japanese fighting man" to his "mental bath in the philosophy of military fascism." In another issue, general Robert Patterson, then the under secretary of war, emphasized ROTC as a vital counterweight to the Hitler Youth, whom, Patterson wrote, had been "subjected to years of toughening." Some military brass at the time were anxious over rumors that Hitler's fighters were being supercharged by anabolic steroids, and remained thoroughly unimpressed with the physical attributes of American military recruits, 50 percent of whom, they claimed, "cannot swim well enough to save their lives, and lack the strength to jump ditches, scale walls, throw missiles and survive forced marches."

In 1941, U.S. military leaders launched a national campaign to promote the importance of fitness, and enlisted Ted Bank, a decorated World War I veteran and handsome former University of Michigan quarterback, to oversee the Army's burgeoning athletics initiatives, where, among other things, Bank developed a fifteen-step workout to build every muscle in the body.

The U.S. military launched a $3 million program to build field houses and gymnasiums across the country and kickstarted a fitness revolution in the ranks, one that included a slate of rigorous training and assessment initiatives, including a new manual that, for the first time, detailed "hand-to-hand fighting" techniques—kicking, gouging, stomping, and choking. One 1942 Army study found that this new regime had produced impressive results after just six weeks, with trainers reporting that troops had achieved a 30 percent increase in pull-up strength, 50 percent increase in push-up and abdominal strength, and an 11 percent increase in muscular endurance. They promoted these gains in splashy recruitment ads featuring impressive before and after photos. The War Department's Manpower Commission also established a "prehabilitation" program, in which local doctors drafted and implemented remedial plans for adult males who didn't meet the service's physical standards. Defending these initiatives before Congress, colonel Leonard Rowntree, the chief physician of the selective service system, explained: "We are accustomed to regard ourselves, as a Nation, as healthy and rugged . . . but when we look at the facts as they are revealed by the statistics on rejection, a very large proportion of our manhood is far below par."

To meet their strength goals, war planners developed the "Victory Corps," which tasked public educators with building war-ready bodies in high school youth. "You must do this," Lieutenant General Brehon Somervell told educators upon its rollout. "Regardless of the cost, time, inconvenience, the temporary sidetracking of non-war objectives, or the temporary scrapping of peacetime courses. No school in America can fail to do its part." By July 1943, more than 75 percent of all American high schools had adopted the Victory Corps curriculum, which could easily eat up ten hours of school time a week. Many middle and elementary schools adopted the corps' curriculum, too.

MacFadden's publishing empire had ignited America's fitness fever, but the Army still kept him at arm's length. He nevertheless claimed direct credit for many of their initiatives, publishing what were almost certainly fabricated conversations with military brass hailing his contributions. In one, General Pershing proclaimed that his fitness regimes had "done much good to the Army." In another, General Robert Bullard said he planned to teach at one of MacFadden's military schools in retirement.

During Franklin Delano Roosevelt's first presidential campaign, in 1932, MacFadden's *Liberty* magazine declared without hesitation that the physically disabled Democrat, who was paralyzed from polio as a child, was nonetheless sufficiently fit for the rigors of the White House. "He is an ardent devotee of physical culture and always has been," MacFadden further assured his readership.

This endorsement had been personally negotiated by FDR's wife, Eleanor, whom MacFadden subsequently made the editor of a new periodical *Babies: Just Babies*, which discouraged pharmaceuticals and vaccines and promoted natural infant care, including breastfeeding. It was aimed at middle-class parents and was launched shortly before election day. *Time* magazine speculated that MacFadden's assistance might land him a role in the White House, but he only secured a weekend there. While he was instrumental in convincing the president to create a cabinet-level health agency, MacFadden was considered too kooky to serve as its inaugural secretary. Nearly a century later, the agency MacFadden helped establish would be helmed by a man similar to him in many ways—Robert F. Kennedy Jr.

The FDR-MacFadden alliance was brief. It ruptured over the New Deal, which MacFadden strenuously opposed as a "fanciful" Socialist experiment. He subsequently tried to outman Roosevelt during the war, authoring a litany of saber-rattling essays to get into the war, then, upon America's entrance, demanding a massive troop increase, arguing that failure to do so represented "an unspeakable national crime." He often made bellicose or plainly racist claims to justify his proposed buildup, including that 250,000 armed Japanese had bunkered down in California. In another case, after Roosevelt demanded, due more to rhetoric than realism, that the

War Department send 50,000 planes into theater, MacFadden insisted that, in fact, 100,000 planes should fill the skies.

AS AMERICA PREPARED TO ENTER WORLD WAR II IN 1941, the men in charge felt cautiously optimistic about their access to manpower. Brigadier General Grant Lowe, who oversaw ROTC and reserve components, proclaimed that "for the first time in our national history, we enter a war for which we are partly prepared." His qualified declaration nodded at the War Department's insatiable thirst for bodies, one telegraphed soon after by Secretary of War Henry Stimson, who reminded his people that they needed to "maintain a steady flow of young men."

By this point, the military had established many spigots: West Point and the Naval Academy, plus many hundreds more private military high schools and college-level officer-training programs. Boy Scout troops were increasingly meeting on U.S. military bases and, beginning in 1911, every U.S. president was ceremonially appointed the honorary leader of Scouting America. President Roosevelt, the first Boy Scout in the White House, actively pitched wartime conscription as fully aligned with the Scouting credo: to keep "physically strong, mentally awake, and morally straight." Again, thousands of Scouts stepped up for the war effort, distributing propaganda posters and salvaging tin, tires, aluminum, and other materials that could be recycled into military equipment. They and other schoolchildren also sold the equivalent of $33 billion worth of war bonds.

Countless other minors did their part, too. In the panicked rush after Pearl Harbor, Valley Forge constructed watch towers and established 24/7 shifts, with young cadets staying up late and peering into the skies for enemy aircraft. Similar outposts were erected at other military schools across the nation.

At the same time, MacFadden stepped up his pro-war propaganda efforts, publishing slick magazine pieces that glorified military service and offered highly sanitized updates from the front lines. One of his G.I. contributors fervently proclaimed that America was a "nation of giants who will assure our place in the sun." Nowhere did his publishing empire examine war wounds or casualties. In fact, the only quasi-negative piece MacFadden printed about the war concerned the nutritional insufficiency of war rations.

Hollywood types, too, promoted the war. One-third of the seventeen hundred feature-length films made and released in America between 1941 and 1945 explicitly supported the military. But the studios were also careful, not wanting to alienate the lucrative German film market through explicit critiques of the Nazis. After 1933, Third Reich entertainment and propaganda minister Joseph Goebbels kept a close eye on Hollywood production and, later, German officials in Los Angeles read Hollywood scripts and weighed in on any representations they felt were problematic for the Nazis. Studios generally complied.

Hollywood production was directly coordinated through the Office of War Information and its Bureau of Motion Pictures, which screened more than fifteen hundred scripts during the conflict and discarded those it viewed as anti-war. Roughly 90 million Americans were then seeing a flick every week, leading the head of the war information department, Elmer Davis, to posit that the "easiest way to inject a propaganda idea into most people's minds is to let it go through the medium of an entertainment picture when they do not realize that they are being propagandized."

Such efforts had far-reaching effects. When Cornell surveyed its student body in 1942, 83 percent said victory in the war was worth great personal sacrifice. Many cadets at Valley Forge were so eager to serve that they abandoned their schooling entirely to enlist as low-ranking soldiers. This created existential enrollment issues and made Valley Forge a victim of its own success in building blind patriotism. In a desperate attempt to retain students, the school screened a brutal real-life combat film called the *Battle of San Pietro*. During the film's most violent moments, some cadets puked or passed out. The Forge's defection problem rapidly subsided.

Despite its tight grip on combat-eligible Americans, the military wanted boys even younger. On August 27, 1942, the War Manpower Commission announced that "all able-bodied male students are destined for the Armed Forces." Soon after, the enlistment age was lowered from twenty-one to eighteen—or, in the case of some branches, seventeen with a parent's permission. The War Department also initiated an exam at thousands of public high schools to students under eighteen that gauged their interest in service and qualifications.

Some military officials worried that younger conscripts would be too weak to serve, though they needed millions of boys and men and were staring down what was then described by the Selective Service System's top doctor as the "bottom of the barrel." As a result, the War Department signed up whomever they could, including countless underage boys—a mission largely carried out by the military's public school capos.

The day after Pearl Harbor, Billie Boyd's high school principal called him and other seniors into his office and made an offer some couldn't refuse: an immediate early diploma should they choose to enlist. Soon after, Boyd, then sixteen, marched into his local recruiting office with his principal and mother. With support from these guardians, he lied about his age. The recruiter didn't ask questions and stamped his passport into combat.

Other American child soldiers from this era similarly characterized recruiters as eager to bend the rules. Some ignored poorly forged documents or even aided in altering birth dates. Others urged schoolboys to fill up on bananas to meet the service's weight requirements. In one case, an underage student who visited a Coast Guard recruiting center with his eighteen-year-old friend was also given forms to fill out, and "being too shy to refuse, complied."

Calvin Graham, an eleven-year-old boy living in an abusive Texas household, deepened his voice, forged his mother's signature, and enlisted. There were myriad signs that Calvin was far too young to be sent into battle, including the fact that he still had baby teeth, which were discovered during Graham's screening by a military dentist, who nonetheless waved him through. Not long after turning twelve, Graham found himself as a gunner aboard the USS *South Dakota*. During the Battle of Guadalcanal, he took shrapnel to the face but kept fighting, earning him the Bronze Star and a Purple Heart.

At fifteen, Alvin Snaper was sent to Bastogne and fought in the Battle of the Bulge. During this hellish, weekslong campaign, he killed a man and was injured. After being patched up, Snaper returned to battle and came under German cannon fire. Among the bombs that rained down was one that exploded right next to Alvin, blowing him into a tree. He was evacuated to Walter Reed Military Hospital, where he recovered for two years. Ray Jackson, who enlisted at sixteen and later chaired the association for Veterans of Underage Military Service, estimated that 100,000 child soldiers served during World War II, Korea, and Vietnam combined.

This unprecedented forwarding of students from the classroom to the front lines made America's citadels of civilian education virtual ghost towns. Take Harvard College, whose undergraduate enrollment had averaged around 3,500 students before the war. By its end, the student body had shrunk to about 850 people. Valley Forge not only lost cadets, but also a band of its best teachers and administrators, including its superintendent, Major Milton Medenbach, who was sent to command an infantry team in Austria. His prompt and unexpected departure exhibited how quickly the school could unravel. Academic vigor declined, supervision suffered, and hazing became rampant. Hoping to reinstall order, a crew of senior cadets created a "Captain's Council" that meted out medieval punishments, including swats by a saber. Conditions became so bad that Forge staff successfully convinced the Army to recall Medenbach back to campus.

THE WAR DEPARTMENT WANTED TO ENSURE American academics' loyalty, cultivating what one military official described as a "consciousness" around their "responsibility to the nation's security." While their rhetorical efforts to sell the war didn't always work, their gobs of research money did. Because, while most nations delegate military research and development duties to government agencies or private enterprise, America assigns this work to her civilian universities. This practice was first established during World War II, when the military plowed the equivalent of $9 billion into academic research. This was the opening salvo in a campaign known now as STEM, which, with its focus on mathematic and scientific supremacy, has long threatened the centrality of the liberal arts in American education.

Early on there was evidence that the military's return on investment would be positive. Johns Hopkins helped establish bomb fuse technology, the California Institute of Technology built Navy torpedoes, and Columbia pioneered improvements to radar technology.

In fact, Columbia substantially remade itself during the conflict, appointing a war research director, John Dunning, who helped steer the school's many war-related initiatives, including a radar technology initiative, a statistical research group, and the Manhattan Project for nuclear weapons. Columbia also transformed a dozen buildings into a Midshipmen's School that trained more than twenty thousand officers for duty, and its medical school established a hospital in Europe to care for the wounded.

Harvard was a top military beneficiary, receiving the equivalent of more than $600 million in World War II contracts to develop everything from night vision to napalm. The school also created a "Fatigue Laboratory" focused on physical fitness and the energetic costs of specific military duties. The personnel tasked with this work were dubbed "Conant's Arsenal," so named after Harvard's president, James Conant, a fierce advocate for American involvement in the war. Conant was himself a trained chemist who served in the Army during World War I, where, among other things, he helped develop poison gases. During the Second World War, he chaired the National Defense Research Committee, which most famously paved the way for the Trinity nuclear test. Later, Conant encouraged President Truman to use atomic weapons on Japan.

By 1941, Conant had suspended virtually all civilian-minded inquiry in favor of war-oriented projects. Harvard Business School all but stopped functioning, while other departments pivoted exclusively to the war effort. Even the school of fine arts stood up a "camouflage program." ROTC cadets also swarmed the campus, their constant drills tearing up the lawn at Harvard Yard. In 1942, Harvard's commencement speaker was none other than Secretary of War Henry Stimson.

BY THE TIME THE GUNS OF WAR WERE PUT DOWN, in September 1945, 15 million people had died in battle, along with many millions of civilians who died of injury, disease, starvation, or genocide.

World War II was run on youth, and it devastated their ranks. The British military reported that the most common age of death in their force was nineteen. America apparently conducted no similar analysis of its 400,000 casualties, but the force's average age was twenty-six. Military schools funneled at least 50,000 graduates into the churn; ROTC contributed another 150,000 fresh-faced officers. West Point suffered the most casualties of any military school, losing 500 young alumni by the time peace was secured. Seventy-two Valley Forge cadets died, and many more were wounded. As devastating as these losses were, officers were generally the most protected men in theater, often strategizing behind the lines. The casualty rate for low-ranking enlisted men was far worse.

The same year as the war ended, Harvard's president Conant acknowledged in his president's report that "it remains to be seen . . . whether this partial conversation to a purpose alien" to Harvard's liberal arts mission "leaves a permanent scar." He believed it wouldn't.

The war's supreme commander, General Dwight Eisenhower, was then harbored similar worries. The war's terrible casualty count was inextricably embedded in the commander's conscience. These were "Ike's Boys," after all, and their deaths formed in him a haunting and relentless sense of loss. Generally, Eisenhower remained stoic about the war, though on at least two occasions he broke down publicly when discussing the conflict.

Days after hostilities ended, Eisenhower called for a moderating of military might, insisting that the best way to honor those killed in battle, and their families, was to ensure "this will not happen again." His commander in chief, President Truman, felt differently. He urged Congress to revive its plans for universal military training, a proposal that excited MacFadden, who wrote to the president suggesting that such an initiative be overseen by West Point's tenacious football coach, Rollie Bevan. MacFadden followed up his note with a series of other missives, most of them bugging Truman aides about the urgency of such a program and seeking an interview with him. One of his messages warned that America's failure to create compulsory military training would confine it to the world's "scrap heap." Fascism may be destroyed, he argued, but newsreels made clear that the Communist Russians were virile, and only becoming more so, while America remained pitifully weak.

His argument was bolstered by Ted Bank, the Army athletic chief, whose thoughts on World War II, unlike Eisenhower's, amounted to cold, corporeal calculations. He saw the high body count as the sign of a weak athletic culture. "Had we had proper physical fitness programs in America for the 23 years prior to Pearl Harbor," Bank argued, "many of our boys that made the supreme sacrifice would be alive today." It was the latest in an escalating series of public programs and declarations tying the American man's strength to national survival and success. Masculine strength was declared the guarantor of everything from economic vitality to familial security. It was a heavy assignment, but one that conferred deep meaning, and many men stepped up to the challenge.

IN THE WAKE OF WORLD WAR II, countless Americans had set aside thoughts of the carnage and clamored to serve. An unadulteratedly evil enemy had been vanquished by American G.I.s, who were then being transitioned back into their communities, heralded by fawning news coverage, ticker-tape parades, and generous government benefits like the G.I. Bill, which was ratified in the waning days of the war.

The Second World War had solidified the glistening image of the officer class, in particular. More than half of the men who fought at the division commander level, or higher, had graduated from West Point, a list that included many of the war's boldfaced heroes, including generals Eisenhower and MacArthur, plus Omar Bradley and, of course, the most colorful man in the bunch, George S. Patton, who, despite his sterling reputation and clear tactical brilliance, was afflicted by a swollen ego verging on lunacy and a poor academic transcript from West Point, having graduated in five years, not four. There were war heroes from other military schools, too, including Army Chief of Staff George C. Marshall, a VMI graduate, and the commander in chief of the Pacific Fleet Chester Nimitz, an alumnus of the Naval Academy.

Historians, journalists, politicians, and military leaders vaunted the battlefield brilliance of these officers and valorized the deaths of the fallen. This reinforced a positive and enduring vision of the American gentleman warrior as someone who is chivalrous, selfless, and who radiates an almost-delusional optimism around the country's loftiest ideals.

This archetype was further fortified by the national media. MacFadden, for his part, published many fawning articles in his popular magazines. One included testimony from a sailor who said that, prior to enlistment, he had been "a coward and a weakling" who "hated myself." The Navy, he wrote, had changed all that, transforming him into a "new man" who can "look forward to a future of unsurpassed happiness and health." In the waning days of the war, NBC aired a thirty-minute program celebrating West Point's 142nd anniversary, produced by the military, featuring marches, military songs, and positive testimonials. Months later, West Point Superintendent Francis Wilby took to the airwaves of Voice of America and hailed his school as a major force for democracy. In February 1945, one patriotic mother on Long Island wrote into *Newsday* urging the paper to print the names of every American military school for enrollment purposes. That May, it emerged that a florist in Queens had ponied up $5,000 to a scam artist who falsely promised to secure a West Point appointment for his son.

Missing from the celebratory headlines were the realities of festering physical wounds and post-traumatic stress wracking millions of American soldiers. Given the understandable exuberance of our success in this "good war," and its defeat of fascism, it was nearly impossible for these complicating details to be heard.

Patriotic fervor persevered through the 1950s, thanks largely to a string of positive Hollywood films, including *The West Point Story* (1950), *Francis*

Goes to West Point (1952), and *The Long Gray Line* (1955). In 1952, Americans also elected, in Eisenhower, a West Pointer as president, signaling that America's positive sentiments toward the military were veering into the kinds of veneration our founders had worried about.

Harvard political theorist (and later the architect of the U.S. military Pacification Program in Vietnam) Samuel Huntington was one of many who held the military sacred. In his 1957 book *The Soldier and the State*, Huntington brashly asserted the supremacy of the U.S. military by negatively comparing West Point's hometown of Highland Falls—"a motley, disconnected collection of frames coincidentally adjoining each other, lacking common unity or purpose"—to West Point, itself a "different world" of "ordered serenity" lacking the sort of "garish individualism" that marked "civilian life." Huntington concluded: "America can learn more from West Point than West Point from America." That same year, Harvard's Department of Government rejected Huntington's request for tenure, worried over what they described as his "authoritarian infatuation with Prussian-style militarism."

AS WITH PREVIOUS AMERICAN MILITARY CONFLICTS, there was a significant demobilization effort after World War II, albeit one far less limited than in the past. While there were roughly 300,000 active-duty personnel in 1939, postwar that figure more than quadrupled, to around 1.5 million, then grew further. As peacetime dawned, the War Department also found itself drowning in $50 billion worth of excess gear. The brass responded by auctioning off industrial war equipment and other gear to civilian scrappers at surplus offices across the country. The tools of war didn't always make sense for civilian spaces, but the military made a hard sell, marketing flamethrowers, for instance, to farmers for weed control. Classic equipment was also deployed to a proliferating number of military museums, while extra clothing fueled an explosion of Army-Navy stores—glamorous new avenues of military propaganda and fashion, respectively, for American boys.

During World War II, the military had launched the monumental construction of the Pentagon, built on 296 acres of land in Arlington, Virginia. Fourteen thousand laborers worked in three around-the-clock shifts. War planners had initially pledged to the American people that this would be only a temporary structure, one to be turned into a hospital or a warehouse once fighting had ceased. But the Pentagon went on to serve as the military's perpetual beating heart, America's largest federal office building and a striking symbol of Washington's insatiable war habit.

In its own rhetorical attempt to temper civilian concerns about fostering a perpetual war footing, Congress renamed the War Department in 1947 the "National Military Establishment," then, in 1949, it became the "Department of Defense" amid concerns that the acronym NME sounded too much like "enemy."

Meanwhile, a subset of military brass were gunning for a forever-war mindset, with saber-rattling assertions coming from figures like Valley Forge founder Milton Baker, who, in the immediate wake of World War II, pledged to stand ready for the next "inevitable war." One West Pointer from this era recalled that amid these "easygoing years of peace," cadets were taught to remain vigilant for the inevitable, catalyzing moment in which they would again "transform a citizenry into an Army." Eisenhower, for his part, offered conflicting messages. When he ventured to Valley Forge on July 4, 1950, to speak before Boy Scouts gathered at their annual jamboree, he at once pined for peace and identified a new enemy: communism.

"That you may not in your young manhood be sacrificed to war is indeed the primary purpose of our foreign policy today," the president told the youngsters. "And you shall not be if the pledge of allegiance stands always before the world as the guiding light of our national life." In other moments, Ike asserted that America needed to maintain its strength. "Every society, every crowd has its weaklings, its cowards, its self-centered individuals," he proclaimed. "We must not be influenced by their actions if we are to escape the shame that is theirs." His words gestured at a new paradigm in American foreign policy, one well in line with MacFadden's beliefs. It was a vision that insisted on strength at all costs, and saw weakness as a debilitating force for failure.

This worldview required unending preparedness, further sustaining military schools while keeping civilian professors unsure of the role they played and susceptible to the whims of the War Department. This latter goal was well articulated by Edward Bowles, the science adviser to Secretary of War Stimson, who solidified an "effective peacetime integration" between academia and the freshly christened Pentagon that came to resemble a permanent military economy. By 1951, the military research budget had basically doubled since the start of World War II, to $1.1 billion, or

$21 billion in today's dollars, part of what sociologist C. Wright Mills described as the capture of America's scientific imagination by the military. "Very few of those engaged in basic scientific research are not working under military direction," he warned.

Here again, Eisenhower seemed conflicted. After the war, he split his time serving as NATO's first Supreme Commander and Columbia University's president. While he was largely absent from campus, Eisenhower supported the dismissal of a left-wing professor and participated in a commission that recommended socialists be barred as teachers. He also oversaw the continued blossoming of martial research, including through the 1951 creation of Columbia's Institute of War and Peace Studies, which, despite its name, was (and is) overwhelmingly focused on military concerns.

A decade later, in his 1961 farewell address as president, Ike warned about the growing influence of what he deemed the "military industrial complex." He initially wanted to use the term *military industrial academic complex*, but scrapped the language so as not to degrade the positive reputation enjoyed globally by America's constellation of colleges and universities. Still, he warned of a future in which "a government contract becomes virtually a substitute for intellectual curiosity."

Chapter 6

Cadets for Christ

In the predawn hours of August 6, 1945, a battle-hardened pilot, Colonel Paul Tibbets, and his eleven-person crew inserted an atomic weapon named "Little Boy" into the *Enola Gay*, a Boeing B-29 bomber that Tibbets had named after his mother. These personifying monikers lent the ordeal a kind of twisted symbolism, representing a sort of sinful antithesis to the immaculate conception. While the biblical Virgin Mary had birthed a savior, the *Enola Gay* would soon deliver a creation of unholy destruction.

With Little Boy was safely stored in the B-29's belly, Tibbets took off from an airfield in the Northern Mariana Islands and flew six hours north, to Hiroshima, Japan. He and his men belonged to the military's recently formed 509th squadron, which undertook both the atomic bombing of Hiroshima, and the subsequent blitz three days later on Nagasaki. In the moment, these men saw themselves as divine and untouchable, masters of a new and awesome power that involved climbing into the heavens before raining hellfire down to earth. This attitude remains within the 509th, which still nods to their celestial self-conception via their official insignia, marked on patches that feature a mushroom cloud hitched to angel wings.

America's development of the atomic bomb armed its military with an unprecedented tool for destruction, one that necessitated distance between attacker and target, making the bomb's grotesque violence a fuzzy abstraction. This sensation was confirmed by the *Enola Gay*'s navigator, Major Theodore "Dutch" Van Kirk, who recalled in his old age that he and his crew were giddy about their mission to Hiroshima. "It was a game for me," he told a reporter while cracking a smile. "I was trying to hit that initial point exactly at nine o'clock. I'm a punctual person. When I say I'm going to pick my daughter up at five o'clock, that's when I pick her up." As promised, Dutch perfectly lined up the path for Little Boy, which fell through the morning air for forty-three seconds before rupturing into a blinding, white-hot fireball nine hundred feet in diameter that killed seventy thousand people instantaneously.

From their vantage point, the men of the *Enola Gay* saw little more than a bulbous cloud and brilliant light. Hiroshima may have looked like it had become heaven on earth. But under the cloud cover was an immediate and unprecedented scourge of death and destruction. In addition to the seventy thousand people who perished instantly, tens of thousands more were injured and poisoned. "Nobody said anything about the people on the ground," Dutch recalled. "That wasn't mentioned at all."

Once America conquered the clouds, it moved expeditiously to protect its new territory. Two years after the atomic bombings, in September 1947, the Pentagon established a new service branch, the Air Force, which was blessed with a massive budget and a mandate for a new service academy fit for the emergent class of gentlemen pilots manning the skies.

From there, the military appointed a committee to pick the rightful site for the U.S. Air Force Academy, or USAFA for short. Its most famous member was Charles Lindbergh, the first aviator to fly solo nonstop across the Atlantic. Lindbergh was also an avowed white supremacist who had quietly allied with the Third Reich while loudly agitating against American involvement in the war. This made his appointment to a U.S. military commission somewhat of an oddity, though after the Second World War, the American military, and the Air Force in particular, brought numerous former Nazis into the fold for the stated purpose of absorbing their technical knowledge. The Air Force Academy itself forged an "overwhelming friendship" via a cadet-exchange program with the postwar German Air Force, then newly overseen by NATO but still largely run by former Nazis. This bond was formed thanks to Horst Judel, a Nazi pilot during the war who, according to an old clipping from the *Colorado Springs Gazette*, was appointed to teach German at USAFA in 1960.

Out of 582 potential locales, Lindbergh and the committee landed on Colorado Springs, Colorado, a sleepy college town that sits at the eastern foot of the Rocky Mountains. USAFA became the first and only service academy to eschew the East Coast and its attendant WASP culture for a locale since dubbed the "Mecca for Evangelical Christians." While some voiced concerns that the Rockies would be too windy and treacherous for flight training, Lindbergh himself soared over the proposed site and declared it perfectly fit for flying. Like the men of the 509th squadron, Lindbergh had become intoxicated by the divine sensation of flight, once reflecting that, as he racked up time in the sky, "I began to feel that I had lived on a higher plane than the skeptics of the ground. In flying, I tasted a wine of the gods of which they could know nothing."

COLORADO SPRINGS WAS CHARTERED IN 1871 by William Jackson Palmer, a railroad baron and former Union general. At the time of his arrival to the region, the Gold Rush was in high gear, flooding the American west with riches, but also vice, largely concentrated in saloons, where gambling, drinking, and prostitution were commonplace.

Palmer, a Quaker, envisioned a wholesome and culturally temperate town. He wanted to attract families. To this end, he deeded a dozen or so of the city's first parcels to religious denominations for the purpose of church building. This foundational culture of faith proved resilient, with more than four hundred evangelical and conservative Christian ministries still in town today. By the 1950s, many local churches had acquired the tools for professional proselytizing, including training centers, radio networks, and publishing houses.

Construction of the Air Force Academy commenced during the summer of 1955, with a mandate to house about 2,500 cadets, or roughly the size of West Point's student body. The first and largest parcel of land purchased for the project was Cathedral Rock Ranch, a 4,600-acre expanse so named for Cathedral Rock, a hulking white sandstone formation on the grounds that abstractly resembles a church.

The campus itself was designed to evoke a modern frontier city, nodding both to its Western locale and the military's imperialistic instinct for expansion. The academy's founding superintendent, Lieutenant General Hubert R. Harmon, ensured classrooms were designed with big wide windows. That way, Harmon figured, cadets could look out on nature and "breathe God's fresh air." The complex's architectural crown jewel is its chapel, which cuts into the sky with sharp, triangular spires. During its 1963 dedication ceremony, speakers praised the chapel as "a symbol for the world to know that the U.S. is truly a nation under God."

The chapel is intended as a multidenominational space. There's a room with a Catholic altar, one for Muslim services featuring partitions and prayer rugs, and a small synagogue space whose foyer features Jerusalem brownstone tiling donated decades ago by the Israeli Defense Forces. But the main area, as with West Point's grand chapel, is designed for Protestant services. It features a 1,200-pound aluminum cross in the form of a cadet saber.

While both the West Point and USAFA Honor Codes ban lying, stealing, and cheating, only the Air Force credo ends with "so help me God." USAFA leaders have long frequented conservative megachurches in town, and invited local religious groups onto campus, forming a deep culture of proselytizing that has hardened many atheists, but also rejuvenated the faith of some cadets and spawned total conversions among others.

GOD HAS LONG UNDERGIRDED AMERICAN MILITARY LIFE, injecting the dubious work of war with a shot of sacred meaning. Religion is a complementary ideology to militarism, a fact stated plainly by an Army major in the trial of a conscientious objector during Vietnam. He cast the objector's conflict between military orders and his personal faith as "a religion butting heads against a religion." In both ideologies, followers must transform themselves into the mold of a higher power. Both also put forth a mission, be it a war or a crusade, and cast death as an honorable sacrifice that secures deliverance. Both belief systems also demand uniformity, hew to rigid rules, and view pain and punishment as pious. In his book *Jesus Was an Airborne Ranger*, military chaplain John McDougall stripped away the softer elements of the savior. He complained that Jesus was too often depicted as a "tender . . . meek . . . long-haired . . . pretty boy." Rather than settle for this "spineless, spiritless, lifeless" Jesus, McDougall and his allies in the military religious corps conceived of a hardcore one. He was called "Christ the Conqueror."

American military religiosity was first spearheaded by Sylvanus Thayer, who imbued West Point with a religious atmosphere described by one scholar as an "unemotional, calculated Christianity informed by the demands of American nationalism." This strain has since strengthened and spread to other military schools, and across all the ranks writ large. One early chaplain at Valley Forge liked to tell his flock that "suffering is good for the soul." General MacArthur made a similar point to West Point cadets in his 1962 acceptance speech for the Thayer Award. "The soldier, above all other men," he said, "is required to practice the greatest act of religious training: sacrifice."

More than anything, the conflation of God and country offers a fragile but comforting justification for troops tasked with killing their fellow men. John Hamre, an evangelical former deputy defense secretary, once articulated how he twisted his faith in ways that helped him sleep better at night. "Jesus wasn't a pacifist," Hamre charged. "I don't think he'd be looking to drop bombs on people all the time, but, on the other hand, there were times when he confronted evil, and he did something about it." A West Point superintendent during this same period made a nearly identical argument during a television interview, claiming that "Thou Shall Not Kill" really meant "Thou Shall Not Murder."

Four-star general and Air Force chief of staff Curtis LeMay, the crazed architect of the aerial campaign in the Pacific theater during the war, including the savage firebombing of Tokyo, and who inspired the unhinged role of General Jack Ripper in Stanley Kubrick's biting satire *Dr. Strangelove*, also coupled his crude love of airpower with religion. "If we maintain our faith in God, love of freedom, and superior global airpower, the future of America looks pretty good," he asserted. Later, LeMay called for first-strike nuclear attacks against Cuba, China, the Soviet Union—and North Vietnam, where he called for the U.S. to "bomb them back into the Stone Age." These plans were ultimately rejected, though by the end of the Vietnam occupation, the military had dropped the equivalent of 640 Hiroshima-sized bombs on the country. In his memoir, LeMay divined his faith from three foundational texts: the Gettysburg Address, the book of Psalms, and the Boy Scout Oath. Harebrained as his ideology was, the Air Force subsequently named its center for Doctrine Development and Education after LeMay, who is today buried a stone's throw from Cathedral Rock.

A TYPICAL CONGREGATION in the Air Force Academy chapel attracts true believers—and cadets bored out of their minds. Truly pious cadets were sometimes called "hell dodgers."

Those who skipped chapel or were caught nodding off would often be punished: put on cleaning detail, given marching tours, or thwacked with a paddle. In the 1960s, one pack of clever cadets responded to these penalties by devising a convincing head prop out of coat hangers.

In 1972, civilian courts ruled that mandatory chapel at the service academies was unconstitutional. A few years after the ruling, Don Gurney,

USAFA's Baptist student coordinator, told a reporter that while chapel attendance had ticked down, "interest in Christian living and the Bible have not decreased among young people." Rather, he declared, they were simply practicing their faith in alternative settings.

Many of these new locales were the conservative ministries dotted across Colorado Springs. One evangelical church held "Salute to the Military" services hosted by Chaplin Mervin Johnson, an ordained minister and at the time the academy's director of cadet activities. A few years later, in 1978, three Air Force professors ventured to Italy for what was billed as a "religious-scientific pilgrimage" to study the long-dubious and since-debunked Shroud of Turin, a cloth relic that many Christians believe Jesus was buried in.

Despite the chapel ruling, cadets across the military schooling system still felt pressured to attend services, which increasingly came to include fiery sermons on holy war, summed up by one evangelical pastor who blessed the work of "putting on one's armor for the Lord."

In earlier conflicts, chaplain work had mostly been undertaken by mainline Protestants, who saw their mission as not to justify warfare, but rather to perform faith healing on the battlefield. They spent the bulk of their time counseling shell-shocked soldiers and helping to bury the dead. This work was not directed toward conversion but rather supporting a service member's own faith to find peace.

Beginning in the 1940s, however, conservative Christian groups launched a quiet but well-coordinated effort to control the chaplaincy. Many covertly inserted evangelical rhetoric into protestant military services. One Navy chaplain bragged in *Christianity Today* that he had converted three thousand sailors. Activist chaplains also seized on America's call for military education by founding dozens of religiously affiliated military schools amid the world wars, including Howe Military Academy in Indiana, whose leader proudly ranked "spiritual integrity" as the "most important thing we can contribute to the educational field." There was also the Massanutten Military Academy, in Virginia's Shenandoah Valley, an evangelical institution founded in 1899 that promises to introduce "a respect for religion and a reverence for God into each boy's life."

Conservative Christians further expanded their influence during the Vietnam War, when many mainline Protestant chaplains became disillusioned by the conflict, and left the military altogether, leading to a sharp spike in chaplains with evangelical and Pentecostal backgrounds. These conservatives provided a more natural fit with the military's neocolonialist and expansionist principles, which mirrored their mission work.

A similar religious transformation played out within the enlisted ranks. That's largely because, after the military draft ended in 1973, the brass turned to a devout evangelical named Bill Brehm to build them an all-volunteer force. Brehm, who served as one of Defense Secretary Robert McNamara's famous "Whiz Kids" before becoming the assistant defense secretary for manpower, ultimately settled on an approach that involved recruiting "increasingly from a segment of society that had strong cultural affinity to the military lifestyle and the values that are enshrined in the military community." Brehm's efforts fostered a force that was "far more evangelical, more Southern, more rural, more conservative."

Hamre, the deputy defense secretary who claimed Jesus wasn't a pacifist, embarked on his own mission to influence the officer class, launching a religious speaking tour at the service academies. This work, he charged, was meant to rebuke America's burgeoning tradition of "enforced agnosticism."

Other military figures established organizations to elevate religious men into powerful military posts. These included the Officers Christian Fellowship and Cadets for Christ. There was also "The Navigators," a sect chartered during the 1930s on the USS *West Virginia*, one of the ships that was badly damaged during Pearl Harbor. The Navigators focused much of their early attention on the naval academy at Annapolis, quickly building a Bible study of midshipmen that was more than three hundred strong. They also focused on the Citadel before establishing a permanent base in Colorado Springs, where they formed their strongest campus ministry at the Air Force Academy, with 85 percent of cadets identifying as Christian.

Amid this increasing concentration of religious cadets, troops from alternative religious backgrounds felt pressured or persecuted. Some were denied accommodations for their religious holidays or claimed that they were denied promotions due to their faith. One Mormon Marine recalled a chaplain who described his church as "satanic." Between 1965 and 1978, the Southern Baptist Convention increased its number of chaplains in the armed forces by about 50 percent. By 2005, the convention had become the largest source of military chaplains—representing 16 percent of the entire chaplaincy corps.

THE MILITARY'S RELIGIOUS SUBCULTURE ALSO SHOWED little tolerance for those who expressed their faith in ways that differed from America's battle plans. This was clear in the case of Dale Noyd, a decorated fighter pilot who, in December 1966, articulated how his core religious beliefs prevented him from supporting the war in Vietnam.

Then an assistant professor of psychology at the Air Force Academy, Noyd had been a star ROTC cadet who was later hailed by his superiors for safely landing a nuclear-armed F-100 jet that had malfunctioned. He was reflexively loyal to the military early in his career, then took a hiatus for graduate school at the University of Michigan. There, Noyd studied psychology and, as one classmate recalled, "his whole intellectual framework changed."

Back at the academy, Noyd submitted an eight-page single-spaced letter seeking to be deemed a conscientious objector for the Vietnam war, which he argued, was "unjust, immoral, and which makes a mockery of both our Constitution and the charter of the United Nations." Noyd based his objections on his belief in religious humanism, which, he explained, "means respect and love for man, faith in his inherent goodness and perfectibility and confidence in his capability to ameliorate some of the banes of the human condition."

His essay acknowledged that the Vietnam conflict was often "obfuscated by cliches and slogans." He put forth a thoughtful indictment that quoted humanistic philosophers, psychiatrists, and other thinkers, including John Dewey, the great humanist educator, and Paul Tillich, the Christian socialist philosopher. During litigation, Noyd secured statements of support from famed theologians, along with statements testifying to the legitimacy of his convictions from two academy chaplains, one of whom said Noyd had "more integrity than any person I've ever met."

The Air Force Academy responded to Noyd's righteous plea for peace by yanking him out of the classroom, denying his promotion to major, and transferring him to a training center in New Mexico, where he refused orders to train a pilot destined for Vietnam. Rather than grant his application, they successfully prosecuted him for refusing an order. Noyd was sentenced to a year in prison, kicked out of the service, and stripped of his pension and benefits. Upon his release, he taught psychology for two decades at Earlham College, a Quaker school in rural Indiana. Hung proudly in his study were two certificates: his military commendation for expertly landing the nuclear-armed plane, and his dishonorable discharge.

JUST AS THE MILITARY ROUTINELY DEFROCKS those who oppose their methods, they also routinely apply the traditional religious tools of remembrance and idolatry to the dead, turning figures who can no longer speak into symbols to inspire sacrifice and give war meaning. Examples dot the grasses of Arlington National Cemetery, and show up in war monuments, many of which are fastidiously cared for by veterans groups or local Boy Scout troops. A granite marker erected at Valley Forge honors the academy's most famous masculine martyr, a World War II veteran named Eric Fisher Wood Jr., who evaded Nazi capture in a Belgium forest and formed a platoon of other separated American soldiers that killed roughly two hundred Nazis before he was cornered and executed.

Eric was the focal point of a 1959 speech before the AMCSUS school association by General Lyman Lemnitzer, himself a proud West Pointer, who deemed Eric an "illustration of courage, of determination, and of indomitable will," praising the influential role that military education played in his life while condemning the "nebulous or amorphous fields" studied in liberal arts environments. Lemnitzer did not lament the fact that Wood's life was grievously cut short. To do so would be to undermine a core tenet of military masculinity, which exalts male sacrifice and, by extension, harshly devalues male life.

In 1976, the Air Force Academy rolled out a similar campaign to canonize Lance Sijan, the first Air Force Academy graduate to be awarded the Medal of Honor, by naming a big, boxy dormitory in his honor. USAFA lost a total of 151 graduates in Vietnam, including Lance, who had been a prisoner of war. Many academy graduates turned fighter pilots became POWs, a testament to the astonishing antiaircraft skills of the North Vietnamese who undercut the reputation of an Air Force still swaggering from the successful atomic bombings of Japan. When his own F-4 went down, Lance landed in a mountainous Laotian jungle. He evaded capture for forty-six days, despite suffering serious injuries. He then briefly escaped his prison before being recaptured. Tragically, Lance died as a prisoner of war on January 22, 1968. He was just twenty-five—the same age as Eric Wood when he was killed.

Sijan Hall includes a painted portrait of Lance that cadets view as a good-luck talisman. Some salute it before big exams or important athletic events. The academy has also displayed some of his personal effects, and produced a video for incoming plebes, or as the Air Force Academy calls them, "doolies." The video casts Lance as a Christ-like male. At certain points, the film's comparisons are right on the nose, as when Lance is depicted bearded and in a shredded flight suit, enduring torture. The reel includes yet another biblical moment, one wherein Lance, facing death in his cell, screams out to the heavens for his father. "Dad, I need you," he proclaims.

Chapter 7

The Bad Apples

Among the things troops carried with them on the battlefields of World War II was the "heart shield bible"—a pocket-sized, government-issued book of scripture, sometimes with a metal cover, that fit snugly in a G.I.'s standard-issue shirt pocket. In at least one remarkable case, this good book acted as life-saving armor. Generally, though, the Bible served its traditional purpose: to calm the conscience and divine celestial meaning. When Jerome David Salinger was drafted, in 1942, and sent to the front lines shortly thereafter, he rejected Christian allegories, and wrote his own saga, complementing his battlefield kit with blank paper and a typewriter. Once, when his unit came under heavy fire, a soldier running for cover caught a glimpse of Salinger hunched under a table, clacking away like a frenzied newsman on deadline.

Now known internationally by his nom de plume, J.D. Salinger, the young conscript experienced many of the war's most terrifying chapters. He stormed the beaches of Normandy, fought in the Battle of the Bulge, and helped liberate Kaufering, a subcamp of Dachau. Partial drafts of his work were carried along with him, soaked in Salinger's sweat and imbued with his raw, instinctive reactions to conflict. His reflections were, in turn, refined into some of the first American texts to unapologetically challenge the pious image of the G.I. and the pretty myths about warfare. Salinger's words also powerfully undercut America's intoxicating model of masculinity, then the major motor driving U.S. military recruitment.

Salinger's piercing stories quickly made him one of the loudest and most successful voices of the so-called Silent Generation. Like many, Salinger emerged from the war severely traumatized. He examined his wartime experience entirely through his writing of fiction. Rarely did he speak or write about his own service record, though his fleeting moments of personal candor were chilling. "You never really get the smell of burning flesh out of your nose entirely," he once confided to his daughter. "No matter how long you live." His thoughts and theories about World War II were often disguised within domestic plot lines or set in military locales away from the front lines. Only once did Salinger write about active conflict, in an unpublished short story called "The Magic Foxhole," which catalogues the lost limbs (and minds) of some of America's "soldier boys" during the bombing of Normandy. It's a gruesome tale, especially for its time, one that feels like Salinger's own tortured mediation on survivor's guilt. It seemed that in writing it, Salinger was trying to negotiate whether his remarkable survival through some of the war's worst gauntlets could be chalked up to dumb luck, or divine intervention.

"The Magic Foxhole" opens with a potent symbol of war's profanity: a military chaplain crawling around frantically on all fours amid crashes of shellfire, searching for his glasses. From there, Salinger introduces a young soldier named Gardner who deftly navigates into all the foxholes spared from bombing. Gardner remains physically unscathed, but his brain has begun to unravel. At one point, he hallucinates another man in his foxhole with a futuristic helmet whom he believes to be his yet-to-be-born son, Earl.

While Gardner "looked nuts," Salinger clarifies that he "wasn't a loony." Rather, he writes, Gardner is overcome with a form of battle fatigue "when you get to look like you're dead, or when you start telling everybody real loud that you wish you was a civilian and not in no goddamn Army." Near the end of the story, Gardner pledges to kill his imaginary son so as to spare him war's toll but then backs out upon his ghost son's wishes. "I was going to shoot him," he explains coldly. "But he said he wanted to be here."

Much of Salinger's other writing during the war was channeled through a thinly fictionalized version of himself named Holden Caulfield. Holden is witty, cynical, and highly acidic, a self-described atheist who ruthlessly assails the war and its attendant institutions. After the armistice, Salinger returned home to Connecticut, where he refined his fragments into a fully coherent novel, *The Catcher in the Rye*. It placed Holden at a private school outside Philadelphia named Pencey Prep, which was a stand-in for Salinger's real alma mater: Valley Forge Military Academy.

Salinger first arrived at the Forge in 1934 after flunking out of the Manhattan prep school McBurney, on Central Park West. Shortly before he matriculated, a cadet fell to his death from an academy window under suspicious circumstances. Like many cadets, Salinger was conflicted about the place. He penned a sentimental poem in his class yearbook that's still recited at school gatherings, and in personal correspondence, he demonstrates a deep affection for the cadets who shared his experience. But he also channeled intense frustrations about the school in *Catcher*. While *Boy's Life* advertised the Forge as a bastion of military leadership, Salinger showed it be a repository for bad apples and lost boys.

"They don't do any damn more molding at Pencey than they do at any other school," Holden reflects on page one. "And I didn't know anybody there that was splendid and clear-thinking and all. Maybe two guys. If that many. And they probably came to Pencey that way."

In Salinger's narrative, Pencey is plagued by a population of troubled youth, crooked teachers, and spoiled rich kids, a mixture that often begat abuse. The Forge was itself becoming exactly this, a mutant form of West Point unleashed on a far younger study body. The school back then had a solid curriculum and robust extracurricular offerings, including a world-class band that played for numerous dignitaries, which later in the century would include President Richard Nixon. But there was also a kinetic, cold-blooded hazing environment thanks to the large swath of unruly cadets of all ages and backgrounds. This included, for a time, King Simeon, the exiled boy monarch of Bulgaria. While spit-shining his boots one day in the fall of 1958, Simeon declared to a local reporter his thirst to regain power abroad. "I was born to the crown," he grumbled, "and I never abdicated, nor signed any papers giving up my reign."

While subsequent military service was not mandatory at the Forge, as with most other schools of this ilk, it nonetheless hosted a strong, voluntary officer commissioning program, plus a recruiting pipeline to the service academies. In turn, schools like the Forge birthed a new military archetype, whose adherents were often privileged, scrappy, and damaged—just as Holden Caulfield was.

Holden eagerly rebels against Pencey Prep, gets the boot, and flees to New York City, a place with its own vices and hazards, but without the sort of propaganda and pretense that obscure the school's dark underside. Like most private military schoolboys, Holden is young. At sixteen he speaks with the resigned tone of a battle-drained war veteran. He's grappling with pent-up sexual energy, a bad cigarette habit, and a bleak view of the world. In their

2013 biography *Salinger*, David Shields and Shane Salerno posit that *Catcher* was deeply informed by Salinger's experience on the front lines. They report that he was hospitalized for psychiatric treatment during his time as an Army intelligence agent, where, among other things, he undertook harsh interrogations. He emerged from this experience "incapable of believing in the heroic, noble ideals we like to think our cultural institutions uphold."

We see Salinger's harsh sentiments about World War II early in *Catcher*, when Holden details the service of his brother, D.B. He informs Holden that the U.S. Army is "practically as full of bastards as the Nazis were." On furlough, D.B. was despondent. "All he did was lie on his bed, practically," Holden reports. "He hardly ever even came in the living room." The passage is eerily similar to Salinger's own state of mind while in uniform, specifically on a day that should have evoked ecstasy. When, on May 8, 1945, the Germany Army finally surrendered, Salinger spent the day in Europe alone, lying on a cot and staring at a .45-caliber pistol clutched in his hand, fantasizing about shooting his palm.

Upon its publication in 1951, *Catcher* quickly became one of the most censored books in America. Another highly controversial text from this time was *End as a Man*. It was also a work of autofiction from a military school alumnus, in this case former Citadel cadet Calder Willingham. First published in 1947, the text similarly explores the violence, hypocrisy, and spiritual void at the center of military schooling through Jocko de Paris, a sadistic and paranoid cadet leader with repressed homosexual urges. Jocko and other upperclassmen unleash hell on those younger and weaker than them. In one case, a band of cadets snatch a picture of a plebe's dead sister, inscribed to him shortly before her passing, and soak it in a toilet bowl.

The New York Society for the Suppression of Vice tried to ban Willingham's work via legal action, alleging that it was an "obscene, lewd, lascivious, filthy, indecent and disgusting book." Lost in this brouhaha was a clarifying truth: that the book in question was not a grotesque fantasy cut from whole cloth, but a fictionalized tale of a real and deeply rotten structure.

WHILE THE AMERICAN BOY'S FEVER for military validation was beginning to break, not everyone would get well. The literary poster child for the old type of soldier was Ernest Hemingway, who, like many men of his generation, had preordained military service as a child. As a kid in the early 1900s,

Hemingway had reasoned simply that war was what "men had always done." His starry-eyed thoughts about the service were blurry, and his vision was, too. After the Army rejected Hemingway from the ranks at eighteen due to his poor eyesight, he joined the Red Cross as an ambulance driver, navigating the front lines of Italy during World War I before being wounded in successive incidents by mortar and machine-gun fire. Hemingway later found a second alternative path to battle, as a newspaperman. In August 1944, as part of his coverage of World War II, Hemingway took up arms to support the liberation of Paris. Soon after, he met with Salinger in the newly liberated city of love, specifically at the bar of the Ritz hotel, where he had spent the lion's share of his time since liberation day, holding court and swigging Perrier-Jouët champagne. Hemingway commended Salinger, then a twenty-five-year-old staff sergeant, on his short stories, and the two conversed for hours. "You have a marvelous ear," Hemingway later wrote to Salinger. "And you write tenderly and lovingly without getting wet."

Salinger saw in Hemingway a writer god and a kindred spirit. Still, he sometimes bristled at Hemingway's unrelenting machismo, which, Salinger felt, often involved withholding the full truth of a soldier's existence. In *Catcher*, Holden derides Hemingway's *A Farewell to Arms* as a "phony book." Salinger's young alter ego also watches a war movie whose sentimentality nearly makes him vomit. Salinger once confided to a friend that he felt negatively toward Hemingway's "overestimation of sheer physical courage, commonly called 'guts,' as a virtue" before admitting that "I'm short on [guts] myself."—a rare admission for Salinger of military masculinity's prevailing hold on his psyche.

Below the surface of Hemingway's puffery was poorly disguised pain. His work is wrought with tension around the invigorating, often self-destructive relationship between the American man and militarism. Nowhere is this interplay clearer than in *The Sun Also Rises*, a book about a war hero whose wounds have rendered him sexually impotent.

Despite the differences between the two writers, Salinger came away from the Ritz rejuvenated to write. He was also surprised and somewhat comforted by Hemingway's soft demeanor in person. Hemingway clearly saw truth in Salinger's overriding thesis: that among the many things war destroyed were important parts of the self, like childhood innocence, inner peace, and optimism. While Hemingway never commented about *Catcher* publicly, he was said to have stored a dog-eared copy of the novel, personalized by Salinger, in his beloved Havana abode.

THE PERSISTENT VISION OF THE FEARLESS, upstanding, and uncommonly patriotic soldier—one whose changes from the war go unexamined—persisted throughout the harsh days of the Cold War, though he struggled mightily. Things got especially bad at the height of Vietnam, when the Pentagon's image curdled, and America saw a whopping 65 percent reduction in its number of military schools. Even the vaunted service academies experienced a recruiting crisis. One West Point professor estimated that between 1969 and 1971, the recruiting situation became "so bad that we accepted the majority of applicants."

This led to increasingly desperate recruiting pleas, which only magnified a growing realization among the public that the military was not simply welcoming in eager young patriots, it was trying to meet quotas by actively exploiting youthful frustrations. As enrollment wobbled, some military schools desperately refashioned themselves as reform schools to stressed-out, self-involved, or impatient parents. Many bought the pitch and pawned off their boys rather than providing them with needed love, support, and assistance.

A major contributing factor to this parenting style was conflict itself, with the world wars turning millions of traumatized men into distant or angry fathers. According to one peer-reviewed meta-analysis, parents who have experienced warfare "showed less warmth and more harshness toward their children." Many fathers who didn't serve, or felt that their service was insufficiently valorous, also ran a cold house, hoping to implant in their boys an aggression that, in their ashamed minds, they didn't sufficiently possess.

Many military schools around this time started welcoming cadets with academic issues, discipline problems, or family trouble, with one official detailing the many parents eager to turn around boys caught "running with the wrong crowd." This planted the seeds of the so-called troubled teen industry, an early and influential spillover of military culture into civilian life and education in which unruly children were prescribed a warrior's way of life. This population included a young man named Charles Manson, who was shuffled between abusive reform programs with a military edge, including the National Training School for Boys. Its superintendent called military culture "particularly suited to the needs of problem boys," praising its ability to inculcate "obedience" and "self-control." As these harsh programs took their toll, Manson came to view himself as a "mechanical boy."

Some bonafide military schools struck deals to admit children from welfare programs, or the juvenile court system. Child defendants in New Jersey could see their criminal records sealed upon proving military enlistment. Other military school leaders claimed these places were ideal environments for children of divorce. What emerged was a volatile mix: state-sanctioned troublemakers, rich kids with absent or overwhelmed parents, and the offspring of working-class families whose parents scraped money together to get their child away from negative influences and into what they felt would be a healthy, realigning experience.

But life at these schools was generally far darker than what was depicted in the brochure. When, in 1964, *The New York Times* visited the New York Military Academy, or NYMA, they compared the barracks to a cellblock. When the reporter asked a random cadet if it was true that the school was a dumping ground for well-off delinquents, he wryly responded: "Don't ask me, I am a delinquent." School officials tried to tamp down negative news reports, pushing their narrative forward in one typical feature in *Town & Country* whose headline reads: "Good Boys Go to Military Schools, Too."

Still, fewer recruits showed up at military schools during the 1960s and 1970s because the military had simply lost its appeal for many young men. In response, the Pentagon concocted a flashy new recruitment pitch that was heavy on sizzle and light on substance. Recruiters shifted attention away from the growing quagmire in the Far East to focus on the service's travel perks and "cool factor." One recruitment poster from the time featured a dapper soldier decked out in civilian garb frequenting an outdoor café in Europe, with a beautiful blonde at his side. This was a stark shift from the image of Uncle Sam, which thrived thanks to a deep well of public belief in the American project. In this wreckage, the military brandished its perks, including the personal status conferred through service. It was no longer a collective force, but an Army of one. The uniform still commanded respect, but because the war behind it was morally compromised, the uniform became an ambiguous signifier and shifted toward being a tool for self-aggrandizement.

This shift arrived with surprising speed, an indication, perhaps, of how soaring rhetoric and codes of honor had worn thin due to the military's brutal and directionless war in Vietnam. The men who harbored dynamic ideas about service were also not long for this world. One was President John F.

Kennedy, a World War II veteran and the much-mythologized man from "Camelot." He sought to revitalize and expand his generation's gallant conception of service, most notably through his 1961 creation of the Peace Corps.

West Point cadet Joseph Zengerle's hopes were high when he marched at Kennedy's 1961 inauguration. He absorbed, in person, Kennedy's rousing call to "ask not what your country can do for you—ask what you can do for your country." Months later, General MacArthur, the hardened old West Pointer, delivered a farewell address to cadets, including Zengerle, that was more humanistic than hard-nosed. Holding court in the cadet mess hall, MacArthur urged the boys in the room "to be proud and unbending in honest failure, but humble and gentle in success; not to substitute words for action; not to seek the path of comfort, but to face the stress and spur of difficulty and challenge; to learn to stand up in the storm, but to have compassion on those who fall; to master yourself before you seek to master others; to have a heart that is clean, a goal that is high; to learn to laugh, yet never forget how to weep; to reach into the future, yet never neglect the past; to be serious, yet never take yourself too seriously."

Months later, Kennedy was assassinated in Dallas, allegedly by Lee Harvey Oswald, a man thoroughly steeped in military culture. At fifteen, Oswald joined an Air Force youth group called the Civil Air Patrol, where he first connected with David Ferrie, a fevered anti-Communist and suspected collaborator in Kennedy's killing. At seventeen, Oswald joined the Marines.

Shortly before his graduation from West Point, Zengerle marched at Kennedy's funeral. The event presaged a darker politics and the continuation of a poisonous war, things that the man in the casket had tried to curb. Per the family's wishes, Kennedy's honor guard that day included a band of Green Berets, one of whom placed his iconic cap on the slain president's grave.

While Kennedy sought to splinter and tame the military establishment, he became fixated on unconventional warfare. He read Mao Zedong and Che Guevara, then, shortly before his death, emboldened America's fledgling sect of shadowy special operators. In 1962, Kennedy officially authorized the green beret as the emblem of these fighters. That same year, in a graduation speech at West Point, Kennedy assured a crowd of Cold War cadets that their service would not "be only standing and waiting."

"You will be privileged in the years ahead to find yourselves so heavily involved in the great interests of this country," Kennedy said, perhaps as a member of the special forces, who, in his eyes, were "growing in number and importance and significance."

Special forces were not deployed en masse to Vietnam until after Kennedy's death. But once their boots hit the ground, they became ensconced in some of the war's ugliest work. The commander of the Green Berets was Colonel Robert B. Rheault, a decorated West Pointer who helped inspire the character of Colonel Kurtz in *Apocalypse Now*. In 1969, Rheault was charged alongside a handful of fellow officers with the premeditated murder of Thai Khac Chuyen, a Vietnamese translator and informant who the operators believed to be a double agent. Following days of merciless interrogation, the men allegedly took Chuyen by boat to the middle of Nha Trang Bay, shot him, and tossed him into the drink.

The case shocked the nation. But in the fall of 1969, the Army suddenly dropped the charges against Rheault and his men, leaving them criminally clear but stuck in a moral gray zone. The case, and subsequent others like it, spurred deep resentment among special operators, who came to feel that the U.S. military was casting war's aberrant behavior as the sole responsibility of a few individuals, rather than the inevitable conclusion of an institution built on violence.

As the Cold War ramped up, an increasing number of troops came to see warfare as a lawless space where violence was always justified. A few years after Kennedy's death, a West Point official quietly offered a newly pragmatic calculus about the academy's true contribution: to keep "killing within the warrior's code so that combat did not generate into blood lust, or decent men warp into butchers." Added another West Point officer more coldly: "We are simply the bullet in the gun."

ONE NAVAL ACADEMY GRADUATE FROM THIS ERA was convinced to attend Annapolis by a slick pitchman who showed up at his Long Island public high school in a metallic blue Corvette and perfectly pressed white uniform. He then screened for students the 1965 propaganda film *Ring of Valor*, a picture named for the coveted rings given to cadets at the end of their junior year. From then on they are "ring knockers," an elite military club whose members make a habit of loudly rapping their bling, often while drunk, on hard surfaces as a show of their status. Class rings as a concept had been invented by West Point in 1835, a status symbol shinier and more conspicuous than a patch or medal.

The 1965 film depicts "ring dances," events of pomp and circumstance during which chrome is awarded. "The glamour of the uniform still works its magic," an announcer croons, before the camera flashes to a pack of young women with rings tied to ribbons. From here, the women ceremoniously dip the rings into a basin filled with "waters from the seven seas," then walk with their men under a massive, trellis-like reconstruction of a class ring. Finally, they place the ring on their cadet's finger, and a kiss on his cheek. A woman who went to a ring dance in the aughts described to me a more awkward ritual, one in which she chugged a glass filled with champagne, and the ring, then, via a smooch, moved the ring to her date's mouth. "I thought I was going to choke," she said.

The military's refashioning of the American troop as a forceful, jet-setting stud seeped deep into the mind of Donald Trump, the most famous bad apple who ever attended military school. In the late summer of 1959, thirteen-year-old Donald trudged into his father Fred's Cadillac, which shuttled him from Queens to upstate New York—five miles north of West Point, specifically, to the gates of the New York Military Academy. He would be schooled there for the next five years.

It was here that Donald began to develop his signature magnetism through a combination of machismo and manifest power. This stiflingly all-male environment was also where he constructed his enduring mythos as a ladies' man, a legend enabled by his parents, oddly enough, who frequently brought pretty girls up from the city for weekend visits. Donald often boasted about their beauty, and, according to a former classmate, also developed a fascination with *Playboy* magazine, a fixation he carried into adulthood, when he allegedly had an affair with a buxom playmate named Karen McDougal. After another cadet got the "Most Popular" superlative one year, a band of loyal classmates rallied to make Trump "Ladies' Man," which, according to another former classmate, "was kind of an inside joke because there really were no ladies." To legitimize Donald's image, cadets tracked down a pretty secretary in an administrative building and had her pose with him for a gushy picture in the NYMA yearbook, called *The Shrapnel*.

Why, exactly, Donald was sent to military school remains unclear. According to *New York Times* reporter Maggie Haberman's biography, *Confidence Man*, some believed Fred sent Donald there after discovering his large collection of switchblades. Others believe it was because he assaulted a teacher at his former prep school, Kew-Forest, in Queens. Longtime Trump chronicler Gabriel Sherman has theorized that Donald developed a budding romance with the mafia that worried his parents. Donald's few cryptic clues about what led him upstate breathe some life into this latter rumor. "I was a wise guy," he once said. "And [my parents] wanted to get me in line."

While Fred's sternness generally fit in the mold of the American father, Trump's mother, Mary, was uncommonly cold and distant, depriving her boy of a mother's softer, more emotional touch. "[Mary] attended to [her children] when it was convenient for her, not when they needed her to," Donald's niece, also named Mary, writes in her frank family memoir *Too Much and Never Enough*. "Often unstable and needy, prone to self-pity and flights of martyrdom, she frequently put herself first. Especially when it came to her sons, she acted as if there were nothing she could do for them."

Once, at his beach club, Fred talked up the merits of military school to a fellow member, Alexander McIntosh, who decided to send his son, Sandy, there, too. Like Fred, Alexander felt his boy was out of control, but for different reasons. While Donald had a hard edge in need of sanding down, McIntosh was seen as too soft. He had spent kindergarten through seventh grade at a progressive Waldorf school, where core activities including knitting, candle-dipping, and baking. "I spent time playing the piano and doing various other things that my father didn't think were masculine," McIntosh told me. "He wanted me to be a man."

On his first day as a "new guy"—the academy's term for a plebe—Donald was outfitted with a plumed parade hat, a deep blue brass-buttoned uniform, a silver saber, and an M1 rifle without its firing pin. He was also assigned a bed in Wright Hall, so named after the school's founder, Charles Jefferson Wright, a white Army officer who commanded a regiment of Black troops during the Civil War. Donald's days featured the typical pillars of military school life: sports, academics, and drills overseen by TAC officers, many of them grizzled World War II veterans. All cadets were expected to become good marksmen and to play tackle football. Donald's austere living conditions were reinforced by a cadet body composed of what McIntosh described as "459 bullies bigger than you." This was unlike anything the spoiled scion and many of his classmates had ever encountered. "It shuts you up very quick," McIntosh recalled.

During Donald's time as a cadet, a faculty member bragged to the *Times* that the academy prioritized "Discipline with a capital 'D.'" Days later, the paper reported that the school superintendent, Army colonel Marvin Coyle, had resigned. The underlying reasons for his departure were unclear, though McIntosh said it stemmed from a brutal attack during the school's seventy-fifth anniversary weekend. It was launched by a tough cadet captain in E-Battery named Michael Scadron after a fellow cadet allegedly called him "a dirty Jew bastard." Scadron responded by grabbing a wooden stick with a metal chain from his bedroom and bashing the kid with it so badly that he required hospital care.

As a resident of Wright Hall, Donald fell under the supervision of the school's longest-serving official, Theodore Dobias, a stern World War II veteran known on campus simply as "Maj'." The son of a Polish butcher who grew up in New York City, Maj' matriculated at NYMA during the war as a sixteen-year-old high schooler. At seventeen, he secretly absconded from campus and joined the ranks of the Army's 10th Mountain Division, where he fought in Italy before being captured. Legend goes that he escaped his imprisonment using the same techniques he had used to elude NYMA's TAC officers at night.

After the war, Maj' returned to NYMA to finish his studies, then stayed on as a staff officer and coach for the rest of his life. He mentored Donald and countless other cadets, including Rich Terlach, who told me that Maj' often carried a stiff wooden paddle, which, he further recalled, he once slapped so hard over a cadet's bare ass that it broke in two. In another case, Terlach saw Maj' screaming orders at a massive lineman on the football team to "man up" and hit him. "The guy leveled Maj'," Terlach recalled. "Then he jumped back up and said, 'Is that all you have, you pussy?'" Some former cadets claimed Maj' could be as helpful as he was harsh. They said he tutored students, trained them physically, and checked in periodically to make sure they were holding up. "He was rock hard, but he cared about every one of his students," Terlach explained.

Donald commanded respect on campus for his die-hard drive to win, but he made few close friends. "People liked [Donald] but he didn't bond with anyone," one classmate recalled. "I think it was because he was too competitive, and with a friend you don't always compete. It was like he had a defensive wall around him."

Maj' coached Donald in baseball, where, according to contemporaneous box scores, he notched a bad batting average. During his sophomore year, for instance, Donald got one hit over ten tries at the plate. Classmates conjured various memories in which Maj' became disappointed by Donald's deficiencies in these and other masculine pursuits, and "pounded the shit" out of him. This began, they recalled, when the Queens scion first arrived on campus, and rolled his eyes in response to an order. "That was his first attitude adjustment," one alum recalled. Added Terlach: "Maj' was the only person I know who could tell Donald to do something, and Donald would listen." Maj' later reflected that Donald was the perfect specimen to shape in his image: "He caught my eye right away because he was so aggressive, and so coachable."

Decades later, the power dynamics between the men had reversed. During Donald's first presidential election, in 2016, he successfully cajoled Maj' to get on the phone with a *Washington Post* reporter and testify to his unwavering excellence. His old mentor further elevated Donald's legend to other reporters, claiming to *Rolling Stone* and the *Daily Mail* that West Point had scouted him for baseball, as had the Red Sox and the Phillies. "He was quite the athlete," Maj' asserted dubiously.

It's unclear what bred Maj's undying loyalty to Trump. Perhaps it was owed to the Cadillac Donald had bought him, or to the fact that a man like Maj' respected hierarchy, and knew that, in the grand scheme of things, Trump outranked him. Still, in private, Donald relied on Maj' for guidance. According to Terlach, the old man was, for a long time, one of just three people outside the presidential candidate's family who had Trump's personal cell phone number. In his comments to the *Post*, Donald described school officials as "really rough cookies." Asked what he learned there, he answered "discipline—how to dish it out and otherwise."

Jack Serafin, who graduated from NYMA two years after Donald did, said the campus was wracked by an atmosphere of nearly nonstop abuse and degradation. "It was a lot like *Full Metal Jacket*," he said, referencing the 1987 film about the Vietnam War, which kicks off with a brutal boot camp section in which a simple innocent boy is transformed into a new figure, the evil-eyed "Gomer Pyle," who kills his drill sergeant, then commits suicide.

McIntosh described the school as an "animalistic" environment rife with acts of chest-thumping dominance. Rich Pezzullo, who arrived a few years after Donald graduated, recalled that there was little adult supervision at night. "You could take any problem behind the gym, where nobody would see you, and you could solve it," he told me.

Then, as now, Donald was a germaphobe and seemed thrilled to uphold the school's strict domestic hygiene requirements. Once, when he felt a smaller cadet named Theodore Levine had failed to properly make his bed, Donald ripped off the sheets. Levine then chucked a boot and a broomstick at him, and Donald charged. "It took three people to get him off me," Levine recalled.

Other NYMA graduates also made violence a core part of their identity. One of Donald's roommates, Art Davie, founded the Ultimate Fighting Championship, a historically lawless martial arts league that, beginning in the 2010s, grew into a global sensation and reliable hub for key figures in the manosphere, including Trump, who made a fight at Madison Square Garden his first public stop following his 2024 reelection. Then there was Cadet Scadron, who beat his classmate with a chain. Scadron was expelled, but Donald was impressed. Years later, he tried, and failed, to hire him for a job.

Some of Trump's classmates were also scions of wealthy and/or infamous Manhattan families, including mobster John Gotti Jr.'s boy. Other mob families sent their children to military school, too. Meyer Lansky's kid went to West Point, while the son of reputed Genovese boss "Matty the Horse" Ianniello matriculated at Valley Forge, which, in Salinger's fictionalized *Catcher*, is depicted as "full of crooks." In *The Godfather*, a film directed by former NYMA cadet Francis Ford Coppola, Al Pacino's Michael Corleone is redeemed by his military service. Similarly, in season three of the TV series *The Sopranos*, Tony seeks to send his listless namesake to the fictional Hudson Military Institute after he's discovered cheating on a test. The mob, it seemed, saw in the military a familiar violence, but understood that the mission undergirding the Pentagon's line of work was considered a just cause.

Corrupt and tyrannical foreign leaders similarly viewed military schools as well versed to teach the traits of a strongman. Valley Forge accepted the offspring of Russian and Bulgarian princes, and years later, Louis Sarkozy, the son of France's strongman president Nicolas Sarkozy. In 2025, Louis fused his love of Trump and Bonaparte to launch a political career on the French right.

West Point also reared foreign boys from powerful families, including Anastasio Somoza Debayle, who followed his brother and father to lead Nicaragua with an iron fist. Before West Point, Somoza attended La Salle Military Academy, a Catholic military school on Long Island, where he was mentored by Stephen Colbert's uncle Andrew Tuck III, one of the youngest paratroopers in World War II. Tuck often invited Somoza to the family's home for the holidays, where he briefly struck up a romance with Colbert's mother. Later, as commander in chief, Somoza instituted martial law with a murderous National Guard force. He also assisted the Americans with the Bay of Pigs invasion, a comically flubbed mission that was largely designed by fellow West Pointer Lyman Lemnitzer.

Other NYMA graduates of the Cold War era told me they went to school with members of the Saudi royal family, and the sons of Latin American strongmen, including Cuban dictator Fulgencio Batista. Serafin recalled swirling rumors that a pack of cadets from Venezuela were "breaking down the school's M1 gun parts and sending them home." McIntosh said he bunked with a Peruvian kid from a powerful government family who once told him dejectedly that, for his entire summer, "my father put me in a brothel to teach me macho." Pezzullo posits that Donald's experience with this ilk primed him for the role of commander in chief. "When he went to meet with Kim Jong Un, he was talking to a dictator's kid, which is a skill he picked up as a boy in military school." The "tough guy" persona Trump built at NYMA made him a natural ally not only of dictators but also of the many mobsters with whom he collaborated intimately as he constructed his mythos as the most canny construction magnate in all of New York City.

BY HIS JUNIOR YEAR, Donald was a towering cadet on campus, physically tall and captivating, though not a particularly outstanding cadet. He had bad grades, a low batting average, and a series of blemishes on his record as a cadet leader. Many of his peers that year were elevated into roles overseeing and mentoring cadets, but Donald was made supply sergeant, tasked not with building character, but with cleaning and overseeing a storage room full of rifles.

Despite his significant limitations, Donald was unexpectedly elevated to a plum position for his senior year: company captain. It was a promotion that the Trump family had apparently paid for. "Everybody knew Fred was pulling out his checkbook," one former cadet alleged. The money angle made sense, for Donald was reportedly an aloof company leader, often cooped up in his room blaring his record player with songs of willful ignorance. This habit got him in hot water when a cadet under his watch shoved a freshman hard against a wall while Donald was cooped up in his room.

After the hazed boy complained about Donald's apathetic leadership style, he was demoted, though he publicly insisted to friends that his new title was actually a promotion. When yet another cadet was assaulted, and his parents threatened to sue, Donald was again reassigned, though he kept his title.

Not long after, as NYMA prepared to march in New York City's Columbus Day parade, Donald was again given a plum position, at the head of the line. On a balmy October day in 1963, he led his fellow cadets down Fifth Avenue before arriving at St. Patrick's Cathedral, where he met Cardinal Francis Spellman. At one point during the journey, alumni contend, he peered up at the city's skyscrapers and remarked, "I'd really like to own some of this property someday." Back at the academy, Donald refused to draw his saber for a yearbook photo. No number of beatings from Maj' or anyone else, it seemed, was enough to curb his indignant autonomy.

Later, when Donald sat for his senior-year portrait, he borrowed the festooned jacket of a highly decorated classmate, which featured medals Donald never earned. With the simple snap of a camera shutter, he secured an apparent promotion. It was an especially brash example of the general atmosphere at these private military schools, which graduate George Witek summed up as "playacting."

Donald took away from NYMA the importance of optics, and how to manipulate them. While the school billed itself as a punishing environment built on sturdy, sanctified codes, Donald seemed to see through the school's shallow culture of solemnity. He could claim adherence to the belief system and, at the same time, actively buck it, discovering that valor could be bought, coerced, or beaten out of someone. This lesson was reinforced by Maj', who hung two gold-lettered signs in Wright Hall that spoke to this stark dichotomy. One articulated his lofty paean to decency. It read: "When the great scorer comes to write against your name, he writes not whether you've won or lost but how you played the game." The other endorsed securing power at all costs: "Winning isn't everything. It's the only thing." The two plainly contradictory messages perfectly represented the military's embellished PR poetry—contravened by its actual orders, given in take-no-prisoners prose.

"I did very well under the military system," Donald said decades later in an interview. It was one of the few credible claims he's made in relation to his past. While he had clear shortcomings as a cadet, Donald demonstrated preternatural abilities to bend people to his will, to push his way up a hierarchy, and to strike fear and loyalty into his peers. "He was so competitive that everybody who could come close to him he had to destroy," one classmate recalled. It was a comment that could have as easily applied to many of the U.S. military's great men, from George Washington to George Patton.

Donald ultimately sapped prestige out of the military system without needing to sacrifice much in return. Upon his graduation, in 1964, the draft was raging. Many NYMA graduates fought and died in Vietnam, with a tall tree standing on campus today in their honor. Donald, on the other hand, secured a diagnosis of bone spurs from a doctor in Queens, avoiding true military service entirely and following directly in the footsteps of his grandfather, Frederick Trump, who was banished from Germany for evading compulsory military service.

This hasn't stopped Trump from receiving his fair share of military honors. When, in 2001, Donald showed up by helicopter to give NYMA's commencement address, he had a young supermodel on his arm and urged graduates to "think big." He then falsely bragged that he had purchased the Empire State Building. A few years after that, he was inducted into the academy's sports hall of fame. In 2016, a gracious military veteran gifted him his Purple Heart on the campaign trail. "I always wanted to get the Purple Heart," Trump responded. "This was much easier." Eight years later, after surviving an assassination attempt, two more veterans gifted Trump their Purple Hearts. "You've got guts," one of them exclaimed during a campaign event, and Trump beamed. He was now technically one of the most decorated war heroes in American history.

Chapter 8

The Death of Honor

As part of Richard Nixon's 1968 comeback campaign for president, the scrappy politician came up with a tricky piece of campaign rhetoric. He pledged to provide exactly what Americans craved: a "secret plan for peace" that would lead to an "honorable end" to the war in Vietnam. It was a vague and open-ended promise, one that kept Nixon's timeline and true aims unclear. As it would later emerge, the candidate had spent much of his campaign season quietly convincing South Vietnamese president Nguyen Van Thieu to withdraw from the Paris Peace Talks, derailing President Lyndon Johnson's muscular efforts to forge a peace agreement before leaving office. Apparently, the details just weren't honorable enough.

Johnson became aware of Nixon's sabotage shortly before election day, and considered making his discovery public. But his advisers, led by Defense Secretary Clark Clifford, convinced LBJ to keep the information secret—arguing that the disclosure this late in the game would reveal that the government had been conducting illegal wiretap surveillance on Nixon and his compatriots. Clifford added that if LBJ went public only to see Nixon win anyway, the new commander in chief would be weakened by his tête-à-tête with Saigon.

Shortly after taking office, in early 1969, Nixon quietly conceded to his National Security Adviser Henry Kissinger that victory in the region was "impossible." Rather than publicly admit this or sketch out a concrete evacuation plan to withdraw and mitigate American losses, Nixon escalated the war and, during his 1972 reelection campaign, derided his anti-war opponent George McGovern for seeking "peace at any price." Needing some kind of Vietnam War message of his own, Kissinger promised that "peace is at hand"—suggesting that negotiations were close to being resolved but without naming any specifics. Nixon then carpet-bombed North Vietnam during Christmas 1972, shortly before being sworn in for his second term.

America had been in broad agreement that its fight against fascism during World War II was honorable, and, despite being marked by numerous acts of brutal inhumanity, the war was considered legitimate and righteous, given the clear and heinous policies of the Axis powers. When the U.S. moved to occupy and attack Vietnam, however, the public couldn't find an easy moral foothold, leading Nixon and others to increasingly invoke the vagaries of "honor" to mask its discredited premise, and the degenerate killing that proliferated. The message became crude and callous: "Do as the military orders and you'll be deemed a hero." In this light, honor was revealed as a synthetic form of selflessness, a plaudit predicated on the whims and wisdom of Pentagon leadership. The lack of moral standing among the officer class that became widely apparent during Vietnam fueled a public backlash to the sterling image of the clean-shaven military cadet and led to an enhanced status of his archetypal opposite—the peacenik.

Nixon's rhetoric around honor was reinforced by his political and military allies, including lieutenant general Albert P. Clark, then the Air Force Academy's superintendent. Echoing Nixon, he proclaimed that America got into the war for "honorable purposes," and it must get out with the same air of integrity. "If we leave dishonorably," Clark asserted, "it will be on our consciences as long as we can remember." When, on January 23, 1973, Nixon announced the end of the war in a short but defiant speech, he asserted that all the proper conditions had been met. In the nine minutes he spoke, he used the phrase "Peace with Honor" five times. This celebration was premature, however—the war lingered on for over two more years.

This notion of military "honor" was hard to square under brutal battlefield conditions in Vietnam, where the targets of our attacks came to include peasants and workers, women and children. Plenty of returning veterans clearly articulated the distance between honor and their own lived experience. Many felt compelled to come clean about the dishonorable things they had done—to begin their long process of healing and recovery.

Officially, though, notions of honor continued to figure prominently among the officer class, which was significantly responsible for Vietnam's failings but showed the least amount of contrition for what had been done. Honor had hovered over every action these officers took while in military school—this was the all-important base of Thayer's much-replicated leadership triangle. Honor had also become a cornerstone for an American masculinity that psychologists diagnosed as toxic, for the societal expectation that men simply accept authority, stand up to threats, and reject vulnerability, often resulting in risky and self-destructive behaviors.

IN 1898, WEST POINT ELEVATED THIS IDEAL when it created its motto—"Duty, Honor, Country"—with its corresponding honor code that demands "a cadet will not lie, cheat, or steal, or tolerate those who do." This code is enforced through so-called honor boards, one node in the military's separate and highly punitive legal system, known as the Uniform Code of Military Justice.

Military honor is traditionally equated with honesty, integrity, and altruism, but definitionally it doesn't require any of these things. In Vietnam, it often demanded just the opposite—as troops were ordered to undertake torture, summary killings, rapes, and their cover-ups. Whistleblowers who adopted the purest form of honor, by disclosing atrocities, were punished, while criminals climbed the ranks.

During the Vietnam War, many came to see the military as not only lacking basic ethics but actively instilling a worldview that was immoral, illegal, and ugly. During World War II, Americans were heartened to read and hear battlefield dispatches describing heroism against heinous Nazis, who rounded up Jews and stormed their way into country after country. Now Americans were repulsed by what was being shown on their TV screens and reported in the papers. Most shocking was the 1968 My Lai massacre, a mass murder of civilians by American troops that left hundreds of women, children, and elderly men dead.

When reporter Seymour Hersh, who broke the My Lai story, visited the mother of Paul Meadlo, one of the privates who followed Army officer William Calley's orders to shoot civilians, she insisted that the military had implanted terrible new instincts in her son. "I sent them a good boy," she told Hersh, "and they made him a murderer."

My Lai was only the most publicized scandal in a pattern of lawlessness defined by the war's infamous order to U.S. soldiers navigating vast "free-fire zones" in the countryside: "Kill Anything That Moves." Virtually all the top commanders who led the charge in Southeast Asia were loyal West Pointers, from the U.S. military's top commander, William Westmoreland, a former first captain expert at covering up the war's failures, to Creighton Abrams, a cigar-chomping tank commander who worked to boost the ranks and weaponry of South Vietnamese soldiers. In concert, they cleared the countryside of people, moving masses of peasants into militarized camps along the protected coast and declaring the vast countryside that remained a "free-fire zone" where anything or anyone that moved was fair game. They also defoliated forests, using highly toxic Agent Orange, so the enemy had no place to hide or move, and covered the countryside in a self-igniting jellied gasoline called Napalm.

The average number of bullets fired per soldier was twenty-six times greater in Vietnam than during World War II. One soldier described the military's campaign in the Mekong Delta as a "My Lai each month." Troops in the Mekong who reported insufficient kill counts were sacked by General Julian Ewell, a West Pointer known as the "Butcher of the Delta." Another West Pointer, George S. Patton III, the son of the famed WWII general, referred to men under his command in Vietnam as "one hell of a bunch of killers"—and he authored a 1968 Christmas card that depicted a pile of dismembered Vietnamese bodies alongside the inscription "Peace on Earth."

President Nixon represented himself as a proud Navy man, which begs the question of how his military training and experience influenced his notions of ethical behavior. Nixon was also a Quaker—but his path to public service was littered with lies, shady deals, the gratuitous targeting of political enemies, questionable financial transactions, the illegal bombing of Cambodia, and the 1972 Watergate affair, which went far beyond the break-in and included Nixon's extorting more than $60 million from American Airlines, oil companies, and others. This was all to fund Nixon's political operations and the White House "Plumbers," an off-the-books unit of dirty tricksters formed to gather dirt on opponents, intimidate them, infiltrate activist groups, spread disinformation, and stem intelligence leaks after the 1971 Pentagon Papers shockingly exposed the true failures in Vietnam.

Not all the president's men had a military background, but many of them did. The chief Plumbers, E. Howard Hunt and G. Gordon Liddy, had military service under their belts as did many of their co-conspirators. Three of the five Watergate burglars were themselves military veterans: Bernard Barker, James McCord Jr., and Frank Sturgis. Nixon's vice president Spiro Agnew, an Army veteran, avoided charges in Watergate, but was later charged with bribery, extortion, and tax fraud stemming from his political rise in

Maryland. Capping off Nixon's crew was his chief of staff during the Watergate fallout, Alexander Haig, also a proud West Pointer.

Military schools were not only producing dishonorable graduates, but their conventional war curriculum, borne by the world wars, was broken and fast-becoming irrelevant. Amid the war's bad orders and ill-planned battles, 7,877 American officers lost their lives out of 58,220 dead American troops total. Nearly 60 officers were killed in more than 1,000 suspected "fragging incidents" by lower-ranking men—a gruesome expression of the inflamed resentments among the enlisted class toward the elite officer corps perpetuating the war and making bad decisions. Another 50,000 American men deserted the military entirely. What was gained from their sacrifice was little more than a devastating path of destruction. At least 3.8 million Vietnamese died violent war deaths, an estimated 11.7 million were forced from their homes, and up to 4.8 million were sprayed with toxic herbicides. This mass poisoning, alongside the presence of millions of unexploded American land mines, has created a death toll that is still growing fifty years later.

DURING THESE YEARS, ANTI-WAR EFFORTS—be they by soldiers, officers, veterans, or civilians—were sharply opposed by military brass, sometimes violently. Shortly after Nixon announced his invasion of Cambodia, in April 1970, student protests popped up on 760 campuses, including at Kent State University in Ohio, where activists had, for months, been demanding trustees abolish ROTC and cease all war-related research. Their peaceful protests were met by a violent pack of National Guard soldiers who, on May 4, 1970, fired about seventy rounds at demonstrators, killing four students and wounding nine others. While eight troops faced trial for their actions, they were charged only with a minor offense—depriving students of their civil rights—and all were acquitted. After the verdict, *The New York Times* found one of the guardsmen on site, sucking down a cigarette and apparently without remorse. "I'm on cloud nine," he said.

Less than a month after the Kent State shootings, Vice President Agnew visited West Point and gave a commencement speech that derided "the charlatans of peace and freedom [who] eulogize foreign dictators while desecrating the flag that keeps them free." Soldiers had just murdered four students in cold blood, and yet Agnew complained of those who "glamorize the criminal misfits of society while our best men die in Asian rice paddies to preserve the freedoms those misfits abuse."

Vietnam exposed the military's lack of a moral center and complicated considerations of right and wrong. America, in turn, became increasingly polarized. Cadets—who were seen by some as exemplifying both militarism and privilege—found themselves increasingly confronted by protesters, an insurgently "cool" archetype showcasing everything military officers were not.

As cadets increasingly faced challenges to their war, their status, and their masculinity, many were receptive to Agnew's remarks. A few months before Agnew's 1970 graduation speech, two hundred Vassar students congregated at West Point's gates where they handed out flowers to cadets and urged them to abandon their commissions. Some cadets snatched their flowers and ate them. Another sarcastically told a protestor that he couldn't speak because he was on his way to "poison gas class." A third, boyish-looking senior vented to the *Times* that the anti-war movement "makes you wonder why the hell you should go risk your neck for those kinds of people." This deep sense of grievance is immortalized in West Point's chapel, which traditionally offers each graduating class a personalized glass pane. When it came time for the class of 1966 to design their sheet, they landed on a depiction of St. Valeria, who was tortured and beheaded by her own people. Other offended cadets around this time insisted that their domestic treatment was so bad that they envied their comrades who had perished on the battlefield.

These were not measured reactions to the substance of the protests, but rather a reflexive resentment over the Army's bruised prestige—and failure to prevail in Vietnam. A more thoughtful cadet from this era observed that "the people here at the Point think this is their own little world, and no one has any right tampering with it."

During and immediately after the two world wars, West Point cadets would proudly don their military dress to venture out to New York City on the weekends. This traditionally assured them of free drinks, cheap meals at luxury restaurants, even hotel discounts. They also enjoyed the assistance of an "academy hostess," payrolled staff tasked with teaching cadet etiquette and developing their social lives, including by fielding letters from girls eager for a blind date with a West Point man.

But attitudes had shifted during Vietnam. While one girl was quoted as saying that West Point cadets were "neater and stand up straighter" than most boys, others had far less favorable experiences. "They're so starved for girls, that when they get you alone—watch out," warned one Vassar student.

Gotham also shifted its attitudes during Vietnam, requiring cadets to abandon their ornamental dresswear. "As soon as we left the gate we went to the closest public bathroom and changed out of our West Point uniform as fast as we could," Robert Caslen, a 1975 graduate turned superintendent, told me. Cadets not only started donning civilian clothes out, but sometimes even wore wigs to cover up their high and tight haircuts. The first few times Caslen ventured to the city in uniform, he alleged, "people would laugh at me, yell at me, and I was spit at." Similar resentments were stoked at the Naval Academy, where protestors sometimes threw eggs at midshipmen, or called them "warmongers."

These were relatively tame protests. Still, the service academies couldn't handle the heat. West Point superintendent major general William Knowlton bemoaned that his beloved academy had become a "stockade surrounded by attacking Indians." He did have some reason to worry. A pacifist contagion had broken out at Culver Military Academy, in northern Indiana, with cadets rebelling against their overseers and painting peace signs all over campus. During the spring of 1970, a recently resigned cadet from the Citadel went as far as to conspire with friends who remained on campus to create and distribute an underground newspaper called *The Vigil*. It railed against cadet mistreatment, officer elitism, and on-campus censorship. That same year, when Dr. Edward Teller, the father of the hydrogen bomb, spoke to a room of West Pointers, one cadet rose and righteously asked: "How can you recommend spending millions researching new weapons systems when we live in such a sick society?"

General Knowlton likely realized that the peace movement had not only articulated a biting critique of the war's failures, it had also popularized a hip counterculture that threatened the Pentagon's long-held dominance over American youth. Perhaps no figure represented the military's fast-diminishing allure better than a ruggedly handsome, whip-smart young Army officer and helicopter pilot named Kris Kristofferson. Kristofferson had a Navy fighter pilot for a brother, a West Point professor for a brother-in-law, and two proudly patriotic parents, and yet still he ditched the service in 1965, turning down a coveted West Point professorship to pursue music in Nashville. "[My parents] sent a letter just flat saying, you know, 'Don't visit any of our relatives, you're an embarrassment to us'—

worse than that, but I ain't going into it," Kristofferson recalled at the time, but still he remained dead set on his one true love. Soon after passing up the West Point job, Kristofferson sold his first song of many, a wrenching anti-war anthem called "The Vietnam Blues."

Knowlton responded defiantly to the surging anti-war counterculture, hanging an AK-47 captured from a dead Vietnamese enemy soldier on his office wall and frequently sharing with cadets sunny stories from his time in Southeast Asia. Still, Knowlton's invocation of triumphalism in Vietnam was undercut by the circumstances surrounding his appointment. In 1970, he had hurriedly replaced Samuel Koster as West Point superintendent—as Koster faced an investigation for his alleged assistance in the cover-up of My Lai. Upon his ascension, Knowlton chose not to discuss Koster's charges or predicament but instead singled out Louis Font, a young West Point graduate who had helped put the My Lai prosecution together. In remarks delivered to the Point's Board of Visitors, Knowlton derided Font as a false prophet, not a true West Pointer but rather a cynical youth there to "ride the education gravy train."

Few service academy graduates spoke up against the wars, a sign, it seems, that Thayer's culture of obedience remained alive and well, strong enough, even, to suppress existential military questions. Font was believed to be the first West Pointer to claim conscientious objector status. "I am not a total pacifist," the lieutenant wrote in his application. "But after con-siderable meditation and study, there exists no doubt in my mind that the Vietnam War is immoral and unjust. To me, in Vietnam, the United States Government is destroying another country and an underdeveloped coun-try, and in the process is destroying itself."

Before he left Thayer Gate for the last time, Koster, the exiting super-intendent caught up in My Lai, ventured to the high stone "poop deck" in West Point's immense mess hall and offered a final indignant order to the school's four thousand cadets: "Don't let the bastards grind you down." It elicited a rousing ovation from the youth, who subsequently marched past his living quarters in a show of respect. One cadet later described this en-thusiasm as more of an acknowledgment of what it's like to be "caught in the bowels of the system," though others blindly defended My Lai actions or were numb to the allegations against him. So, too, was the military jus-tice system. Koster's war crimes charges were eventually dropped in favor of a rank reduction and formal letter of censure.

The muddying of ethics and morality surrounding the My Lai massacre was further complicated by another West Pointer, brigadier general John Donaldson, who disposed of military records pertaining to the massacre. This was part and parcel of what Edward King, a retired lieutenant colonel, described in the *Times* as the "West Point Protective Association." Donaldson, King noted, had been separately accused of murdering six Vietnamese civilians and assaulting two others, charges that another West Pointer in power dropped. For his service, the Army transferred Donaldson to a plum, quiet post in Paris.

"West Point classmates learn to stick together, cover each other, and not to ask questions about the actions of senior graduates," King warned in the paper. "The public should not have to continue to pay excessive costs to maintain a military educational institution which chiefly serves to perpetuate a system of elitist control and an Army leadership more dedicated to protecting itself than the best interests of the nation."

VALLEY FORGE SUPERINTENDENT WILLARD PEARSON was another brash example of a military officer class that, since the end of World War II, had become unrepentant and out of control. A gray-eyed commando, Pearson had served as a low-ranking officer in World War II before serving as a general during Vietnam. There he worked closely with Westmoreland commanding the 101st airborne division, a legendary brigade known colloquially as "The Screaming Eagles," which was famously depicted, in its World War II iteration, in the 2001 HBO miniseries *Band of Brothers*. In Vietnam, Pearson ran a bloodthirsty brigade that specialized in guerrilla warfare and conducted brutal night raids. Over one seventeen-month span, Pearson bragged, the Eagles killed or captured 3,300 so-called Communists.

Upon his 1973 appointment to lead the Forge, Pearson defended private military programs by deriding public schools as overrun with "drug addiction, alcohol abuse, racial tension, overcrowding, a poor curriculum, teachers' strikes, crimes against youth, and a permissive atmosphere."

Behind the scenes, however, Pearson pioneered an organizational model later copied by other military schools, called the "3-S Program." It prescribed three orders for military school success: increased enrollment, fatter endowment funds, and cost-cutting. Pearson's austerity policies led the Forge's alleged culture of corruption to fester, although he publicly asserted just the opposite. "Military academies are remarkably free of" crime, substance abuse, and miseducation, Pearson asserted, explaining that this purity was achieved through traditional military values, like honor, discipline, patriotism—edicts, Pearson concluded, which "made America great."

But a rotting culture was germinating, one wherein the performative culture of optimism and ethics that long pervaded military schools was being replaced by the bald brutality and corruption of Vietnam. In the years after the war, the Forge, like Trump's alma mater, fueled what a former Title IX officer deemed a "'Gomer Pyle' method of training," referring to the brutally hazed Vietnam conscript in *Full Metal Jacket* who commits a murder-suicide.

Scott Eberly, who graduated from the Forge during Vietnam, told me the school "taught me how to take shit" and "taught me how to be tough." When, upon his graduation, he moved on to a civilian college and joined a fraternity, he laughed at the lightness of their freshman initiation rites, one of which was to do ten push-ups. "I was like, are you kidding me." The Forge of Vietnam, Eberly concluded, "was a pretty autocratic thing," adding, "it made me able to survive and stay sane under a repressive regime."

ONE OF THE MILITARY'S MAIN TACTICS to undermine the anti-war movement was to cast its adherents as feminine and weak. One of the louder voices in this chorus was Frank Kobes Jr., a hulking colonel and longtime leader of West Point's PE department, a position so vaunted it is given the title "Master of the Sword." From his West Point perch, where he sat between 1953 and 1974, Kobes scolded the "Space Age child" as "overfed" and "underactive," a proverbial boy seized by "abstract intellectualism." He also authored a questionable study asserting that physical education was conclusively tied to emotional maturity.

Some cadets embraced Kobes's stance. "You can look at a man and tell if he's West Point," one said. "He stands up straighter, he speaks more forcefully, he looks better. Just look at his belt buckle—it's always properly lined up." In their piercing 1973 exposé *West Point: America's Power Fraternity*, Vietnam veterans K. Bruce Galloway and Robert B. Johnson Jr. report that the academy went so far as to hire recovering drug addicts with a hippie sensibility as groundskeepers—a move meant to negatively model the civilian counterculture to cadets. West Point, they observed, "is there to help this poor creature, and also make him a living exhibit of the moral degeneracy in the outside world." In this same way, school administrators studied civilian college practices, but only to amass evidence of West Point's superiority. This was part of the academy's efforts to insulate itself from what it considered the "contaminating impurities of the world." Administrators enacted special punishments for behaviors associated with the counterculture, like hitchhiking and smoking doobies, dismissing at least sixteen cadets found in possession of marijuana.

West Point administrators also looked to choke the flow of outside information available to cadets. It wasn't until 1920 that cadets were first permitted to read daily newspapers, though this particular policy was short-lived, reversed, it seems, after a pack of "disgruntled old grads," known colloquially as "DOGs," made a stink with the administration. By the Vietnam era, the academy had produced a short list of acceptable magazines to which a cadet could subscribe. Anyone who wanted to venture outside this collection had to formally seek authorization for a new magazine, explaining how the selected periodical was pertinent to their studies.

At the time, all West Point administrators and permanent faculty were in the military. Many were service academy graduates deeply loyal to the institution, combat veterans who didn't meaningfully question the war, or both. Andrew Bacevich, a 1969 West Point graduate, told me that his professors "did not encourage cadets to think critically about what was happening, and about the war we were about to join. Conformity was encouraged." When a young midshipman named Oliver North arrived at Annapolis in 1963, he similarly discovered a radically sheltered place, one where "we didn't really know what the rest of the world was thinking." Eberly, the Forge cadet, agreed. "We were pretty closed off from the rest of the world."

Bacevich said that while many cadets were latently aware that the war was "going badly," all had made indelible service commitments. Complaining at this point simply didn't seem productive, plus America's victory in World War II was still animating the institution with a patina of invincibility and military prowess. "We had just ascended to a position of global supremacy," Bacevich reasoned. "We were numero uno." Nixon himself tapped into this nostalgia, which included watching and rewatching the hagiographic biopic *Patton* while pushing plans to invade Cambodia in the spring of 1970.

A screening of *Patton* at West Point aroused a similarly enthusiastic reception, with cadets cheering loudest following Patton's grisly pledge at the beginning of the film that: "We won't just shoot the sonofabitches. We're going to cut out their living guts—and use them to grease the treads of our tanks." It was a loud indication of the violent fervor then sweeping the campus—and evidence for World War II's dehumanizing effects, even on its most noble heroes.

When Lucian Truscott IV arrived at West Point in the summer of 1965, he expected an environment dripping with noblesse oblige. Truscott's grandfather, who shares his name, was a legendary World War II commander, a man important enough to be depicted in *Patton*, where he's shown coordinating the allied invasion of Italy.

Young Truscott's hopes were dashed on his first day as a plebe, when a major advised him and other cadets that securing a position to see action in Vietnam was a good idea, not necessarily because it was the right thing to do, but simply because it would enable an "escalator to Army success."

Truscott knew from his grandfather's travails that war was hell. Now, here was a major describing conflict in breezy terms, almost as if it was a networking conference in Orlando, Florida. "What the fuck is going on here?" he thought. Truscott quickly became a noted agitator on campus, successfully challenging the legality of mandatory chapel service. Later, at Fort Carson, Colorado, he wrote articles about heroin addiction in the ranks. When brass threatened to send him directly to Vietnam, he resigned his commission. Decades later, Truscott remains profoundly disillusioned with the myths his alma mater tells about itself. "West Point," he told me, "exists to pass the secrets of power from men to boys."

THE PENTAGON BECAME DEEPLY WORRIED WHEN, in the summer of 1971, Captain Michael Rose, a young Air Force Academy graduate, kicked off a mission to expose highly sensitive secrets, thereby violating the institution's unofficial omertà code. Over a few months, Rose visited all five service academies, plus VMI and the Citadel, investigating the "infirmities of the military academies' conduct, honor, and ethics systems." Rose's findings would be published two years later in a meticulous and damning 253-page report titled "A Prayer for Relief."

A 1969 USAFA graduate, Rose had researched the report as part of his juris doctorate at NYU Law School. His inquiry was powerfully co-signed by a contingent of federal lawmakers, who explicitly counseled the service academies to accommodate Rose's requests for access. They did so begrudgingly, especially West Point, which gave Rose the chilliest reception and frustrated his efforts. "The military police there were following me," he said. West Point also refused to connect Rose to James Pelosi, a cadet then facing a gauntlet of hazing for failing to immediately put down his pencil at the conclusion of a test.

Rose ultimately navigated around the wire, sneaking one night into West Point's Camp Buckner, located just north of the academy on Lake Popolopen, where he went tent to tent looking for Pelosi until he found him. "Then he and I went into the latrine, and I tape-recorded him for an hour." Pelosi's assessment of the cadet corps was unsparing. "I'm disillusioned with the air of elitism, of perfection, around here," he said. "People think that just by being here they're automatically a little bit better than anyone else. But they're not."

Rose's resulting thesis was simple but devastating: the military's festering morality crisis—evidenced by "pandemic drug addiction, racial tension, sedition, common crime, refusal of combat duty, widespread assaults and murders of officers [and] rapidly increasing desertion and decreasing reenlistments"—could be traced back to training and leadership failures germinated at places like West Point. His argument was crafted by a powerful combination of legalistic analysis and hundreds of vivid interviews from sources in all roles at military schools. During his frenzied investigation, Rose's monthly phone bill often spiked to $200, or roughly $1,500 in today's money.

Rose's report largely zeroed in on the service academy's judicial system, known as "honor boards," sketching out scenes that seemed plucked from a hard-boiled police drama. He documented tainted investigations and corrupt cadet interrogators, some of whom turned off their tape recorders to scream threats at defendants. During a pulse-pounding interrogation session in 1967, one high-ranking cadet seeking information on a burgeoning cheating scandal lashed out at a new plebe who had just laid out what he knew. "Do you expect us to believe that shit?" he screamed.

Few of those who found themselves in this alternate legal system were afforded the right to remain silent or provided counsel from military lawyers. Some cadet committee members also ignored exculpatory evidence or dozed off during testimony. Unlike in civilian trials, the jury was composed not of impartial outsiders but of classmates who knew the defendants intimately. As a result, rulings and punishments were often biased and freighted with personal baggage. The chairman of one honor board stated his hostility toward a cadet on trial. "This guy has been in trouble before," he said. "And we don't want that kind around." Cadets who sought to appeal their honor board decisions were often threatened with a more serious military court-martial, which, due to the military justice system's punishing and capricious nature, could entail imprisonment at Fort Leavenworth.

Prosecution could stem from any number of offenses. Hundreds of regulations dictating cadet life were itemized in a standard issue manual known as the "Blue Book." Infractions were often vague, making them easily exploitable. They included "general inattention," "carelessness," and exercising "poor judgment." Cadets were technically considered in violation of the honor code for asking a fellow cadet how to spell a word for an essay assignment, or for telling a fib. One cadet who told a superior he had done twenty push-ups when, in fact, he had done eighteen had the book thrown at him. Another who lied about shaving was expelled.

Admitting one's failings could also end in expulsion. "The code," one West Pointer explained, "weeds out some cadets who are honest enough to report themselves for honor violations." Even cadets who reported others for wrongdoing were sometimes expelled for "tolerating" bad behavior, forming what some administrators quietly worried was a warped lesson, namely that "those who said 'no comment' or lied fared better than those who told the truth."

One West Point professor argued that these "seemingly purposeless rules breed resentment," which, in turn, curdle into a full-blown rejection of morality. The honor code was a stand-in for respectable behavior, and yet cadets found it nearly impossible to stay in the code's good graces. It could be fairly reasoned from here that the code was simply too rigid, and that rule-breaking was the only way to survive. "Cadets," the report concluded, "learn by example that deceit and deception are 'standard operating procedure' when the image of West Point or the Army is at stake." His assertion was backed up by cadets and service academy psychiatrists. "I hear leaders talking about integrity and spirit and intent," confessed one cadet. "But I see few who live by their preaching."

As the Vietnam War dragged on, *Time* pointed out that impressionable officers in training were being taught by men known for "falsifying body counts, concealing the bombing of Cambodia, [and] covering up My Lai." By the time the war ended, cadets had little respect for notions of honor. Sixty percent of West Point cadets, for instance, asserted in a 1974 survey that "adherence to the spirit of the Honor Code is deteriorating." This, according to an accompanying study, could be traced back to Thayer's "sanctimonious" belief in honor, which obscured the true knottiness of ethics. One post-9/11 West Point graduate theorized why Thayer had initially set up such a ruthless system. "The stupidest things were treated with life-and-death importance; meanwhile actual life and death was treated with flippancy," he explained. "This is both one of the greatest paradoxes of military indoctrination and one of its critical linchpins."

THE MOST PROMINENT REJECTIONS OF THE HONOR CODE took shape as cheating rings. A series of major cheating scandals at the service academies broke out during the Cold War: in 1951, 1967, 1972, and then, not long after the fall of Saigon, in 1976. Air Force Academy dean Robert McDermott blamed the 1967 scandal on civilian counterculture, testifying to congressional investigators that dozens of identified cheaters had hailed from a clique "symbolized by kooky music, long hair, and a few other things." A subsequent report penned by a committee of retired brass and academics disagreed, blaming the behavior on an academic environment concerned with "the symbols of achievement, sometimes at the expense of reality."

Perhaps the system's most extreme response to cheating emerged during the 1972 scandal, at the Air Force Academy. Administrators and senior cadets carried out an operation of coercion, interrogation, and mass prosecution via the school's honor committee, one composed of a few dozen older cadets and overseen by a few senior officers, plus the superintendent, who held the ultimate power to confirm, reverse, or revise a decision by so-called honor boards. This largely cadet-run justice system was established by the same man who wrote the honor code: Douglas MacArthur. As West Point superintendent in 1922, he had formalized the boards to professionalize the academy's covert and volatile "vigilance committees" composed only of cadets.

The first whiff of cheating emerged when, after six long hours of questioning, a USAFA cadet standing trial for an unrelated petty theft charge broke down and confessed to participating in a widespread cheating ring. His admission came in the middle of the night, but the honor committee was undeterred. They rustled awake roughly 125 cadets and requested their attendance at an "important meeting." These boys were subsequently escorted to guarded rooms and interrogated by fellow cadets, often for hours.

One claimed he was confined for eighteen hours before being fully briefed on the conditions of his detention. Others said that committee members falsely claimed that other cadets had signed statements incriminating them.

As time wore on, some cadets fell asleep in their chairs. Others were forced to stand at attention and brace, a hazing rite pioneered during West Point's early days in which cadets were forced to crunch their heads downward, into their necks, a position that, held over long periods, can lead to nerve damage and temporary arm paralysis.

Some interrogators cut cadets' hair and screamed at them. One cadet said the pressure became so bad that he vomited. Others compared the experience to the mock prisoner-of-war interrogation training that Air Force Academy officials had instituted a few months earlier. This ad hoc training camp included tents and isolation boxes, and it landed fifteen cadets in the hospital. *The New York Times* reported that cadets "entered the camp with laundry bags over their heads, were made to squat for hours at a time, interrogated frequently and slapped with open hands or hit with tree branches and sticks." Some were also waterboarded. Academy officials downplayed reports of torture, then asked taxpayers for $244,000 to build a modernized interrogation facility, a request one Wisconsin lawmaker deemed a "ghoulish expenditure."

"Reform," Rose concluded in his report, "cannot be expected to come from within the military itself, for the Armed Forces are so steeped in tradition as to be both incapable of perceiving the need for reform and unprepared to yield to it."

In the months leading up to the report's release, the Pentagon tried desperately to undermine Captain Rose and his cause. One Air Force official preemptively labeled his report "very shallow." Another compared Rose to "a high school student interpreting the law." The service further labeled him a puppet of the peaceniks, pointing out that his project had received modest funding from Harvard professor Marty Peretz, the publisher of *Ramparts* magazine and *The New Republic*, as well as "The Fund for Tomorrow," which, they warned, was tied to various anti-war figures, including actress "Hanoi Jane" Fonda.

The Pentagon also looked to tarnish Rose by leaking his so-so USAFA academic records to the press, and charging him, without evidence, of cheating. Genuine worry lay behind their bravado. One military official fretted that Rose's analysis might provide solid legal footing for a variety of judicial challenges to the service academy structure, and the uniform code of military justice, two systems Sylvanus Thayer had yoked together in his desperate efforts to control cadets.

Rose's "Prayer of Relief" ultimately went unanswered. Not just that, but the Air Force's judge advocate general declined to certify Rose as a military lawyer. By the summer of 1974, brass coerced him to resign. Predictably, the issues he had spotlighted continued bubbling up to the surface, mostly in the form of cheating scandals. In 1976, more than 150 West Point cadets were charged, this time within the academy's most storied and prestigious department: electrical engineering. Some assessments later indicated that as many as six hundred cadets had cheated, but even the smaller statistic qualified the 1976 affairs as the worst cheating scandal in military history. One of the many cadets forced to resign was Robert K. Koster, son of Samuel Koster, the My Lai cover-up man who once ran West Point.

THE SHEER SIZE AND SCOPE OF THE 1976 CHEATING SCANDAL forced the Army to form a special investigative committee, one manned by a bishop, two civilian college leaders, two retired military men, and the chairman of West Point's Board of Visitors. The committee's illustrious chairman was Frank Borman, a West Point graduate turned fighter pilot who, in 1968, commanded the Apollo 8 space mission. Borman was the kind of guy West Point loved to spotlight: blond-haired, blue-eyed, fiercely smart, and modest. He and his Apollo brethren were also named *Time*'s 1968 man of the year. In his work as chairman, Borman didn't hold back.

The committee's subsequent findings—dubbed the "Borman report"— found that the cheating practices inside the engineering department were just the "tip of the cheating iceberg," declaring further that "all aspects of the Academy" demanded reform. It echoed Rose's report in many respects—and the 1901 congressional investigation launched after the death of nineteen-year-old Oscar Booz. Among other things, Borman warned that West Point had delegated a worrying amount of authority and supervision to cadets, creating a culture of favoritism, corruption, and abuse. Many of the school's so-called honor representatives had themselves been found complicit in acts of "dishonesty, toleration, and, on occasion, misconduct."

Ultimately, the cheating scandal had ended up ensnaring twenty-three cadets on the honor committee. One had been previously exonerated by eight honor boards, thanks to his successful efforts to fix the panel with friendly cadets who would vote "Not Guilty" no matter what. The committee also unearthed evidence that honor boards were fixed through bribery, with the *Times* reporting that "sums of up to $1,000 reportedly had changed hands in efforts by accused cadets to find the single vote that would bar prosecution and perhaps save a career." Even as they fixed honor boards, cadets on the honor committee adopted a "holier than thou attitude." Some outsiders began sarcastically calling them "the guys with the black hoods."

This cloak-and-dagger reputation was fortified by the case of Steven Verr, a slight nineteen-year-old plebe and champion marathon runner who was seen one night leaving the mess hall with tears in his eyes. His emotional outburst followed days of being berated and denied food by upperclassmen. As a runner, he normally consumed 12,000 calories a day, but upperclassmen had restricted his intake to around 1,000. As a result of this deprivation, Verr fainted on campus and fell down some stairs. When a cadet leader in the mess hall ordered Verr to say why he was weeping, the young plebe offered an off-the-cuff, disjointed lie: that his parents had been in an automobile accident. When cadets discovered that wasn't true, they charged him with an honor code violation. When West Point's superintendent reversed their decision, cadets took justice into their own hands. As part of their hazing response, they stole Verr's mail and ransacked his room. Then a school official overheard a threat on Verr's life, leading West Point to provide him with twenty-four-hour security.

Borman's committee chalked up this atmosphere to a series of factors, including the simple fact that West Point offered a single ethics course, an elective that was only available senior year. They also found that school leaders had failed to express true reverence for academics, treating them instead like an afterthought to military training, which, in turn, bred cheating, anti-intellectualism, and dishonesty.

Accountability was also scant. Borman charged that West Point's Board of Visitors lacked the resources to provide effective and consistent external review. The current slate seemed eager to cover up problems, not address them, a fact made clear during meetings in which they were briefed about the West Point cheating scandal. After one such meeting, the board took a single action: "urging improvements in the Academy's athletic and other facilities."

Borman recommended the creation of an oversight body more akin to a traditional board of trustees, one removed from politics and more engaged with school activities. Around this time, cadets filed an unsuccessful suit against the honor code, arguing it was unconstitutional for, among other things, presuming cadets guilty, not innocent.

West Point fired its hard-charging commandant, Brigadier General Walter F. Ulmer Jr., who had allegedly harassed military lawyers assisting cadets with their defense, and, in a tacit acknowledgment of their heavy-handed practices, allowed ninety or so cadets implicated in the cheating scandal to return. But the academy didn't create a new board structure, didn't reform the honor code, and didn't crack down on corrupt honor board members. Meanwhile, the cadet ruling class narrowly defeated a proposal that would have created a more flexible penalty system for honor violations. The student body further voted by a wide margin to eliminate administrative oversights of honor boards and assume complete responsibility.

Shortly after Borman exposed the school's brittle honor code, his son, Frederick, a West Point cadet, was accused of taking a $1,200 bribe as an honor board member, an allegation he declared a total fabrication meant to get back at his dad. In the decades that followed, dishonesty continued to flourish. Major cheating scandals again broke out at the service academies in 1984, 1993, 2020, and 2025.

These days, certain cadets have come to see deception as an ingrained part of military life, represented by a long-circulating joke about West Point's motto. It goes: "Duty, Country, Hon—well, two out of three ain't bad."

Chapter 9

The Silence

When Lloyd Austin first arrived at West Point in the summer of 1971, he was taken aback by the campus's uncanny uniformity. "It was unlike anything I'd ever seen in my whole life," he later reflected. "The grounds were perfectly groomed, and they seemed to be filled with perfect people." All were professional, athletic, well-spoken. Most of them were also white. "I don't think they ever even blinked," Austin recalled.

Austin was one of about two dozen Black cadets in a class of roughly one thousand. At the time of his matriculation, West Point had yet to admit women. But a few years later, when Pat Locke touched down from Detroit to become one of West Point's first two Black female cadets, she was similarly startled. "Oh my gosh," she thought. "Where are all the Black people?"

By this point, American lore firmly cast the military as at the forefront of civil rights, thanks largely to President Harry Truman's 1948 executive order desegregating the institution. But the president's decision was borne more out of practical consideration than soaring idealism. Truman himself harbored racial animus, making grossly prejudicial statements in private throughout much of his life. His order was spurred by intense civil rights activism on his left, plus a series of publicized beatings and murders of recently returned Black G.I.s. While Black troops have served in vital enlisted roles dating back to the Revolutionary War, they had often been treated viciously, and were long frozen out of the officer class.

The Naval Academy, for instance, didn't graduate its first Black midshipmen until 1949, nearly eighty years after Harvard recognized its first Black graduate, Richard Greener. Black midshipmen at the Naval Academy were met with a litany of racialized hazing rites geared toward getting them out. Some were whitewashed with paint. Others were chased up trees by rabid freshmen barking like dogs. At least one Black midshipman was even tied overnight to a buoy on the Severn River, a tidal estuary that surrounds the Annapolis campus.

Vietnam saw the highest proportion of Black soldiers up until that point in American history. In 1965, 31 percent of combat troops in Vietnam were Black, despite making up 12 percent of the general population. These men were serving under a virtually all-white officer class, creating a military racial and class disparity that was impossible to ignore. During Nixon's inaugural parade to celebrate his 1968 presidential victory, many Black onlookers protested over the nearly all-white contingent of West Point marchers. It was around this time that West Point first started tracking Black cadet admissions and hired its first Black admissions officer, who was ordered to quickly increase the share of Black cadets.

During the summer of 1969, West Point admitted forty-seven Black cadets, dwarfing the number enrolled over the previous nine years combined. One of the cadets West Point recruited in this gambit was Eric Evans. He proved too rebellious for West Point's staid culture, transferring to Cornell where he served as the "minister of defense" for the Ivy's Afro-American Society, and helped coordinate an armed thirty-five-hour takeover of Willard Straight Hall to spotlight racial injustice on campus and demand reform. This moment was captured in a Pulitzer Prize–winning photograph from the AP showing the former West Point cadet sporting a bandolier and armed with a shotgun. Such brash action spooked Cornell administrators, who promptly undertook reforms to the University Senate and the Board of Trustees, refigured the campus judicial system, and founded an Africana Studies and Research Center. They also agreed to absolve Evans and other students of legal liability.

West Point's class of 1975, to which Lloyd Austin belonged, was essentially the first in the academy's history with the adequate numbers to form a distinct subculture. "Until these plebes arrived, it wasn't possible to have a Black identity," one cadet recalled. "There just weren't enough of us." Months before Austin's arrival, the *Times* reported that racial tension within the military was at a boiling point. "Race is my problem," a white noncommissioned officer told the paper. "Not the Russians, not Vietnam, Jordan nor maneuvers. I just worry about keeping my troops—Black and white—from getting at one another."

The paper's report further laid out evidence of Ku Klux Klan activity within the service, plus a corresponding surge of Black Panther activity. At Cam Ranh Bay naval base, Black troops had revolted when white soldiers celebrated the death of Martin Luther King by raising the Confederate flag. The NAACP later opened a branch near a base in West Germany, after the organization's investigators had found institutional discrimination, including "the extensive use of pretrial confinement for Negro soldiers, the alarming degree to which nonjudicial punishment was meted out to Blacks, the deplorable practice of housing discrimination by German landlords, and the ever-present problems of inequities in the promotion system."

Amid this flurry of bad headlines, the military pledged to address discrimination and racial tension and relieved a dozen or so white officers because they "could not relate to policies designed to ease racial tensions." They pledged to finally empower Black officers, recruiting people like Austin to West Point, and established ROTC and JROTC programs in majority Black colleges and high schools. The military also deployed more recruiters in Black communities across America.

LLOYD AUSTIN GREW UP IN THOMASVILLE, a small city in southwest Georgia still plagued by the vestiges of Jim Crow. Austin attended a segregated middle school, then helped desegregate his high school. Along the way, he earned good grades, found kind mentors, and became driven to become one of West Point's "perfect people." He matriculated at the academy hoping to make good on the Pentagon's meritocratic promise but was more aware than most of the potential pitfalls for a military man of color. Many men in Austin's family had served, including his reputed grand-uncle, Henry Ossian Flipper, another Thomasville native who, in the spring of 1877, became West Point's first Black graduate after enduring a relentless campaign from the academy's entrenched white power apparatus.

Like traditional college fraternities, West Point confers valuable privileges and connections to its graduates, including a clear path to America's most hallowed government corridors. While Greek life offers economic perks, power and prestige are what the military promises—perhaps even the chance to go down in the history books. But these opportunities are closely guarded, and only selectively proffered, historically to white, conservative men, who, in turn, have sought to drive out cadets whom they deem weak, different, or otherwise underserving of military power. To shore up this hierarchy, West Pointers have turned to an age-old shunning practice called "the silence."

Even when it has failed to push cadets out, the silence reinforces a vital lesson: that cadets must receive orders without debate, maintain discipline even when they disagree, and fully reject their individual identities should they hope to secure acceptance, communal support, and military authority.

After arriving at West Point, Henry Flipper experienced intense prejudice from his white counterparts, including a particularly nasty bout of the silence that stripped him of all human connection. He had no roommate, no one to study with, no one to eat with in the mess hall, no one to cheer with at sporting events. Silenced cadets have seen their mail destroyed and been banished from school dances. Some have broken under this isolation and resigned their commissions. Others who persevere are ordered by their cadet superiors to refrain from ever wearing their class rings, the all-important membership totem of the West Point Protective Association.

Flipper was born in 1856 to parents who were enslaved. After the Civil War secured his family's emancipation, Flipper took an interest in the Army, and, in 1873, secured a congressional appointment to West Point. He was clear-eyed about the threats on campus, but he ventured north nonetheless, arriving on campus "tremblingly yet confidently," wary of the "dread of inevitable ostracism." Flipper knew that Black cadets before him had been run off campus through relentless hazing or discharged on flimsy academic or administrative grounds.

Terrible abuse had befallen Johnson Chestnut Whittaker, a cadet from South Carolina born into slavery who had been mentored by Richard Greener, Harvard's first Black graduate. During his senior year at West Point, Whittaker, then the only Black cadet on campus, was found in his room unconscious, bound by his feet and hands, with his head shaved and his ears cut. Burnt pages of the Bible were strewn across the floor. Whittaker said he had been attacked by three cadets, but West Point chose to court-martial him for perpetuating a hoax instead. He was found guilty at trial and expelled.

The same year as Whittaker's abuse, West Point superintendent major general John Schofield articulated racial animosity as school doctrine in his annual report:

To send to West Point for four years competition a young man who was born in slavery is to assume that half a generation is sufficient to raise a colored man to the social, moral, and intellectual level which the average white man

*has reached in several hundred years. As well might the common farm horse
be entered in a four-mile race against the best blood inherited from a long
line of English racers.*

Flipper recalled that the sustained silence he faced produced in him
"weary barren wastes of loneliness." In 1877, Flipper graduated fiftieth in
his class of seventy-six. Over his next four years in the military, Flipper did
well. He devised a drainage system at Fort Sill that eliminated a series of
ponds harboring malaria. He also became the first non-white officer commanding members of the 10th Cavalry, an all-Black unit that was deployed
to frontier outposts and fought in a series of skirmishes during the American Indian Wars. Regardless, he was unjustifiably discharged after being
falsely accused of stealing commissary funds.

In 1885, West Point's second Black graduate, John Hanks Alexander, described his "silencing" as akin to his being "in the confines of the highest and
most secluded peak of the Himalaya Mountains." Charles Young, West
Point's third Black graduate, hadn't been admitted on his first attempt to
matriculate, even though he had scored second highest on the entrance
exam. He graduated in 1889 after being forced to repeat his plebe year. He
was "silenced," too. It would take another half-century before West Point
saw its fourth Black graduate, Benjamin O. Davis Jr., an academic whiz who
was silenced for all four years by a student body that, for a time, included the
great-grandson of confederate general Stonewall Jackson. Davis Jr. went on
to a remarkable military career, including as the respected commander of
more than a thousand brave Tuskegee Airmen during World War II.

MUCH HAD IMPROVED AT WEST POINT by the time of Austin's arrival in 1971,
but not nearly enough. In 1931, the school had installed a portrait of Robert E. Lee, the slave-owning Confederate general and former West Point
superintendent. It depicted him in his blue U.S. Army uniform. In 1952,
this portrait was supplemented with one in which Lee sported Confederate gray, with an enslaved man guiding his horse behind him. West Point
named a road, a gate, a barracks, and a childcare center after Lee. An eponymous award for the famed Confederate was created for the graduating
cadet with the highest mathematical proficiency. In 1961, the school
sought, and was granted, a formal military legal opinion supporting use of
the "silence." Four years later, the academy affixed a bronze plaque to its

science center featuring a hooded figure holding a rifle and the words "KU KLUX KLAN."

These and other environmental markers sought to suppress Black identity, and they achieved this goal. But West Point could also spawn defiant shows of activism and solidarity. One Black cadet from Austin's era reflected that he identified much more with the civil rights movement after landing on campus, largely because his martial conditions exacerbated latent inequalities: "[I'm being] ordered around by white people," he explained. Austin's senior yearbook page indicates that he may have experienced a similar metamorphosis. It shows him sporting an afro and his entry begins with four bolded words: "YOUNG, GIFTED AND BLACK."

It's unclear if Austin's stance redounded in the "silence" or any other abuse or prejudice. Speaking in 2017 for West Point's oral history project, Austin diplomatically declined to detail any specific harassment he faced on campus, explaining that, as a plebe, "I don't recall . . . [being] the object of racist activity." Later in the interview, Austin acknowledged "people with different types of attitudes" and said that the school's older Black cadets helped him "get through some things."

At first blush, Austin's career offers strong evidence that America has achieved a post-racial military meritocracy. After graduating from West Point, he became the first Black officer to command a division in combat, then a full theater of war. He became a four-star general in 2010 and retired in 2016, at which point he parlayed his status into advisory roles for Raytheon and United Technologies, work from which he reaped more than $1 million. In 2021, he returned to service as America's first Black defense secretary, a tenure that included proxy weapons shipments to Israel and Ukraine, work that enriched his former employers to the tune of billions of dollars.

Austin's meteoric rise cleared room for other Black officers to thrive, just as Austin had been elevated and mentored by other pioneering Black officers, including General Colin Powell, who, as the first Black chairman of the Joint Chiefs of Staff, hung a print of Flipper on his office wall. Still, these men had limited bandwidth to increase diversity or spur change, adopting the stoic endurance and muted protestations showcased by Flipper, which typify an old piece of advice given to cadets: "cooperate and graduate."

In a speech as defense secretary, Austin declared that Flipper "turned the tide of history" without protesting, or joining a movement, or standing on the steps of the mess hall and making "an impassioned speech." There is something truly remarkable that Flipper and scores of other Black officers endured the humiliations of this system without vocally agitating against it. These tactics were often effective in forcing the military to follow through on their promises of merit-based promotions. But these passive tactics ultimately yielded to the military's expectation that soldiers subvert their own identities on behalf of the institution. "[Flipper] brought about needed change by simply setting an example," Austin marveled near the end of his remarks. "He did so without uttering a single word."

Weeks into Austin's plebe summer, Percy Squire, an older Black cadet, launched a peaceful takeover of the Contemporary Affairs club after West Point leaders refused to let cadets form a Black Pride one. From here, this de facto Black student union developed a series of demands.

Squire was the son of a Youngstown, Ohio, steel worker who understood the power of collective bargaining. He was a senior during Austin's plebe year, and the two were in the same company. "We tried to make the planet hospitable for him," he told me, which, he added, was easier said than done. "Part of the DNA at West Point is racism." Squire faced his fair share of racial epithets as an underclassman and witnessed a highly offensive skit put on during a summer training course that featured white cadets depicting Black ones as "fawning sambos." Other "outsiders" also faced heat back then. Squire recalled that a pack of West Point WASPs had run out a Jewish classmate on account of his religion.

One of Squire's closest friends was David Brice, a Black cadet from South Carolina who had been class president and valedictorian of his segregated high school. When his nomination to West Point was first announced in the local paper, the Ku Klux Klan burned a cross on his family's front lawn. At the academy, he was paired to room with an avowed racist from Meridian, Mississippi, a town with a dark history of race riots and Klan killings. Like their Black forefathers, Brice, Squire, and other cadets weathered rough treatment for years, while turning to each other for quiet support and solidarity. Collectively, their frustrations were rising, fueled by the growing civil rights movement outside the gates and finally unleashed by the commander in chief.

RICHARD NIXON VISITED WEST POINT only once during his presidency, in May 1971. By then, the Vietnam War had become an unmitigated quagmire, punctuated by major tactical missteps and mounting evidence of war crimes. During his visit, Nixon chose not to engage with these twin crises, both of which were extremely salient to the pack of fresh lieutenants soon to be sent into the suck. Instead, the president projected a sunny optimism, declaring that no American conflict has ever been motivated by "conquest, territory, or selfish aims," and pledging that an armistice was close at hand. "The seeds of peace are planted," he asserted, but, in a preview of his coming reelection rhetoric, warned that this germination would be compromised should America get "lulled into wishful thinking and passive policies."

At the time, West Point was probably the only college in the nation that would permit Nixon's appearance, and the president found himself thoroughly charmed by its warm fidelity to him, remarking that the visit provided a "great boost to my morale." He faced no vocal opposition during his remarks, no screams or protest signs, and he lingered on campus after the ceremony, inviting Superintendent Knowlton into his Lincoln Continental for a tour of campus.

As they rolled along, Nixon asked Knowlton why there was no campus monument to the Confederate Army. Were he properly steeped in West Point history, Nixon would have known that the academy's outsize role in training Confederate generals had nearly led to its demise. General George W. Cullum, West Point's superintendent at the tail end of the Civil War, had argued that the school must never forgive its Confederate turncoats, whom, he charged, had "forgot the flag under which they were educated to follow false gods."

West Point harbored racist undercurrents before and after Cullum's decree, but, for a long time, the dominant view of Confederates as traitors kept the allure of the Lost Cause howling at the gates. No Confederate was ever buried in West Point's cemetery, and no flag for the failed nation ever flew on school grounds, though plenty of cadets had tacked some version of the Dixie flag up on their bedroom walls.

Nixon inquired about a monument because he had his finger on the quickening pulse of white racial resentment. He theorized that erecting a Confederate monument in the North would provide a potent political symbol, one that could shore up his support in the South, where he might again face the electoral threat of George Wallace, a Jim Crow Democrat.

"This is the theme of my administration—bringing us together," Nixon explained to Knowlton, "and you've got to get a monument up here to those Confederate dead." Nixon tasked Alexander Haig, a loyal general and West Point graduate, to pester Knowlton on a near-daily basis about the project. Haig stressed that his boss wanted it done in time for the 1972 Republican National Convention.

Knowlton begrudgingly followed his commander in chief's orders, drafting and promulgating plans to fund the monument through the school's powerful association of graduates. This elicited a contentious debate among alumni, though many prominent figures supported the idea, including former chairman of the Joint Chiefs of Staff Lyman L. Lemnitzer and general Harold K. Johnson, former chief of staff to the Army.

On October 23, 1971, Knowlton summoned Squire to his office and explained what was soon to happen. Squire was the highest-ranking Black cadet on campus, and Knowlton hoped he could help "minimize Black rage" over the monument's erection.

Two days later, Squire and Brice convened a meeting of Black cadets to discuss the memorial. It ignited a righteous, hours-long venting against the conditions Black cadets then lived under. Some called for sit-ins, or a mass resignation. Another fifteen or so argued for more radical, even violent action.

Squire and Brice channeled this anger into a six-page manifesto. It included a thirteen-point list of "abuses and usurpations," many of which concerned the lack of diversity and respect across campus. The thirteenth grievance was Nixon's monument, which they declared an abomination, in part by reminding Knowlton that no foe in American history had killed more Army officers than the Confederates. Their well-reasoned polemic took inspiration from the manifesto written two months prior, during the 1971 uprising at the Attica prison in Buffalo, New York, but also, as one West Point scholar noted, "evoked the American colonists' petitions against the British government leading to the American Revolution." The authors further framed their arguments around the military oath, hoping it would increase the manifesto's appeal to white cadets. It was signed by every Black cadet, and all but one of the Black staff officers.

On November 9, Black cadets delivered their manifesto to Knowlton, who immediately understood the potentially disastrous path in front of him. In short order, he worked to calm tensions through a litany of relatively radical actions: establishing monuments to Black service, renaming the school's parade ground to honor the Buffalo Soldiers, and commissioning a bust of Flipper. He mandated twelve hours of race relations classes for cadets, and sixteen hours for officers and staff. He also banned the playing of "Dixie" at football games and welcomed on campus a series of speakers, including Nation of Islam spokesman Louis Farrakhan, who urged the cadets to stay woke. "Don't be lulled to sleep by the fact that you're at West Point," he said. "There's no place in the West where you are respected."

Knowlton even lent his large boat to Black cadets for a dance party on the Hudson. Up until then, most sock hops had strictly featured rock 'n' roll and white girls. For this affair, cadets organized a bus full of Black women from Hackensack, New Jersey, then danced the night away to the soulful stylings of the Delfonics and Marvin Gaye.

Finally, Knowlton notified his powerful Army overseers in Washington that Nixon's Confederate statue was set to unleash intense campus activism, creating a publicity nightmare that would almost certainly devastate the academy's burgeoning minority recruitment efforts. Scrapping the project, Knowlton pledged, would "weaken" the radical Black elements on campus. Roughly a month after the manifesto's creation, the White House quietly terminated the project, and Nixon moved on to another topic ripe for demagoguery: school desegregation. Meanwhile, Knowlton not only preserved but expanded his recruiting pathways into minority communities, including a partnership he forged with the Urban League of Chicago.

Knowlton's response to the manifesto had improved the quality of Black cadet life and culture in meaningful ways. Austin's yearbook quote is a testament to this change, as is his afro, which Knowlton had also newly permitted as part of his package of concessions, supplementing West Point's Italian barbers with some Black ones, too. Still, the lion's share of these changes were cosmetic, acts of symbolism that did little to meaningfully elevate Black military power, or stifle white hate.

It wasn't until a year after Austin's graduation, in 1976, that West Point first appointed tenure to a Black faculty member, physics professor James Stith. (Two days after Stith and his then pregnant wife arrived to their on-campus quarters, he told me, someone scrawled the N-word on their garage door.) Three years after Stith's appointment, a local paper revealed that several West Point cadets had donned Ku Klux Klan robes and tormented a cadet in the shower. Superintendent Andrew J. Goodpaster, a lieutenant general, told a reporter that there was no racial animus involved, and that the cadets had simply masked themselves in sheets "because it was humorous and that was what was most available." A similar incident occurred in 1987 at the Citadel, when five white cadets dressed in sheets entered the room of a Black cadet and left behind a charred cross.

COUNTLESS POLITICIANS SINCE TRUMAN HAVE WIPED AWAY the complicating facts of Black military service to tell a compelling story of racial progress in America. In his June 1991 West Point commencement speech, President George H.W. Bush took his turn. It had been three months since the racialized beating of Rodney King by Los Angeles police, and Bush was scrambling to calm the ensuing firestorm, in this case by highlighting an institution supposedly free of racial animus. "Our armed forces have shown what Americans can do when they see themselves not as white and Black and red or brown but as one people united in common purpose," Bush said. That year, West Point graduated its thousandth Black and female cadets, facts that Bush proudly highlighted. "America's task is to achieve nationally what we celebrate today at West Point," he charged.

The diverse cadet body before Bush suggested that perhaps the academy finally had exhumed its prejudice. Months later came another encouraging sign. The Board of Visitors at the Citadel, in South Carolina, urged leadership to outlaw the flying of the Confederate flag at sporting events, along with the fight song, "Dixie."

Less than forty-eight hours after the school announced its intention to ban the song, a Black cadet, Berra Lee Byrd Jr., was walking in a parking lot near his dormitory when a bullet tore into his chest and exited out his back, just missing his heart. Berra screamed in anguish and fell to the ground, blood soaking through his dress grays. He crawled toward the mess hall, where someone spotted him, delivered aid, and called an ambulance. Berra survived and went home to recuperate, while the Citadel launched an investigation.

Berra had harbored dreams of military service since high school, where he was twice named the most outstanding cadet in his JROTC program. Once his wounds healed, he defiantly returned to the Citadel, dead set on graduating. Shortly thereafter, another Black cadet discovered a noose on the floor of his dorm room, which the Citadel dismissed as a harmless prank. Then the administration reversed itself, declining to ban the playing of "Dixie" and refusing to police Confederate flag-waving at games.

The Citadel's investigation of Berra's shooting also yielded nothing. At one point, they identified Berra as to blame, theorizing that he had been shot over a drug deal gone bad, or over a woman, or even that he had set the whole thing up in a deranged plot to embarrass the Citadel—an uncanny echo from when West Point alleged that cadet Chestnut had arranged for himself to be bound up and abused. Citadel staff interrogated Berra, threatened him with expulsion, and ordered him to submit to a lie detector test, which he refused.

State law enforcement ultimately took up Berra's case, but the force was stacked with Citadel alums, seemingly eager to protect their alma mater. It took months for police to uncover a bullet at the scene. They also failed to identify witnesses or chase leads. "Somebody had to see something or hear something the way I see it," Berra told a local paper in 1993. "I was shot in broad daylight."

As the investigation stalled, the NAACP called for a federal investigation and got one. FBI agents spent four years interviewing hundreds of students and staff before identifying a white former cadet named George Cormeny III as the potential shooter. When they tracked him down, Cormeny admitted to the shooting, but swore it was an innocent mistake. The feds bought his story, charging him only for unlawful gun possession. Berra was furious. "[Cormeny] left me for dead," he vented to the *Boston Globe*. "The authorities aren't taking this seriously. Why did he have a gun at the Citadel? What was his motive?" He was backed up by his white ROTC mentor, Ted Ballard, a former Air Force pilot and Vietnam POW who grew up in South Carolina and was intimately familiar with its ugly underbelly. "I don't think that shooting was an accident at all," he said.

In 1994, Berra proudly walked at graduation and received a degree, though his dreams of Marine service had been dashed by his injuries. Two years later, just after the feds had extracted Cormeny's confession but before they publicized it, Cormeny called Berra at his home, told him he was in town, and dropped by. There, he confessed to the shooting, apologized, and said he had been saved by God. Berra was overwhelmed by shock, while Cormeny seemed eager to turn to other subjects. When his father returned home, Berra whisked Cormeny out of the house without explaining the circumstances, and the two took a walk, during which Cormeny turned to a bit of haunting small talk. "[He] told me how he had spent part of his summer," Berra recalled. "He said he did a lot of hunting. And that he was a pretty good hunter. Now, when I got back to my apartment, I got to thinking that, in light of what all has happened, that was a mighty strange thing to tell me."

Chapter 10

The Last Class
with Balls

West Point's class of 1979 witnessed what they viewed as the tragic end
to their all-male power structure. They called themselves the "Last Class
with Balls," or, conversely, the "Last Class Without Bitches." Some memo-
rialized this grubby distinction on their class rings, with the acronym
"LCWB."

Over the preceding decades, lawmakers and military leaders had worked
desperately to keep feminine energy out of the officer class. In 1944, Georgia's Democratic representative E.E. Cox floated legislation to establish a
separate service academy for women, one in which they were educated in
"clerical, scientific and other duties" so that, once fighting broke out, "the
able-bodied man may do the advanced work of fighting in the front lines."
The military later concocted a harebrained scheme to integrate the service
academies that involved injecting female cadets with testosterone to make
them more aggressive. By the time the Air Force Academy was constructed,
in the late 1950s, women had been serving in official military capacities for
decades, and yet still the school hung a large plaque at its entrance reading
"Bring Me Men."

The service academies were ultimately opened to women only thanks to
hard-fought federal legislation first introduced in 1972 by Senator Jacob
Javits of New York. After years of opposition, it was ratified in late 1975
with a stroke of President Gerald Ford's pen. This was partly a push toward
equity, but also a practical response to the personnel problems created two
years prior with the end of military conscription.

Every academy superintendent opposed Javits's bill, with West Point Superintendent Sidney Berry personally lobbying President Ford against its passage, trying his damnedest to keep women from joining his secretive fraternity of military elites. Another powerful opponent was Army secretary and West Point alum Howard "Bo" Callaway, who argued that women would dilute the system's "spartan atmosphere." A lawmaker supporting integration responded that, on the contrary, women might help tame the system's "Neanderthal" traditions. The public seemed mostly to be on the military's side. Ahead of the law's passage, one constituent argued in a missive to Senator Barry Goldwater of Arizona that the world had seen only one successful female combat officer. "That was Jeanne D'Arc," he wrote, "and she was a saint. Also, she did not menstrate [*sic*]."

The most prominent argument that women were unfit for the military came in a 1979 essay in *The Washingtonian* by future Navy secretary and U.S. senator from Virginia Jim Webb, who then taught literature at the Naval Academy. Webb's brash polemic was entitled "Women Can't Fight," though the text itself mostly rehashed the stereotypical indicators of masculinity that his sailors clung to. "They drive fast cars, usually sports cars," Webb writes. "They play hard. They drink hard. They are physical, often comically abusive among each other." Despite this behavior, Webb insists, these men are "not trying to prove their manhood," they are simply celebrating hard-coded instincts that make them ideal warriors. "Every citizen who may someday send a friend or relative into war should rejoice that these future professionals develop and retain such qualities," he concludes, "because combat is competitive, vulgar, and tough."

For his part, General William Westmoreland, who served as West Point's superintendent before becoming commander of U.S. forces in Vietnam, declared that any woman able to succeed at his alma mater was "a freak, and we're not running the military academy for freaks." His words seeped deep into the minds of many male cadets, who, in their early treatment of their female peers, adopted and systemically applied Westmoreland's worldview. One early female cadet recalled being endlessly gawked at in the mess hall, made to feel like "a freak at a freak show."

Westmoreland's dire warning about female officers seems particularly rich considering his own Neanderthalic reputation. Academically, Westmoreland ranked right in the middle of his West Point class but excelled in the nebulous specialty that is "leadership" and in the gritty arena of military training—a skill set recognized upon his 1936 graduation through the issuance of a ceremonial sword named after General John J. Pershing. Westmoreland was brawny and liked push-ups, rising through the ranks far faster than more academically gifted peers even as he repeatedly failed to devise smart military strategies, or evince basic competence. Biographers wrote that Westmoreland wasn't much of a reader, and was driven largely by racial prejudice, a belief he almost certainly nurtured at West Point as a member of the class that silenced Benjamin O. Davis Jr. Colleagues found him dull and incurious, including Air Force general Robert Beckel, who bluntly deemed Westmoreland "rather stupid."

AS REVANCHIST BRASS AND MILITARY SCHOOL ALUMNI loudly inveighed against the prospect of female cadets, feminist leaders were conflicted. Some felt that increasing women in the ranks would be positive for the movement, providing the final nail to men's claims of higher standing. Others, such as Representative Patricia Schroeder, a Colorado Democrat, argued that "if equal rights is all about insisting that women should be as warmongering as men, then we've blown it." Betty Friedan, author of the landmark book *The Feminine Mystique*, called the pitched debate "a red herring." In the end, the feminist movement avoided deeply engaging with the issue, or supporting the women looking to break into the military officer class. The same year that Ford integrated the service academies, Representative Bella Abzug, cofounder of the National Women's Political Caucus, flitted away a question on the issue. "I do not regard women in the military as my first priority," she said.

Conservative activist Phyllis Schlafly filled the void, cynically invoking the prospect of female combat service as a key plank in her sustained and ultimately successful push against passage of the Equal Rights Amendment. At her rallies, children were given signs that read "Please don't send my mommy to war." William Rehnquist, a proud Army veteran and future Supreme Court Chief Justice, adopted Schlafly's framing in his role as an assistant attorney general for President Nixon, drafting a memo opposing the amendment in which he warned it could make women "eligible for the military draft."

The 1976 integration of women into the powerful and ultra-secretive service academy system landed a direct blow to the heart of America's most masculine enterprise. The military had long thrived by concocting a specific conception of manliness, then facilitating a training ground to prove these traits. This scheme was plainly reflected in service academy applications, which long judged prospective cadets against a series of metrics known collectively as the "Whole Man" score. The military's psychological grip on young men depended on a weak and largely subservient feminine construct, one in which women not only relied on, but were endlessly impressed by, male strength. Before the introduction of women, military school was viewed as the purest test of masculine bona fides. Those who failed were labeled with derogatory feminine terms like "pussy," "lady," or "fairy." Now, one school commandant worried, "if women can make it, can it really be tough?"

Cathy Long, one of West Point's first female cadets, routinely witnessed this masculine panic on campus. Before her arrival, she asserted, military school was a place "where a little man could go and feel like a big man." She dealt directly with many of these guys, including one stunted upperclassman who screamed guttural insults in her face daily. Once, she looked deep in his eyes and realized that, under his bluster, was real worry. "We took away his masculinity," she said.

WHEN JAVITS'S LAW FINALLY PASSED, it bound only the federal service academies. The network of other private, religious, and state-chartered military schools resisted gender integration for as long as they could. The Virginia Military Institute, for instance, didn't become co-ed until a 1996 opinion from Supreme Court Justice Ruth Bader Ginsburg specifically ordered it to do so. The Citadel took a similar route, not admitting its first woman, Shannon Faulkner, until 1995, when she challenged the school in court. A few days after the judgment, cadets wheeled a huge sign to the highway. It read "DIE SHANNON." She ultimately lasted about a week. In 2007, Valley Forge became one of the last private military schools to admit women, a decision that evoked a vehement response from powerful alumni, who complained that the school was "losing its character."

Faced with their own binding congressional mandate, service academy recruiters moved with characteristic swiftness to find their first female cadets, who enrolled into the class of 1980. Officials fanned out to high schools across America and sent more than 18,000 letters to guidance counselors seeking athletic women with high ACT and SAT test scores. They also scoured the enlisted ranks.

Many of the students the military found harbored other dreams. But West Point made a powerful pitch, promising to turn them into heroines in the mold of MacArthur, Patton, and Eisenhower. None really knew what this transformation would entail, thanks largely to the school's euphemistic recruitment materials, which vaguely indicated that the environment would be "taxing," but that ultimately it would forge a "very special woman." Those who accepted a service academy commission basked in positive attention from their friends, family, neighbors, and, often, the press. "As soon as I got the nomination, the newspapers and radio station came to my house," one female cadet recalled. "[They] built it up so big I couldn't have backed out if I'd wanted to." When a UPI reporter later checked in on West Point's first female plebes, one co-ed urged any women curious about military school to "investigate" its history and culture, so that they "know what they're really getting into."

West Point's inaugural batch of female cadets first walked through Thayer Gate and onto the parade lawn on July 7, 1976. There were just 119 of them among a class of 1,400. Roughly half would survive through graduation. Some had become enchanted by West Point's romantic pitch, though many others signed up simply to secure a free education. Some hoped to escape their home lives or boring hometowns. Others wanted to prove their worth, to themselves, maybe, or, as with many male cadets, to impress their gruff veteran fathers. By this point, nearly 14 percent of all West Point cadets had been raised by career military officers.

No matter their motivations, though, these women proved highly unlikely to fully define themselves by their military lives. Contemporaneous school survey data shows that male cadets were nearly four times as likely as female ones to view their soldier status as deeply important to their self-perception.

One of the first women West Point plucked from the ranks was Pat Locke, who had been serving as a private at Fort Folk, in Louisiana. Shortly after Javits's law was ratified, Locke's battalion commander whisked her into his office and asked if she wanted to attend West Point, insisting that she needed to answer on the spot. Locke had grown up surrounded by deep poverty and violence in Detroit, reared in "a house where we had a gun under every mattress." She knew nothing about West Point but felt she could handle the intensity of whatever the Army threw at her. Plus, the pitch made the academy seem like a regal, exceedingly academic place, one where she might feel "free to breathe and do something other than just survive."

Without much hesitation, Locke said "Yes" to her commander. Hours later, she was on the road to upstate New York, where she would become one of two Black women in this inaugural class. "The women shared a race, the men shared the commonality of being male, and with me I was Black and female, so I shared almost nothing with the majority," Locke explained in a 2015 interview for a West Point oral history project, adding she was also one of the few cadets who had been raised in poverty. "They didn't know what to do with me."

Another early female West Point cadet was Cathy Wells, a California kid who loved the classroom, notched great SAT scores, and dreamed of becoming a teacher. She had already been accepted to UC Davis, but her mother was "tickled pink" by West Point's recruitment offensive. The prospect of her daughter becoming an Army officer felt like an important rejoinder to her era of homemaking. Wells applied to West Point and was accepted shortly after her mother died tragically in a car accident. She had her doubts about the Army, but wanted to honor her late mother's wishes, and accepted her nomination. "It's a major institution, it's run by the government, I never thought it would be an unsafe place for me," she reasoned. "I didn't have any qualms about it." Cathy Long had wanted to be a veterinarian. But her dad had died in Vietnam, and her stepdad was a general, so her path was preordained. "I wasn't allowed to be me," she told me.

Valerie Coffey's dad had gone to West Point, but he didn't think women belonged there. She matriculated because she wanted to prove him wrong. "There wasn't a lot of thought put into it." Before seventeen-year-old Kris Fuhr landed at West Point in the summer of 1981, she had already been marked a freak. Upon her nomination to the military academy, the family of Fuhr's high school boyfriend successfully pressured him to break up with her. According to Fuhr, her own mother labeled her a "camp follower," a demeaning term to describe women who, during the Revolutionary War, cooked for soldiers, washed their clothes, and, it's believed, sometimes provided sexual services.

DURING WEST POINT'S INITIAL CHARM OFFENSIVE for female cadets, one high school girl asked, "Do you have to be a virgin to apply?" Technically you didn't, but as the school prepared to welcome its first female cadets, administrators seemed singularly worried about the prospect that some in their coming class of plebes would become pregnant. This, one administrator explained to the press, would restrict them from participating in West Point's "vigorous year-round activities."

The far more ominous prospect was that a group of eighteen- and nineteen-year-old girls was about to enter a militant, all-male environment with a two-hundred-year history of violent initiation rituals. The Air Force Academy took modest steps to protect their inaugural class of 157 female cadets, appointing a crew of active-duty female officers to serve as "upperclassmen" during the first two years of integration. This smoothed the transition through mentorship and protection, with female Air Force cadets making progress at similar rates as their male counterparts.

West Point's leaders, however, treated the prospect of female integration with lackadaisical cruelty. Regimental commander James Hall told a local reporter that hostilities on campus would simply "take time to work out." Asked if he would recommend to his daughter that she commission on campus, Hall coldly responded, "I would not."

The academy's laissez-faire and, at times, callous approach to its new crop of women was apparent in decisions large and small. The uniforms assigned to female cadets, for instance, were poorly designed and constructed, with plastic zippers, unlike the men's metal ones. The women's bathrooms had also been quickly retrofitted, and many still had urinals. For a time, the dorm room windows didn't have curtains, and the dorm room doors didn't have locks. This latter policy was a dubious outgrowth of the honor code's ban on stealing, which cemented the delusional belief among administrators that the edict alone could ensure privacy and security.

West Point was aware that female cadets would face threats, but their main response was to teach them how to fight. The school employed Susan Peterson, who, in 1979, wrote a book called *Self-Defense for Women: The West Point Way*, as director of Women's Self-Defense. Dotted throughout the pages of her book are photos of female cadets performatively gouging eyes, kicking groins, and knuckle-punching male cadets. The book profiles various common criminals, among them the "street bum," the amateur thief, and the rapist, described as someone between eighteen and thirty who is unmarried, unskilled, low intelligence, and "unsure of his masculinity." The book mostly fearmongers about the dangers of the "urban jungle," when, in fact, danger—in the form of male cadets and officers—stalked the academy's grass-and-stone campus.

As for the prospect of pregnant cadets, the school banned them. Some medical staff at service academies also recommended female cadets go on birth control, even if they weren't sexually active. "You never know what might happen," one explained.

While female cadets were derided as soft, all were subjected to West Point's classic hazing rituals—punched, kicked, screamed at, and spit on, among other humiliations. They all faced the stressors of drill and other stringent military regulations. One early female cadet, like Oscar Booz before her, would, while sleeping, shout "Yes, sir!" and "No, sir!," and sometimes even sleep march.

In addition, female cadets faced a battery of gendered attacks that at once sexualized them and stripped them of their femininity. During a summer survival camp at nearby Camp Buckner, in 1979, one female cadet was forced to bite the head off a chicken, a ritual that Superintendent Andrew Goodpaster insisted applied to both sexes. Not long after, though, a male cadet announced in mixed company that he would shoot in the back any woman he served with should she prove ineffective in combat.

Male cadets endlessly flung vulgar insults at women, calling them "cunts," "bitches," and "whores." They developed a glossary of military specific digs, joking, for instance, that a pool of swimming West Point women was called "The Bay of Pigs." Girls at the Naval Academy were derided as "dumb, ugly bitches," or "DUBS." Many cracks concerned the physical appearance of female cadets. Classmates barked that the difference between a female cadet and a squad car was that "it takes two squad cars to make a roadblock." Others fake diagnosed larger women as being struck by "Hudson Hip Disease." All of this was made worse by public company weigh-ins, a vestige of Sylvanus Thayer's fixation on physical attributes.

In response, many female cadets developed eating disorders. Like Joan of Arc, many also stopped menstruating. Cadet Susan Spieth broke out in a stress-induced rash from her head to her toes. "I tell people it altered my DNA," she told me. "It probably wasn't the best place for me, but my dad was tickled proud."

Cadet Carol Barkalow experienced what felt like an elemental metamorphosis during an evening trip off base for a meal at Arby's. There, an attendant at the cash register asked, "Can I help you, sir?" Later that night, Barkalow locked herself in a bathroom and stared in the mirror, sobbing. "I felt so confused," she writes in her memoir. "Did I look like a man? What was West Point doing to me?" Cadets at VMI sought to force a similar transmogrification, buzz-cutting women's heads and lodging charges against those who wore skirts.

Male cadets led the charge against female ones, but faculty and staff sometimes piled on, too. Barkalow recalled one teacher musing in class that she and the rest of the women's basketball team were all "dykes." Another professor gave a female cadet a "C" on a military science paper simply because "a woman shouldn't be doing well in tactics." Some squad leaders took bets with male cadets on which women would fall out of running exercises or cracked jokes about having sex with them.

During West Point's plebe summer initiation program, known as Beast Barracks, Susan Spieth's squad leader ordered her out with him on three-mile runs every night. It was purportedly to improve her stamina, but the male cadet simply wanted to rag on her. "The whole time we would run he would talk to me about how MacArthur and Pershing and Eisenhower are turning in their graves because I'm there," Spieth told me. During one session, the cadet leader pushed her to the ground. "I got up and gave him a look like, 'Leave me the fuck alone,'" she recalled. "And he did."

MUCH OF THE ANIMOSITY TOWARD WOMEN EMERGED from a single cadet company, B-1, which unofficially referred to itself with the longhand "Boys Won." The company was driven by a psychosexual desire to entirely rid the school of women. They summed up their intent cryptically in West Point's 1983 yearbook, which features their onetime battle cry: "B-1 or Be Gone." A photo in that yearbook also shows a male cadet next to a female cadet, alongside a caption that reads: "That's right, she's mine."

Barkalow appears to make a veiled reference to B-1 in her memoir, vaguely invoking a company that formed a "secret committee that would target one female a month and harass her until she quit." This mission passed down to subsequent generations, and infected other companies, too. When Valerie Coffey arrived for Beast Barracks two years after Barkalow, in 1981, a cadet leader screamed, "I'm gonna get every one of you fuckin' bitches out of here!" At the conclusion of Fuhr's successful plebe summer, one in which she often outran the boys, a senior cadet kicked open her door one day and screamed, "You're going to B-1—be male or be gone and you will be gone!"

The campaign to oust women, known colloquially as "Project Zero," included sexually charged shows of force, often under the cover of dark. In one case, a cadet snuck into the women's changing room at night and, according to Barkalow's memoir, "discovered an anonymous way to express his feelings on the subject of women at the academy. The next morning, my classmate found her bathing suit sticky with his opinion." Fuhr shared a litany of stories from her year in B-1. There was the guy who ordered her every month to come by his room when his new *Playboy* arrived and critique the centerfold while he sat behind his desk and masturbated; then there was the guy who had somehow figured out how to spy on Fuhr, and each morning whispered in her ear what color underwear she had on; there was also the guy who stole all her underwear; and the guy who stalked Fuhr and attempted to rape her before she violently screamed and a squad leader came in and pulled the cadet off her. That same cadet was commissioned as an Army officer at the end of the year.

Many female cadets were scared to be in the hallways at night, and at least one urinated in her room's sink as a form of self-protection. But because there were no locks on the doors, women's rooms made easy targets. Some male cadets pierced female cadets' pillows and mattresses with their ceremonial sabers, or left condoms on their bunks. Others intruded into women's rooms while they were asleep, sometimes simply to scare them, other times to assault them, or, according to former cadet Luci Fitzgerald, to "get their jollies off." One repeat offender always wore a black ski mask.

During Cathy Wells's second year, she was assigned to B-1 and became a target. During the day, B-1 boys called her a "whore" and a "slut" ad nauseam. Her female friends knew of the company's nasty reputation, and thus didn't venture over much to visit her, which only deepened her sense of isolation. One night, when her roommate went off campus for a sporting event, Wells woke up with someone on top of her. "I don't know who it was, and I don't even remember to this day if anything really awful happened," she told me. "I didn't see his face 'cause it was dark, but I don't remember a mask." While the night remains largely fragmented in her mind, she clearly remembers shoving a chair under her doorknob after the intruder left, and staying up the rest of the night, terrified.

Incidents like this were frequent and normalized. "I had people come in my room at night and touch me in ways they probably shouldn't have," Fitzgerald told me matter-of-factly, explaining that female cadets routinely spent their evenings in a state of "low-grade vigilance," and that she and her roommates, including Spieth, often put a trash can near the door to alert them to any intruders. One night, Spieth recalled, "my roommate woke up, saw the masked man, screamed bloody murder and he went running out."

There was no acknowledgment by the administration of this nighttime terror, no public warnings from staff about the various men stalking the campus. Instead, women set up a whisper network. They warned each other about the masked intruder and also noted that a Peeping Tom frequented the women's showers. Coffey told me that a friend of hers "was raped, she reported it, and nothing happened to him. Then she was raped again, and she didn't report it." Another female cadet woke up being assaulted in her bed with a pillow over her face. She never saw the man who did it and figured there was nothing she could do. "What am I supposed to report?" she thought.

A cadre of upstanding male cadets began to guard women's rooms at night, but B-1 boys allegedly ordered some of them to stop. An internal West Point study from this time found that at least forty female cadets had been visited by late-night intruders. Brass responded to these numbers with relief. "I thought it was more than that!" one officer said. In exit interviews over many years, female cadets urged the school to install locks on their doors. West Point didn't do so until the early 1990s.

Not long after Cathy Wells was violated in the night, a B-1 boy accused Cathy Long of an honor violation. Long told me the charge stemmed from an incident in which some male cadets ordered her to rearrange her hat, which, as with so many other elements of female West Point dress, didn't sit well on her head. "It doesn't fit right," she barked at the nitpicky cadet, whom, she claims, went on to falsely accuse her of telling them to "fuck off."

Cathy Wells had no direct knowledge of the incident, but the tattle fell squarely in line with the campaign to push women out, especially because one of the accusers was a notorious B-1 leader. Wells offered to provide supportive contextual testimony in Long's case, describing her own torment by the accuser, and his company. In the days leading up to her testimony, he and his B-1 cronies repeatedly ordered Wells to stay silent. In one particularly unnerving instance, a male cadet cornered her alone in a stairwell and promised that she would regret her testimony. "I felt physically in danger," Wells told me. "I tried to find myself not alone anywhere. It was really a terrifying time. I was hypervigilant. There was no place I felt safe."

As her scheduled testimony approached, Wells began suffering sharp stomach pains, and realized that if she backed out, B-1 may finally leave her alone. But she ultimately believed that silence violated military virtues. "You're supposed to follow the truth, that's the honor code: you don't lie, cheat, or steal," she told me. Wells ultimately testified, and Cathy Long won her case, only to be expelled her junior year following another trumped-up honor charge. B-1 immediately retaliated by silencing Wells, a practice the school had technically retired nearly two decades earlier. Male cadets also frequently knocked her books to the ground as she walked between classes, ransacked her desk, and stole her plebe yearbook, along with a necklace her father had given her.

Wells wanted to leave, but waited until the last possible moment, after the B-1 cadet who led the charge against her had walked at graduation. "I wasn't gonna let that bastard see me go," she said. After he was officially commissioned as a second lieutenant, she met with her TAC officer and formally resigned. He didn't ask why she was leaving so abruptly, only what she planned to do next, a reaction, Wells believes in retrospect, that indicates the TAC knew about the B-1 campaign. "[The West Point administration] absolutely knew it was going on," Fuhr echoed. Her own attempted rapist, a B-1 boy, was simply moved to another company far away after the incident. Years later, as Fuhr and other early female graduates began to compare notes on their campus experiences, they collectively discovered that Fuhr's attacker had potentially assaulted six to seven other women.

When Wells arrived home, her brother brushed off her treatment as small potatoes, basic "boys will be boys" behavior. Her father, a Navy veteran, told her she was weak and stupid for leaving, comments for which he wouldn't apologize until many years later. Wells internalized these judgments and didn't talk about West Point for decades. After facing the academy's gauntlet, she couldn't really be around people, or make friends, and bounced around aimlessly for years. She landed at San Jose State and got a part-time job at a grocery store, but couldn't balance both and dropped out. A woman who once dreamed of being a teacher now couldn't focus on school. She didn't secure her degree until she was forty-six, through an online program from the University of Phoenix.

THE SINGLE UNIFYING TRAIT AMONG THE EARLY CLASSES of female cadets was their strength and self-esteem. All were highly accomplished, both physically and academically. All were also uncommonly brave. Male West Point cadets did everything in their power to disabuse them of these traits and run them out, but by and large the women demonstrated that they could succeed. Female cadets outperformed male ones in English and foreign languages. They held their own in other courses, and in physical drills, too. "The women, we found, are more willing than the men to push themselves past stress barriers," explained one West Point official.

As women prepared to enter the Air Force Academy, the chief of staff's son, himself a cadet, warned his father that this new crop wouldn't be able to stomach even a week of drills. "I was your typical male chauvinist pig: Varsity football player, the whole bit," he acknowledged to the *Belleville News-Democrat* in 1980. "But they were there . . . doing things I did as well or better." When, around this time, the Army first integrated women into field exercises, they discerned no negative results. In 1981, Kate Wilder became the first woman to complete the Green Beret course, outperforming some of her male peers. The military reacted to her historic achievement with new regulations explicitly barring women from taking the course.

Women's pioneering military achievements were often curtailed, minimized, or met with terrifying aggression. Susan Golden, a member of West Point's class of 1980, compared her psychological status upon graduating as akin to that of a battered spouse. For Spieth, "I came out of that place very much feeling like men had the upper hand and could be and would be violent and domineering and hateful and hurtful. I really hated men for a while."

On her graduation day, all Pat Locke wanted to do was "get my diploma and get in my car and drive as fast as I could away from West Point." Locke hoped that her abuse in the military was over, that she had proved her worth. Then an officer told her that while they had failed to drive her out of West Point, "we'll take care of you out in the Army." In that moment, she realized she was "a long way from being safe."

Marene Allison, another graduate that day, was proud to have broken the school's glass ceiling but reflected that the experience left "some shards . . . embedded in my shoulder." Decades later, these women still feel ripples of West Point in their daily lives. "I'm a bit OCD-ish," Fitzgerald reflected. "That has permeated my cells." When Fitzgerald returned to West Point for a friend's retirement ceremony, she was reminded of her many female classmates who've never been back. "They've dropped off the face of the earth because they have such horrible memories," she said.

During the 2020s, one of Cathy Wells's female cadet friends gifted her a bayonet from Russia, a country she had taken a keen academic interest in while at West Point. She now keeps the saber below her headboard, in case some bastard sneaks up on her. "For years, I could not reconcile what happened to me with the ideals that I signed up for and really believed in," she concluded. "But I still live by the honor code. There's nothing better in life than to have a code like that to live by."

In her taped oral history interview, Locke exudes perfect poise, even as she recalls memories of intermittent silencing, punctuated by a pattern of fights and physical abuse involving cadets and instructors. Remarkably, she graduated from West Point into two successful decades of service, including as an Army adviser in the Pentagon. At one point, she begins to describe a particularly bad altercation, at which time we see a brief flash of pent-up emotion crossing her face. "I've got to stop for a minute," she informs the interviewer, and the screen goes dark. When Locke reappears, she pivots to a new topic.

THE PIONEERING WOMEN AT OTHER MILITARY SCHOOLS faced similarly hellish environments. After the Citadel pushed out Shannon Faulkner, packs of cadets viciously harassed other women and even set their clothes on fire. Members of the mounted calvary unit within Texas A&M's military corps allegedly attacked a female cadet hoping to join them. In 1987, at Kemper Military School, the so-called West Point of the West, a male cadet killed a female classmate in an "act of passion."

In 1990, *The Baltimore Sun* chronicled the story of Julie Simas, a Naval Academy midshipman who hadn't been allowed to go to the restroom without permission during her period, even after blood had soaked through her uniform. "They just made a joke out of it," recalled Simas, who resigned shortly after the incident. Around this time, Gwen Dreyer, another midshipman, claimed she was dragged from her room and handcuffed to a pipe over a men's room urinal, where a bunch of boys jeered and took pictures. A subsequent investigation from the Navy's inspector general identified "a breakdown in civility and discipline, which contributes to an environment conducive to sexual harassment and discrimination."

A year later, the *San Diego Union* broke the military's first massive sexual abuse scandal. Their story zeroed in on the Tailhook Association, a fraternal organization of Navy and Marine Corps aviators, many of them Naval Academy graduates. The organization's name derives from the pegs on fighter planes that, amid landings on aircraft carriers, catch an arresting wire.

Tailhook confabs had long been debaucherous affairs. The organization's board had, for instance, convened a special meeting to reckon with the 1985 convention, which, according to notes from one member, included binge drinking and property destruction among aviators who become so trashed they resembled "walking zombies." The member further detailed "dancing girls performing lurid sexual acts on Naval aviators in public." Little had been done to reel in these urges by September 1991, when Tailhook convened its largest convention ever, at the Las Vegas Hilton. Many attendees arrived fresh off disappointing deployments to Desert Storm. The Navy's role in the Persian Gulf had been relatively minor, in large part because they had no counterpart Navy to battle against, leading the Air Force to control most of the skies. When a batch of Navy Hornet planes did fly in combat, they struggled with projectile dysfunction, their laser-targeting systems largely unable to accurately lock missiles onto targets.

These emasculating failures seemed to swell members with performative swagger and unearned bravado. Tailhook attendees were further juiced up by the recent release of *Top Gun*, which fictionalized a real training program then overseen by Tailhook's venerated president Captain Frederic G. Ludwig Jr., whose call sign was "Wigs." His son, Eric, recalled that after the blockbuster was released, crowds would sometimes roll out a red carpet for "Wigs" when he got out of his jet.

Tailhook conventions had a professional veneer, with daytime forums focused on war policy and new technology. The nights, however, were really what everyone was there for. Tailhook dropped over $35,000 for alcohol on the 1991 bash, fueling boozy banquets that led into sweaty, deviant afterparties overseen by blitzed-out aviators. The weekend was shot through with a nervous and threatened energy, thanks to the Navy's embarrassing role in the Gulf, plus rumblings of military downsizing and growing discussions about empowering women to serve as combat aviators. During one forum, a female sailor asked an all-male panel when women would be allowed to be fighter pilots, to which the panelists, and many men in the audience, loudly laughed and jeered.

At night, one aviator donned a shirt that read "Women Are Property." Others hired strippers, flopped their penises out of their pants, and formed a swarm of bodies on the third-floor hallway of the Hilton they called "the Gauntlet," which they forced people to pass through. Over the course of the convention's final evening, officers sexually assaulted at least seven men and eighty-three women, including an intoxicated underage girl who allegedly had her clothes removed. Many flag officers and other top brass were in attendance, including Navy Secretary H. Lawrence Garrett, who sipped drinks with Navy pilots on an outdoor terrace near the Hilton hallway where the "Gauntlet" assaults took place.

Garrett resigned under pressure in 1992. Washington spiked the careers of a few other aviators, but no one was criminally prosecuted. Meanwhile, the Navy hurriedly declared a sea change in its treatment of women. In short order, they permitted women to compete for combat pilot positions and opened nearly all naval vessels to their service. Tailhook also pledged to clean up its act, only to declare that it was moving its conferences from high-flying Las Vegas, to Reno—a location arguably less notorious but every bit as debauched.

Still, many more allegations of grievous sexual misconduct, often referred to as flare-ups of "Tailhook syndrome," continued to pervade the military. Not long after Tailhook, a horrific, historically large Army rape ring was exposed at Aberdeen proving ground, in Maryland. A subsequent survey on the progress of gender integration at the military academies showed intense animosity, with more than 50 percent of women at the Army, Navy, and Air Force academies reporting sexual harassment at least twice a month. This behavior again burst into public light a few years later at the Air Force Academy, where 12 percent of women in a class survey claimed they were survivors of rape or attempted sexual misconduct. Seventy percent said they had faced sexual harassment, including "pressure for sexual favors." These statistics, and many more to come, completely undermined the military's long-articulated contention that military service is simply too harsh for women. The glaring truth is that military women often face far harsher, more violent conditions than men, facing threats from multiple fronts, chiefly foreign adversaries, but also the twisted bands of brothers that walk beside them.

Chapter 11

Soldier of Fortune

Over the course of the Vietnam War, the U.S. military cycled more than 2.5 million combat troops in and out of Southeast Asia. On March 29, 1973, Master Sergeant Max Beilke became the last one to leave. His eight-month stint in-country was focused on getting all the remaining men out, including American prisoners of war. Beilke's remit made him a clear-cut symbol of imperial surrender, though he viewed the job's practical requirements as a point of pride. "When you're responsible for moving the people out of here," he said, "it's nice to know you're the last man out."

His departure was treated warmly by Bui Tin, a North Vietnamese officer who had helped ensure that every living American got out of the country safely. He shook Beilke's hand, said "Peace," and offered him a parting souvenir: some postcards of Ho Chi Minh and a bamboo scroll with a painting of a pagoda on it. Beilke then boarded a Lockheed Starlifter filled with sixty-seven men, and, minutes later, took off for the homeland. "This is an historic day," Tin declared from the ground. "It is the first time in 100 years that there are no foreign troops on the soil of Vietnam."

About twenty hours later, the troops landed on the tarmac of Travis Air Force Base, in California, where military officials held the last of their red-carpet welcome home events for planes holding former prisoners of war. The plight of the war's prisoners, and those mythically "missing in action," had by then been made the centerpiece of an archconservative movement that, according to historian Rick Perlstein, propelled President Nixon's drive "to justify the carnage in Vietnam in a way that rendered the United States as its sole victim." The black-and-white flag of the POW/ MIA movement shows the haunting profile of a captured man. His Vietnamese captors are not depicted, though the flag clearly insinuates their cruelty, worthy of whatever hellfire we rained down upon them. The POW/ MIA movement's tagline is "You Are Not Forgotten." In truth, Vietnam is a conflict that everyone wants to forget but will never be forgotten, creating contradictory pressures that suggest it may not ever be remembered right.

At the core of the POW movement is the claim, made entirely without evidence, that heroic Americans are still languishing in Southeast Asia—left behind. This false contention poisoned the Pentagon's well and promoted a warped lesson to soldiers and civilians alike, namely that America got out too early and didn't go hard enough. This elegy later served as an accelerant after the September 11 attacks, propelling America into a conflict that was as factually and spiritually bankrupt as Vietnam, if not more so. As blinding feelings of revenge took root in the military, Beilke came to represent the last of an old military guard that, despite its flaws, valued facts as the necessary prerequisite to sound decision-making. Beilke's mission in Vietnam was a clear rebuttal to the false and poisonous legend of the POW. Decades later, he revived this ethic in a newsletter called "Max Facts," in which he addressed and dispelled the myths and concerns of military veterans.

Beilke spent the final part of his military career in an unsexy Pentagon job, as the deputy chief of the Army's Retirement Services division, where he secured better benefits for troops. In an eerie historical footnote, the American Airlines jet that plunged into the Pentagon on September 11, 2001, directly hit a conference room that Beilke was occupying, killing him instantly and adding extra weight to the old adage that "the first casualty of war is truth."

AFTER VIETNAM, political theorist and Vietnam policy adviser Samuel Huntington prescribed compartmentalization as the best postwar remedy. "It is conceivable," he argued, "that our policymakers may best meet future crises and dilemmas if they simply blot out of their minds any recollection of this one."

This same posture widely characterized the professorial ranks at military academies, sparking curses and ghosts of Vietnam that remain to this day. The American military has never been able to escape the memory of that war because it has never effectively processed its losses and learned from them—a willful blindness that led to a series of spectacularly similar military mistakes during the War on Terror. Defiance took the place of reckoning, and shame was superseded by pride and triumphalism. This stance seeded a darker, more violent and more conservative military establishment. Between

1976 and 1996, the share of senior military officers identifying as Republican jumped from one-third to two-thirds.

In his book *The Cost of Loyalty*, civilian West Point law professor Tim Bakken cites various studies indicating how this burst of conservatism translated to tactical actions. "Simply put," he writes, "the conservative brain . . . is more likely to spot conflict where there may or may not be any."

In the waning days of the Cold War, a debate over future military curricula at the academies heavily featured discussions involving POWs. One Navy admiral who had been in captivity for eight years said his POW experience justified his alma mater's harsh hazing practices. "I came out of prison being very happy about the merits of Plebe year at the Naval Academy," he said. "You have to learn to take a bunch of junk and accept it with a sense of humor."

Others offered a more holistic course. Andrew Bacevich, a West Pointer who had fought in Vietnam before returning to the academy in 1977 to teach history for a few years, argued against a military curriculum focused solely around managing and applying violence. He advocated for a new military doctrine to incorporate "diplomacy, information policies, economic leverage, and the imperatives of culture and morality."

Retired Army lieutenant colonel Edward King argued that the war's failures could be traced to West Point's "sterile educational environment" and "inbred characteristics" of its mostly alumni military faculty. "[West Point] has played a primary role in creating an institutional system that has brought about the moral decay of the Army and the failure of Vietnam," he wrote. "If public apathy lets this system remain largely unchanged, then we must be prepared for more My Lais, probably both at home and abroad."

When, in late 1963, Westmoreland was first tasked to lead in Vietnam, he dropped by West Point to speak with cadets, then ventured to a gilded suite at the Waldorf Astoria in Manhattan to seek advice from famed graduate Douglas MacArthur. Both men had been named first captain at West Point, the highest attainable rank for a cadet, and yet their discussion of the war was obtuse and unsparing, with MacArthur advising Westmoreland to treat the South Vietnamese officers soon to be under his command with the same hazing regime that had been applied at West Point. He also warned that the conflict's guerrilla warfare justified a "scorched earth policy."

IN 1982, THE AIR FORCE ACADEMY'S ENGLISH DEPARTMENT compiled a slim volume of essays from military men arguing that literature and the liberal arts offered the clearest path to process the traumas of Vietnam and understand the broader pitfalls of imperialism.

They recommended texts like Joseph Heller's *Catch-22* and Joseph Conrad's *Heart of Darkness*. In one of the pamphlet's essays, Lieutenant Bill McCarron argues that literature is a vital counterweight to war. Combat, he asserts, is a brutish tool for death, whereas literature illuminates the many textures of human life. Cadets must therefore be exposed to more writing, McCarron argues, so that they may not only know "the value of what they are seeking to preserve, but of what they may have to destroy."

While some POWs argued that hazing's art of practiced persecution prepared them well for detention, others became disenchanted with military doctrine. One of them, Colonel Dave Burroughs, called the humanities "the real life-saving stuff," not the pretend POW camps. He defined the humanities as "Books. Plays. Poems. Philosophy. The big ideas. The persistence of values." Former POW and presidential candidate John McCain agreed. He said he stayed sane by reciting poetry. Another former POW, Hervey Stockman, similarly credited the preservation of his mental faculties to a pencil stub and paper he secured in his cage. He used these simple tools to ruminate on Shakespeare and the Declaration of Independence. Stockman also wrote short stories and poems about the bugs, lizards, and other creatures that crawled around his cell, writings he later compiled into a yearbook he distributed to fellow POWs. It was called "Gecko."

Many high-ranking military men liked a black-and-white world, one free of the pesky word *failure*, or even the more nuanced prospect of a "stalemate." Their attitudes were later summed up by an Army report that described West Point's "relatively humorless atmosphere," where "grimness" prevailed and cadets robbed themselves of joy, levity, or vulnerability. One Air Force Academy professor recalled a cadet in his English class complaining that the assigned readings, which included *Antigone* and *Moby-Dick*, focused on failure, and that it was improper to introduce such a demoralizing idea to a budding military officer. He would have presumably been far more open to West Point's English class offerings, which, according to one former cadet's memoir, assigned literature that argued man is intrinsically predatory.

By closing off their emotions, cadets foreclosed on their ability to honestly study and understand Vietnam. Many professors and guest lecturers had themselves just returned from Southeast Asia and seemed uninterested or unable to rationally teach the conflict. The Army study called this "intellectual inbreeding," in which malformed lessons passed from general to cadet.

West Point Superintendent William Knowlton did his damnedest to defend and justify the Cold War, including by recruiting a South Vietnamese cadet, Tam Minh Pham, whom, he hoped, would offer an approachable face for America's nominal new ally. After Pham arrived on the Hudson in 1970 he generally assimilated well into the corps, even dating a general's daughter, though his company gave him the nickname "Gooky," a derogatory term for people of East and Southeast Asian descent. It was apparently coined by Marines during the Philippine-American War before becoming the slur-du-jour among American G.I.s in Vietnam.

Pham's appointment as a cadet was essentially the beginning and the end of West Point's reckoning with the war. While the men in charge had just bungled a classic counterinsurgency mission against guerrilla forces, the academy declined to create a mandatory course on the subject. On the contrary, brass expunged counterinsurgency materials from their curriculum and kept it out of training manuals, leading political science professor Dominic Tierney to muse that the military was worried that simply "saying the name of the guerrilla bogeyman might summon it again."

There were, of course, enough primary documents to justify a litany of classes. This trove included the Pentagon Papers, a RAND Corporation study commissioned by Defense Secretary Robert McNamara that provided a frank and comprehensive assessment of the war's failures. There was also a new set of critical texts on military schools written by military men, including *The Brass Factories* and *West Point: America's Power Fraternity*. The latter book, published in 1973, exhaustively traces the West Pointers involved in brutal and disastrous military decisions, only to be protected or further emboldened. The book sums up its cynicism toward the military's role in civic life with a quote from noted sociologist C. Wright Mills, who warned that "alongside the corporate executives and the politicians, the generals and admirals—those uneasy cousins within the American elite—have gained and have been given increased power to make and to influence decisions of the gravest consequences."

IN 1977, BRIGADIER GENERAL DOUGLAS KINNARD, a West Pointer, published a bombshell book called *The War Managers*. It featured candid insights from 173 generals who took Kinnard's survey, then sat for follow-up interviews on the strict condition that their insights be cited anonymously. Unsurprisingly, the West Pointers in the bunch were far more optimistic in their reflections about Vietnam than nongraduates. Still, the group's overall conclusions were scathing.

A majority said America should have never been involved in Vietnam. Under the veil of anonymity, others admitted that the war planning and assessments had been injected with gross exaggerations, even "blatant lies." A colossal 55 percent agreed that Westmoreland's kill-ratio strategy was a "misleading device to estimate progress." One wrote: "I shudder to think of how many of our soldiers were killed on a body-counting mission—what a waste." Another called Westmoreland's strategy "strategically bankrupt," one built on "blood in lieu of brains."

Westmoreland publicly responded with muted defensiveness to Kinnard's book, arguing that it was "written with the benefit of hindsight." In private, though, he pestered Kinnard unsuccessfully to reveal his sources, then marked up negative notes on nearly every page of the book and sent it to him for consideration. Unlike other assessments of the era, Kinnard's book was unemotional, but nonetheless damning, depicting an officer class that was urged to keep quiet about the war's elemental failures. "Perhaps the main lesson for the future," Kinnard concluded, "is that the system will have to permit more dissent without exacting the sacrifice of careers as the price."

Soon after, a CBS investigative report found that Westmoreland had aimed to "suppress and alter critical intelligence on the enemy" to substantiate his optimistic reports on the progress of the war. Westmoreland, desperate to preserve his own reputation and complicate any honest reckoning of the war, responded to the CBS findings with a $120 million libel suit against the network. It quickly backfired. As part of the discovery process, one of Westmoreland's key aides, major general Joseph McChristian, who had participated in the initial CBS program, powerfully testified that his boss had explicitly sought to suppress the troop strength of the enemy, recalling his worries that accurate figures would "create a political bombshell" in Washington and "embarrass my commander in chief." As Westmoreland pondered how to handle the suit, a bunch of his "friends" told *The New York Times* that he was shocked McChristian was willing to "break the old West Point tie."

Westmoreland ultimately dropped the suit but still managed to convince CBS to release a statement saying that while they stood by their reporting, the network did not intend to suggest Westmoreland "was unpatriotic or disloyal in performing his duties as he saw them."

Westmoreland's campaign in Vietnam may have been racked by cooked books, war crimes, and strategic failures, but it all occurred within the Pentagon's approved framework, and that made it inherently honorable. As Westmoreland saw it, he had simply been doing the government's bidding—all in perfect harmony with his alma mater's venerated honor code.

Despite Westmoreland's myriad military failures, his reputation was fundamentally revised via a biography written by West Point's chair of American history. He was further mythologized at Valley Forge Military Academy by its president Willard Pearson, the former Screaming Eagles commando whom Westmoreland had himself highly recommended for this top military school job. In 1978, the Forge presented him with its highest honor, The Order of Anthony Wayne. It was a fitting tribute. Its eponymous figure, a Founding Father and major general nicknamed "Mad Anthony," had been a forceful but not altogether effective military leader, contributing to Revolutionary War losses in Philadelphia that forced General Washington's bitter retreat to Valley Forge. After a sumptuous award dinner in Valley Forge's Eisenhower Hall, Westmoreland gave a speech in which he stressed the importance of "moral fiber."

As people with rap sheets like Pearson and Westmoreland reached the military's pinnacle, the Army's soldier archetype started to reshape itself, from the modest G.I. loyal to his country to the pugnacious mercenary, focused not on winning the war, but simply securing a high body count—just as Westmoreland had ordered.

THIS CULTURAL MUTATION IS WELL REPRESENTED in popular culture. Clint Eastwood, for instance, went from playing noble cowboys to, in 1971, *Dirty Harry*. The ultimate lone wolf warrior emerged in 1982 with Sylvester Stallone's *Rambo*, a Vietnam War veteran grappling with PTSD following his torture at an enemy POW camp. A Green Beret, Rambo hates bureaucracy, rejects orders, and relishes killing, leaving one *Washington Post* critic to quip "Sly's body looks fine. Now can't you come up with a workout for his soul?" In the franchise's second installment, Rambo is reinstated in the Army and sent to Vietnam to capture the POWs America left behind.

This was followed in 1986 by *Top Gun*, which helped precipitate a 10 percent jump in applications for the 1987 Naval Academy class. Another factor, school officials joyfully reported to *The Baltimore Sun*, was the increasing popularity of military books by local author Tom Clancy. The military image these products sold was devoid of modesty, community, or even basic morals, replaced instead by rugged individualism, beautiful violence, and cover-the-earth imperialism.

The military seemed thrilled with any attention that boosted recruitment. The brass could also cynically scapegoat this toxic culture when it suited their interests. Some, for instance, blamed the Tailhook scandal on a "Top Gun Mentality," a charge that rang as clear deflection even as it spoke to how a film glorifying partying naval pilots could help seed negative behavior.

In 1990, lead actor Tom Cruise cautiously distanced himself from the film in an interview with *Playboy*. "Some people felt that 'Top Gun' was a right-wing film to promote the Navy," he said. "And a lot of kids loved it. But I want the kids to know that's not the way war is." He assured readers that he was not some reflexive war propagandist. "That's why I didn't go on and make 'Top Gun II' and 'III' and 'IV' and 'V,'" he explained. "That would have been irresponsible." Three decades later, of course, in 2022, Cruise starred in a second *Top Gun*, which made a boatload of money and again helped spur Naval enlistments, again at a critical juncture in the wake of a highly unpopular conflict: the Global War on Terrorism.

Cruise got his first big break in *Taps*, a 1981 film that follows a crew of cadets who violently rebel against the planned closing of their beloved Bunker Hill Military Academy. There is a dark moral void at the center of this insurgency. Cadets as young as eight reach for weapons, form a militia, and instigate a pitched standoff with the National Guard in a vain defense of their military identity. Many so value the rank and respect conferred by their uniforms that they would rather die than lose this special status—and many of them, including Cruise's character, later do.

The film's director, Harold Becker, scouted numerous military schools before landing on Valley Forge. Administrators bristled at the plot, but the school was facing dire financial straits, and leadership couldn't easily turn down the $100,000 offered by 20th Century Fox. The shoot itself exposed the decay at the heart of the Forge. "I saw things there that people would say I was satirizing if I had put them into this film," Becker explained during the press tour. He was perhaps alluding to the strife between a pack of cadets and the film's lead, Timothy Hutton. Vic Quarato, a Forge cadet, charged in the local press that Hutton had become "Joe Cool Cadet," assuming the high rank of his character and insisting that real cadets salute him. "Wars broke out over that," he contended. One night after filming, Hutton allegedly got into a spat with a few cadets and called them "faggots." They responded, in turn, by kicking and punching him, causing bruising and swelling bad enough that the production had to rearrange its schedule to allow him to heal.

In his press tour, Hutton strongly cautioned parents from sending youngsters to military school, calling it a "dangerous" environment that forms in children a "distorted sense of reality through an abstract code of honor that has no specific meaning." Cruise was more positive, insisting that schools like the Forge "break you down and then build you up to what they need."

LIKE WESTMORELAND'S BATTLEFIELD INSTRUCTIONS, the tagline for the hard-edged Cold War magazine *Soldier of Fortune* explicitly endorses indeterminate killing. It simply reads: "Kill 'Em All and Let God Sort 'Em Out." The periodical's title itself nods to the killer without a country, a mercenary who will do anyone's bidding so long as the price is right.

The periodical was in some sense a more violent precursor to *Vice* magazine, but controlled by veterans. It launched a few months after the fall of Saigon, in 1975, by Robert Brown, a disaffected former Green Beret known to friends and magazine employees simply as "The Colonel." In his 1994 book *Warrior Dreams: Paramilitary Culture in Post-Vietnam America*, James Gibson writes that the magazine's "position was explicit from the start: the independent warrior must step in to fill the dangerous void created by the American failure in Vietnam." Despite his fringe beliefs, "Colonel" Brown was a product of officer candidate school and, after Vietnam, was invited to lecture on guerrilla warfare and communism at the U.S. Army War College and the Air Force Academy.

Soldier of Fortune, or *SOF* as it was colloquially called, was a far cry from *Boy's Life*, which depicted an earnest, innocent Norman Rockwellian world. The pages of this new magazine were thrumming with an emergent masculine id, one formed largely from the psychological depths of Brown and other damaged Vietnam War veterans. Feeling acutely aggrieved and somewhat dazed by their war's indefinite closure, Brown and his buddies identified new enemies, and salivated over more lethal weapons.

It was during this time that military guns were first marketed to civilians. In 1989, the Department of Alcohol Tobacco and Firearms estimated that as many as three million military-style rifles had hit the streets since the Vietnam War ended. *SOF*'s pages romanticized rapid-fire machine guns and World War II–era pistols, profiled legendary POWs, slapped Rambo on the cover, and provided swashbuckling tales about new Cold War enemies. It told these and other amped-up stories through the magazine's "participatory journalism," a gonzo approach in which the stable of staff writers, many of them veterans, would often provide tactical support and engage in battles. Some served as supplementary forces in Afghanistan to the Mujahideen Islamic fighters battling the Soviet army. "We'd carry guns," Brown explained. "If we were shot at, we shot back."

Much of the magazine's coverage was meant to shame America for getting out of Vietnam early, including a cover story written by Thomas Marks, a West Pointer and *SOF*'s chief foreign correspondent, headlined "Ho Chi Minh City's Living Dead."

It chronicled the experience of Tam Minh Pham, the South Vietnamese West Point cadet nicknamed "Gooky." After graduation, Pham became a TAC officer at the Vietnamese National Military Academy, in Da Lat, which was formed by French colonizers before the Americans took it over. After the fall of Saigon, Pham was targeted for his ties to West Point and the U.S. He was detained by the new government while evacuating the academy, which imprisoned him for nearly six years. Amid the chaos of his arrest, Pham lost his coveted class ring.

Marks's piece reduced Pham down to a casualty of cowardly war planners that prematurely "pulled the plug." His story spoke more to the military's total removal from the aftereffects of war, and its fleeting support for local partners. When Pham contacted his classmates, in 1989, he nodded to this disparity, writing "you must be in pretty much better shape than I am."

ANOTHER OF *SOF*'S STAR WRITERS was a 1979 West Point graduate named Lance Motley. Lance was a particularly hardcore cadet, forming a Tactics Club at the academy before becoming a local legend for ruck sacking in West Point's woods during a category four storm. The school's commandant later found him passed out under a tree.

One of Motley's classmates, Vic Robertson, wrote that Lance was "'hard' to the extreme." Others who knew him recalled that his dad, a Marine Corps sergeant, "was all hard and no soft," and that Lance emulated him to the point that he became "as solid as a tree." Robertson added: "He was never at peace. He was at war with himself, I think, and wanted war as an outlet."

Lance wore his thirst for violence on his sleeve. One plebe who trained under Lance described him as a "menacing terror." Once, during history class, Lance volunteered a solution to discourage new American enemies on the battlefield: put their heads on pikes as a warning. Some saw Lance as an ideal soldier, comparing him favorably to General Patton. Others said he was more like Colonel Kurtz, the cannibalistic madman at the center of *Apocalypse Now*. "He was crazy, he was warped, he was intense, he was single-minded, he was 90 degrees off or 180 out," Robertson observed. "He wanted to kill."

Lance left the Army after his initial five-year commitment because he was bored by the vague peace of the Cold War. He wanted to fight. He found an outlet on the *SOF* masthead, where he visited conflict zones in places like Lebanon, Honduras, Nicaragua, the Philippines, and Guatemala.

His final assignment took him to eastern Burma (now Myanmar), where he embedded with the Karen people, an ethnic group locked in a prolonged civil war for their autonomy. On May 29, 1989, Lance was grievously hit by a mortar round while out with the guerrillas. He died a day later. An official West Point remembrance called him "the genuine thing." It concluded: "For all of his extremism, one has to admire his patriotism, dedication, honesty, and motivations. He lived Duty, Honor, Country." Once Lance's body was recovered from Thailand, he was buried in West Point's cemetery.

Years later, it emerged that Lance's valiant death may have been yet another glossy myth in the miasma of Cold War revisionism. A few years after he died, Kent Shreeve, himself a former Army officer turned freelance journalist, landed in Burma on assignment and heard from sources on the ground that Lance had not died from an incoming Burmese mortar shell, as *SOF* had reported, but instead perished while "trying to show us how to turn an unexploded mortar round into a booby trap and the mortar round blew up on him."

Shreeve reported that the locals made up a story so that Lance could have "a soldier death." It seemed that a soldier's death was all Lance wanted, or perhaps, amid the dark moral void of the American empire, the last noble thing that he felt was guaranteed.

BY THE EARLY 1980s, nearly 200,000 Americans subscribed to *SOF*, and many more were enticed by its themes. Its core readership was eighteen- to thirty-four-year-old white men. Many wore uniforms but couldn't credibly call themselves heroes. This constituency included noncombat veterans, cops, security guards, and guard-dog breeders. The magazine's classified pages offered opportunities to both look the part of a fighter and become one. Inserted next to gun adverts was a notorious classifieds page that sometimes contained thinly coded requests for assassination services.

SOF always operated on the fringes, but it built an influential audience, and its ideas percolated into mainstream pockets of America. Those eager to live the *SOF* lifestyle could visit a popular paintball field opened in the Mojave Desert called Sat Long Village—meaning "Kill Communists" in Vietnamese. Players were given three mock battlefields: Vietnam, Cambodia, or Nicaragua.

Even some Boy Scouts succumbed to this new paramilitary-like strain. In 1980, a bunch of Scouts and Civil Air Patrol cadets, some as young as thirteen, trained on tactics in a swampland site near Houston run by Louis Beam, a decorated Vietnam War helicopter gunner turned Grand Dragon of the Texas Ku Klux Klan. The AP reported that the boys were taught "how to strangle people, decapitate enemies with a machete, and fire semi-automatic weapons."

President Ronald Reagan and some of his top lieutenants also embraced this new mindset, with one Reagan-era CIA officer claiming that the White House seemed stuffed with "an awful lot of *Soldier of Fortune* readers." Reagan deemed Vietnam "the noble cause" and stoked anger among veterans by telling them they had been "denied permission to win." He also said Rambo offered a road map for what to do "next time."

FEW WERE MORE DEEPLY STEEPED in the military educational culture than Oliver North. He was first a Boy Scout, then attended Christian Brothers Military Academy, a high school in upstate New York, before enlisting in an ROTC program at SUNY Brockport. From there, North transferred to the Naval Academy, where he stayed for five years. His extended run there was owed to a terrible car accident North and fellow classmates suffered during their plebe year. It killed the driver and left North in a full-body cast, wracked by serious knee and back injuries. At the time, doctors said he might never walk again.

North went home to recuperate, where, a neighbor recalled, he regained his strength by routinely jumping off the roof of his parents' garage. When he returned to Annapolis, to repeat his plebe year, North still walked with a limp, but he played football and became a competitive boxer who won a string of bouts, including one against Jim Webb, the future Navy secretary who penned the polemic against women in combat.

North was the kind of cadet who liked the academy's rigid structure, an environment, he recalled, where "everybody got up in the morning headed in the same direction." He described the Naval Academy as a mix between a monastery and a prison work camp, one that was tough but created a "protective coating that serves you well in war." North was recalled as a cadet leader who "fried" his fair share of plebes but abstained from the worst abuses. "He wasn't a fanatic like some guys who made you eat bowls of ice cream until you passed out from the cold," one classmate testified.

While North harbored respect for his fellow cadets, he developed a putrid sense of loathing for those outside the gates. "You soon come to understand that most civilians are inferior beings," he said, "whom you can identify first by the length of their hair, and then by the absence of shine on their shoes, the lack of a close shave, and their generally flabby and slovenly appearance."

This sense of superiority muted his own moral code. One night, a fellow midshipman caught him limping in the direction of the academy's personnel office, seeking to remove the medical records of his injuries so that the Marines would deem him "man enough" to serve. His classmate was impressed and let him proceed. When the Marines nonetheless raised concerns over his health post-crash, North played footage of his win over Webb, which helped him secure his commission in June 1968.

North later served on the front lines of Vietnam, where he was uncommonly cool under fire. During his service, he killed numerous enemies and was repeatedly wounded. He came away with two purple hearts, plus silver and bronze stars. But his fidelity to the rules only extended to the sorts of performative customs that are penalized at the academy. Unlike many others, he always wore his flak jacket, always buckled his helmet, always shaved every day. During the Paris Peace Talks, though, he concocted and undertook a highly inappropriate nighttime operation named "Hot Tamale," to find and capture a North Vietnamese soldier serving in the demilitarized zone. Along with his team, North crossed the 18th parallel, saw the guard, shot him in the jaw, and brought him back to base for interrogation. "Don't write home about this," he allegedly told his troops.

North later served as a character witness for his war buddy, Randy Herrod, who had been credibly accused of premeditated murder of five women and eleven children in the Que Son Valley. North had, by this point, returned home to teach tactics to Marines at Quantico, but he paid his way back to Da Nang, where he offered stirring testimony about how Herrod had saved his life after he was wounded in 1969 by rocket fire in Cam Lo. Herrod was ultimately acquitted, thanks largely to North's compelling story.

Two years later, North publicly defended the atrocities committed by American soldiers at My Lai. After that, he served as a character witness for another national security buddy, Thomas Reed, who was accused of securities fraud. (Reed was also acquitted.)

In 1974, North was psychiatrically hospitalized in Bethesda. News reports allege that he was suffering from war trauma and threatened suicide with a .45-caliber service pistol. Whatever the case, North reportedly convinced an officer buddy to scrub these details from his military file. He joined Reagan's national security council in 1981, where he was fixated on Communist foes. He also started to spin his own incredulous legend, inflating his already impressive Vietnam war record, and overstated his planning roles in the invasion of Grenada and the bombing of Libya. When he traveled out of America for work, he assumed an alias: "Mr. Good."

North's most famous misdeed was the Iran-Contra Affair, during which the administration covertly and illegally sold weapons to the Iranian regime to help smooth the release of hostages in Lebanon, then illegally funneled the profits to the brutal right-wing Contra rebel group in Nicaragua. North helped establish the secret channel of funds to the Contras, in defiance of a congressional statute explicitly banning such behavior. He then lied to the press, lied to Congress, and altered and shredded documents, including, perhaps, evidence that he had personally profited from the sales. When the scandal broke, Reagan blamed the press and called North a "hero."

Rather than shun North's alleged law-breaking, the military school establishment rallied around him. In December 1986, some of his Annapolis colleagues from the class of 1968 met for lunch at a motel in Virginia, where they conceived of what would become the Oliver North Legal Assistance Fund. That next August, retired Marine Corps lieutenant general Edward J. Bronars left his post as executive director of the AMCSUS military school association to run the fund.

These leaders raised millions for North's defense and formed a separate trust to provide for his family's security, and other related expenses. As part of all this, they pushed out direct mail and advertisements defending North, including a splashy ad in the *Wall Street Journal* that cast him as a man singularly driven to "rescue hostages, combat terrorism and fight Communism." Their work quickly generated $1 million. As part of his own defense, North derided the investigative journalism that exposed his misdeeds as the slanted work of the "liberal media."

In December 1987, *SOF* featured North on its cover. Inside, they "exclusively" published fifty-seven slides he had presented to Congress on the "Soviet threat" as part of the Iran-Contra hearings. Many slides dwelled on Nicaragua, including one that declared the Soviets viewed the country as "the best opportunity for advancing their cause in the hemisphere."

SOF publisher Robert Brown was also a vocal fan of the Contras, claiming at one point that he had supplied them with one hundred American mercenaries, plus millions of dollars in supplies. In his 2025 essay on *SOF* for *The Baffler*, Caleb Brennan connected the magazine's various causes to current Republican orthodoxy, including their pitched anger in the early aughts about "illegal aliens" on the southern border. *SOF* demanded a military response to this threat, one later realized during NYMA graduate Donald Trump's second term as president.

SOF's defense of North also presaged the successful campaign, launched during Trump's first term, to defend credibly accused war criminals from prosecution through a mixture of crowd-funded lawyers, fearmongering over the enemy, and righteous declarations that brave troops were being prudishly targeted for the routine work of an ugly profession.

When North went on trial, in 1989, prosecutor John W. Keker repeatedly invoked his time at the Naval Academy, contending that his indiscretions were especially remarkable considering he had been thoroughly educated in honor and the rules of warfare. North countered that military regulations are often impractical, and rarely applied, delivering an oblique line that could have been ripped from Rambo: "I had to live within the rules of what I thought was lawful."

Chapter 12

Shit Screen

Some of the sharpest criticism regarding the Iran-Contra scandal came from an unexpected figure: Senate Majority Leader Robert Byrd. If there were anyone to endorse unorthodox, extrajudicial ways to defeat communism it would have seemed to be this good old boy from West Virginia, who had long seen Reds around every corner. As a young man, Byrd was drawn to the Ku Klux Klan by its "fraternal appeal," but also by what he later conceded was its two-pronged exterminationist plan for Black people, and communism. "I felt in those days we were becoming too buddy-buddy with Russia," he recalled.

These twin fears fused into Byrd's worry that the civil rights movement was a Commie plot. He later became a vociferous supporter of the Cold War, first voting in 1964 to authorize the Vietnam War, then working to expand it into Cambodia and Laos. In 1972, Byrd also used his perch as Senate majority whip to gum up congressional attempts at peace with a resolution making the war's defunding contingent on the release of all prisoners of war, and an internationally supervised ceasefire.

The contra rebels that the Reagan administration had covertly armed were crazed anti-Communist commandos fighting to topple Nicaragua's leftist government that had dethroned ruthless dictator (and West Point alumnus) Anastasio Somoza. Byrd nonetheless felt that the government's illegal and clandestine efforts to fund their work was evidence of a deep moral decay. "The White House became a haven for a conspiracy of silence and cover-up fundamentally at odds with our constitutional system of openness and checks and balances," he contended. "The rule of law was flagrantly disregarded, and habits of power inherently undemocratic were fostered and encouraged."

As he searched for the source of this depraved behavior, Byrd landed at the Naval Academy, which hadn't just reared North, but also, Byrd realized, two other principles in Iran-Contra: former national security advisers John M. Poindexter and Robert C. McFarlane. Also involved in the scheme was a West Pointer, Richard Secord, the logistics man for the "Enterprise," the cutout firm that facilitated the Iran-Contra supply chain. This logistics network came to include a ship, planes, and Swiss bank accounts. Millions moved through the Enterprise, mostly for weapons transactions, though it was alleged that Secord dipped into the fund to purchase himself a $32,000 Porsche and a private plane.

Then there was President Reagan, the authority figure for key parts of the affair, who was ordered to active duty in 1942, but because of his poor eyesight, was excluded from combat work. While his real military service was limited, Reagan became intimately familiar with the military honor code thanks to his star turn as a VMI cadet in the 1938 film *Brother Rat*.

Despite his conservative beliefs, Byrd believed deep down that when a country's most elite military graduates "responded to orders that were probably illegal and used shredders to destroy evidence, something is clearly wrong." He pushed hard for answers on the moral curriculum being taught at the service academies, only to run headfirst into a cocksure defense secretary named Dick Cheney, who responded to Byrd's inquiries with a boilerplate report asserting that the honor code was not ailing at all, but, in fact, the "greatest strength" of military schools.

Byrd charged that Cheney's Pentagon "fell far short" of what lawmakers had asked for, concluding that there simply wasn't "a great deal of interest" internally to tackle the problem. Cheney's disinterest may have stemmed, in part, from his old friendship with McFarlane, whose fiftieth birthday Cheney had attended a few years earlier despite simultaneously serving on the House committee investigating Iran-Contra.

Contrary to Cheney's proclamations, however, there was clear evidence that the honor code was ailing, with 90 percent of Naval midshipmen in one 1990 survey describing the prevailing ethical winds on campus as "something is only wrong if you get caught." Byrd felt that military morality could be remedied by empowering the service academies' small band of civilian academics, a generally more independently minded bunch. Several of them were, in fact, at odds with the Naval Academy's dean, Robert Shapiro, who had recently fired the chairman of the Electrical Engineering

Department after he had refused orders to inflate grades. Byrd secured language in the 1990 defense spending bill mandating an overhauled ethics curriculum at the service academies, one that would focus largely on the necessity of civilian-military relations, the proper response to illegal orders, and the misuse of military power.

Three years later, lawmakers floated additional language in their annual defense bill seeking civilian parity with military school faculty. The justification for this proposed shift was simple: to add a "fresh and often provocative world view not bounded by military culture," one informed by "doctoral-level currency and depth." Military brass managed to dilute this proposal, with the final language requiring that military leadership only appoint as many civilians as it "considers necessary."

Byrd hoped these reforms would ensure that the academies would no longer produce Ollie Norths, though one retired general emphasized to me that, internally, these dictates were strenuously opposed. "This is something Congress drugged [the military] into." Publicly, the Naval Academy declined to confront or condemn North during the scandal and imposed a sweeping gag order on faculty and cadets from uttering a word about the infamous alum. Then, in 1991, after North successfully vacated his convictions, Annapolis administrators invited North on campus to promote his new memoir, *Under Fire: An American Story*.

The book is more of North's blustery mythmaking, though there are brief moments of candor, as when he discussed his strained family dynamics. North writes that he was "too busy being the tough guy to see into my own heart." In general, though, North twists himself into knots trying to justify his off-kilter moral compass. "I know the difference between right and wrong, and I can tell good from bad," he writes. "But I also know that the more difficult decisions come when we have to choose between good and better. The toughest calls of all are those we have to make between bad and worse."

This equivocating gobbledygook served as a guiding light for the 750 or so midshipmen who lined up on a chilly December afternoon to buy North's book, and have it signed, in person. Midshipman George Segredo, then nineteen, loudly whooped after taking his picture with North. "A lot of us think what he did was right," Segredo said. "And a lot of us tend to idolize him for that." Twenty-one-year-old Steven Delazaro agreed: "He's been called a hero, and my opinion is that he did what he was supposed to do. I don't think that can be held against him. As an officer in the Marine Corps, you're supposed to do what you're told."

AS BYRD HARPED ON THE ETHICAL FAILINGS of the officer class, he invoked a series of recent hazing incidents, including the torturous tribulations of midshipman Victor-Hugo Vaca Jr. When, in the summer of 1989, the baby-faced nineteen-year-old arrived at the Naval Academy, he had a "Hollywood image of the place," thanks, he said, to *Top Gun* and the saccharine Richard Gere picture *An Officer and a Gentleman*. It wasn't long, however, before Victor-Hugo suffered a plebe's worst fate: being labeled a "shit screen," a vulgar term for someone destined to catch every upperclassmen's grief.

The slang itself was a new coinage, though military academies have, since their invention, assigned certain cadets to the lowest, most humiliating rung on their campus ladder. Many shit screens rightly feel that their designation is conjured arbitrarily, though most do not realize that while they've been deemed worthless, they are essential to the structural integrity of a military hierarchy, and to the ruthless culture of success that permeates the place. The prestige of military promotions is driven by pride and ambition, yes, but also desperate survival instincts to avoid the hacksaw that is hazing. Everyone wants to avoid the sorry fate of the poor saps suffering at the bottom—who help to keep the overall system humming.

Perhaps the most famous shit screen was Oscar Booz, who received his fateful, scarlet letters for flashing sparks of personal independence and insubordination to what he saw as a hypocritical culture. Integrity and personal sovereignty are signature traits that lead to the marker, though there are other routes to it, from simply looking different to making one of a million arbitrary mistakes. Asked by the *Baltimore Sun* what spurred his targeting, Victor-Hugo replied, "I tried to stick up for my rights and that's what got me into trouble. Nobody likes to hear they're wrong, especially from a lowly plebe. They can just back you up against a wall and use the honor system against you."

Once an influential sect of midshipmen had settled on Victor-Hugo as a shit screen, they ordered him to articulate his own worthlessness by referring to himself as "Caca"—a derogatory version of his last name that is Spanish slang for "shit." They would also routinely ask him, "What do you have?"—a question he was expected to answer with: "No redeeming characteristics whatsoever, Sir!" Victor-Hugo painstakingly chronicled his plebe-year abuses in a journal, which ranged from being force-fed to violent threats. One day, an older midshipman swung a pool cue wildly in his direction and declared ominously: "I'd love to bash your head in."

Once Victor-Hugo's parents heard about his abuse, they became acutely concerned for his safety and contacted the school for help. Administrators pledged to handle the matter, but wouldn't say which midshipmen, if any, they counseled, or what, if anything, had been done. The ultimate result of whatever the administration did redounded negatively on Victor-Hugo. Once his tormentors became aware of his family's complaint, their behavior worsened. At one point, a pack of midshipmen surrounded Victor-Hugo in a tight circle, at which point one of them mimicked shooting him through the skull, and another pledged to kill him. He wasn't allowed to eat dinner that night. At the end of his plebe year, Victor-Hugo resigned his commission—a move an academy administrator deemed a "wise decision." The school vaguely stated that his abusers were somehow punished, though all remained aspiring Naval officers.

AT THE EXACT SAME TIME AS VICTOR-HUGO WAS ENDURING his mistreatment, a Valley Forge cadet 130 miles north, Jesse Holland, was also navigating life as a shit screen. When Jesse arrived as a fifteen-year-old plebe, his expectations of military school, like Victor-Hugo's, were shaped by popular culture, in this case the Rambo movies, Arnold Schwarzenegger, and G.I. Joe, whom Jesse dressed up as for Halloween nearly every year.

Jesse alleged that his dad, Christian, often beat him, and his Cub Scoutmaster did, too. Jesse felt deeply ashamed for never fighting back, and he frequently daydreamed of a life in which he could "stand tall and be proud." But aggression simply didn't suit him. His father was performatively aggressive, especially when socializing with his drinking buddies, many of whom were Vietnam veterans. Jesse today reckons that this posturing was a response to his father's shame over the fact that he never served, a shame, it seems, that also drove him to want a hardcore son.

Jesse always tried to meet his dad's high bar. Once, after he won an arm-wrestling match at school, he rushed home and excitedly shared the news with him. Not to be outmanned, pop slapped a $100 bill on the table and told his boy that it was his, should his son beat him. Then he called Jesse's mom into the room to witness the matchup. "Not only did he need to win, he had to pulverize me," Jesse recalled. "I couldn't move my arm for like a week."

There were few stereotypical tropes or talismans associated with American masculinity that Jesse's father didn't embrace. He bought his boy a pocketknife, enlisted him in the Scouts, and took him hunting and fishing. When Jesse caught his first fish, his dad ordered him to yank the hook out of its mouth, an act of disfigurement to the animal Jesse couldn't will himself to perform. "The fish is in agony, and I'm a disaster," he remembered. "I couldn't kill an animal, I didn't have it in me." Jesse had a similar but more visceral experience when, on a pheasant hunt, his dad ordered him to strangle out a bird he had clumsily wounded with buckshot. "The bird wasn't dead, it just couldn't fly," Jesse recalled. "I'm wringing its neck, and it's kicking me and making noises, and I'm doing my best not to burst into tears."

Perhaps Christian's most bizarre and embarrassing gambit occurred on his son's thirteenth birthday, when, in the cadence of a scuzzy nightclub promoter, he told Jesse: "I don't have a gift, but I know this chick who will do anything for $10." Jesse, who felt like his dad was genuinely trying to get him laid by a hooker, froze up. Then he meekly shook his head no. "Oh good, that was just a test," Christian clarified nervously, never to speak of the moment again.

Jesse's parents were in their early twenties when they had him and didn't really know what they were doing. At times, it felt to Jesse like they resented him for interrupting the prime of their lives. Then, at fifteen, they sent him to a place that would nearly destroy him. Schools like the Forge have long advertised themselves, among other things, as a guilt-free option to pawn off a boy, a place "to clean up my parents' mess," in Jesse's words, and make him a man. "My parents didn't want to go that deep into me, or them, or us," he told me. "It was so much safer and more comfortable to have a relationship at a distance."

On the late-summer day in 1988 when Jesse was dropped off and made a plebe, the Forge looked like a well-honed masculine breeding ground. He was excited. Weeks later, he informed his folks in a letter that it had all been a mirage. "The minute you left they broke out the whips and chains," he wrote, comparing his experience thus far to "a party in hell."

For most plebes, the devilish deeds eventually end, and the cadets graduate into the upper ranks, rewarded with status, power, and a vengeful path to heal their old wounds by imparting fresh ones on a new round of plebes. Not Jesse, who was a prime target for the older boys, physically weak and emotionally vulnerable. "I was scared of my own shadow," he told me. Many of the upperclassmen, by contrast, were first-wave gym rats, and some, according to Jesse, were using steroids. "They were monsters," he recalled.

Early in his plebe year, a couple older cadets beat him up in the gym, though most of their bullying was mental—messing up his room, screaming at him, and refusing to promote him within the cadet-run hierarchy. At first, Jesse tried to make the best of his bad situation. In letters home, he reported getting "a lot skinnier" and "a lot stronger." He was performing well academically, too. While he wasn't promoted within the cadet-run corps, teachers recognized his smarts with a red star pin that declared him a "meritorious student."

When Jesse returned home for fall break, however, his low rank didn't register with his parents. In his military parade uniform, Jesse cut the figure of a war hero, and his dad was thrilled, trotting him out repeatedly in full get-up to a nearby Italian restaurant, fittingly called Liberty, to show him off. "I was a piece of shit, and now I'm somebody," Jesse thought over bites of spaghetti. "I'm the golden boy."

Jesse's powerful if fleeting feelings of pride were enough to make his freshman year bearable. When he returned to the Forge for year two, he anticipated finally earning some respect. He was no longer a plebe, but an "Old Man," in campus parlance, who had paid his dues, and was surely on a path to success. "I can't make any promises," he wrote his parents at the beginning of his third semester. "But, as usual, I will try my best!"

Jesse's hopes were dashed weeks later, when he entered the Forge's "Old Man" lounge only to have an upperclassman quip, "Who let the plebe in here?" That night, a pack of tormentors trashed his room. Jesse was the latest in a long line of shit screens whose party in hell would seemingly never end.

Part of what was so frustrating about these conditions was that Jesse saw no clear path out of them. He was working hard, following the rules, enduring the pain. Meanwhile, hellions and rulebreakers were being promoted. Some of their parents, Jesse told me, were donors.

When, finally, Jesse was promoted, it was to a demoralizing position. "I was made the lance corporal of the fucking janitor's closet. I wasn't doing anything except all the shit work." Around this time, he started losing focus in class, and his grades plummeted. "I felt like I was in hell," Jesse said, "and all I wanted to do was get out." At one point, he wrote a letter to his dad begging to be picked up and brought home, but then he crumpled it up and threw it in the trash. "I couldn't face being vulnerable and being weak and being rejected."

One day, when he was cleaning the broom closet, a Black cadet started teasing him and called him a "honky," a softly derogatory term for white people. "I snapped and said something to the effect of, 'You should be back here. You should be the slave.' So, then he goes and tells one of the other African-American students, who was a star football player, and huge. And he came down and humiliated me in front of everybody and I was crying, and it was ugly and messy." At one point, the football player punched Jesse in the chest, then, when Jesse didn't punch back, called him a "pussy."

A few nights later, Jesse took out the pocketknife his dad had gifted him and starting crudely cutting his wrist. "The blade was dull, and it was a painful, protracted process. And because it was so dull, I couldn't really hit any veins. And I was just like, 'I can't believe I'm a failure at this, too. I can't even get this right.' So, finally, I gave up and went downstairs, and the barracks commander was in his office, just by chance. And I'm crying and I'm holding a knife and I have a bloody arm."

Jesse was rushed to a nearby hospital, where his wounds were bandaged and he was placed in a psychiatric unit for a few weeks. When his parents first arrived at his bedside they were supportive, but then his dad made an ugly proclamation: "We wouldn't be in this mess if my son wasn't always feeling sorry for himself." At this point, Jesse remembers, "it was kind of the end of me being his son."

On October 31, 1989, Jesse articulated his wrenching isolation in a poem published by the *Bryn Mar Hospital Psych News*, a weekly digest "by patients for patients." It reads:

> *Leave me alone.*
> *What do you care?*
> *Mind your own business,*
> *Get out of my hair.*
> *If I wanted you to know,*
> *I would have whispered your name,*
> *I close up for a reason,*
> *It's my personal game.*

A few months later, Jesse, now sixteen, returned to his local public high school in South Brunswick, New Jersey. He was still reserved, but in a new way, one tinged with anger, hardness, and resentment. His classmates were impressed. From then, Jesse understood that he could use his time at military school "as some sort of mystique."

He ultimately went to great ends to maintain this status. After high school, Jesse attempted to join the Army but was disqualified because of his suicide attempt. He then went to community college and tried to join the Marines, but, he recalled, they had met their quotas for the year and declined to offer him an enlistment waiver. From here, he signed up again for the Army via ROTC, but this time he lied on his forms about his mental health crisis and was initially accepted. He thrived in this program, but his paperwork moved slowly, and, when he turned twenty-three, ROTC ruled him out. He was too old.

From here, Jesse transformed into a hollow simulacrum of a soldier, taking jobs "as long as there was a badge." First, he tried to become a cop, then worked as a bouncer, where he became jacked and often got into fights, only to feel ugly afterward. He also spent years in the security industry, including stints at several of Trump's Manhattan properties. Still, he felt empty. "You could have put a mannequin at the front desk," he explained. "It wouldn't have mattered."

Once, while working security, Jesse had an emotionally clarifying moment, nabbing a kid who had been goaded by his friends into stealing. After hearing this, Jesse saw parts of himself in the boy. "This kid had a complete and utter breakdown, because this was not who he was, and he regretted not being strong enough to resist."

Jesse eventually stopped chasing badges, but still he couldn't shake his thirst for service. At the gym, he sometimes wore an Army T-shirt. "I was doing a stolen valor shtick," he admitted with a sharp sigh. Once, when someone asked if he served, he lied and told him that he had been in Mogadishu. "Immediately after I said it, I regretted it," he said. "I thought about the real people who died there."

Three and a half decades after his suicide attempt, Jesse still thinks about Valley Forge a lot. The bathroom in his New Jersey condo features the towel and laundry basket the school issued him. His old uniform also hangs in his closet, and most of his computer passwords include some play on the school's name. Now in his early fifties, Jesse can see that he spent his youth "chasing something that wasn't me." I asked him if he would enlist today should the military bend their age and mental health rules, and Jesse immediately responded "Yes."

"Maybe," he reasoned, his thirst for hero status and martial glory "hasn't died." He paused. "It's still present," he told me. "But I don't know why."

A FEW MONTHS AFTER JESSE ATTEMPTED SUICIDE, four older Valley Forge cadets were arrested and charged with beating two fifteen-year-old cadets under their command. One of the tormented teens, Ryan Dever, told the *Philadelphia Inquirer* that older cadets had thrown darts at him and another boy, shot at them with a BB gun, and beaten them with wire hangers and lacrosse sticks. He also said that he had been personally forced to massage upperclassmen or face beatings, and that a cadet had snuck into his room at night and assaulted him. Another cadet claimed that, rather than simply giving demerits, upperclassmen would "hit you." Administrators denied these allegations, while the local cops downplayed the problems on campus. "I've been here 32 years and I've never seen any major problems," a local police superintendent told the *Inquirer*.

Once these allegations hit the paper, however, many parents freaked out, and, virtually overnight, the Forge saw a 23 percent drop in enrollment. The school responded by hiring a new superintendent, retired Navy admiral N. Roland Thunman, who pledged to assess the school from "stem to stern." In September 1990, Thunman announced that he was eliminating hazing, in large part by imposing twenty-four-hour supervision over the middle schoolers. "I believe we can turn it around," he told the *Inquirer* in September 1990. "This is a fine school."

And yet at the same time, Thunman slashed the school budget, harming academics, supervision, and everything in between. During his first year, two of the four cadets charged in the criminal hazing ring returned to the Forge. One of them regained his senior rank, and the power that went along with it.

Weeks after Thunman's announcement, West Point followed suit, dramatically pledging that hazing would be abolished entirely. In its coverage of the academy's announcement, the *Los Angeles Times* suggested that its current hazing culture was tame, even academic, a series of hokey and harmless traditions far more elevated than the "mistreatments piled on unlucky civilian college fraternity pledges." Plebes were expected to memorize how many ice cubes go in the drinks of upperclassmen, the paper reported. Every morning, they also studied the academy's acceptable news organ, *The New York Times*, and were expected to repeat articles verbatim.

West Point has perennially pledged to eliminate hazing, but never put the final nail in the coffin. In the wake of the Civil War, West Point's superintendent deemed hazing "essentially criminal" and a "vicious and illegal indulgence," but did little to meaningfully address it. In 1901, following the death of Oscar Booz, the academy first "abolished" hazing, but nothing really changed. When hazing faced renewed public scrutiny in the 1950s and '60s, former Vietnam War chieftain and then-superintendent William Westmoreland pledged to impose "enlightened discipline." In 1977, another West Point superintendent, Andrew Goodpaster, said somewhat abstrusely that he would abolish plebe "abuse," estimating that "we've just about got it eliminated, and we won't let up."

In 1874, Congress technically outlawed hazing at the Naval Academy, but abuse continued to fester. A patchwork of state and federal bans emerged over the following century, but they were rarely enforced, especially in a military context. When, in 1987, South Carolina passed its own anti-hazing law, it explicitly exempted military training. Six years later, this law led hazing charges to be dropped against two Citadel cadets who were accused of beating, kicking, and pulling the chest hair from a pair of plebes.

The stark contrast of these many military figures talking tough on hazing while, in practice, offering unwavering leniency shows that the brass has forever seen harsh physical and psychological contact as indispensable to their formula for success in turning boys into men. While often blamed on coarse forms of youthful transgression, hazing and hierarchy are, as writer Elizabeth Schambelan argues in *N+1*, "a violent resocialization that better equips young men to wield privilege, put down challenges to existing hierarchies, and police the status quo."

WEST POINT'S TRUMPETED 1990 DECISION TO RESTATE its perennial pledge to outlaw hazing was likely meant to preempt the blow of a coming report on military school abuse from the Government Accountability Office (GAO). It was also a reflection of changing cultural mores, and attendant admissions problems that were afflicting the entire military schooling system.

Staff at Norwich University, founded in 1819 by Sylvanus Thayer's nemesis Alden Partridge, were then grumbling that the baby boomers had molded Generation X in their image. "We're dealing with a whole generation of parents from the 60's who were anti-war and antimilitary and are now rearing their children that way," one school official vented. A by-product of this kinder, gentler parenting phenomenon was West Point cadet John Edward, who ranked in the top 5 percent of his class, but, as a senior cadet, in 1988, was dismissed for refusing to engage in the plebe hazing system. His stand caused reflection from at least one West Point elder, a 1943 graduate and former assistant secretary of state for Kennedy, Roger Hilsman, who told the *Houston Chronicle* that the plebe system "brought out the worst of sadists."

As a more holistic child-rearing mindset took hold, Culver Military Academy, in Ohio, responded by recasting their programs as "military with a small m." Culver's dean, Ralph Manuel, a former administrator at Thayer's alma mater, Dartmouth, pitched his programs as a positive countervailing force to "the Me-Generation and to self-indulgence." He predicted a post-hippie cultural realignment, contending that Culver's ranks included many "children of the flower children."

When the GAO report dropped, in November 1992, it severely undercut West Point's sunny PR promises made two years earlier. It found that hazing on military school campuses was far more rampant than top officials let on. It also reported that senior school officials rarely punished cadets appropriately, given that federal regulations justified expulsion. Instead, cadets were often slapped with minor charges and retained. Accountability was especially lax at Oliver North's alma mater, the Naval Academy, which hadn't secured a single hazing conviction between 1986 and 1990.

The GAO estimated that the most common forms of hazing were verbal, but found evidence of physical abuse, too, including "dunking fourth class students in toilets, using physical restraints, covering fourth class students with shaving cream or other substances, or spraying them with water." The watchdog uncovered cases of physical assault and monthslong harassment campaigns, plus the persistence of the infamous "white tornado," wherein a plebe rapidly consumed everything on their mess hall table, including condiments.

Most damning was the GAO's conclusion that "the typical offender is not a renegade or sadist, but rather a highly committed and strongly motivated high performer." Hazing, in other words, was part and parcel of school success. In the rare cases when prolific hazers were hauled before disciplinary hearings, records showed that their case files often included "strong endorsements from their officers and faculty that they be retained."

The GAO found, too, that contrary to military orthodoxy, the stressors imposed on cadets were unhelpful. Quite critically, they didn't emulate the pressures of active-duty service. Far from being the glue that bonded the cadets together, hazing was also correlated to higher rates of "physical and psychological stress symptoms, lower grade point averages, more frequent thoughts about leaving the academy, and lower motivation toward making the service a career."

Academy administrators had been shown ample evidence of the negative consequences of this stress, including a 1988 inspector general report that derived "very little" positive leadership development value in the plebe system. A year after that, the Bethesda Naval Hospital's Psychiatry Department reported that a plebe's debilitating headaches were the result of hazing stress. More than 50 percent of cadets at the Army and Air Force academies similarly reported to the GAO that they suffered "frequent symptoms of psychological distress."

This anxiety could emerge from intense hazing, or simply the school's frenetic schedule. "I have had eighteen-year-olds in my office sobbing because they can't devote the time they'd like to their studies," one Naval Academy professor told the GAO. "These are kids who were valedictorians, and they come here and are told to memorize menus." Another West Point cadet testified, "we usually have to blow off homework so that we can shine shoes, etc. It is better to get a D- than to be hazed by an upperclassman."

The Pentagon vehemently disagreed with the GAO's findings. They insisted that hazing did not occur more frequently than the small number of officially charged cases. They further defended their policies and promised only modest changes. Crucially, they also declined to create reprisal protections for those who brought issues forward. A separate GAO report from this time detailed a persistent lack of oversight for the service academies, revealing that neither the Pentagon nor the Board of Visitors "has conducted regular, systematic, comprehensive management reviews of academy costs and operations or the performance of academy graduates."

Whatever academic and administrative failures these schools were grappling with, they were largely succeeding in spawning a hard-edged belief among male cadets that pain was good for the soul. "We are the last of a dying breed," one Air Force Academy cadet told the GAO. "Please, leave us alone, look away, and let the tradition continue." Another cadet called for West Point to "get rid of politically correct leftists [*sic*] influence and focus more on hardening its cadets for war." Added a third: "We should be about warfare preparation, not sensitivity training." As these schools were increasingly challenged, their air of nobility partially lost its power, and leaders embraced base instincts. As hazing allegations piled up at the Forge, for instance, a school spokesperson explained that a philosophical cornerstone of the academy was teaching cadets "not to be intimidated by anyone."

A few months later, retired lieutenant general Willard Scott Jr., the president of the AMCSUS military school association, complained to *The Cincinnati Enquirer* that military school leaders "resent" the fact that their programs were being cast so harshly. You would think these places were prisons, Scott griped, but he clarified, "there are no bars on [the windows]."

WHEN, IN 2011, MARK JONES FIRST ARRIVED at the Columbia Correctional Institution, in Tampa, Florida, he noticed uncanny similarities to his alma mater. "When I got to prison," he told me, "I said, my goodness, this is just a watered-down version of West Point."

Both institutions enforce a set of rules meant to produce conformity. Both have a mandated uniform. Both also share a volatile social hierarchy. In Mark's estimation, West Point's culture is more intense than that in his prison, where the wardens and others in power simply aren't "as disciplined."

Mark's childhood in Marlton, New Jersey, had been highly regulated by his father, Lewis, an exacting FBI agent who served the bureau for three decades. He set strict rules for Mark and his brother, Robert, and would often activate his investigative skills to enforce them. If Mark took the car out late, for instance, his dad would root around in it the next morning, searching for contraband. When Mark was left home alone for a weekend, Lewis would later gather and interview his friends, probing for evidence of hijinks.

Mark respected his father's rules because he respected his father's moral compass. Lewis believed deeply in freedom, liberty, due process, and justice, and he had risked his life enforcing these principles. Over a storied career, he had investigated spies, bankers, and, during a particularly gnarly assignment in Georgia, the Ku Klux Klan, a mission where he had a shotgun pulled on him.

Mark was a Boy Scout, an athlete, and a big believer in public service. For years, he harbored dreams of being a high school math teacher and football coach. But he was seized with patriotism watching the Gulf War play out on the television. After that, his brother Robert went to West Point to play football. When the family first visited campus for a game, Mark was bowled over by its atmosphere. "All the ritualism and camaraderie was overwhelmingly impressive, a whole different ambiance," he told me. "I was intimidated by it, but I thought it was a good thing, I thought there was a reason for all of it. At that time, I wanted to be part of it."

At nineteen, Mark followed in his brother's footsteps, arriving at West Point for Beast Barracks in the summer of 1992 with a spot on the football team. It had been two years since West Point had nominally abolished hazing, two years since school leaders pledged to "remove stress" from cadet life. But all Mark saw were cosmetic changes.

West Point had recently rebranded their initiation rites as the "Cadet Leader Development System," what one brigadier general boasted was "the most coherent and progressive system of overall leader development ever established at West Point." Gone was Thayer's cruel and simplistic leadership triangle, replaced by a convoluted military chart featuring arrows and buzz words that all coalesce into one big channel representing "Duty, Honor, Country."

Despite the rebrand, Mark found that the classic stressors were all still there. He objected less to their intensity and more to how unnecessary they felt in service of building leaders. "I would often question things at West Point," he explained. He was especially vocal about his treatment on the football team. "It wasn't about developing me as a person, it was just a bunch of bully stuff," he said.

The team has long enjoyed universal reverence on campus, which has translated to special perks and administrative deference. Players have historically spearheaded their own intense initiation rituals, some of which involved heavy drinking and violent subjugation. Mark emerged from some team bonding events with fractured ribs and concussions. "It was bad, the kind of treatment where I lost consciousness multiple times," he said. On numerous occasions, he was secured to an immovable object and beaten in the head. "I didn't come here for this garbage," he told himself, and repeatedly raised issues to the coaching staff, including a future NFL coach. They did nothing, Mark said.

Meanwhile, players got wise to Mark's disclosures and sought to stop them. One night at around 2 a.m., a drunken teammate banged on Mark's dorm room door until he opened it, then tried to intimidate him into silence. On two other occasions, after practice, teammates surrounded Mark in the locker room and imposed brutish hazing practices. Decades later,

Mark still won't detail exactly what happened, saying only that he experienced acts of intense sexual abuse that he still hasn't fully recovered from.

In the aftermath of this torture, Mark became wildly anxious, struggled with memory issues, and was frequently haunted by nightmares. Often only alcohol could put him to sleep. Certain things that triggered his abuse—like the smell of cleaning chemicals or the din of loud voices in an echoey space—made him unspool entirely. Mark's dad had always preached the virtue of commitment, and so Mark stayed on the team for part of another season. At some point, though, he couldn't handle it anymore and quit West Point altogether. For years, he didn't tell his family why.

The year that Mark would have graduated—1996—the football team quietly adopted a new motto: "God Forgives, Brothers Don't." Whether the team knew it or not, their new phrase had been originally coined by a neo-Nazi crime syndicate in Texas known as the Aryan Brotherhood. It was their omertà code. Just as Army football borrowed the brotherhood's menacing tagline, the Texas gang adopted a stringent military-style chain of command, complete with soldiers, captains, and generals. Both organizations also cultivated loyalty by ferociously punishing insubordination.

After Mark washed out of West Point, he landed at West Virginia University, where he got an undergraduate degree in statistics, then a master's in industrial engineering. Then he got married. At the same time, he developed a nasty drinking problem to cope with his undiagnosed PTSD. Some nights Mark ventured into the woods to sleep because it felt safer there. One day, Mark's mother told him she had started to see him fall into "your dark place," and wondered what was bringing him there. Still, he wouldn't say.

Mark's marriage quickly fell apart, and he racked up a string of petty theft charges that culminated in 2010, with his imprisonment for stealing a drill from Home Depot. In prison, he was paired with a counselor, who linked him to care at the Department of Veterans Affairs, which ultimately diagnosed him with PTSD.

Once he was out, Mark went into a VA treatment program, in Orlando, but he got into trouble for drinking and was unable to secure a bed at an intensive impatient program in Bay Pines. "I feel like I am being thrown aside," he told a counselor at the time. A few months later, on a hot June afternoon in 2011, he was blindingly drunk in the parking lot of a Publix Grocery store in Altamonte Springs, Florida. At some point, he leaned into the rolled-down car window of a sixty-nine-year-old woman, grabbed her by the arms, and demanded her car keys. He was unarmed, but physically imposing. She screamed, and he quickly left her alone. Later that day, though, Mark was arrested and charged with attempted carjacking. As cops drove him to jail, Mark told them, "I'm a freak show, man."

He was found guilty and will now sit behind bars for the rest of his life without the possibility of parole, thanks to Florida's notorious two strikes law, one of the strictest sentencing statutes in America. The woman he grabbed has publicly stated that Mark's fate is far too severe, but that hasn't mattered. Neither has the fact that Mark has shown himself to be an excellent inmate, a law clerk at the prison library who takes various vocational classes, works out, and prays. The only option at this point is clemency, and Florida governor Ron DeSantis, himself a former Navy lawyer, has shown a general aversion to granting such requests.

Mark directly attributes his path to imprisonment to West Point. "At that age you're developing your identity, who you are as a person, and when something rocks your personal security like that it's devastating," he said. "It's bends and shapes your life." He's relying on his Christian faith for light, as well as on his second wife, Rose, who makes the three-hour drive from their Orlando home every month to visit him. Both of his parents have died since Mark was incarcerated, but he still holds close the words of his dad, who, shortly after he was imprisoned, said, "You can handle this, son."

"I'm severely disillusioned by the fact that I'm so cynical now," he told me. "I look at what these places take, you know—young, bright minds—and then you go to cadet basic training, and it's designed to break you down and build you back up. Well, I was built already. I didn't need to be broken down. I didn't want to be formed and molded in your image. I was an adult. I was raised by a decent family. I knew what I felt was right and wrong, and I knew what my goals and aspirations were, so I wasn't looking for that. But that's the design."

Before the time on our crackly prison call expires, Mark makes sure to clarify his abiding respect for the military. "I'm not one of those guys that serve in the Army and comes back with a lot of animosity. I feel like it's still an honorable institution. The actions of a few people aren't going to ruin it." His enduring loyalty is embodied by a decorative West Point mug that proudly sits on the mantel in his living room, a place Mark hasn't kicked back in for years.

Chapter 13

Strange Love

Smack dab in the middle of the Naval Academy's breezy, coastal campus stands an erect, twenty-one-foot obelisk honoring William Lewis Herndon, a fallen Navy commander. Every spring, the statue is coated in two hundred pounds of creamy white Crisco. The monument is then enveloped by a writhing pyramid of plebes. Shoeless and often shirtless, they crush their bodies against the cool granite and each other, rushing to scale the slippery statue and place a sailor's cap on its tip. The fastest recorded time belongs to the class of 1972, which climbed the obelisk in less than two minutes, albeit without the impediment of shortening. Since the advent of grease, the climb usually takes at least two hours.

The Navy pitches this rite of passage as one in which climbing cadets come to embody the spirit of Herndon who, in 1857, helped save the lives of 152 women and children when his boat became caught in a hurricane. After sending up a distress flag and facilitating tricky evacuations onto a rescue vessel, Herndon ultimately went down with the ship. In so doing, he was, as his monument notes, "forgetful of self"—an instinct that the military rears and relies on.

The Herndon climb is today considered a dazzling spectacle of teamwork, determination, and core military grit, one meant to reinforce the military's expectations that service members commit all of themselves to the mission. "Captain Herndon's story is one of bravery," academy superintendent Yvette Davids remarked during the 2024 climb. "And one that says fight to the end."

While the climb is today heralded as the ultimate test of core battlefield tenets, the tradition was originally born through the release of pent-up sexual energy. The obelisk is located on what was once called "Love Lane," a yard at the academy where, before the school became co-ed, was one of the few places where, on Sundays, male midshipmen could fraternize with women. For decades, Love Lane was only available for upperclassmen. When, at the end of their first year, plebes finally earned the right to stroll the lane and flirt, they started the tradition of swarming around the monument in celebration. By 1940, the year cited as the origin of the climb, the festivities had evolved into a long awkward shimmy up the granite phallus.

Since 1976, when the Naval Academy became co-ed, women have partaken in the climb, too, though nearly all the plebes who have placed the cap on top of the monument have been male—a record prized and preserved by the men, who generally shunt the women to supportive roles, at the monument's base.

At once a showcase of old school manliness and a vivid display of homosocial bonding, the climb and other traditions like it are intended to foster loyalty and cohesion—transforming fresh-faced recruits into a tribe, boys into men, with the girls given tertiary positions. The climb also nods to the military's tight regulation of intimacy and emotion, aiming to harness these strong forces lest they get out of control.

Many have stereotyped the Navy, and its jurisdictional partner, the Marines, as the two most homoerotic service branches. Naval service, in particular, offers an especially romantic allure to disillusioned or dislocated people, queer or otherwise, offering an escape, on a boat, far out to sea. Recounting his experiences in the British Navy, the flamboyantly gay raconteur Quentin Crisp once theorized that "perhaps the act of running away to sea was an abandonment of accepted convention." Many join the military to escape a bad life, or prying eyes, with one pithy Navy adage declaring that "it's only queer if you're tied to the pier." Crisp crassly observed that "after a strange sojourn in strange ports," many sailors return with "their outlook, and possibly their anus, broadened." The added benefit was that one could explore an alternative lifestyle, while, in the estimation of one Marine, still enjoying the military's patented "guise of masculinity." Others, like Adam Schuman, hoped the Naval Academy would be genuinely transformative, a "military conveyor belt," in his words, "where I'd come out straight at the end."

Some of the most colorful military initiation rites originated on Naval ships, from tattoos and nipple piercings to what's called "Crossing the Line," a ceremony in which young sailors, after traversing the equator for the first time, are subjected to sadomasochistic party games. The night before this ritual, ships would often throw bawdy talent shows in drag. The next day, sailors would get naked and hose each other down. Sometimes there would be simulated anal and oral sex. Young "wogs" were also made to suck olives out of the belly button of the ship's fattest chief petty officer.

Then there's the Herndon climb, a land-locked, very public ritual at the academy that trains officers for both the Navy and the Marines. Queer outlets sometimes cover the extravaganza, with one headline reading: "Here Are 10 Sexxxy Not-Safe-For-Work Pictures of Navy Boys Climbing a Greasy Obelisk, And Now You Are Gay." Navy and Marine archetypes break down semi-neatly across various queer groupings—tops and bottoms, beards and twinks, with seamen seen as the sweeter, more gentle folks, while Marines are more macho and aggressive, according to author Steven Zeeland, who interviewed scores of queer troops for his three books untangling homoerotic subcultures across the military. One gay graduate of the Naval Academy told me that Marines had far higher rates of internalized homophobia, desperate to make love to a sailor while also calling them out for their "faggoty white uniforms."

Other anecdotal evidence has long bolstered these stereotypes. Many early gay American havens were formed in port towns, and many early gay models, it seems, had previously served. In an old interview, the editors of *Physique Pictorial*, a queer gentleman's magazine founded in 1951, remarked that a lion's share of their subjects came from the Navy and the Marines. Decades later, the military's extensive testing data for HIV antibodies showed the Navy with the highest positivity rate. In 2015, the RAND Corporation conducted the first-ever estimate of the military's LGBT population. Their results further corroborated the old cliché, with the Navy reporting the largest share of queer service members of any service branch. The outsized presence of queer seamen has created two powerful but contradictory forces: a significant underground culture and an intense fixation and fear of gayness, one that has spread throughout the military, leading the men in charge to strictly, and sometimes violently, police love, intimacy, and manhood.

THE MILITARY'S ESPECIALLY PRIMITIVE EQUATION of gayness and softness motivates young recruits to ardently prove their straightness but also punish peers who deviate from the norm. In his 1995 book *Sailors and Sexual Identity*, Zeeland details troops ceaselessly jockeying to be labeled the most homophobic of their bunch, all operating within a reward structure where "being acknowledged as less gay . . . is more warrior-like." In his memoir *Honor Bound*, Joseph Steffan, a brilliant Naval Academy midshipman expelled weeks before his 1987 graduation after disclosing his own homosexuality, writes of a close friend naturally prone to sensitivity and kindness, only to lash out against these instincts anytime someone publicly pointed them out with a "stream of searing profanities or a quick punch to the shoulder." Years later, when a West Point cadet created and circulated a PowerPoint presentation titled the "Class of 2000 Homo Factor Report," it was not intended to out actual gay people but instead zeroed in on the cadet companies that had the fewest number of graduates headed to the studly world of combat arms. A decade later, members of West Point's rugby team operated an email chain rife with showy heterosexual posing, as when one player allegedly "headbutted a dude over thanksgiving and broke the fags [*sic*] nose after he tried to stop [said cadet] from hitting on a girl."

The actual rooting-out of suspected homosexual behavior in the military was similarly theatrical and cruel. Joseph Steffan, for his part, was wracked with anxiety over being outed, knowing full well that it would fatally compromise his career, but also that it could result in serious bodily harm. He had heard tell of two male midshipmen caught together in bed a year before his arrival; they were dragged from their rooms by fellow midshipmen, wrapped in blankets, and senselessly beaten. Many years earlier in 1919, the Navy launched an intense but sexually confused dragnet campaign at a training center in Rhode Island, with admirals ordering putatively straight sailors to entrap "queers" by having sex with them.

As Zeeland sees it, homoerotic dynamics—positive and negative, latent and overt—pervade military life. "A desire to be in close quarters with other military men in a tightly knit brotherhood might be homosexual," he writes. "Navy initiation rituals involving cross-dressing, spanking, simulated oral and anal sex, simulated ejaculation, nipple piercing, and anal penetration with objects or fingers might be homosexual. An officer's love for his men might be homosexual. The intimate buddy relationships men form in barracks, aboard ships, and most especially in combat—often described as being a love greater than between man and woman—might be homosexual—whether or not penetration or ejaculation ever occur."

A more family-friendly analysis emerged in a July 1993 *Newsweek* cover story headlined: "Homoeroticism in the Ranks." The piece noted obvious military regulations with homoerotic undercurrents, like shared bathrooms, showers, and sleeping quarters in the barracks, plus the service's long history of drag shows. One scholar quoted by *Newsweek*, citing military hazing rituals like paddling, declared that the Pentagon had a special fixation on "the male buttocks."

The magazine piece was published just as President Bill Clinton entered office with a sweeping mandate to support the cause of gay service members. Clinton was the first American politician to champion gay issues, helping stitch this vital constituency into the Democratic Party tent. He made his pledge in part to support his old friend David Mixner, a gay man and powerhouse organizer.

The two men had first connected in 1969. Mixner was then a rising figure in the anti-war movement, his activism fueled by the four family members he lost in Vietnam. Mixner worked as a young aide on Eugene McCarthy's 1968 presidential campaign and was beaten by police on the streets of Chicago during the convention. The next year, he became one of the four national co-chairs for the Moratorium to End the War in Vietnam.

Clinton was then a young Rhodes Scholar awed by the anti-war movement's tactics and power. He spent a summer working for the cause in Washington, D.C., crashing on Mixner's couch. Clinton then helped with a satellite protest against the war in London. He had personally avoided Vietnam through two educational draft deferments. Then, when the law changed, and he received his draft notice, Clinton leveraged his connections to join the ROTC at the University of Arkansas, which newly allowed him to avoid the war and return to Oxford.

After the war ended, Mixner turned his attention to gay rights, organizing closely with the pioneering San Francisco gay activist Harvey Milk, who, in the early 1950s, served on Navy rescue submarines before being discharged due to his sexual orientation. In 1976, Mixner helped launch the Municipal Elections Committee of Los Angeles, the first gay and lesbian political action committee in the country. When, two years later, Californians faced a ballot measure to bar gay men and lesbians from working in public schools, Mixner organized like hell, and defeated it, largely by successfully convincing then-governor Ronald Reagan to vocally oppose it. Also included on Mixner's roster of victories is the U.S. Senate re-election campaign of Virginia Democrat Charles Robb who, thanks to Mixner's effective organizing, defeated Oliver North in a 1994 race, one in which North fearmongered over Robb's support of openly gay service members.

When Clinton first sought Mixner's help in his 1992 run for president, his old friend was skeptical, noting to the Arkansas governor that, on the topic of queer advocacy, "you have no public record to speak of." Mixner had been betrayed by his fair share of politicians, including Reagan, who, as president in 1982, instituted the government's first formal ban on gay service members. (Its implementation further confirmed the Navy's especially strong queer subculture: while the branch accounted for just 27 percent of the armed forces, it experienced 51 percent of all discharges for homosexuality.)

Clinton asked Mixner what he desired, and his old activist friend made two simple requests: a Manhattan Project–style initiative to fight AIDS and the repeal of the federal ban on gays in the military. Clinton assured Mixner it would be done, then boldly announced to America's gay community that he would deliver on their agenda. "I won't be in the closet on this issue," he pledged.

The election was gearing up to be the first in which issues important to gay and lesbian voters were receiving major attention. All five candidates in the Democratic presidential primary endorsed a repeal of the ban on gays in the military, and the official party platform prioritized the repeal, alongside AIDS research and a gay and lesbian civil rights bill.

After initially pledging not to hire homosexuals for any government jobs, independent presidential candidate Ross Perot, himself a Naval Academy graduate and keen barometer of public opinion, reversed his position, albeit cryptically, promising to hire based on "merit."

Incumbent president George H.W. Bush offered a more muddled message. Rather than demonize gays outright, Bush stressed the importance of "family values," while campaign surrogates disparaged Clinton and his running mate, Al Gore, as "pretty boys." On the sidelines of the Republican National Convention, First Lady Barbara Bush wore the red AIDS ribbon, but took it off before joining her husband at the podium. Gay activists at the convention reported being shut out of policy meetings and ridiculed on the convention floor. Some claimed they were Bush's "new Willie Horton." In his convention speech, neoconservative firebrand Pat Buchanan derided Clinton as a "militant leader of the homosexual rights movement," while pastor Pat Robertson, a key conduit to evangelicals, explicitly condemned Clinton's pledge to open the military up to gays.

Clinton's political bet, however, turned out to be the right one. Queer voters responded with overwhelming hope and energy in the 1992 election, defeating discriminatory ballot measures and electing openly gay and lesbian judges, lawmakers, and other local officials across the country. They also fueled Clinton's win. One exit poll found that 89 percent of openly gay and lesbian voters broke for him. Mixner and other activists were also able to raise millions for Clinton from affluent gay donors. "This is a rite of passage for the gay and lesbian movement," Urvashi Vaid, the executive director of the National Gay and Lesbian Task Force, excitedly declared in the afterglow of Clinton's win. "For the first time in our history, we're going to be full and open partners in the government."

THE MILITARY, HOWEVER, STILL OPENLY CAST homosexuality as a plague. Two years before Clinton's win, in 1990, representatives from Washington D.C.'s gay and lesbian community visited with Marine general Alfred Gray amid a series of escalating altercations with his men at a nearby gay bar and offered to provide them with sensitivity training. Gray nixed the idea, feeling that such interactions would "likely be used to recruit enlisted Marines to a homosexual lifestyle."

A month after Clinton won, the Joint Chiefs of Staff told the president-elect that they would resign en masse if he forced the gay issue upon them. Clinton initially defended his proposal as akin to what President Truman had done in 1948 when, via executive order, he racially desegregated the service. But Colin Powell, then the chairman of the chiefs and the most prominent Black officer in America, disagreed. Speaking before an audience at the Naval Academy, Powell argued that Clinton had falsely conflated the discrimination of Black and Gay troops. Race, he argued, involved "benign" characteristics. Sexuality, he charged, was different.

Later, Powell told *U.S. News & World Report* that opening the service to gays would force a "constant pressure to show equality to a community whose mores we don't understand." Perhaps the crassest comments came from General Carl Mundy, then the commandant of the Marine Corps, who predicted that a Marine coming out to his squad mates would spur a reaction akin to if he copped to being a rapist, a Nazi, or a card-carrying member of the Ku Klux Klan.

Hidden under this bluster and fearmongering was an institutional worry: that the introduction of openly gay troops, as with the integration of Black and female ones, threatened the fragile ideals at the heart of the American military. To have an openly gay soldier be as effective, or more so, than a straight one would certainly bruise the egos of the men in charge. It would also reduce the allure of service as a proving ground for one's manliness.

The military has, in general, long sought an antiseptic, asexual service environment. Many brass aim to disabuse their men of intimate interpersonal connections—be they homosexual, heterosexual, or familial—worried, perhaps, that such bonds may undermine institutional loyalties or warm the coldness their training regimes inculcate. "Where love is absent, power fills the vacuum," goes a famed Jungian adage, one that perfectly typifies a military environment. A version of this idea is now clinically described as "masculine discrepancy stress," in which boys and men, believing they have failed to meet gender norms, increasingly engage in risky behavior and all forms of violence, including of a sexual nature. This stress can easily fracture a man's interpersonal relationships, but it forms the exact instincts that the military requires.

One Marine confessed to Zeeland that his own sexual proclivities were shaped in part by his military training, which is largely built around withholding approval, and, in the Marine's words, instills "a need to take orders and be dominated." Another said, "there is a craving to serve, to win approval, or even love . . . when I play bottom, I get no physical enjoyment out of it; I go through the abasement and pain out of a sense of duty." He paused. "You could almost say that being the bottom is mission oriented."

Former Army officer Erik Edstrom, who is straight, echoed these sentiments in his memoir, comparing West Point cadet training to BDSM. "Initially the academy takes away your humanity, and sometimes your human dignity," he writes. "But then they give it back to you sparingly, in smaller parcels, rebranding it a 'privilege.'"

AS PART OF THE MILITARY'S TIGHT REGULATION OVER INTIMACY, leadership long discouraged dating, and public displays of affection were banned. Should cadets leave campus for a break or weekend away, they were made to swear upon their return that they had not gotten married. For many decades, tying the knot while serving as a cadet was expressly banned. Up until 2023, every service academy also banned cadets from becoming parents.

Love was once largely dosed out at West Point in small portions by a "Cadet Hostess," one in a pack traditionally composed of military wives and organized into an official West Point office that still exists to this day. The women were den mothers and matchmakers, screening and busing in "femmes" or "drags"—"dragging" meant taking a woman on a date—for sock hops and other special occasions. These included overnight sojourns, though the prevalence of in flagrante delicto among these visiting girls is unclear. Because sex at military school was so rare, it intensified sexual energy and elevated the act as a sacrosanct marker of one's manliness. When, at the Naval Academy, the rare midshipmen managed to sneak a sexual encounter, he would then proudly denote the accomplishment by hanging a Chiquita banana on his door. To many, sex became yet another highly regulated obstacle course, an exploit turned transactional, with some cadets grading girls on a Thayerian scale from zero to three. (Those girls considered least desirable were stamped as L.P., or "lemon pie.")

Publicly, however, the cadets were perfect gentlemen, taught by their cadet hostess certain noble deeds, like how to handle a teacup or dance the foxtrot. For many years, the military cadet was in high romantic demand, with young girls flooding the cadet hostess office with letters seeking love.

One of West Point's more infamous pairings occurred in the fall of 1973, when Holly Knowlton, then a student at Dickinson College and the daughter of West Point Superintendent William Knowlton, needed a date for a football game. West Point's assistant brigade adjutant was tasked with this mission, scouring the cadet rolls before landing on a promising cadet named David Petraeus, and ordering he accompany Holly to the game. Petraeus was fast at track, a soccer whiz, and a "Star Man," meaning he had placed in the top 5 percent of his class academically. The future general also earnestly defended the school's ethos of discipline, much to the administration's delight.

A few months after the game, on Petraeus's West Point graduation day, a local paper reported that the young lieutenant, then just twenty-one, "got a diploma from the U.S. Military Academy—and the boss' daughter as well." The fledgling couple was already engaged and, a few weeks later, would be married at West Point's chapel.

Not many cadets tie the knot with each other, but when they do, it's generally consummated, in part, for practical considerations. It's helpful to marry another person at the whims of the same controlling institution, someone who understands that, at the end of the day, the marriage comes second, and the military comes first. These dynamics are summed up by the "2 Percent Club," named for the small slice of service academy cadets who manage to sustain relationships with their high school sweethearts through graduation. This trend continues after graduation, with the Pentagon sustaining a divorce rate higher than any other career field.

TRY AS IT MIGHT TO MASTER LOVE, the military has never quite been successful, especially because deep interpersonal affection so often flourishes under shared duress. Air Force Academy surveys from the early 1970s indicate that, as many cadets progressed through training, they became increasingly loyal to their fellow cadets and increasingly detached from academy officials and other military authorities. "Loyalty is like an onion with many skins," one cadet noted. "At the core is your family, it radiates out from that point. Family and friends are the only things you have when everything else is in chaos. The family is the only thing that anyone is bound to protect. I am not here to protect some abstract cause, such as liberty and honor, I am here to one day fight to protect my family."

Before women were allowed at West Point, male cadets frequently entered into quasi-domestic relationships with their roommates, whom many called their "wives." These deep bonds further flourished on the battlefield, as in the World War II dispatch from legendary war correspondent Ernie Pyle, who, in searching for words to describe what American G.I.s were fighting for, landed not on fascism, but "each other."

"When I became captain of a submarine, my gaydar failed," mused Steve Clark, a 1975 graduate of the Naval Academy, explaining that "every one of your sailors looks like a guy coming onto you at a gay bar." Clark ultimately developed a heartwarming explanation for his handicap. "It's because they have deep respect for the captain, and they want to be seen by him as a good sailor."

Cohesion and community may be the most beautiful facets of military life, but they are fragile and easily perverted by the military's training regime, which often stunts natural love and forces intimacy in false directions, confusing a genuine thirst for close bonding with puerile practices and nonconsensual bodily debasement.

Under ideal circumstances, repressed military men engage in harmless initiation rites tinged by their pent-up horniness. Such traditions date back to West Point's earliest days, when upperclassmen would soap down bathroom floors and force naked plebes to slide across them. Or they would force naked plebes to run down a street while being doused in cold water. Entire cadet companies have semi-ritually masturbated together in the showers, or all shit surrounded by each other in the same, wide-open room.

Clark recalled a pack of sailors holding "a jerk-off contest" to see who could "squirt the furthest." The mess was subsequently wiped up, he added, with "the towel of a sailor they didn't like."

Naval graduate Adam Schuman recalled a half dozen instances on his ship where his roommate, slightly tipsy, "climbed into my bunk instead of his." He clarified: "It was never anything sexual." This behavior may be formed in equal parts by the packed-like-sardines nature of the job, and by the natural desire for bodily intimacy with those for whom you share your life with. No matter the underlying instincts, this behavior could easily get out of hand in military environments and become semi-sadistic. The most common form of military sexual assault has long been hazing. The breadth of harsh, homosocial bonding routines is too immense and too dark to fully catalog here. Sometimes, senior cadets would hold down plebes, stain their nipples black with shoe grease and write "I love cock," on their arms and backs. On the other end of this spectrum are the bands of older cadets who have forcibly sodomized younger ones.

Then there are all the examples in-between. At the Naval Academy during the summer of 1989, for instance, there emerged an example of sexual humiliation and, perhaps, warped courtship. A senior midshipman took special interest in a plebe, forcing him to eat in a sexually suggestive manner and requiring him to squeal like a pig while standing, bent over, on his chair in the dining room. Afterward, he questioned the plebe's sexual orientation. It seems, perhaps, that the older boy was intensely repressed. Perhaps he even saw a glint of something similar in the young plebe he gravitated toward. But real love wasn't possible in a place like this, and so power filled the vacuum.

In his jailhouse interview, Mark Jones described the football team's treatment as a "mutant" form of bonding, something so totally debased that it shatters the possibility of any real connection and instead establishes a ruthless social stratum. When, two decades later, another young West Point footballer attended training camp, older players made their dominance clear by storming his room while he was sleeping and beating him senseless with big black dildos.

Sandy McIntosh, Trump's old classmate at the New York Military Academy, told me that his experience in an all-male hierarchy certainly stunted his sexual maturity, creating "artificial love" through *Playboy* magazine and promoting what he called "animalistic" behavior, "like when a dog humps another dog, not for sex but just to gain supremacy." Cadets hosted contests over who could wet dream first, groused conspiratorially that school officials were dosing their food with potassium nitrate to curb their testosterone levels, and carried condoms that remained unused but which left small distinct marks on their leather wallets.

At some point during the Cold War, it seems, cadets at Valley Forge established an especially violent tool of assault as a tradition for building brotherhood and reinforcing authority. It was called "tooth-pasting," and it was passed down over decades. The practice usually involves older cadets ambushing younger ones, then forcibly sodomizing them, often with a broom or a lacrosse stick or a coat hanger. It seems that, by highly conservative estimates, dozens of Forge cadets were exposed to this practice over many decades. It's also true that although tooth-pasting was repeatedly raised as problematic to school senior administrators, they always permitted it to continue.

When, in 2009, fifteen-year-old Forge cadet Ryan Niessner was first ambushed in the shower, he tried to ward the cadets off. "I struggled for a little bit, but five, six other people—numbers just kinda won that," he told me. Soon after Niessner's first assault, he fought off another tooth-pasting attempt. Hoping to thwart such attacks, he and some fellow cadets took on overnight surveillance shifts. "We were the only adults in the building with high schoolers and middle schoolers," he recalled.

In an affidavit, Niessner testified that when he reported his abuse to the Forge, an officer asked, "Will your parents sue?" (They did not.) "After this meeting," he testified, "I was discouraged from reporting this incident to anyone else." When a Forge administrator reported a different tooth-pasting attack to her superiors, she told me "they didn't do anything about it." Ray Bossert, a retired colonel who worked at the Forge between 2018 and 2020, added that some of the dozen or so cadets thought to have participated in tooth-pasting assaults during his tenure were dismissed, only to return the following semester. None of them tried it again, to his knowledge. "But think of the type of kids that would do that," Bossert said. "They are going to do hell across the board."

After Niessner graduated and entered a civilian college, he became withdrawn, depressed, and eventually had to take medical leave. The mother of another Forge graduate who was sodomized told me he now drinks to excess and sleeps with a hunting knife under his pillow.

Many other forms of sexual misconduct pervaded Valley Forge, and scores of other military schools across this era, much of it exclusively involving men. One case involved Bret Lewis, who, after landing at the Forge as an eleven-year-old cadet in 1982, was groomed and then sexually assaulted by an older cadet and scion of the Genovese crime family. His major coping mechanism became drinking, which he started doing at age fourteen. Then he became a raging homophobe in high school. Brett told me he now has three DUI convictions and was married once, but only for a year. "I have trouble keeping relationships," he said.

A *NEW YORK TIMES* POLL CONDUCTED SHORTLY before Clinton's 1992 victory showed a 57 percent approval rating for homosexuals openly serving in the military. Other allied nations were then opening their ranks to gay members without issue, leading the GAO in 1992 to assert that the ban had "no validity according to current scientific research." Reagan's ban had also cost the Pentagon a half-billion dollars to separate and replace the 17,000 gay troops who had been subjected to it.

Clinton's pledge to overturn the ban had drawn several notable and surprising allies. One was Lawrence Korb, who had previously enforced the ban under Reagan as the Pentagon's leading personnel official, but now said he could find "no convincing evidence that changing the policy would undermine unit cohesion." Even Barry Goldwater, a retired Air Force general and archconservative, was in favor of lifting the ban, writing "you don't need to be 'straight' to fight and die for your country. You just need to shoot straight." Further bolstering Clinton's case was a recent federal court decision deeming the ban unconstitutional, plus a seven-hundred-page Navy report from 1957 which found that homosexuals posed no risks to the service and advocated for dishonorable discharged based on sexual identity to end.

Nonetheless, the week after Clinton's election, he pivoted his campaign pledge of an "immediate repeal" to a mealymouthed plan to "consult with a lot of people" for an indefinite period "about what our options are." Behind closed doors, Clinton sought to minimize his commitments to the queer community. "I'm not doing this for gay groups," he explained. "The people I would like to keep wouldn't show up for a Queer Nation parade." In his deeds and actions, President Clinton expressed an intensely scrutinized version of one of the era's cornerstone anxieties: he was afraid of being called "gay."

When, on January 29, 1993, the freshly minted commander in chief showed up for his first White House press conference in office, he was already resigned to a toothless compromise. He announced the Defense Department would spend the next six months studying the problem, thereby gifting the decision to the generals. Mixner and other advocates spent the following months pushing the administration to stick by their pledge. So, too, did Vice President Gore, who got into a bitter argument with Clinton, saying the president should make the decision unilaterally, claim it as part of his commander in chief powers, and then see where the chips fall.

Clinton adviser turned ABC News star George Stephanopoulos was then Mixner's incommunicative point person. When the two did talk, Mixner felt Stephanopoulos was "feeding me a line of bullshit," mostly vague platitudes aimed at placating him and the movement. Then, on July 19, 1993, Clinton marched onto the stage of the National Defense University, where he formally announced, "Don't Ask, Don't Tell," which he described in Nixonian terms as "an honorable compromise." The "compromise" was basic and pathetically unambitious: recruits would no longer be expressly asked about their sexual orientation.

In her book *On the Edge: The Clinton Presidency*, reporter Elizabeth Drew describes the scene as little more than a cowardly surrender: "[Clinton] was virtually begging for the military's approval," she writes. "'I'm here because I respect you,' [he said.] He didn't look like a commander in chief." Clinton concluded his remarks with a telling admission: "Our military is a conservative institution," he said. "And I say that in the very best sense."

Clinton's new policy, Mixner charged, "merely gift-wraps a horrendous policy of prejudice and hatred." Not long after, Mixner led a protest against "Don't Ask, Don't Tell" outside the White House, and was arrested. His protest spurred a counterdemonstration from the ACT UP AIDS Coalition, which felt that gay activists were focusing too much attention on the military issue. Media coverage of the protest was robust, and much of it noted Mixner's rich history with Clinton. This strongly provoked the president's ire. A message from the Oval Office subsequently went out saying that neither Mixner nor any interest he supported or was consulting for was welcome at 1600 Pennsylvania Avenue. In a flash, Mixner lost all his clients, and much of his money. "At the end of the four years I was selling watches to pay my rent at pawnshops," he later recalled.

Clinton's betrayal was sharp and stinging, significant enough to fundamentally question his support for queer Americans in the first place. In retrospect, it may have been inauthentic from the start. Clinton had, after all, considered Senator Sam Nunn as his defense secretary, even after it was revealed that the conservative Democrat from Georgia had fired two aides after learning they were gay. The actual drafting of the "Don't Ask, Don't Tell" policy was left to Nunn, the powerful chairman of the Senate Armed Services Committee, who held days of hostile hearings on the policy, in which he and others spewed ugly stereotypes about gay Americans as sexually deviant. To reinforce his position, Nunn toured a Navy ship in Norfolk, Virginia, pointing out worriedly to the press that as many as three sailors sometimes shared bunks. "It is a very close-quarters situation," he protested.

Nunn's final text, tucked into the 1993 defense bill, deviated from Clinton's rhetoric, allowing for recruits to still be asked about their sexual identity at the discretion of the defense secretary. The final policy also failed to equally apply the military's anti-sodomy laws to gay and straight troops. And it did not institute vital protections to prevent witch hunts against gay service members.

As *The Detroit Free Press* saw it, Nunn was casting blame in exactly the wrong direction. As the paper looked for the true culprit of military sexual abuse, it landed on the Tailhook scandal. "If the military has a problem with sexual misconduct in close quarter, gays aren't to blame," the *Free Press* opined. The military's light treatment of the Tailhook perpetrators extended to countless other acts of sexual abuse. Two sailors around this time who had sex with a woman without her consent and filmed the encounter were given nonjudicial punishments and stayed on their ship. Decades later, data corroborated what many gay service members, especially assaulted sailors, have long been saying: they constitute an outsized proportion of military sexual survivors.

CLINTON'S COMPROMISE ON GAY TROOPS REPRESENTED a dangerous two-step: spotlighting gay service members, then failing to protect them. As discussion of the ban reached a fever pitch in the weeks leading up to the 1992 election, sailor Terry Helvey and an accomplice killed a gay shipmate, Allen Schindler, leaving him so disfigured that his family could only identity him by his tattoos. After reading the coroner's findings, his mother reported that "just about everything was damaged except his heart." A few months later, four sailors and two Marines in San Francisco lured a gay man from a bar and beat him. Then three Marines at Camp Lejeune mercilessly attacked another gay man, screaming "Fag, you should die!" and "Clinton must pay!"

A year later, when "Don't Ask, Don't Tell" was formally enacted, Clinton promised it would bring personal privacy, but the opposite happened. Troops suspected of being gay were often branded "one of Bill's," and discharges related to sexual identity spiked, with roughly ten thousand gay people being kicked out of the service during the first decade of the policy. At one point, the Navy went so far as to investigate the online activities of a decorated sailor suspected of being gay, tracing him to a screen name on a gay website, then discharging him. In 2003, John Huston, a longtime judge advocate general in the Navy, penned an article in the *National Law Journal* pointing out the obvious: "rather than preserving cohesion, [the ban] fosters divisiveness."

That same year, the Naval Academy's alumni association refused to formally recognize a chapter of gay, lesbian, bisexual, transgender, and supportive heterosexual Naval Academy alumni, contending it needed to be geographically chartered. When, in response, the pack reoriented as the "Castro Chapter," so named for the queer district in San Francisco where a dozen or so members lived, the alumni association again rebuffed their request.

These alumni hoped the chapter would form a mutual support network and also create conspicuous role models for lonely queer sailors and midshipmen still living under "Don't Ask, Don't Tell." Even as it denied the Castro application for a second time, the Naval Academy released a sham press release claiming a "commitment to diversity and inclusiveness." Months later, the academy threatened to arrest a few dozen outside activists planning to protest Clinton's infamous policy on campus.

A school spokesman justified their threats with yet another hypocritical statement, this one touting the military's vital role in defending free speech while also asserting its "obligation to ensure our mission and activities are free from disruption." The Naval Academy was one of numerous stops on a planned protest tour. Another was the Falwell family's evangelical college Liberty University, in Lynchburg, Virginia. One organizer told *The Washington Post* that while the Naval Academy had blanket-banned their demonstration, "ironically, Jerry Falwell allowed us onto the campus, and we had a fruitful dialogue."

Chapter 14

No Child Left Behind

On the clear, crisp morning of September 11, 2001, a Boeing 767 jet operated by American Airlines and featuring red, white, and blue stripes, took off from Boston's Logan International Airport with an official destination of balmy Los Angeles. The plane, known by the soon-to-be infamous moniker "Flight 11," was piloted by two military veterans: John Ogonowski, who had flown an Air Force transport plane during Vietnam, and his first officer, Tom McGuinness, a Navy guy who had attended the esteemed Top Gun academy.

A few minutes after the plane, and its people, left the ground, it was hijacked by five Al-Qaeda terrorists, who either killed or incapacitated the two military veterans manning the controls. One of the hijackers, Mohamed Atta, then took over. He stayed on course for about fifteen minutes, at which point he saw the Hudson River glistening before him, and veered hard to the left.

The American military has viewed the Hudson as a tactical vulnerability since the earliest days of independence. For British forces, it was a naturally frictionless path from their New York City stronghold to important rebel outposts in the north. Colonists erected West Point explicitly to deter the British Navy, imbuing the place with a mission that, in General Washington's eyes, made it "the most important post in America."

Washington anxiously dotted other strategically placed, bomb-proof fortifications along the shores of the Hudson, which were all designed and supplied to sustain a ten-day siege. While the crown tried repeatedly to overwhelm these forts—even aided at one point by intelligence from infamous turncoat Benedict Arnold—the Red Coats never captured West Point.

Two centuries later, a new enemy—Al-Qaeda—was, wittingly or not, cribbing British imperial military tactics, using the river as a waypoint to attack the beating heart of American capitalism, the World Trade Center. Over the course of a few fleeting seconds, the 767 passed imperviously over West Point and its four thousand or so cadets. A few minutes later, at 8:46 a.m., the plane became a shot heard across the world, one that would engross America for decades and entangle new generations of soldiers, a selective few of whom had been inexorably marked by the attack before it even happened.

Minutes after Flight 11 hit the North Tower of the Trade Center, a second plane out of Boston hit its twin to the immediate south. A third hijacked plane hit the Pentagon, while a fourth one, destined for the U.S. Capitol, crashed in a rural Pennsylvania field following a passenger revolt. Nearly three thousand people were killed within minutes, leading the American political, military, and pundit class to promptly cast the attacks as a modern-day Pearl Harbor. Both incursions were on American soil, both unexpected and shocking, and unfathomably destructive. But the historical parallels basically ended there. When a reporter for *The New York Times* visited West Point four days after 9/11, he observed a school struggling to contextualize what had happened, and unprepared for what came next. "In 1941 the enemy was clearly defined: across an ocean, over the next ridge," the reporter wrote. "Now everything was as gray as a cadet's uniform."

For the country's premier institution of military learning to be caught flat-footed in this moment fit a pattern of historical myopia. By the time of the attacks, the American military had waged numerous campaigns against nebulous, non-state actors, from its earliest skirmishes with Native American forces to the Philippine-American War, and, of course, Vietnam. The national security state had also been fixated on the Middle East for more than a decade, and Osama bin Laden, in particular, who had been implicated both in the 1993 bombing of the World Trade Center, and the bombings of American embassies in Kenya and Tanzania five years later.

Nonetheless, in 2001, West Point's counterterrorism curriculum consisted of a single elective, coupled with limited offerings in Arabic and the Middle East. Many senior military leaders were nostalgic for the winning strategies of World War II and also haunted by the stinging losses of the Cold War. This created confusing and contradictory conditions, forming a potpourri policy environment that endorsed counterinsurgency and guerrilla tactics, but remained stubbornly loyal to certain state-based strategies.

While military brass had experienced the acute challenges of confronting a fluid and formless ideology, like communism, their thinking was fatally compromised by the deceptive myths about Vietnam then swirling around the Pentagon. More than anything, the brass was dead set on winning, summed up by the so-called Powell Doctrine, a vaunted war selection process, of sorts, that emphasized conventional conflict and clear exit strategies. The doctrine was drafted by Colin Powell, who had come away from his service in Vietnam believing that America should only fight wars that, first and foremost, had clear national interests—and would be short, popular, and winnable.

The Gulf War had, in basic terms, aligned with the Powell Doctrine, though its whiz-bang brevity meant that the military's mind remained largely stuck in Southeast Asia. On the day that the twin towers and the Pentagon were hit, West Point cadets still learned a marching cadence that talked about "killing Commies." One former TAC officer added that, at the onset of the Global War on Terrorism, or GWOT, as it would come to be called, staff were also still training cadets decked in old combat fatigues and armed with out-of-date guns. "It was a bit Mickey Mouse," he told me. "They looked like kids from Vietnam." A report from this time further detailed how one West Point first sergeant motivated new plebes by reading Vietnam-era Medal of Honor citations he had dug up on the internet.

In the immediate aftershock of the attacks, West Point brass pledged to *The New York Times* that America's freshly brewing war would be met with "new thinking." In service of this mission, faculty instructors hurriedly reframed their syllabi around guerrilla warfare, homeland defense, and civil liberties. For the first time, mock civilians were placed into battle drills, and West Point developed a new course on counterterrorism. One professor crudely sketched a graph with "security" on one axis and "liberty" on the other. "What is the proper balance?" she asked.

The Air Force Academy boosted their Middle East offerings, too, though these efforts appeared half-hearted. As part of his broader complaint alleging cronyism and poor academic credentialing, a civilian Air Force professor claimed that the school brought on an Arabic instructor who had little more than a master's degree in business administration.

The Pentagon's purported academic push toward the future seemed to scarcely disabuse military school campuses of Cold War thinking. When, after the attacks, a West Point professor asked his class how to defeat terrorism, Cadet John Rowold volunteered that "one thing you could do is topple governments," reasoning "we used to do it in South America every day." Another cadet suggested cribbing British tactics from World War II.

A third, more thoughtful cadet worried that, as the war commenced, the American military was in "one of the worst positions we've ever been in." He continued: "We're looking at fighting an enemy that we can't really identify, in a land that we can't really identify. And we know at this point that nonretaliation is not an option. But we also know any retaliation is going to breed more hatred against us in an Arab world."

The cadet's professor deemed this a "smart point," but then pronounced "excellent" a call from his classmate to go to war with all forms of terrorism, "including those who operate within our allies, like the [Irish Republican Army]."

President George W. Bush and his select war planners similarly favored a more global framing. One of the loudest voices for this expansive approach was former Secretary of State Henry Kissinger. When, in September 2000, Kissinger visited the West Point campus to receive the Sylvanus Thayer Award, he proclaimed that conflict was inevitable, then presciently prophesized a war.

Kissinger also praised Al Haig and Brent Scowcroft, two West Point graduates turned Nixon aides who had helped enable Vietnam. That conflict, Kissinger asserted, was not a lost war, but one that had simply proved vexing to end. His major piece of advice to cadets cribbed the Powell Doctrine: never again "enter a conflict whose successful end we cannot describe."

Hours after the 9/11 attacks, however, Kissinger completely dispensed with his own wisdom, advocating in a manic *Washington Post* editorial for a brash multinational military campaign to destroy terrorism wherever it existed. In it, Kissinger admitted that the war on terrorism was unlikely to have a "definite end," but proposed nonetheless to extend our aims beyond Afghanistan, to what he knew to be a favored White House target: Iraq. "The issue is not whether Iraq was involved in the terrorist attack on the United States," Kissinger asserted in the *Post*, but rather that its leader, Saddam Hussein, had a cache of biological and chemical weapons and was developing nuclear capacities—none of which was true.

President Bush was himself brazenly incautious about war, eager for it, even. He wanted to take out Hussein, a longtime former ally and tyrant his father had failed to kill or unseat during the First Gulf War. In June 2002, President Bush expressed his impatience for war in a West Point commencement speech. "If we wait for threats to fully materialize, we will have waited too long," he argued. The cadets sitting before him were the school's vaunted bicentennial class, and Bush seemed excited to enlist this anomalous crew into what he cast as the Pentagon's coming "drama." Already, his administration had sharpened the campus's edginess by deeming West Point a potential future target for terrorism, a designation that led New York State to station armed national guardsmen at the gates.

The American public writ large did its best to swallow their post-9/11 anxieties, largely through an omnipresent but artificially induced "rebirth of patriotism." This was coupled with a renewed prestige for the American soldier, which, in 2003, was named *Time*'s "Person of the Year." Amid a driftless, increasingly divided American society, the country's soldiers, and their new wars, offered, at least in *Time*'s estimation, a perfect chance to recapture the greatness of our past. In his comments to the magazine, however, Defense Secretary Donald Rumsfeld articulated no galvanizing moral center to the conflict. Instead, he adopted the traditional tone of a military school superintendent overseeing a bunch of "bad apples." He pledged that the war, if nothing else, would institute a new era of honor, work ethic, and discipline.

Rumsfeld griped that the incoming generation of young military recruits "have purple hair and an earring, and they've never walked with another person in step in their life." Military culture, he bragged, changed that. "They become part of a unit, a team."

A FEW WEEKS AFTER 9/11, the annual Army-Navy game offered the public a perfect opportunity to witness America's martial excellence through sport. West Point has long viewed the gridiron as a strong proving ground for martial excellence. Famed general George Marshall once said that, when faced with a "secret and dangerous mission," he often ordered his staff to "send me a West Point football player." The event drew more television viewers than any college football matchup in the preceding decade, though, in a worrying omen for the war to come, both teams were historically bad. The Navy had lost all nine games it played that season, while the Army had only won two.

These losing records went unmentioned by President Bush when, before the game, he visited the locker rooms for both the Army and Navy service academies. A former middling owner of the Texas Rangers baseball team, Bush gave short, awkward remarks, promising his players, who were also his military recruits, that the impending war would be a good one. "Should you ever enter theater, the cause is just, it is, uhh, right what we're doing. And we'll win. There's no doubt in my mind we'll win." Bush's spiel paled in comparison to the howling pep talk given to the Army squad that same evening by General "Stormin'" Norman Schwarzkopf, himself a former West Point football player. "Men," he said, "today you are going to war and the U.S. Army does not lose wars!" The room exploded in roars.

Schwarzkopf had attended Valley Forge before the Point and viewed both institutions as deeply formative. "West Point prepared me for the military," he once reflected. "Valley Forge prepared me for life." Schwarzkopf was the first distinguished general since Patton who was both colorful and smart. His pièce de résistance was the Gulf War, a relatively clean, tactically sound six-week blitzkrieg with easily identifiable good and bad guys spread across the flat, open desert. In short order, Schwarzkopf liberated tiny Kuwait from Iraqi forces led by Hussein and his Republican Guard, with few American casualties. This led President H.W. Bush to declare that the nation had finally "kicked the Vietnam syndrome once and for all."

Schwarzkopf's warm reception in the locker room may have stemmed, in part, from the widespread hope among a team of soon-to-be soldiers that the new war in the Middle East would be as quick and relatively painless as the general's campaign in the Gulf, in which battlefield casualties were so low that it became statistically safer to wage war for Bush and Schwarzkopf than to live in most American locales.

In a West Point footballer's mind—and in the hearts of many Americans for that matter—were reasons to be hopeful. After all, this was seen as simply a new Gulf War, one that would again be orchestrated by a WASPy commander in chief with "Bush" as a last name, and by the smartest soldier scholars the world had ever seen. There were, however, uncomfortable truths contravening Schwarzkopf's legend, West Point's track record, and H.W. Bush's war. "Schwarzkopf's enormous air, sea and land forces had overwhelmed a country with a gross national product equivalent to North Dakota's," *The New York Times* noted in the general's 2012 obituary. Their point was simple: the first Gulf War had been less a war and more a multi-week bombing campaign, one, it's worth noting, that leveled Iraqi infrastructure in the process, creating an acute humanitarian crisis while failing to dislodge Hussein from power or meaningfully damaging his military capabilities.

But now it was the winter of 2001, and there was little public interest in nuance, especially at the Army-Navy game. The crowd at Michie Stadium, so named for the godfather of West Point's football program, roared in approval when the Army's Black Knights stormed onto the field, brandishing a black flag and their motto, borrowed from the Aryan Brotherhood: "God Forgives, Brothers Don't." In the end, the Army won convincingly: 26 to 17. Two of the game's players later died in action in Iraq and Afghanistan, respectively, but, in this fleeting moment, everyone on the field appeared awesome and invincible. Cadet life was, if only briefly, back in vogue.

Days before the game, Representative Sue Kelly, whose district included West Point, told *The New York Times* that high schoolers were newly eager to join the service. "There is enormous respect for the Point now," she said. "The young men and women applying, when they meet the cadets, you should see their eyes light up." Many were Boy Scouts, a constituency that was now making up as much as 20 percent of any given academy class. In comments discussing West Point's enrollment surge, its director of admissions, Colonel Michael L. Jones, noted with mixed feelings that his son, a West Point graduate, had, on 9/11, cut short a job interview in Toronto to reenlist. "That really refocused his mind," Jones said with a nervous laugh. "I know how my parents felt when I was in Vietnam now."

West Point's rapidly regenerating reputation was assisted by an expensive spit shine from affluent alumni. A business group composed of West Pointers had recently partnered with the Army on a $26 million renovation of the school's historic Hotel Thayer, which, according to a fawning news report from the time, offered a Sunday brunch that couldn't be beat. In 2002, another group of graduates forged a marketing partnership with ABC that included a two-hour television special to commemorate the two hundredth anniversary of West Point. A year after that, Vincent Viola, a West Point alumnus made billionaire from oil trading, served as the major funder for West Point's Combating Terrorism Center, which in the two decades since it was founded, has published a few dozen, non-peer-reviewed reports, one of which endorsed "Stealing Al-Qaida's Playbook."

The media placed many additional cherries on top of these image-boosting activities. While GWOT coverage would darken considerably over the course of the conflict, it was, in its fledgling years, remarkably upbeat and optimistic. This sampling included a 2002 Disney film called *Cadet Kelly*, in which Hillary Duff plays a misbehaving teen who finds purpose thanks to a series of gung-ho commandos at the fictional George Washington Military Academy. A few years before its release, David Lipsky, a *Rolling Stone* journalist, was deeply embedded on West Point's campus, where, purely by chance, he directly experienced 9/11 and its historical aftershocks.

The book Lipsky produced in 2003, however, was no gonzo takedown but an uplifting tome, *Absolutely American*, which immediately became a national best seller. Lipsky didn't trace any fear or loathing on campus, asserting instead that West Point cadets were the "happiest," most purely idealistic young people he had ever met. Some of the characters in his book truthfully meet this definition, though Lipsky did little to examine how their optimistic energy could be diluted or curdled through service.

Lipsky's acknowledgment of the school's dark past is often credulously contextualized by his description of current campus efforts to create what he calls "The Nice Guy Army." These efforts included promoting "wellness" on campus, reducing stress, and encouraging volunteerism. Many cadets looked down on this curriculum, and Lipsky did, too, writing that it was likely an overcorrection, one seemingly dictated through "transmissions from Oprah."

At times, Lipsky's writing verges on a full-on recruitment pitch, chronicling, for instance, "a uniform standard of prettiness for cadet girlfriends." He also promotes the $18,000 loans the academy was granting to juniors at impossibly low interest rates, allowing them to purchase flashy cars or glitzy class rings—and maybe even make some prudent investments.

THE MILITARY'S DISTINCTIVE BRANDING PUSH as "The Nice Guy Army" seemed a conspicuous effort to move on from the intense violence and futility of Vietnam, reaching back further to World War II, where soldierdom was envisioned more as a form of community service, not simply an internecine proving ground for male power. This revival was perfectly complemented by the 2001 HBO miniseries *Band of Brothers*, a heroic World War II tale about a remarkable group of soldiers in the 101st Airborne that premiered two days before the 9/11 attacks. Its noble ideas and sentimental tropes were frequently applied to the GWOT, most obviously through newspapers' breathless accounts of various "bands of brothers" deploying to the Middle East from New Jersey, Nebraska, and everywhere in between.

The GWOT and World War II shared a kernel of similarity—that of the devastating air attack by foreign invaders. This alone helped reignite the old school ideas of the Second World War, which, in turn, injected the military with positive public sentiments and concurrently enhanced parental interest in military schools still suffering under the cloud of the Cold War.

At the onset of the GWOT, the Forge had, during previous decades, seen its enrollment steadily decline from an early–Cold War high of 1,100 cadets, to just a few hundred. The place was on the verge of bankruptcy. But the school's new superintendent, an impressive-looking Naval Academy graduate and retired rear admiral, Peter Long, laid it on thick. He loudly played up Schwarzkopf's connections to the Forge after the 9/11 attacks, while also promising parents that he would turn their unruly boys into men worthy of gracing the cover of *Time* magazine. He pledged specifically that, by the time he was done with them, Forge graduates would show "courtesy," "orderliness," and compliance.

Long's message resonated with parents, who showered him with their boys, boosting enrollment. Roughly two dozen new military academies also opened their doors, many of them charter schools concentrated in low-income, Black and brown neighborhoods. In 2002, Cincinnati's school district created Ohio's first public military high school. The Chicago Public School District established six charter military schools, including one built in the mold of the Air Force Academy. California opened seven military charter schools, including an institution in Oakland championed by many of the state's most powerful Democratic leaders, including Dianne Feinstein and Jerry Brown. In 2003, the Delaware Military Academy opened as the first and only charter school specifically oriented around U.S. Navy tenets. It was funded, in part, by a $300,000 Pentagon grant.

Taxpayers were also paying $300,000 per service academy cadet—or roughly double the cost of an ROTC officer reared at a land grant. Some pundits and lawmakers objected to this hefty price tag, reviving the age-old argument that military service academies were elitist, anachronistic, and way too expensive. Writing in *The Washington Post*, war correspondent Thomas Ricks argued that in addition to being far cheaper, ROTC trainees also benefited hugely from attending civilian colleges and universities, since "their assumptions will be challenged." Congress, in sum, paid these arguments little mind. In 2002, lawmakers authorized bigger budgets for the service academies, issuing mandates that they significantly grow their student bodies.

Congress essentially gave the military a blank check after 9/11, supercharging a steady trend of military budget bloat since World War II. This vastly enhanced the Pentagon's scope of influence in American life—especially education—and inhibited any sort of ambitious domestic agenda. A vivid symbol of the military's slow cannibalization of the budget, and America, can be seen in West Point's hometown of Highland Falls. During the last century, the town has lost roughly 95 percent of its land to the Army through campus expansions guaranteed through eminent domain. This has ravaged Highland Falls's base of taxable property, limited its economic and development dreams, and, at one point, even threatened townspeople's access to drinking water.

As America's war planners became increasingly flush with land, cash, and ammunition, there existed few concrete oversight metrics to guide the education of a twenty-first-century version of the gentleman officer. In 2003, the GAO reported that the federal government had no "formal goals and measures" over the service academies, and that such regulations were sorely needed. As evidence, the watchdog revealed that about 60 percent of students at the Army and Naval Academies and 70 percent at the Air Force Academy "reported that quality-of-life problems are openly confronted and/or solved to some, little, or no extent." Between one-quarter and one-third of cadets also rated their academy's standards for developing officers from "generally too low" to "much too low."

Per Sylvanus Thayer's enduring order, the academies' Boards of Visitors remained largely toothless, armed with no dedicated staff and bound to agendas largely dictated by military officials. Site visits weren't well attended, and board members were often conservative, recalcitrant, and stuck in the past. VMI's board, for instance, resisted shedding its confederate symbols, while Valley Forge's trustees wasted meetings with gauzy nostalgia. "Everyone told war stories," one former trustee told me. "We didn't get anything done." An internal audit later warned that "Valley Forge is not going to survive by looking backwards." The authors laid most of the blame on the trustees' hasty "Ready, Fire, Aim" decision-making style. After a few reform-minded members authored a report with similar takeaways, the Forge disbanded its Board of Visitors entirely.

DURING THE TWELVE MONTHS FOLLOWING 9/11, the military enjoyed a recruitment bonanza, with the active-duty and reserve ranks rapidly swelling by roughly 250,000 people. Still, the brass seemed to sense that it might be a fleeting rush. It was. By 2005, all components of the Army, the Air National Guard, and the Navy Reserve had missed their recruiting goals, even though most had reduced the number of enlistments it sought. At the same time, 40 percent of troops who had enlisted in the Army National Guard in the wake of the attacks failed to complete their initial term of service.

The Pentagon fought against these headwinds through an aggressive, multipronged military recruitment campaign, one fueled by a threefold increase in its advertising budget. In January 2002, Congress quietly assisted in this work by granting the military sweeping new powers in the "No Child Left Behind Act," an educational reform bill focused chiefly on testing policies for disadvantaged schoolchildren. Saddled within it, however, was a provision arming recruiters with unprecedented access to the personal data of American students, including minors.

From here, recruiters spammed youngsters with phone calls, visited them at their homes, and camped out in their school's hallways, with internal military regulations directing staff to ply administrators with flowers, tchotchkes, and donuts. Data obtained through the Freedom of Information Act by writers Scott Harding and Seth Kershner found that recruiters most aggressively targeted America's most vulnerable communities, sometimes visiting a single school more than a hundred times a year. Most recruiters would set up tables, but some coached sports, or even lectured in history classes, all part of an internal plan to secure "school ownership."

The recruitment pitch itself could be prolonged, intense, and misleading. Eighty-six percent of Texas students in one survey reported that their recruiters never floated the bodily risks associated with service. In another especially troubling case, a military recruiter assured a prospective high schooler that "we're not even in a war anymore"—in 2006. When high schooler Seth Dvorin told a recruiter that his mother had questions about him signing up, the official responded, "Aren't you man enough to sign on the dotted line yourself? Who wears the pants in your family?" Seth ultimately joined the Army following years of incessant recruiting, then, in 2004 at the age of twenty-four, he died in Iraq from a roadside bomb.

RUMSFELD'S PENTAGON ALSO REASSERTED ITS POWER in the corridors of civilian higher education, threatening to withdraw hundreds of millions in federal grants to Harvard Law School unless it agreed to allow military recruiters back on campus. The Ivy quickly caved. "This university cannot accept the loss of federal funds," its law dean explained. Other spooked colleges soon folded under similar threats.

This capitulation was strong proof that the military's campaign, first launched during World War II, to secure a chokehold on civilian universities through research dollars had been a smashing success. At the GWOT's onset, nearly 350 colleges and universities were conducting Pentagon-funded research. The Defense Department had hefty influence in many departments, including around Thayer's academic specialty of engineering, then providing a whopping 60 percent of all university-based engineering research in America.

Between 2003 and 2004 alone, the Pentagon's power skyrocketed even more, as its research and development budget grew by $7.6 billion. This appropriation was eagerly endorsed by the Association of American Universities, which, in 2006, released a paper supporting stepped-up resources for America's defense and security interests, largely by incentivizing schools and professors to expand their Science, Technology, Engineering, and Mathematics offerings— or STEM—and aggressively recruit students to study them.

Other national security agencies also redoubled their recruiting relationships with academia. In 2002, *The Wall Street Journal* reported that the CIA was becoming a "growing force on campus." Three years later, the FBI launched the National Security Higher Education Advisory Board, a body composed of sixteen civilian college presidents and chancellors and led by then-FBI director and future Russiagate special counsel Robert Mueller. He hoped the board would "foster exchanges between academia and the FBI in order to develop curricula which will aid in attracting the best and brightest students to careers in the law enforcement and intelligence communities."

In 2004, Congress created the Pat Roberts Intelligence Scholars Program, a spy state tuition assistance fund for students who pledged to enter the intelligence community upon graduation. The program was, ironically, named for a Republican senator accused of a whitewash in his role co-chairing the committee investigating intelligence lapses in the run-up to the Iraq War. Roberts had repeatedly cautioned against reforming the intelligence agencies after 9/11, leading his Democratic counterpart, Jay Rockefeller, to accuse him of taking "all his talking points from the White House." Roberts repeatedly punted on releasing the committee's core findings, first until after the 2004 election, then until after the 2006 midterms, leading the *Los Angeles Times* to dub his panel "the Senate Coverup Committee." (A comprehensive report was not released until 2008, after Roberts had left the committee and it had reverted to Democratic control.)

AS RECRUITMENT WANED, the military began seeking high school dropouts and those who had scored low on its aptitude tests. Between 2003 and 2006, the number of waivers granted by the U.S. Army for recruits with criminal backgrounds also jumped by nearly 65 percent. Despite renewed national interest, schools like the Forge were similarly still relying on the tuition dollars of "bad apples," including bullies and purported gang members. Eager to stem parental fears, Superintendent Long announced in 2003 that the school had hired a pack of psychologists to help these troubled teens. Long also introduced merits for "good behavior."

These tools proved grossly insufficient. Months after Long's announcement, in January 2004, a seventeen-year-old Forge cadet was slapped with abuse charges concerning three cadets, including stalking, statutory sexual assault, and "involuntary deviant intercourse"—a category of felony crimes ranging from forced oral and anal sex to other forced non-vaginal penetration. While the report didn't clarify whether this was yet another act of "tooth-pasting," it sure sounded like one. That same year, the Board of Trustees voted unanimously to boot Long for an alleged pattern of sexual harassment. Long later sued the school, claiming the allegations were cooked up by a board member who disapproved of his management style. The two parties settled out of court, but the whole affair elicited more embarrassing headlines in the local press.

In 2006, AMCSUS, the powerful association representing private military schools, hired a new executive director, Rudy Ehrenberg, a Vietnam veteran and West Pointer. He told me that service academy staff worked "very closely" with his member schools, counseling senior leaders and maintaining a postgraduate pipeline to their more affluent campuses. Ehrenberg said the biggest threats he faced in his seven years on the job concerned the public perception that member schools, like the Forge, were rife with hazing and bad students. The association responded, Ehrenberg acknowledged, mostly through increased marketing.

The Forge, for its part, often responded to internal strife or damaging headlines through poorly enacted cover-ups. "The school was constantly worried about themselves and covering their own asses," a gruff Marine Corps veteran and longtime TAC officer told me. "All they cared about was that there was no negative press, even if it meant that kids were being sodomized or kids were having inappropriate sexual relations, or getting drunk or getting high, or whatever. They didn't care."

When, for instance, a whistleblower stepped forward with credible allegations of rampant sexual misconduct and hazing among cadets, the school tried to fire him, leading a Forge lawyer to warn that doing so would amount to "retaliatory discharges." Sources told me that J.J. Rivera, a brutal Marine helicopter pilot in Afghanistan turned Forge commandant, allegedly slow-walked investigations—including one that involved a rape. When another TAC raised concerns about Symantha Hicks—a Forge guidance counselor who, according to police records, was suspected of giving alcohol to minors and performing oral sex on a sixteen-year-old—a school official allegedly tried to convince him not to go to the cops. Hicks denied engaging in sex with the boy, but was convicted of "corruption of minors." The Forge had hired her to replace another female counselor whose comportment with students came under scrutiny. But when an administrator raised concerns with the HR office about that counselor—who was later convicted of sexually assaulting a fifteen-year-old at another school—"I was told that it was none of my business, to just stay out of it."

"At Valley Forge, it's all about how things look," one former cadet told me, echoing others. "How the school acts is much different." As the Forge adopted a stance of "image over everything," rules lost all meaning and abuse skyrocketed. In 2007, two parents told the *Philadelphia Inquirer* they were pulling their sons from the Forge after one of them, age sixteen, was savagely beaten by peers. The other, a thirteen-year-old, was "repeatedly tormented," kicked while doing push-ups, and branded with a five-pointed star. Another suit details other allegations, including that after a thirteen-year-old cadet reported his own abuse to school officials, his tormentors branded his flesh with a "B"—for "bitch."

In this lawless environment, some cadets felt emboldened to target staff. In a 2008 wrongful termination suit, a Forge security officer claimed he had been attacked by two intoxicated cadets. A former chemistry teacher also claimed in court that a group of students broke into his classroom with a long knife and demanded a cell phone he had confiscated. As conditions at the school became unbearable, some cadets tried to escape. Most were hunted down by TAC officers, some of whom were former cops and corrections officers. "It's kind of like prison," one former cadet told me, echoing sharply the observations of Mark Jones, the incarcerated former West Point footballer.

AMERICA'S SHORT, SUGAR-LIKE OPTIMISM for the war crashed hard. Military recruitment collapsed, and military school enrollment did, too, exacerbating budgetary problems and precipitating cuts. As the war dragged on, campuses started to reflect the Pentagon's beleaguered image. The Air Force Academy faced food shortages, while the Merchant Marine Academy was marked by "crumbling facades, leaking pipes and water damage." At one point, the Forge barracks became infested with rats, cockroaches, and water leaks, and school leaders scaled back their toilet paper purchases. Bread in the chow hall was often covered in shamrock-green mold, leading cadets to call hamburgers by another name: St. Patrick's Day patties.

Supervision at the Forge also evaporated, spiking violence and drug abuse. Cadets often snuck nips of liquor into their rooms. In one grainy cell phone video I obtained, a cadet is seen in the Forge barracks ripping a bong, then blowing the smoke into a friend's mouth through the barrel of an AK-47. A father of two boys who attended the Forge said some trustees were getting trashed, too, and even got in fights downtown. "Between the board and the cadets, I'm not sure who was crazier on alcohol," he said.

As adult leaders shirked their responsibilities, various senior cadets stepped up. Some rushed students to the hospital who had become dangerously intoxicated or injured from fights. Another cadet leader, then twenty, temporarily filled in as the school's chaplain, holding religious ceremonies and counseling suicidal cadets as young as twelve. Some stationed themselves in children's rooms to ensure they didn't hurt themselves. Others were put on shifts to hunt down and capture cadets fleeing campus. "There are many fights—I mean many, many fights—I have seen that played out completely, where one student was beaten to a bloody fucking pulp before anyone intervened," one former Forge cadet told me.

Depression became a way of life at the Forge, especially in the winter, which cadets called "the dark ages," and at West Point is known as "the gloom period." Cadet suicide has long been a hallmark of military school life, and a few contagions marked the early years of the war. Between 2002 and 2004, the Air Force Academy saw eighteen suicide attempts. On December 8, 2008, Alfred Fox, then a junior at West Point, checked himself into a motel off campus and killed himself by inhaling helium from a tank as he slept. Another West Point cadet committed suicide off campus shortly thereafter, then a professor and staff member committed suicide, and two more cadets attempted it.

"People need to know that it's not a normal college," West Point plebe Matt Sinclair told *The New York Times* after this spate of suicides. "You're going to be stressed. Sometimes it can feel overwhelming. If you have family problems, and it's really bothering you, West Point is not the best place to try to resolve them."

In 2015, a twenty-year-old cadet in H-1 company named Nick Wright killed himself. A few years later, another twenty-year-old West Point cadet in H-1 named Kade Kurita became dangerously disillusioned with the academy's pedagogical environment. This was a tectonic shift for a boy who, throughout middle and high school, stayed at least two weeks ahead on his homework and who, for his Eagle Scout project, chose to refurbish his beloved fifth-grade classroom. Kade was sold on West Point's lofty claims of academic excellence, only to land in an environment hyperfocused on combat and obedience at the expense of scholarship.

"West Point's supposed to be this amazing school, but it's looking mediocre to me," he confided in his mother, Anita. He further expressed his distaste for firearms. "I can shoot, but I don't like it," Kade told her. "It's safe to say that I don't want to be in combat."

During a vacation home his sophomore year, Kade asked his mom cryptically, "What happens if your commanding officer orders you to do something that is morally wrong?" His stepdad, a hard-assed former Los Angeles sheriff, quickly interjected. "You need to be loyal," he said.

A few months later, Kade was set to compete in a military skills competition. Around this time, he snuck some ammunition for his M4 rifle out of the armory. Then, on October 18, 2019, Kade disappeared. Four days later, he was found dead on campus.

WHEN, JUST LIKE WITH VIETNAM, the American public soured on the GWOT, many military schools abandoned their pretense of moral superiority and embraced a more cutthroat, but also corner-cutting, modus operandi. Rather than revise their own effective discipline structure, Forge administrators sloppily copied the rulebook from the Virginia Military Institute, an ironic move given that plagiarizing is universally considered at military schools to be an honor code violation.

Around this time, the GAO found that West Point wasn't even bothering to teach the honor code anymore. Some West Point faculty openly showed contempt for the law, with one colonel questioning the efficacy and expectation that troops abroad follow the laws of war. "War crimes go on all the time," he said. "You can't expect soldiers to memorize the [Uniform Code of Military Justice]. Things are mushy." Another agreed. "The lawyers have hijacked ethics," he said.

In 2005, when Lieutenant General John Regni became the Air Force Academy's superintendent, he discovered a similar decline. Fitness and academic standards "had been lowered" since his time as a cadet in the early 1970s. Also, he told me, the academy's Center for Character and Leadership Development had "died on the vine."

Military schools became infected by the war's worst impulses, owing, according to interviews, to a subset of battle-drained veterans. "Many of the TACs who came back with combat patches were hard on cadets in all the wrong ways," Riz Shah, a former West Point TAC officer, told me. When, once a month, TACs would convene to discuss West Point's state of affairs, Shah said he often made his disappointment clear. "You guys need to spend more time actually mentoring these cadets," he said. "We were no longer in the military, we were civilians," Shah concluded. "We were there to be a role model for these kids, not a drill instructor. Many of my co-workers didn't understand that. They ruled by intimidation and fear."

A Forge TAC similarly recalled the time he heard that a veteran co-worker had brutally beaten up a fourteen-year-old cadet from Texas, which he confirmed by speaking to the cadet, who was badly bruised. This TAC angrily confronted his co-worker, stripping the military bars off his uniform and challenging him to a fight. "I'm going to make you pay for what you did to that little boy," he seethed.

One of the harshest post-9/11 TACs at Valley Forge was onetime commandant and Afghanistan veteran J.J. Rivera. He once declared his intention to give cadets an experience he likened to a deployment in "one of the shit-istans." A former cadet summed up Rivera's outlook as: "Toughen the fuck up! If I hear you have problems, then fucking leave . . . I don't need a broken soldier." In a grainy video shared with me, Rivera can be heard screaming "Shut the fuck up!" at a whimpering young cadet. Then he grabs the boy, and the video cuts to black.

The Forge also briefly employed Steve Stefanowicz, a towering former Navy officer who had been a key player in the Abu Ghraib torture scandal. He was tasked with overseeing the middle schoolers, aged ten to fourteen, until a staffer's chance Google search uncovered allegations that the six-foot-five Stefanowicz had previously ordered underlings to violently interrogate Iraqi detainees.

Some military school cadets came to embrace the war's signature torture methods. In one case, a pack of VMI upperclassmen darkened out a dorm room, bound the feet of two plebes with duct tape, and played an Islamic call to prayer over a loudspeaker. "It's time for some Abu Ghraib shit," one of them said. Then cadets placed a towel over the face of a plebe and waterboarded him.

ONE MONTH AFTER NEWS OF ABU GHRAIB BROKE, on a windswept afternoon in May 2004, Defense Secretary Rumsfeld arrived at West Point to deliver a commencement address. In the spring of 2001, he had reportedly been "too busy" to fulfill invites to the West Point and Naval Academy graduations, but now the campus offered a safe space from gnawing scandal, one where Rumsfeld could wax poetic and bask in unearned acclaim, just as Nixon, Kissinger, and countless other war planners had done before him.

As protesters outside the school's gates spotlighted the injustices of Abu Ghraib, and demanded Rumsfeld's resignation, West Point's graduating class cheered him on. Rumsfeld delivered rote remarks that stressed the importance of "moral clarity" and conflated the conflicts he was overseeing to the Second World War—already a grossly overused analogy by the Bush White House to squeeze every last bit of goodwill from that old war for the aims of this new one. In Rumsfeld's simplistic telling, both conflicts were about "defending freedom."

At the conclusion of his remarks, Rumsfeld was presented with a ceremonial saber from the class, then jumped on a plane and flew back to Washington for the dedication of the World War II memorial, yet another attempt to ease public dissatisfaction with a nostalgic salve.

A few years later, in 2008, when Bush gave commencement remarks at the Air Force Academy, he also sought to exhume the noble ghosts of World War II for the purposes of defending the GWOT. "We are once again facing evil men who despise freedom, and despise America, and aim to subject millions to their violent rule," Bush said, though he steeled the crowd for a victory that would feel far different this time—"maybe even like nothing at all."

"In the past," Bush concluded, "there were public surrenders, a signing ceremony on the deck of a battleship, victory parades in American cities. Today, when the war continues after the regime has fallen, the definition of success is more complicated." Bush's battleship reference was particularly conspicuous, coming exactly five years after his disastrous "Mission Accomplished" speech aboard the USS *Abraham Lincoln*, in which he very prematurely signaled an end to fighting in Iraq.

The unmitigated failure of the PR stunt was, strangely enough, softened by Bush's own incompetent but quasi-harmless public image, a man seen as slaphappy, foolish, and profoundly naïve. There was something comforting to voters in Bush's theatrical incompetence and fratty affectation, a cultural progenitor, perhaps, of the ascendant power of the hard-drinking manosphere and Barstool Sports.

Bush's identity was formed at his father's alma mater, Yale. By his own admission, Bush "didn't learn a damned thing," except perhaps how to get drunk and torture plebes, including perverse branding ceremonies, as the president of Yale's DKE fraternity chapter. Then, to avoid Vietnam, Bush joined the Texas Air National Guard, where he essentially washed out due to his poor attendance record. His vice president, Dick Cheney, was also a draft dodger, but had become a keen operator of military bureaucracy as H.W. Bush's defense secretary. Cheney was effectively deputized to prosecute the war from the guts of the Pentagon, while W. Bush stuck to scripted public events.

Bush ruled during a moment of popularizing fraternity culture, epitomized by a glut of comedies like *Old School*, a 2003 picture starring Will Ferrell, who had become famous for portraying a dull but humanizing version of Bush on *Saturday Night Live*. Bush nurtured this culture, and benefited from it, even though he was sober by then. The public didn't seem to matter. In a poll during his 2004 reelection, many members of the public overlooked their deep disaffection with Bush's foreign policy agenda for his affable demeanor. In their eyes, he was the ultimate dude to grab a beer with.

Bush capitalized on his barstool persona to help clinch a second term, and often turned on the charm, including at the 2008 Air Force graduation. After his hyperserious remarks about the war, Bush concluded with a series of playful send-offs to graduating cadets. Mostly, he shook hands, then sent the cadets into battle. In some instances, though, Bush hugged graduates, even kissed them. When, at one point, a beefy airman from his adopted home state of Texas ventured onto the stage, the commander in chief chest-bumped him.

Chapter 15

The Crusade

President Bush usually took pains to cast his Middle East wars in explicitly secular terms, highlighting, for instance, the "vital" roles Muslim leaders played in fighting extremism. In an example of his put-on podunkness, he sometimes labeled the enemy simply as "evildoers." But on the first Sunday after 9/11, as church organs across the country rang out with heartfelt strains of "America the Beautiful," the commander in chief slipped up. After attending chapel services at Camp David, Bush returned to the White House, gathered reporters on the south lawn, and pledged his "faith in our military." Then things got pastoral, fast. "This crusade," Bush continued, "this war on terrorism is going to take a while. And the American people must be patient."

Bush's use of the term *crusade* was seen by his defenders as an unfortunate gaffe and by his detractors as an unvarnished admission of the war's true aims. Many in the president's war cabinet repeatedly cast the fight in explicitly religious terms, a reflection of the canny, decades-long campaign among evangelicals to capture the officer class. No matter the war, faith generously covers the cursed ground of death with a somber hue of just cause. The GWOT, however, became indelibly marked by deeper, more radical Christian undercurrents, by dint of the simple fact that it was being fought against a series of Muslim-majority countries, often in locations featured in the Bible.

Years after his deployments had ended, Major General David Petraeus buzzed when he recalled the moments he and his troops "liberated" the ancient religious city of Babylon, and "the biblical Nineveh," for which God had prophesized its destruction. At churches and prayer breakfasts shortly after the 9/11 attacks, Lieutenant General William Boykin had himself declared that God sent Bush to the White House, and that the war in the Middle East was a fight against "Satan." Boykin had previously cast his involvement in the 1993 Battle in Mogadishu in similarly sacred terms, even asserting that a photo he took during his deployment revealed peculiar black marks in the sky that, in his view, showed that the Muslim-majority city was cursed by a demonic presence. Defense Secretary Rumsfeld declined to denounce Boykin's post-9/11 rhetoric and had also privately evinced contempt for Islam, asserting in one memo that "oil wealth has made Muslims averse to physical labor."

In 2004, Boykin and a half dozen other high-ranking military officials appeared in a video promoting a powerful evangelical organization called "Christian Embassy" that was partially filmed at the Pentagon. In it, West Point Commandant Robert Caslen claims that the embassy's flock includes many high-ranking officers, adding that, whenever he runs into one, "I immediately feel like I am being held accountable because we are the aroma of Jesus Christ."

ONCE BUSH AND HIS MEN CLUMSILY SET THEIR SIGHTS on America's new enemy, West Point became convulsed with a jittery, jingoistic campus energy, one fueled by the stomach-turning anticipation of deployment to a war zone. As in other wars, young cadets knew their commitment, gritted their teeth, and puffed up their chests. "I'm ready to go," swore one cadet while fidgeting with his class ring. "I wanna die with this ring on me." His friend added coolly: "The bullet hasn't been made yet that can kill me."

This warrior bravado was amped up through rowdy social events with darkly violent tunes like the nu metal anthem "Let the Bodies Hit the Floor." A crew of self-styled badasses named "The Goodfellas" talked about "how much war matters to us." These conversations often included a percolating, venomous undercurrent of revenge for the perpetrators of 9/11, and, sometimes, undisguised Islamophobia. Posted in the school gym were signs reading: "The Taliban didn't skip leg day, how about you?" Pictures of Osama bin Laden were displayed in bar urinals just off campus.

In his memoir *Un-American*, West Pointer Erik Edstrom ticks off the common slurs circulating on campus when he arrived as a plebe, in 2003, including "haj," "towel head," and "goat fucker." Edstrom's platoon sergeant also marched him and his fellow underclassmen to a violently Islamophobic chant that went, in part: *"I went to the mosque, where all the terrorists pray / I set up my claymore and blew 'em all away!*

Edstrom was part of the first batch of high schoolers to apply post-9/11. It was a class that became forever stamped as the one that "answered the call." Edstrom, for his part, applied mostly for practical reasons, and got in because he perfectly fit the bill. He was smart, physically fit, and came from a home that couldn't easily send him to college. He matriculated with no righteous zeal for the enemy, no lurking desire to kill. He had been recruited by a member of West Point's savvy network of "Old Grads," who trawl their towns and jingle their medals for ripening talent.

Edstrom went to the academy without much forethought; the "Old Grad" he met seemed pretty well off. He later reflected that he had signed up at an age "when I was a virgin, had never drunk alcohol, had an 11 p.m. curfew, couldn't tell you three facts about Iraq or Afghanistan, and briefly thought about getting a tattoo, in Japanese, saying 'Death Before Dishonor.'"

"I knew nothing," Edstrom concluded. "And yet I was willing to sacrifice everything."

Early on, Edstrom committed hard to the program. He built his body and opened his mind. It soon became filled with visions of carnage and killing, thanks to a particularly barbaric form of inculcation: showing young cadets a "highlight reel of death and destruction" from Iraq. Edstrom recalled what he saw: real blood, explosions, and body parts. After the tape rolled, an Army captain justified the killing, saying "the insurgency is a threat to Christianity."

Screenings like this apparently became commonplace at military schools. More than a decade after Edstrom's screening, Air Force Academy cadet Joy Metzler said she and a thousand other cadets were taken inside an auditorium near her campus's stately chapel and shown a kill cam from a plane's-eye view. Some cadets burst into laughter as combatants got blown to bits, Metzler recalled. "I understand that they have to glorify killing or else no one's going to kill for them," she reasoned, but the footage felt a step too far. Soon after, she applied for conscientious objector status.

The military employed other tools to dehumanize the enemy and glorify his death. This is a staple of American warfare, of course, though what had once been voluble essays on the evils of the British crown's tariff policies had, by now, become a shamefully racist curriculum that pervaded all ranks and backgrounds.

As early as 2002, reports emerged that military guards at Guantánamo Bay were desecrating the Quran. When, in the mid aughts, a Muslim West Point graduate landed at his first active-duty base, in Kuwait, he saw a mural featuring a biblical passage about the Crusades. A weapons contractor supplied rifle scopes to some troops imprinted with coded references to biblical verses. A Marine veteran of the War on Terror turned Forge TAC recalled a case in which a cadet "beat the shit" out of a Muslim classmate, then threw bleach in his eyes. In 2004, Seymour Hersh, the reporter who broke My Lai, surfaced the grisly allegations from Abu Ghraib, in which U.S. troops imposed terrible bodily and psychological torture on a population of predominantly Muslim prisoners.

When, during inspections, cadet squadron leaders ripped up rooms, some screamed "there's a terrorist under your bed." Cadets "cast" as enemy combatants in military trainings were outfitted with scarves to look like they were from the Middle East. A former Air Force Academy staffer recalled a scuffle that broke out after a cadet desecrated a Quran.

By his third year at West Point, Edstrom had developed an Islamophobia that ran deep, evidenced by the target photo of a mean-looking Arab he dubbed "Abdullah" that he tacked on his dorm room wall.

These instincts were further nurtured by academics like Dave Grossman, a former Army Ranger who taught psychology at West Point. Grossman was also the founder of the "Killology Research Group," which studied how to motivate killing from the premise that man is not inherently violent. His work examined specific Pavlovian processes used by militaries to train and calibrate aggression, and claimed to be able to inoculate against battlefield stress, forming "the bulletproof mind."

Because PTSD contributed so immensely to the dark mark left on Vietnam, the GWOT generation became swamped with suggested treatments—some legitimate, others snake oil—to cure their psychic wounds. These included advanced psychotherapy techniques and holistic remedies, like horseback-riding and marijuana. There were lots of pills, too, and secretive labs that developed neuro-chips aimed at creating super soldiers who need little sleep, feel little pain, and experience little fear. "It is possible that we may one day be stupendous at brainwashing; that is replacing adverse and intrusive memories with benign ones," mused Dr. Steven Hyman, director of the Stanley Center for Psychiatric Research at MIT and Harvard. "We might in that sense 'cure' PTSD, but we may also cure the conscience."

The military's anti-Muslim sentiments were given an academic patina by a short-lived West Point law professor, William Bradford, whose writings, surfaced by the *Guardian* in 2015, led to his expulsion. Bradford had deemed Middle Eastern schools, media outlets, and Islamic holy sites as legitimate targets during the war, "even if it means great destruction . . . and civilian collateral damage." Bradford may have been booted, but educational materials at the Joint Forces Staff College still proposed "'Hiroshima' tactics" for mosques and other holy sites.

"There was definitely a right-leaning conservative slant to almost everything," recalled John Schmitt, an ROTC graduate from UC-Davis who worked as a Black Hawk helicopter pilot in Iraq and taught chemistry at West Point between 2009 and 2012. Schmitt told me he was frustrated that the cadet curriculum didn't meaningfully grapple with moral injury and the ethics of killing. "When I would ask cadets, 'Where do you get your moral authority to break shit and kill people?' many would often say 'God.'" While he technically taught science, Schmitt tried to widen his cadets' aperture for war information, in part by covertly screening Al Jazeera segments in class.

Perhaps the military's most expensive effort to "understand" the enemy was through Project Minerva, a social sciences research consortium named after the Roman goddess of wisdom. It was launched in 2008 by Defense Secretary Robert Gates as a redux of sorts to Project Camelot, an ill-fated Vietnam-era operation largely run out of American University that aimed to study and psychoanalyze the political cultures and revolutionary tendencies of developing Communist and Socialist nations.

Minerva was initially given a $50 million research budget, immediately making the Pentagon one of the largest funders of social science research in America. Secretary Gates cast this work as vital to America's national security, though not before lightly deriding his gestating crop of academics as "eggheads," a juvenile dig, it seemed, meant to reaffirm the age-old schoolyard hierarchy of brawn over brains. A few years into Minerva's rollout, the number of academic articles focused on terrorism increased sevenfold, leading Catherine Lutz, professor of anthropology and international studies at Brown, to prophesize that the military's dalliance with psychology, sociology, history, anthropology, and other fields, would fundamentally reframe them around "the military definition of reality." This "entails seeing the world as a series of threats to be dealt with," she wrote, "sorting people into enemies and allies, and focusing on the use or threat of force."

Secretary Gates was well connected on campuses, a former president of Texas A&M University who maintained close ties with the Association of American Universities. Many schools marshaled themselves into his cause, including Yale, which took $1.8 million of Minerva cash to set up a "center of excellence" focused on improving military interrogation techniques. It was to be led by Charles Morgan, a professor of pyschiatry who had previously studied how to tell when Arab and Muslim men are lying. Before long, Yale abandoned the center following revelations in the press that its research subjects were largely being pulled from New Haven's immigrant communities.

Many Minerva-backed projects focused explicitly on the Middle East—covering everything from the Iraqi government under Saddam Hussein and the Taliban to "the role of Islamic madrassahs as incubators of violence." Many studies utilized the five million or so documents that had been plundered by troops during the initial 2003 invasion, in flagrant violation of international law. These materials were later transferred to Stanford University's Hoover Institute via the Iraq Memory Foundation, formed by an Iraqi exile and Bush's favorite academic: Kanan Makiya.

Just as West Point conjured in the public imagination the idea of the invulnerable soldier scholar, Makiya served as a uniquely powerful validator of the White House's case for the invasion, pledging that American ground troops would quickly incubate and hatch Western-style democracy. At one point, Makiya promised the president that American troops would be greeted by civilians with "sweets and flowers."

In 2002, Makiya drafted an idealistic, Bush-backed plan for bringing Iraq "forward," including through a skelton constitution he wrote for the country. He also lambasted the Muslim world. In one scathing interview with PBS, Makiya dismissed Islam as a "medieval" religion obsessed with obedience and fatalism. He further scolded the Arab world for letting "the darkness of religion flourish." In exchange for his helpful research and rhetoric, the Pentagon granted Makiya and his team $5 million.

A few years later, in 2008, the Air Force Academy hosted a four-day symposium on "Dismantling Terrorism" that largely reinforced the military's rigid conception of the Arab world. Centerpiece remarks were delivered by three known fabulists posing as reformed Islamic extremists. All depicted Islam as inherently violent, with one proclaiming that converting to Christianity had saved his life. They were paid $13,000 for their services by private donors.

WHEN ERIK EDSTROM FIRST ARRIVED for Beast Barracks at West Point in the summer of 2003, he and his fellow plebes were sorted by religion. Unsurprisingly, Christianity dominated. Atheists, he recalled, were disparaged as "heathens." West Point had Muslim cadets, but not many of them. At the time of the 9/11 attacks, just nine of West Point's four thousand cadets practiced Islam. Shortly after 9/11, *The New York Times* talked with three of them, all of whom said they had been approached since the attacks by fellow cadets and officers with questions about their faith. "Some asked about Koran passages; others wondered if Osama bin Laden was really from a wealthy family," the paper reported. "One cadet asked Cadet [Amir] Bagherpour if the Koran condemns suicide."

Noor Merchant was the only woman among the trio of Muslim cadets interviewed by the *Times*. She told the paper of her practical impediments in practicing her faith, including her packed academic schedule, which allowed for prayer only twice a day, not five times, as is expected. West Point's exhausting physical regime also made it virtually impossible for Noor to fast for Ramadan. "I'd probably faint," she reasoned. At the time, the school didn't offer services for Shia Muslims like herself, so her uncle picked her up on weekends and took her to a mosque in Poughkeepsie.

In an interview decades later, Noor told me that her time at West Point was mostly positive, insisting there "wasn't a lot of ignorance." One of her Muslim classmates similarly observed that Islamophobia was generally reserved for the enemy. "There were cadets from my class who had Confederate flag tattoos, and are as racist as it comes," he said. "But if something happened to me, and I called them, they'd have my back."

Noor had wanted, as a child, to be a doctor, but when she didn't get into her preferred medical school, she had what she now views as a childish rebellion, telling her parents, "Screw this, I'm going to go to West Point." Today she likens her education to a drawn-out indoctrination. "The discipline and structure of cadet life does something to your brain," she said.

For Noor, it forced a fast maturation that kept the war in front of her strangely abstract. "When you're at West Point things just don't feel as real," she explained. The conflict, she remembered, "seemed scary, but also felt really far away." In 2006, Noor, then just twenty-three years old, first faced the reality of war, landing in Afghanistan and tasked with running a platoon. "I still kinda felt like a kid," she said. "But I was a young lieutenant in charge of people's lives and well-being. It was a huge responsibility, and it was scary as shit." Some lower-ranking enlisted soldiers were older than she was.

Noor's sixteen-month deployment in-country was "horrible and hard." Her most trying professional moment came when American troops had shot at a vehicle thinking it was the enemy when, in fact, it held a mother and her newborn coming home from the hospital. The baby was struck with a bullet and died. "They had me go visit her in the hospital to represent the Army," Noor explained. "I was very disturbed and angry about the incident. And I apologized."

During her stint at Forward Operating Base Salerno, in southern Afghanistan, Noor said she was sexually assaulted by a superior. She filed a complaint and requested a base transfer, but neither appeal went anywhere. Once the superior caught on that she had reported him, he also allegedly ordered his colleagues to silence her. Noor was cut off from her family, isolated from teammates, and emotionally wounded. "It was a whole lot of fucked up shit happening," she told me, and so she, like many of her Christian brethren, looked to the skies. "I turned to my faith then because I didn't have anything else," she said. "And it kind of got me through."

THE SAME YEAR NOOR MERCHANT DEPLOYED to the Middle East, Lauren Baas, then eighteen, flew West, to Colorado Springs and the Air Force Academy. As the wheels of her plane touched the tarmac of her new home, Lauren dreamed of becoming a fighter pilot. She had been raised devoutly Catholic, but many of her peers at the academy were more fervent than she. By the early aughts, 90 percent of cadets identified as Christian and the school's chaplaincy office had become dominated by evangelicals. Some staff felt their colleagues allocated resources unevenly, to boost Christian-based activities. Islamic services, they alleged, were scheduled to conflict with compulsory academy activities. Many senior school leaders were part of this evangelical flock, too, including the academy's commandant, Brigadier General Johnny Weida, and head football coach Fisher DeBerry, who plastered a sign in his locker room reading: "I am a member of Team Jesus Christ." Brigadier General Dana Born, dean of faculty, was also known to hand out Bibles at faculty meetings. In a survey taken shortly before Lauren's arrival, 30 percent of cadets reported pervasive proselytizing by their evangelical peers.

In the early aughts, the Air Force Academy logged nearly sixty complaints charging religious discrimination. West Point, by contrast, logged one. The Naval Academy—zero. Some of the worst treatment at the Air Force Academy, and elsewhere, concerned Jewish cadets, one of whom said he had been told that the Holocaust had been a righteous revenge for the death of Jesus. Another Jewish student was reportedly called "Christ Killer." In 2005, Air Force Academy Superintendent John Rosa candidly admitted to the Board of Visitors that the religious atmosphere had become untenable. "The problem is people have been across the line for so many years when you try and come back in-bounds, people get offended," he explained.

Academy chaplain MeLinda Morton harbored similar worries. A mainline Lutheran, she told me she saw her evangelical peers leverage the stressors of academy life to proselytize, intervening with cadets at their weakest moments to "introduce theological concepts and religiosity." Morton's observations were subsequently confirmed during a site visit by officials from Yale Divinity School. In their 2005 report, the Yale team detailed "stridently evangelical themes" across campus life, including during dangerous training situations, where staff egged on cadets with a divine promise: "Jesus will save you."

The Air Force Academy responded to these revelations with new guidance, championed by Rosa, that banned some public prayers and discouraged discussions of faith between commanders and lower-ranking personnel. But soon after, Rosa left Colorado Springs to run the Citadel. He was replaced in 2005 by John Regni, an academy graduate and former altar boy who was Roman Catholic to his core, having earned his master's degree at St. Mary's University, the oldest Catholic University in the American southwest. Nonetheless, Regni was aligned with Rosa's campaign against too much evangelicalism. In his four years as superintendent, Regni supported the newly created interfaith council and kept his own faith in private. "I basically took four years off from the church," he told me. "I wasn't going to cadet chapel in my uniform." He also engaged with the sharpest critics of the academy's religious culture, even texting a particularly zealous critic a photo of a Jewish star hanging in front of the cadet chapel, which seemed to soothe his opponent. Evangelical groups, however, lobbied successfully to soften the Air Force's guidelines shortly after Regni arrived. The new rules allowed religious discussions so long as they weren't deemed "coercive." Lauren arrived at the Air Force Academy soon after this regulatory rollback.

When, during Vietnam, Regni had attended the academy as a cadet, religious activities had been limited to mandatory Sunday chapel service. Now, cadets were being enticed by zealous school officials, plus megachurches off campus, sometimes even whisked away to their spaces on nights and weekends. Certain sects were given classroom space, even key cards for the dorms. "That was different from what I had experienced as a cadet," Regni recalled.

One of these ministries was "The Navigators," a sect tied to evangelical leader Billy Graham, which assigned two chaplains to proselytize on campus full-time. There was also the fourteen-thousand-member New Life Church, whose famed pastor, Ted Haggard, was a familiar figure on campus until 2006, when it was reported in the media that Haggard had had sexual relations with a male escort and used amphetamines.

Lauren was targeted by a small ministry called "Cadets for Christ," run by an older couple named Don and Anna Warrick. She began attending their weekly Wednesday-night Bible study, then participated in frequent "retreats" at the Warricks' palatial, five-bedroom home, which sat, according to property records, atop a hill in Colorado Springs and featured photos of many "Cadets for Christ" who had come before her.

Lauren's parents felt a bit uncomfortable by the speed at which the Warricks burrowed into their daughter's life. But as her mother, Jean, explained, "you're 1,000 miles away and you trust your kid has a good head on their shoulders." She didn't then understand how thoroughly military training can scramble one's mind. "During those first six weeks, they tear those kids down, they make them subservient, they make them follow commands. That's why the church can get their tentacles in these kids." Her family's concern spiked to alarm when they discovered a "Baa Baa Sisterhood Cookbook" the Warricks had gifted to their daughter. Inside the cover, they inscribed it to "Sheep Lauren." Months later, Lauren abandoned her plans to be a pilot, shifting to the less rigorous missile program.

Former chaplain Morton corroborated this kind of behavior to me, saying that religious figures within the academy's orbit "encouraged women cadets in general, and several women cadets specifically, to choose military career paths that would enable them to more easily marry and quickly bear children." She said this advice was generally framed within a "rather imperialist interpretation of Genesis 1:28—a biblical creation story where God commands humankind to 'be fruitful and multiply' and 'have dominion' over the earth."

Another set of Air Force Academy parents whose daughter arrived the same year as Lauren also described to me their experiences with the Warricks. It featured many of the same beats. This second family, who insisted on anonymity, called Cadets for Christ a "cult," with the father saying, "these kids didn't drink Kool Aid, but they might as well have." They alleged that, in their case, the Warricks attempted to isolate and dominate their daughter, including by whisking her away to Florida on a trip without informing them.

When Lauren's mother, Jean, began vocally raising concerns about the Warricks to Air Force Academy officials, they "did nothing." (Regni, for his part, claims that Lauren's case never crossed his desk. "It's not ringing any bells at all," he told me.) The academy's alleged passivity permitted Cadets for Christ to strongly calcify Lauren's faith. By the time she graduated, in the spring of 2010, Lauren was fully committed to the Warricks' flock, having been paired with a male "Cadet for Christ" two years her junior that snowballed into an engagement shortly after graduation.

Regni's replacement, Michael Gould, quickly showed himself to be far less open to tackling religious intolerance than his predecessors. A few months after Lauren graduated, Gould tried to preempt the release of the school's latest religious climate survey, in which 41 percent of non-Christian cadets reported being subjected to unwanted proselytizing over the previous year.

Its findings spurred Jean to shoot off a rageful email to the Warricks. She copied Gould. It charged that the religious couple had "taken Lauren's mind and soul and twisted it to your fundamentalist Christian liking." Jean alleged that Gould never responded to the thread, or meaningfully reined in the Warricks. On the contrary, a few months later, Gould hosted a National Prayer Luncheon on campus and invited as its keynote speaker Clebe McClary, a highly decorated military veteran who had lost his left eye and left arm in hand-to-hand combat in Vietnam. After the war, McClary had become a motivational speaker, generally for NFL teams and military audiences, where he discussed his wartime record as well as his ongoing service in the "Lord's Army."

A few weeks before McClary was set to deliver remarks, a pack of five academy professors sued to prevent his appearance, arguing it was unconstitutional. Four of the five plaintiffs had joined the suit anonymously, worried that any public "dissent from the 'party line'" would yield "serious negative consequences" from academy administrators. The sole public plaintiff was David Mullin, an evangelical economics professor and self-identified Republican who nonetheless believed strongly in the separation of church and state.

Whispers around campus alleged that senior academy staff had ordered a "counterinsurgency" against the plaintiffs, but Mullin was undeterred. In addition to the suit, he also alleged that senior school administrations had hired dozens of uncredentialed military instructors, then lied about their qualifications to the school's accrediting body.

Not long after Mullin's vocal protestation, on the day before Easter 2011, he and his wife attended church with their black lab, Caleb, who, during the services, began acting strange. Hours later, Caleb started suffering from massive internal bleeding and was rushed to a veterinary hospital. The dog survived by the grace of God—and three blood transfusions. A veterinarian subsequently informed Mullin that his dog had ingested a slow-acting poison. This led Mullin to speak out once more, charging that Caleb had been covertly poisoned on a recent visit to campus, an act of heartless retaliation for blowing the whistle. Not long after that, the Air Force Academy terminated his teaching contract. If Mullin's instinct about his dog is to be believed, then it stands that figures within America's most pious military service academy perpetrated a deeply sinful deed. This is startling but not altogether surprising news, a logical endpoint for a place that, since its founding, has been in direct violation of God's sixth commandment: "thou shall not kill."

Chapter 16

COIN of the Realm

America aimed to steel itself against the mistakes of Vietnam chiefly by injecting the Global War on Terror with perspective and intelligence. This work was largely accomplished by handing the reins to West Pointers, chief among them General David Petraeus, one of the academy's all-time golden boys. Upon his graduation, Petraeus had gone on to earn a PhD at Princeton where, over two painstaking years, he penned a dissertation that promised to definitively explain the "lessons of Vietnam."

Petraeus carefully cultivated his image as a quintessential soldier-scholar with reporters, politicians, and the public. He leaned on his academic credentials and turned up his personal charm. This led him to receive the same prestigious job twice, first commandeering President Bush's troops through a surge in Iraq in 2007, then, in 2009, architecting a similar campaign in Afghanistan for President Barack Obama. Petraeus's ability to flip his reputation and ingratiate himself to the famously cerebral Obama impressed observers. In 2007, as an Illinois senator, Obama derided the general as a spin doctor, accusing him publicly, during the Iraq surge, of setting "the bar so low that modest improvement" was considered success. Despite Obama's overall vibe during his 2008 campaign of being a peacenik, he had only contended that he wouldn't fight "dumb wars." Once he became president, Obama embraced Petraeus, who pledged to give him a smart one.

Petraeus's pitch was optimistic and impeccably delivered. His public persona offered everyone everything, all at once. Here was a man who was both bookish and grandiose, fast and strong, technocratic and lethal. The war strategy Petraeus laid out to Washington's decision-makers embodied all these shifty terms. It was known as counterinsurgency, or COIN.

COIN's steely acronym belied its purportedly soft focus. Basically, it theorized that the best way to win an irregular war was to court civilians and use force judiciously. COIN was an attractive strategy because it placed a moral core at GWOT's center, obscuring firefights and fatalities with infrastructure improvements and the grand dream of a Western-style civil society in the East. Petraeus cast himself both as a loyal public servant to the American people—and to the men and women of Iraq and Afghanistan. He drove this point home on the walls of his well-appointed Kabul office, which featured poignant photographic portraits of locals.

Petraeus pursued the GWOT largely by reeling in the military's "Rules of Engagement," which dictate when troops can shoot, and launching a flurry of humanitarian projects. Education was something he frequently singled out, a tool he viewed as critical to the region's stability. In Iraq, Petraeus helped reopen the University of Mosul, earning him the local moniker of "King David," then he and his wife Holly funded a scholarship at the American University of Afghanistan. The general also supported the Afghan Military Academy, modeled after West Point and located near Kabul.

An ardent devotee of PowerPoint, Petraeus liked to inject Ted Talk–like flourishes to his military campaigns. He presented, for instance, color-coded charts on suicide-bombing trends to reps on Capitol Hill, which he complemented with impossibly vague and aspirational military aphorisms like "the surge that mattered most was the surge of ideas," or "money is ammunition." But Petraeus's baseline strategy was crude—an overwhelming deployment of mostly male bodies. In 2007, he surged 30,000 troops to Iraq. Two years later, he flooded 33,000 more into Afghanistan.

Petraeus believed that inundating the region with more troops would force a fragile calm that could allow new nations to flourish. This tactic helped foster impressive reductions in violence, but they were fleeting, and sometimes accompanied by lucky local developments. The temporary territorial gains and general stability secured through Petraeus's Bush-era surge, nicknamed "the new way forward," was vitally aided, for instance, by the "Anbar Awakening," in which 100,000 mostly Sunni men fed up with Al-Qaeda allied themselves with U.S. forces. This ephemeral progress, which evaporated once troops left, was secured through a hefty price in blood. The year of Petraeus's first surge ended up being the deadliest yet for American service members in Iraq.

Petraeus minimized questions about casualties or strategy with political sleight of hand. In his Princeton dissertation on Vietnam, he embraced a co-equal belief in optics and progress. "Perception" is key, he wrote. "What policy-makers believe to have taken place in any particular case is what matters—more than what actually occurred." Nowhere were his skills in the dark art of deception on better display than in the fall of 2007, when Petraeus provided his first public update on the war before Congress. The press breathlessly declared it the most anticipated war update since Westmoreland had urged Congress to stay the course in Vietnam four decades earlier.

Petraeus borrowed much from his legendary West Point forefather. The White House intentionally scheduled Petraeus's testimony to occur on the sixth anniversary of 9/11, hoping to strike a potent public chord about what America was fighting for. At the same time, a fledgling dark money group called Freedom's Watch, funded largely by conservative casino magnate Sheldon Adelson and led by former White House press secretary Ari Fleischer, blitzed the airwaves in twenty states with $15 million worth of ads championing the war.

Petraeus seemed unfazed but physically uncomfortable in his Capitol Hill hot seat. This could have been due to the lingering symptoms from a pair of noncombat injuries: an accidental bullet wound to the chest in 1991 from a soldier under his command and a broken pelvis suffered a decade later after falling sixty feet when his parachute went screwy. On top of this, Petraeus hated the feel of the chairs themselves. "You can't adjust the height. You have to sit on the edge of them," he groused to *The New Yorker*. "Actually, I really had back pain, which I don't normally have," he said, "just from sitting there for ten hours that first day. So, it was just something to be endured, candidly."

Petraeus's bones may have ached, but he still appeared put-together, brandishing a high-and-tight haircut and more ornaments on his chest than a Christmas tree. When his time came to speak, the general reported "success" in Iraq and predicted ultimate victory, albeit one that would be "neither quick nor easy." He urgently counseled that a rapid pullout of the sort then being advocated by Democrats would be foolish and dangerous. The next day, many American newspapers reacted skeptically to Petraeus's words, reporting that, in the day before the general had hyped up the war, nine American soldiers had died.

More than four thousand American troops perished in the Middle East during the first six years of the war, more than the number of people who died on 9/11. Most of the administration's projections of progress since the initial 2003 invasion of Iraq had not been borne out. By then, only 5 percent of Americans trusted the administration. This was similar to Vietnam, when, in 1967, Westmoreland ventured to Capitol Hill and promised, much like Petraeus, that the American military would ultimately "prevail in Vietnam over Communist aggregation"—so long as he was backed by a big bag of cash and a deep well of public "patience."

Les Payne, a former Westmoreland speechwriter turned journalist, saw in Petraeus a slick operator in the mold of his former boss. "Westy, as we called him, was as eager to please LBJ as Petraeus is to please Bush," Payne reflected in the wake of Petraeus's remarks. "No four-star general arrives at his post by displeasing officers and politicians above him."

Three years later, in 2010, Petraeus returned to Capitol Hill to testify on his newest surge, in Afghanistan. By this point, Afghanistan had officially outpaced Vietnam as America's longest war, and public sentiments had become distinctly worse, though less vocal. This time, Petraeus failed Capitol Hill's test, even as Congress remained stubbornly divided over the Global War on Terror. Not long into his hearing, the general became flustered, then lost all bodily control. His ultimate collapse came as Arizona senator John McCain, generally a defender of Petraeus and his wars, was lightly inquiring about the feasibility of a timetable for withdrawal. As soon as McCain headed to the meat of his question, the general wobbled in his uncomfortable chair, then fainted, his face slumping into his stack of well-prepared policy papers. A minute later, a phalanx of fellow military officers briskly whisked a dazed Petraeus out of the room. He returned shortly afterward to applause.

PETRAEUS WAS EXPOSED TO MILITARY SCHOOLING from an early age. He grew up just seven miles west of West Point, raised by a stoic military veteran in Cornwall-on-Hudson, home to Trump's alma mater, the New York Military Academy, and a small slice of West Point land. In her fawning biography *All In: The Education of General David Petraeus*, Paula Broadwell, a fellow West Pointer and later Petraeus's mistress, and her coauthor, describe Petraeus's father, a World War II Merchant Marine named Sixtus, as an "austere perfectionist." Other veterans populated David's youth, too, and he molded himself in their image. These figures included his high school soccer coach, who had previously captained West Point's team, and the academy's director of admissions, who lived just around the corner. In high school, David also dated the daughter of an Air Force officer in town, and, according to *All In*, was significantly influenced by his "demeanor."

He then briefly courted and married Holly Knowlton, the daughter of West Point Superintendent William Knowlton, where, in visits to the superintendent's cushy quarters, he was regaled by the aging general with exciting war stories from World War II and Vietnam. In 1974, Petraeus's commencement speaker was yet another unrepentant cold warrior, Army Secretary Howard "Bo" Callaway, a West Pointer who prosecuted much of Vietnam for President Nixon. It was Callaway who reduced the military sentence of, then paroled, William Calley, the officer chiefly responsible for My Lai.

Superintendent Knowlton was especially animated about a modest Vietnam counterinsurgency campaign he had been involved with, one orchestrated through the office of Civil Operations and Rural Development Support, or CORDS. It was putatively in keeping with President John F. Kennedy's "hearts and minds" strategy, though Joseph Zengerle, the 1964 West Point graduate who attended Kennedy's inauguration and funeral, told me that, in his subsequent work with Westmoreland in Vietnam, a much blunter maxim circulated among the brass: "Grab 'em by the balls and their hearts and minds will follow."

CORDS involved pacifying popular fronts in Southeast Asia—and America, for that matter—by employing a sheen of humanitarianism to the war in an effort to earn morality points and defang critics. In basic terms, it was an aid and infrastructure program. Military forces constructed roads and waterways, and provided residents with medicine, education, and other services. One project involved American forces building thousands of "strategic hamlets," work nominally intended to move civilians away from warfare but really aimed at strangling South Vietnamese recruitment efforts. Ultimately, many of the people displaced were resentful about it. The plan backfired, with most hamlets becoming infiltrated or overtaken by revolutionary forces. CORDS came late in the war, leading its godfather, a former CIA spook and powerful White House surrogate named Robert Komer, to later concede that it was "a small tail to the very large conventional military dog."

Petraeus would one day wag this dog, but, again, his gains would prove modest and impermanent. No matter its size and scope, a military's humanitarian work is fundamentally compromised by its overarching campaign of death, destruction, and displacement. All of CORDS's accomplishments could never take away from the fact that, in Vietnam, millions of men, women, and children were being killed. Millions more were made refugees or sickened by Agent Orange and other pollutants. During the initial 2001 invasion of Afghanistan, a similar pattern played out when the Bush administration committed billions of dollars to warfare while pledging just $300 million to humanitarian aid, representing about 2 percent of what the United Nations then estimated would be needed to stabilize the country and empower its people.

No matter the balance sheet on aid, many officers saw a fallacy in the idea of an occupying force winning over the locals. During Vietnam, one general bluntly acknowledged that "foreign troops . . . never win the hearts of the people." Three and a half decades later, as COIN was implemented across the Middle East, this same observation was noted by Karl Eikenberry, a retired Army lieutenant general and former chief of Combined Forces Command in Afghanistan: "The typical 21-year-old Marine is hard-pressed to win the heart and mind of his mother-in-law," Eikenberry said. "Can he really be expected to do the same with an ethnocentric Pashtun tribal elder?"

CORDS had, at times, seemed chiefly focused on creating a false sense of humanity in a war zone, fomenting what one scholar described as the "illusion of progress." Among its most harebrained gambits, CORDS created a fool's paradise for a *Newsweek* reporter, bringing him on a purportedly "unescorted automobile tour" to tout progress in the Mekong Delta region while the skies and roads were heavily buttressed by a large but well-hidden military presence. It was not unlike many of the "embedded" but highly regulated reporting trips outlets would take to war zones in the years following 9/11.

PETRAEUS DIRECTED THE GWOT alongside prominent West Pointers, including Stanley McChrystal, H.R. McMaster, Lloyd Austin, John Nagl, and Robert Caslen—a loose crew of ring-knocking whiz kids known in some Washington circles as "the COINdinistas." Together, they promised to avoid a flare-up of President H.W. Bush's dreaded "Vietnam Syndrome," even as they all shared an alma mater forever gripped by the disease. The school's main prescription for moving past Vietnam seemed to be heavy doses of myopia. When asked by a reporter, around 2008, what impact Vietnam had on him as a cadet and a young officer, Petraeus weirdly answered, "[it] was not that significant, believe it or not."

Four years prior, Petraeus helped organize a conference on irregular warfare at the Marine Corps base in Quantico, Virginia. A well-regarded professor of security studies called it a flagrant exercise in ego and a historical optimism. "[The officers] looked at all these failed counterinsurgencies and decided that we knew why they failed and put together a doctrine about why we would win," she recalled.

If there was anything West Point was good at teaching its elite recruits, it was unconstrained confidence. This was clear in Douglas Kinnard's 1977 survey of 173 generals for his book *The War Managers*. Of those surveyed, the West Pointers in the bunch were far more optimistic in their reflections about Vietnam than nongraduates. Decades later, Lark Escobar, a civilian who worked at the Afghan Military Academy, found the campus rife with "pissing match" energy between the packs of mostly West Point officers vying for control of the academy and jockeying for awards. "There was so much arrogance," she said. John Schmitt, a man who became an officer through ROTC channels before serving in Afghanistan, similarly concluded that "the shittiest officers, those who were most out of touch and the most arrogant, were always fucking West Pointers."

Schmitt's attitude was borne out by a 2020 military study of new officers from different commissioning channels. It found a stark mismatch with how officers viewed themselves versus their immediate superiors—a gulf that was most stark among West Point grads. They had the highest levels of self-assurance, a trait Petraeus perfectly embodied. When the Obama administration evinced initial skepticism for his Afghanistan plan, Petraeus expertly manipulated press and policy figures to box the administration into his plan, brashly asserting that the White House was "fucking" with the wrong guy.

The unctuous overconfidence of West Point's COINdinistas was perhaps best personified by General Stanley McChrystal, a self-styled badass who quoted Bruce Lee and carried a custom-made set of nunchucks into battle. He was a man who would make fitness zealot Bernarr MacFadden proud. McChrystal ran operations in Afghanistan when Michael Hastings famously profiled him in *Rolling Stone*. The piece begins with McChrystal at a chichi hotel in Paris, dreading a meeting with NATO allies. "I'd rather have my ass kicked by a roomful of people than go out to this dinner," McChrystal tells Hastings. "Unfortunately, no one in this room could do it."

Hastings found that McChrystal's cockiness belied his remarkable ability to navigate the chain of command. "The son of a general, McChrystal was also a ringleader of [West Point] dissidents—a dual role that taught him how to thrive in a rigid, top-down environment while thumbing his nose at authority every chance he got. He accumulated more than 100 hours of demerits for drinking, partying, and insubordination." Despite all this, cadet McChrystal could honestly grapple with the complexities of war. One short story he wrote for West Point's literary magazine followed a nineteen-year-old soldier who kills a boy he mistakes for a terrorist.

Once in charge, however, McChrystal defended the Army zealously. When football star turned soldier Pat Tillman was killed by friendly fire in April 2004, the general tried to cover it up by awarding him a silver star, which suggested that Tillman had been killed by the Taliban. A few years later, a civilian law professor at West Point organized a screening of a documentary film examining Tillman's story. West Point initially blocked the showing, then allowed it to move forward but limited the number of cadets able to attend and sent an Army lawyer to deliver company talking points afterward. A few months later, the professor who had organized the screening was terminated for so-called budgetary reasons.

After Hastings's *Rolling Stone* profile of McChrystal hit newsstands, Obama fired him for his criticisms of leading administration officials. This provided a clear but limited repudiation of the sort of hypermacho, increasingly nihilistic culture then pervading the military ranks, especially among the largely lawless special operations units that operated on McChrystal's watch. Rather than widely condemn these tenets, let alone tame the swaggering violence and policy daftness of the GWOT, Obama continued to co-sign the campaign, albeit by adding within his killing matrix newly technocratic elements, most famously drones. This created surreal conditions in which an out-of-shape military tech whiz, programming a drone from thousands of miles away, could boast a body count on par with a member of SEAL Team Six. For locals, this phenomenon created new types of terror in the air. The guys on the ground, meanwhile, turned more madcap and reckless, following their basic orders while simultaneously pursuing an outside mission to be known as the last true men of the military.

COIN'S POLITICAL BRILLIANCE RESULTED from its deep-rooted rhetorical ambiguity. Petraeus expertly leveraged this like a Rorschach image, emphasizing the war as deeply humanitarian to some audiences and playing it up as kickass to others. When, for instance, a prominent former military intelligence official wrote to the general worried that his plans were too tame—religious extremists, he warned, were "not susceptible to friendly persuasion"—Petraeus moved to soothe him. "Let me assure you there is no reluctance to kill religious extremists," he replied.

In 2006, Petraeus published a 419-page counterinsurgency field manual for the Army and Marine Corps, cowritten with Nagl and others. It was positively reviewed in *The New York Times* by Samantha Power, foreign policy adviser to Senator Obama, and given a fawning introduction by noted Harvard security professor Sarah Sewall, who wrote that Petraeus's tome "challenges much of what is holy about the American way of war." While the manual was long, two respected scholars argued that it was only remedial, describing basic elements of insurgency but not the vital specifics. This was reflected, they documented, by how the military reduced the region's complicated web of religious, ethnic, and political movements under the single ambiguous umbrella of "insurgents."

At some point during the War on Terror, the term *counterinsurgency* became so overused and underexplained that it started to lose all meaning, even, it seemed, to Petraeus. In August 2010, he issued a three-and-a-half-page counterinsurgency memo to U.S. and NATO forces bursting with beguiling aphorisms like, "Be first with the truth," "Hold what we secure," "Live our values," and "Win the battle of wits." That same year, Army Captain Tim Hsia wrote that many of his peers used COIN as shorthand for "what it is not—conventional warfare," meaning, warfare that is good and cutting edge. In some circles the term degraded further, serving as nothing more than a stand-in for the word *complexity*.

While COIN in its most eloquent interpretation preached understanding and nuance, senior military officers generally offered only the most remedial trainings. One was Lieutenant General H.R. McMaster, who had, by 2006, become commander of the Army's 3rd Armored Cavalry Regiment. McMaster, like Petraeus, was the rare senior military officer with a doctorate, but he taught his men only the most basic regional lessons via a three-week course in Arabic language and culture. As part of this, they dressed up in Arab dishdashas, or "man dresses," as soldiers called them, before acting out kinetic scenarios. McMaster taught his soldiers to kill Iraqis, but also never to swear in front of them, or call them hajjis, an honorific for those who had been to Mecca—which the force had perverted into their war's version of "gook."

Like Petraeus, McMaster claimed chiefly to be working for the locals. "You have to really listen to people," he told *The New Yorker*. Nagl agreed. "What we want for them," he told *The New York Times* in 2004, "is the right to make their own decisions, to live free lives." At times, this optimism among the officer class veered on delusion. The rhetoric did little else, it seemed, other than soothe the tortured conscience of the war planners.

Critical feedback from locals went largely ignored. "The United States is using excessive power," a Sunni chieftain working with the Americans told the *Times* in the same 2004 story. "They round up people in a very humiliating way, by putting bags over their faces in front of their families. In our society, this is like rape. The Americans are using collective punishment by jailing relatives. What is the difference from Saddam? They are demolishing houses now. They say they want to teach a lesson to the people. But when Timothy McVeigh was convicted in the bombing in Oklahoma City, was his family's home destroyed?"

In 2008, Petraeus was promoted to head the United States Central Command. During a visit to Pakistan, president Asif Ali Zardari raised alarm over the rise of American drone strikes, which he argued "result[ed] in loss of precious lives and property, are counterproductive, and difficult to explain by a democratically elected government." Zardari publicly warned after a meeting with Petraeus that these attacks were "creating a credibility gap." The general didn't publicly comment on the president's critique, or respond to immediate questions from the press. Instead, over the coming years, he increasingly turned to drones as a key tool in his arsenal. McChrystal, for his part, deployed special operators on a campaign of night raids in Afghanistan he deemed "F3EAD," short for Find, Fix, Finish, Exploit, Analyze, and Disseminate. His technocratic acronym belied the mission's base brutality, in which more than half the Afghans killed or abducted in this campaign were targeted by mistake.

Robert Caslen, who served as West Point's superintendent from 2013 to 2018, perfectly though unintentionally exposed COIN's infeasibility in his own written defense of it: "On one block," Caslen wrote in 2011, "we may be engaged in a vicious fight. On the next block, we may be building a school; and on the third block, we may be restoring water and power—with all of this being done simultaneously." What Caslen imagined was COIN's impossible premise, of building peace amid war, making allies with one person while killing another, building society while destroying it, or what some COIN advocates described as "armed social work."

A MAJOR PLANK OF THE GWOT COIN PLAN INVOLVED bringing enlightenment to the region through education. In 2011, President Hamid Karzai ventured to the Afghan Military Academy, located just west of Kabul, in Qargha, and publicly positioned it as the key predicate to successfully assuming security duties from the Americans. "The Afghan nation doesn't want the defense of this country to be in the hands of others anymore," Karzai said. "This is our responsibility to raise our flag with honor and pride."

Often, a new COIN initiative seemed plagiarized from an old one, and the Afghan Military Academy was no exception. It was a near carbon copy of the Vietnamese National Military Academy that West Point cadet Tam Minh Pham, derided as "Gooky," had worked at before it was overtaken by Communist forces. Both were founded on the impulse to instill military excellence and "independence" in occupied regions.

A few years into the GWOT, leaders in the Air Force, Army, and Naval Academies teamed up for this ambitious mission: to convert Afghans, via education, into Western-style soldiers and gentlemen who could curb the regional unrest that had flummoxed the West for decades. American forces failed to realize, it seems, that it had been decades of war, displacement, and economic hardship that had fueled violence, resistance, and corruption in the Arab world. According to sociological data, men in the Middle East, as in America and countless other locales, feel a strong pull to be seen by their families as respected providers, protectors, and decision-makers, instincts that, in a forever war zone, can turn them into fierce fighters, cynical power brokers, or domineering warlords.

The site America ultimately chose for the Afghan Military Academy was on the bones of an old Soviet flight school first established in the 1980s as part of the Communist superpower's woefully intractable Cold War proxy campaign there. One would be hard-pressed to find a more obvious symbol of the perilousness of foreign occupation in the Middle East than this Soviet relic. When Air Force Academy officials initially visited the site, they discovered a room filled with physics books in Russian, which they attempted to toss, only to be rebuffed by an Afghan commander, who explained, "No, no, we'll keep them. We're not sure how long you'll be here."

A 1984 CIA assessment detailed the Soviet Union's many challenges in training Afghan officers. Their chief obstacles were corruption and a vexing indoctrination environment. The country's citizens, the CIA concluded, are "unwilling to forsake Afghan traditions or Islam to embrace the brand of Marxism-Leninism." Somehow, academy officials presumed that the all-American principles and practices of Sylvanus Thayer, a stern Puritan from New England, would be a more natural fit in the Arab world.

One former adviser at the Afghan Academy told me that West Point officials developed the academy "soup to nuts," retrofitting an honor code, an engineering curriculum, and more from the banks of the Hudson. While West Point is symbolized by the long gray line, the Afghan academy's color would be purple, to evoke democracy, since citizens had their fingers stamped with violet ink after voting. The initial price tag for the complex, which included a police academy and a language institute, came in at around $90 million, but school leaders insisted it would yield major dividends for the country's future. One report from the time deemed its graduates "the kernel of Afghanistan's future leadership." Democracy, the military pledged, was ready to pop.

The Afghan Academy opened its doors on February 3, 2005, welcoming an inaugural class of 106 cadets amid roaring snow and record-cold temperatures. While American service academies sometimes struggle to integrate their classes of cadets from all fifty states, the situation in Afghanistan was on a whole other level. The first cadets hailed from virtually all Afghanistan's thirty-four provinces, many of which had conflicting regional, religious, and tribal allegiances. School leaders hoped to erase these lines by mixing cadets up and bunking them six to a room. Lieutenant Colonel Scott Hamilton, then the academy's support team chief, was bullish on this forced integration. "They're coming from all over the country," he told a U.S. Air Force publication in 2007. "All the provinces are represented, all the ethnic groups are represented, and it's a great opportunity. It starts them off on a career and it really is building a nation."

Hamilton's heady hopes for camaraderie were quickly dashed. According to Ahmad Shahpoor Askarzada, a law lecturer at the academy from 2006 to 2014, cadets frequently called each other names and sometimes fights broke out across sectarian lines. He told me this included one nasty bout in the mess hall where a Tajik cadet and a Pashtun cadet were both bleeding after bashing each other with glass dishware.

The academy complex was itself overrun not only by U.S. military forces, but also by representatives from dozens of other NATO countries, all of them vying for influence and some promoting their own unique military schooling formulas and goals for modernizing the Middle East. For their part, the British attempted to set up a version of their famed Sandhurst Academy, whose alumni include many royals, English and otherwise, including princes William and Harry. The Germans, meanwhile, touted their own program, which American forces were quick to point out neglected to teach key military skills, like map reading. "We used to joke that it was like 47 people in a canoe trying to row in 47 different directions," recalled Bill Schustrom, a former adviser to the Afghan academy from West Point.

Many Afghan commanders at the academy had previously worked with the Soviets, spoke Russian, and were skeptical of American forces, who struggled to understand the region's many complexities. Hamilton told me he devoured as many books as possible on the Middle East before, and after, he arrived—but it wasn't enough. "About the time I left was probably when I was most useful, because I was starting to understand things," he reckoned.

While most cadets only spoke Dari or Pashto, the textbooks at the Afghan Military Academy were in English. At one point, sources told me that the Pentagon dropped a bunch of money on a contract to have their tactical training books translated, only to hire a company that used a crude machine-learning program lacking critical Pentagon oversight and quality control. When, after the printing, Schustrom provided one of these shiny new texts to an Afghan colleague, he couldn't make heads or tails of it. "What language is this in?" he asked.

As in many American military schools, the composition of cadets at the Afghan Military Academy was young, volatile, and academically uneven, thanks to rampant cronyism among some of the academy's Afghan partners. Hamilton recalled that while the school had devised a meritocratic admission process predicated around an SAT-style test, the final list of admitted students ended up differing significantly from those who showed up on campus. This was due, Hamilton claimed, to pressure exerted by regional power brokers who wanted their sons and daughters to attend. In one case, Afghan academy colleagues told Hamilton they felt pressured to admit the offspring of a powerful Afghan prison official. "If we don't admit his son," they were counseled, "he'll release everybody."

As "bad apples" populated the Afghan academy, cheating became rampant, and bullying was common. While Askarzada, the longtime lecturer who served in the Afghan National Army, said he strictly followed an old regional edict to "lead with love," many of his fellow commanders were violently harsh. He counseled cadets who had suffered scars, bruises, and, in one case, a lost tooth from being abused, often over trivial matters, like failing to salute properly or taking too long to boil tea. "If a guy was goofing off in class, they would take a stick and beat him," recalled Lark Escobar, the civilian educator and one-time chair of the Afghan Academy's English department. "You were trained to be tough," Khan Shinwaray, a former cadet, told me. Like Noor Merchant, Shinwaray had long dreamed of being a doctor, but found that a military route was the most feasible career path during the American occupation.

Commanders and plebes also allegedly engaged in sexual harassment, and, in numerous instances, rape. Askarzada claimed he investigated, corroborated, and pushed forward on these charges, only to have his commander order him to keep the issue "inside the academy." "They were hiding cases, like rape and sexual harassment," he told me.

Askarzada claimed many of the most troublesome cadets were related by blood to senior officials in the defense ministry and other powerful government bureaus. As such, they were allowed to act out and cheat with impunity. After Askarzada failed the nephew of one of these officials, he said, a senior academy leader ordered him to change his grade, reasoning that a poor mark could end in severe retaliation from the family, maybe even his death. In another similar case, Askarzada said his Afghan military overseers threatened to transfer him to a dangerous province. Again, he was undeterred, hailing from strong military stock in a country racked by decades of proxy war (his last name roughly translates to "son of soldier"). He stood tall in the face of this latter threat and didn't budge. "I know how to defend myself," he charged. Escobar once squared off with an Afghan professor she had failed to certify in a teacher training course due to his habitual tardiness. "He shouted at me, threatened me, then stormed outside and wrote 'Die Pig' on the dusty window of an SUV," she recalled.

THE AMERICAN MILITARY VIEWED THE AFGHAN ACADEMY as a feather in its cap, but it was inconsistent about its future, variously surging and depriving resources. Western academic advisers were also cycling in and out quickly. Hamilton insisted that many of them "purposefully didn't want to know what the person before them did because they had their own plan. It wasn't this consistent effort of support."

Nasima Omari Sayar, a civilian geography professor between 2011 and 2013, told me that many of the cadets she taught were motivated and smart. She indicated that regional tensions had abated by the time she arrived, more proof of the military's ancient track record of forging unbreakable bonds. But Omari acknowledged that many male cadets bristled at her gender, and that she sometimes felt unsafe on campus, in part because, at first, men and women shared the same restrooms.

Lieutenant Colonel Hamilton described terribly inconsistent security across campus, with NATO officials being denied entrance while "so-and-so's cousin" could just walk in. Some cadets took advantage of this situation, smuggling out everything from printers and paper to shoes, uniforms, and pistols. Askarzada said many pilfered American goods ended up at a flea market in Kabul long known as the "Bush market," so named for the presidential dynasty fixated on the Middle East.

Around 2012, the Army decided to sharply scale back its support for the academy, creating an immediate fiscal crisis that starved the place of faculty, equipment, and other resources. In the years after this, Schustrom recalled, American advisers would occasionally check in on the ailing academy, often for little more than a "photo op," if they happened to be in Kabul, a pattern of scattershot attention he compared to "drive-by shootings."

On the morning of August 5, 2014, an Afghan soldier then training at the academy complex quietly entered a bathroom, stuck an M16 rifle through its window, and opened fire on a visiting military entourage. In seconds, he wounded eighteen people and killed Major General Harold Greene, the highest-ranking officer to be killed in combat since Vietnam. The Pentagon had formed the academy as a symbol of integration, stability, and democracy. Now, a tragic school shooting transformed it into yet another reminder of American failure and chaos overseas.

A subsequent military investigation uncovered no ties between the soldier and the Taliban, or any other terrorist group. "It may be that the shooter was self-radicalized, or that he suffered from some sort of psychological condition," it stated. Tucked away in the report was the fact that the shooter's chain of command had denied his request for leave to celebrate Eid al-Fitr, the Muslim holiday marking the end of Ramadan. A more effective counterinsurgency force might have accounted for the importance of giving locals grace for this holiday, but the Pentagon missed it.

After the attack, the Afghan academy came to be seen as scarred, cursed ground. It withered further in the months after Greene was killed. For two years beginning in July 2017, Schustrom said he was the only American adviser at the complex. "I was pretty well armed, but I was an army of one, that's for sure," he half-joked. Lieutenant Colonel Hamilton's diagnosis of the academy's problems doubled as an indictment of the war. "We put in a lot of money, but I'm not sure we really had a big strategy," he said, adding that the U.S. military didn't view the academy as a cohesive, twenty-year project, but rather "twenty one-year wars."

When, in 2021, the real war finally ended and America shambolically withdrew from Afghanistan, the academy's garrison commander successfully held back the Taliban for a couple weeks, but America's enemies ultimately took it over. "I feel embarrassed, and I feel sad for the situation," said Shinwaray, who, after graduating, wrote engineering texts and taught for a while. "Me and my other colleagues, we did a lot of work. And our work has been lost." He and other sources told me that the Taliban is running the academy to this day, armed with some of the same staff and much of the same resources and curriculum, albeit scrubbed of its "western ideology."

IN TIME, OTHER WESTERN EDUCATIONAL INITIATIVES in the region failed, too, including the American University of Afghanistan, where Petraeus and his wife had endowed a scholarship. In 2016, it was attacked by the Taliban, leaving about twenty people killed and dozens more injured. "I remember talking to one of those women wounded," Petraeus recalled years later. "And she said, 'General, I will die to get an education.'" Petraeus paused. "There are all these inspirational stories like that."

It's been clear since at least the late aughts that Petraeus's counterinsurgency strategy was a failure reminiscent of Vietnam. The similarities persisted all the way through America's haywire withdrawal in Afghanistan, a hasty and heartless exit echoing the fall of Saigon. In both cases, Chinook helicopters evacuated their respective region's American embassies. The Afghanistan exit left scores of translators and other local U.S. military employees and allies to languish in a country immediately taken over by Taliban forces eager to exert retribution. During the maelstrom of the exit, thirteen American service members also died.

Nonetheless, Petraeus and his crew were able to successfully leverage their self-spun legends and fully rebound from their failures. Five years after the affair with his biographer was made public, the general was invited to West Point to counsel cadets and offer "leadership skills." One frustrated post-9/11 West Pointer cited the perpetuation of "ontological incest," in which military brass in their twilight years pass down their failed ideas to fresh-faced cadets.

There are countless examples of this phenomenon of imprudent, inter-generational military guidance. One example came in 1964, when Westmore-land met with General MacArthur in the Waldorf Astoria. Spurred on by his excitement, Westmoreland adopted an unrestrained bombing campaign in Vietnam like the one his idol, MacArthur, had undertaken in Korea. A decade after this, Petraeus sat at Knowlton's knee, learning about CORDS and coun-terinsurgency. Petraeus then made his own massive imprint on the officer class, teaching many West Point cadets and officers at Fort Leavenworth, as well as writing war manuals, authoring books, and appearing on television. In 2007, he was also appointed to the panel that selected full Army colonels for promotion to brigadier or one-star general.

A similar pattern of sustained influence and success struck other COIN-dinistas. Nagl, who wrote an influential book on COIN called *Learning to Eat Soup with a Knife*, secured teaching jobs at the Naval Academy and Georgetown, then, somewhat discordantly, became headmaster of the Haverford School, which had been founded in 1884 by pacifist Quakers. In 2016, while at Haverford, Nagl become violent after finding marijuana on his son. According to a police report, he confiscated his son's pot, took away his cell phone, and put him a chokehold.

In 2018, Valley Forge named its center for security studies after H.R. Mc-Master, who had graduated high school there before entering West Point. Caslen served as West Point superintendent from 2013 to 2018. Among other things, Caslen, a former West Point football star, was accused of going light on a string of serious misdeeds among football players. McMaster, a former West Point rugby player, had similarly allowed two young academy gradu-ates from the team to attend Army Ranger School despite them being under criminal investigation for sexual assault.

In 2015, Caslen oversaw a fanatical iteration of the annual plebe pillow fight, in which cadets suffered split lips, concussions, and at least one bro-ken bone. "My plebe was knocked unconscious and immediately began fighting when he came to," one upperclassman wrote on the social media platform Yik Yak. "I was so proud I could cry." Caslen banned pillow fights in response. As key details of the embarrassing maelstrom had first emerged online, he also instituted newly restrictive policies on what West Pointers could share with the public.

Four years later, in 2019, Caslen was appointed president of the University of South Carolina, a job for which he was paid a yearly salary of $650,000. Many opposed his ascension, including the university's faculty senate, which unanimously approved a no-confidence vote shortly after he arrived. During his 2021 commencement speech, Caslen, dressed regally in royal black robes with red accoutrements, seemingly slurred his words, and mistakenly referred to the South Carolina residents before him as "the newest alumni from the University of California." Later, it was revealed that he had plagiarized parts of his speech from remarks given by William McRaven, a Navy SEAL turned University of Texas chancellor who oversaw the mission that killed bin Laden.

McChrystal started a lucrative consulting firm and reeled in millions serving on boards and giving corporate speeches. He wrote several books, including one on risk that is chock-full of the kind of empty bromides part and parcel of the general class. At one point, McChrystal argues that "adaptability requires the ability, willingness, and, I'd argue, courage to dare to become something different."

These men's legacy was further solidified by soft, even positive academic assessments of COIN and GWOT. One came in 2010 from two Army men, one a former professor at West Point, the other from the Army's Command General Staff College. That same year, another sunny article appeared called "The Surge: General Petraeus and the Turnaround in Iraq." It was written by William Knowlton Jr., the son of West Point's former superintendent and Petraeus's brother-in-law.

Chapter 17

Lifting the Veil

In a radio address two months after 9/11, First Lady Laura Bush declared that "the fight against terrorism is also a fight for the rights and dignity of women." It had been just a few weeks since troops had touched down in Afghanistan, but already, Mrs. Bush falsely insisted, "women are no longer imprisoned in their homes. They can listen to music and teach their daughters without fear of punishment."

That same day, the State Department released a report on the Taliban's repression of women. Then *Time* published a cover story on the topic headlined "Lifting the Veil." Support for Afghan women's rights was a pillar of America's COIN strategy. It also provided a comforting rationale in the minds of many citizens of the war's noble aims. Bush himself had made misogyny a focal point of his 2002 West Point commencement address, declaring that "brutality against women is always and everywhere wrong."

This was a highly effective message, but a deeply reductive one. Left unsaid were many uncomfortable facts, including that America had once fueled religious fundamentalism and its attendant misogyny in the region. This took the form of billions of dollars provided to the Mujahideen, the militant group that mounted a defense against the Soviet Union's 1979 invasion of Afghanistan. For years after the Soviets left, America continued to tolerate a spin-off group, the Taliban, viewing it as a helpful counterforce to Iran that, in an ideal case, might stabilize the region to the point that the Texas oil firm, Unocal, could erect a massive pipeline. In 1995, an uncomfortable symbol of this aspirational symbiosis emerged when Unocal unintentionally rented office space in Kandahar just across the street from one of bin Laden's compounds.

The basic truth was that America hadn't had an issue with how women were treated by these mercenaries fighting the Soviets during the Cold War. Now, in the GWOT, it was all anyone could talk about, even as the military's declared achievements, and Laura Bush's declarations, were egregiously overstated. Afghan women faced violence and oppression throughout more than two decades of conflict, including years of monstrous acid attacks on Afghan school girls. In total, 400,000 Afghan civilians died in the so-called War on Terror, many of them women and their children.

Many local women in Afghanistan rejected America due to its violence in their country, and its ignorant assumptions about their faith, evidenced by our country's obsession with the veil. When Bush and his team first rolled out their rhetoric, Rina Amiri, an Afghan-born American diplomat, presciently warned that it would be all symbols and no substance. "If we cast a glance backward through the annals of Afghan history," she wrote, "we see that women have long been the pawns in a struggle between the elite modernists, usually defined as pro-Western, and the religious and tribal-based traditionalists."

IT WOULD BE SUPREMELY BAD OPTICS if a military hell-bent on defeating violent misogyny abroad was flagrantly anti-women at home. In recognition of this potential public relations nightmare, and thanks to activism by many American military women, the Pentagon launched in concert with the War on Terror a domestic campaign to support, promote, and protect women in the ranks. This self-imposed "lifting of the veil" resulted in a series of glass-breaking career achievements among long-struggling American military women. As always, there were practical considerations at play, including acute U.S. manpower needs in Afghanistan. The region's gender and cultural dynamics also caused female troops to be vital vectors of intelligence gleaned from local women. Many female troops who had been passed over for years were recognized and elevated. These included Ann Dunwoody, who, in 2008, became the first female four-star general in American history.

Pentagon policy then prohibited women from serving in direct combat roles. But these lines had been blurred in the GWOT from the beginning. Military brass routinely placed women in combat environments while formally depriving them of the recognition that their roles were just as dangerous as the combat positions in infantry, tank, and artillery units, all of which were reserved for men. These female soldiers operated dangerous checkpoints, searched towns for explosives, and provided convoy security on frequently booby-trapped roads. Ultimately, more than a thousand women in the U.S. military were wounded in the GWOT, and 166 died.

One of the true badasses of the war in Iraq was Leigh Ann Hester. On Palm Sunday 2005, she and nine other National Guard soldiers were tailing around thirty supply trucks on a dusty road southeast of Baghdad when they heard the faint sounds of gunfire and explosions at the head of the convoy. As they sped toward the sound, the Humvee in front of Hester was hit with a rocket-propelled grenade, blocking the road and, according to the military's account, "stopping the convoy in the kill zone." Her unit, known as Raven 42, was outnumbered five to one by Iraqi fighters, who, per the Pentagon, wanted hostages.

Hester and her squad leader, Timothy Nein, acted quickly. She ordered a gunner to fire toward the fighters' position in a nearby orchard, then started shooting her own M4 rifle. She and Nein directed their team to a flanking position, where, over forty-five minutes, they cleared trenches and killed combatants. While three members of her unit were wounded, all survived. Three months later, in a ceremony at Camp Liberty, in Baghdad, Hester was awarded America's third-highest combat decoration for valor: the Silver Star. She was the first woman to receive the honor since World War II, and the first woman ever to receive it for combat action.

A few months after Hester's firefight, a brash, handsome twenty-five-year-old Army lieutenant named Pete Hegseth landed in Iraq, not far from where the Raven's convoy had been hit. Hester and Hegseth were both part-time soldiers attached to state National Guard units, but their civilian lives looked very different. When she wasn't serving as a Raven, Hester managed a shoe store in a strip mall. Hegseth's day job was as an equity markets analyst at Bear Stearns. Hegseth leveraged his elite connections to secure a slot as a platoon leader in the 101st Airborne, a U.S. Army division that had gone mainstream four years earlier thanks to Spielberg's *Band of Brothers*. (At least one former officer serving with Hegseth rightly predicted that he would eventually parlay his deployment into public office.) In Iraq, Hegseth oversaw about forty men in a bloodthirsty brigade nicknamed "Kill Company" that tallied their body counts on a whiteboard. Shortly after he moved on from the company to a civil affairs post, the brigade was ensnared in a war crimes case after soldiers let three Iraqi detainees loose and shot them in the back as they ran away.

People who served with Hegseth generally agree that he was a good leader, and cool-headed in combat. But his conduct was not especially remarkable. Hegseth came away from Iraq with a Bronze Star to Leigh Ann Hester's Silver. His, it's worth noting, was issued without valor, a lesser version of the medal that, according to *The Washington Post*, was "issued somewhat liberally" during the War on Terror. Some in the enlisted ranks joked that this decoration was little more than a "participation trophy" for needy officers. Hegseth's award citation is dry and formulaic, chock-full of the White House platitudes used to sell the public on the war. It asserts that Hegseth "contributed immeasurably to the success of building a free and democratic nation for the citizens of Iraq." Hester's citation, by contrast, reads like an excerpt from a Tom Clancy novel. It lays out her conditions that day—"75 degrees and sunny with a 10 knot breeze from the southwest"—before chronicling the "well-coordinated ambush" and Raven 42's canny tactical response, detailing the "heavy volumes" of grenade launcher and machine-gun fire Hester directed at "an overwhelming number" of fighters as she also fired away.

This discrepancy seems to have weighed on Hegseth. In his 2024 book *The War on Warriors*, Hegseth casts Hester's actions as an aberration in his broader quest to keep America's pantheon of military gallantry the exclusive domain of men. As part of this, Hegseth takes issue with the military's "political" awards process, musing conspiratorially over the fact that Hester's star was issued relatively quickly, within a matter of months. "Nothing happens that fast," he claims. "Unless there is an agenda." Hegseth is sympathetic to his former sergeant major, Eric Geressy, who had his own grievances about women in combat. Geressy specifically griped about Monica Brown, a combat medic who earned a Silver Star in 2008 after delivering life-saving aid in Afghanistan as "rounds were literally missing her by inches," according to a member of her platoon. Hegseth quotes Geressy's complaint that he found it impossible to escape Brown's story, whining that the Army plastered her picture in chow halls and military balls. "Why is that?" he asked. "None of my guys had their picture on the wall."

Other military males—cadets, troops; both officers and enlisted— shared Hegseth's animosity against military women. They wanted the veil to remain. In 2003, 63 percent of midshipmen at the Naval Academy charged in a survey that their female peers received preferential treatment during the admissions process, even though the women were, on average, earning higher grades than they were. Despite their general excellence, female cadets were still graduating at lower rates, an indication that the long-running tradition of driving out women remained alive and well.

In their attempts to rob military women of their ambition, cadets and troops alike classified them as sexual objects. When, for instance, the first nine women arrived at Valley Forge in 2007, some male cadets posted claims on MySpace that they were only there to have sex with them. "The rumors were that we were all sluts, and that we were easy," Cadet Lauren Perry told a local Pennsylvania newspaper.

Years later, two other female cadets at the Forge were caught trying to sneak off campus by J.J. Rivera, a senior TAC officer who had served as a helicopter pilot in the Marines. He threatened to look in on their rooms at night when they slept. Another former female cadet told me Rivera allegedly flirted with her repeatedly, and even said she reminded him of his wife. In addition, Rivera reportedly advised a male cadet, then still a minor, to check out a strip bar near their shared ROTC base called Club Risqué. Some male West Point cadets made their obsession with women clear in depraved marching chants, including one that went *"I wish that all the ladies were holes in the road, and I was a dump truck / I'd fill 'em with my load."*

A similar chant at the Air Force Academy described cutting a woman "in two" so that they could keep "the bottom half and give the top to you." Some West Point faculty also joked openly with male cadets about hooking up with their female classmates, even urging them to "seize any chance to have sex," an attitude echoed by some of the academy's rugby players who, on an internal email chain, called girls "rando skanks" and ordered a teammate to "get your girl on a leash." While the Bush administration's proud defense of Afghan women was often splashed on the front pages of newspapers, shorter items in the back pages periodically reported on military sexual offenses.

PUBLIC ATTENTION TO THE PLIGHT OF FEMALE TROOPS spiked in January 2003, after an anonymous source sent an email to a group that included top Air Force officials, politicians, and reporters. It claimed that the Air Force Academy had a massive sexual abuse problem. This helped spur an inquiry from the branch's inspector general, which found that 12 percent of the women in the Air Force Academy's class of 2003 were survivors of rape or attempted rape. A whopping 70 percent said they had experienced sexual harassment, including pressure for sexual favors. The watchdog also found that school brass had often sought to cover up this behavior or blame the women. In one case, the academy charged a rape victim with having sex in the dormitories.

Just as this report broke, seven male Air Force cadets were caught drinking with underage high school girls in a Colorado Springs hotel room. Johnny Weida, the senior evangelical Air Force academy official, pledged to fix the problem, more, it seemed, out of his loyalty to the academy and its future than to any of the victims. "We are warriors," he reminded his student body. "If we don't reverse this trend, the very existence of this institution is threatened."

A year later, in 2004, Mark Conliffe, an offensive lineman on the West Point football team, was criminally convicted and sent to Fort Leavenworth for taking semi-nude pictures of eight female cadets without their consent. Shortly thereafter, in a survey of women across the service academies, 10 percent reported being sexually assaulted. While the accuracy of the military's sexual misconduct data had been suspect from the start, the available information was deeply troubling, suggesting that females at military academies were five times more likely to face sexual assault than those at civilian schools.

As the scope of this predatory behavior became apparent, and more military sexual assault survivors began to speak out and organize, the Pentagon briefly abandoned its long-standing claim that this behavior was the result of a "few bad apples." For the first time, officials promised systemic reform. In 2005, the Pentagon created its Sexual Assault Prevention and Awareness Office, which started systematically tracking sexual misconduct cases. It seemed, for a moment, that this would be a meaningful fix. In 2006, West Point senior Lonnie Story became the first cadet convicted of rape since the school began admitting women. Then, in 2008, President Bush approved a death sentence for an Army private convicted in the late 1980s via court-martial of numerous rapes and murders—the first death sentence approved for a troop since 1961.

Many female troops and advocates remained skeptical, though, insisting that the Pentagon remained a boys' club incapable of truly investigating itself. "The Pentagon does not have the ability to change its ways," Dorothy Mackay, the executive director of Survivors Take Action Against Military

Personnel, told the *Chicago Tribune* in 2005. "It would be like asking Saddam Hussein to change his stripes."

Mackay's point proved prescient. Bush may have executed one soldier for rampant sexual misconduct, but many more evaded punishment altogether. None of the incidents that surfaced as part of the 2003 Air Force Academy scandal, for instance, led to convictions. Many other defendants pled down their charges or successfully appealed their convictions. One was Jacob Whisenhunt, a West Point cadet who returned to campus after his three convictions for sexual assault were speciously vacated by an Army judge. Some of the strongest evidence of rot within the oversight system emerged in 2013, when the Air Force colonel in charge of overseeing his entire branch's sexual assault prevention program was charged with sexual battery after he approached a woman in a parking lot near the Pentagon and, according to a police report, "grabbed her breasts and buttocks" before she fended him off and called 911.

As more allegations leaked out, the Pentagon introduced additional programs, task forces, reviews, and regulations. Each was ballyhooed as a silver bullet that would stem the crisis. Most of it ended up being window dressing, creating illusory conditions that one former military school official described to me as "a chocolate-covered onion." In 2011, the Defense Department admitted that West Point was "not in compliance" with sexual assault training policies and was providing a "deficient" prevention program that failed to meet "the Department's minimum standard." That same year, Sarah Locke—whose mother, Pat, had been one of West Point's first two Black female cadets—arrived at West Point, steeled by her mother's horror stories. Conditions were generally better than in the mid- to late 1970s, she told me, though one evening bore an uncanny resemblance to the elder Locke's tenure.

It came during West Point's so-called Night of the Firsties, when seniors go drinking at West Point's exclusive upperclassmen club. Ahead of this, a leader came to Sarah and said, "Make sure you lock your door tonight, a lot of the Firsties are going to come back drunk and I don't want them coming to your room."

Sure enough, a band of blindingly drunk cadets stumbled back to the barracks hours later. One cornered a female in a stairwell, Sarah recalled, while another broke into a room and urinated in the wardrobe. At one point, Sarah and her roommate heard someone struggling to pry open their door. "Neither of us slept that night," she told me. "I would have expected this in the 1970s, not 2012."

PERHAPS THE MOST SUBSTANTIAL COVER-UP of military school sexual abuse occurred at the Coast Guard Academy. An internal investigation, launched in the early 2020s and dubbed "Operation Fouled Anchor," quietly concluded that roughly a hundred assault cases dating back to the 1980s had been grossly mishandled by school officials, with data often played down or withheld entirely from Congress and the Coast Guard's criminal investigative service. This smoothed the way for many credibly accused cadets to graduate and rise into senior military positions.

Certain details that surfaced through Fouled Anchor are eerily reminiscent of West Point's early years with women, including that numerous assaults were enabled thanks to the Coast Guard's stubborn refusal to put locks on the doors. One female cadet claimed she had been assaulted twice, first by a cadet and then by an officer. Another cadet who reported her rape was punished for "engaging in lewd acts" and told she had not rebuffed her attacker's advances strongly enough.

A similar pattern of obfuscation struck the Air Force Academy, where brass doctored misconduct cases before sending reports to Congress, according to Teresa Beasley, the academy's longtime sexual assault response coordinator. "Officers think they'll get fired if they have a lot of assaults," she explained. Eventually, she ditched the Pentagon's poorly built and easily manipulable systems and created her own tracking tool via an Excel spreadsheet. Among other things, she stitched together a worrisome trend: assaults spiked every Halloween. One year, six cadets reported being assaulted that one day. Beasley pushed her superiors to increase training and vigilance leading up to the holiday, but her superiors belittled her analysis and did nothing. She subsequently filed a whistleblower report and, in 2017, was forced out of her job after thirty years of service.

Riz Shah, the former West Point TAC, told me that sexual abuse and other misdeeds were made "hush hush to keep West Point's reputation clean." Among West Point's many bureaucratic tricks for obscuring data, Shah said, was separating guilty cadets under academic rules rather than using the Uniform Code of Military Justice, a more serious lane that would be recorded in publicly accessible government data sets.

Shah was the rare outsider at West Point, not a ring knocker but a kid who enlisted as a private and earned his way into the officer class. This breed of officer, known as the "Mustang," commands a certain respect within the military, but is also seen as less loyal to the officer class. Indeed, Shah was shocked at how fanatical the school was in protecting its reputation and hiding issues, especially if it involved a graduate. "Those cases," he said, "never hit the news."

In 2021, at the age of twenty-two, Air Force Academy graduate Caitlin Foster committed suicide. She left a note reading: "Do all that you can to make sure I am the last one." Her family later discovered that she had been raped at the academy, and that, instead of seeking military justice, the school quietly disenrolled the perpetrator for "academic reasons," and gave him an honorable discharge.

A *New York Times* investigation the next year found at least sixty JROTC instructors had, over the previous five years, been credibly accused of sexually assaulting female cadets in high school. One Tennessee cadet told the *Times* that her JROTC instructor "warned that he had the skills to kill her without a trace if she told anyone about their sexual encounters." Another student, in Missouri, said she was "forced to kneel at her instructor's bedside, blindfolded, with a gun to her head." The military had received reports of this abuse for years, but had not imposed any additional oversight, or, in many cases, fired the instructors, one of whom had told a high school girl under his care that "sexual submission was expected of women in the military."

UNLIKE FEDERAL SERVICE ACADEMIES LIKE WEST POINT, Valley Forge and other private military schools operated, beginning in 1972, under the auspices of the Title IX statute, which mandates schools to address and prevent sexual discrimination and violence as part of their mission. These regulations forced certain positive reporting and oversight requirements; though, due to the sharp enrollment slumps that have long afflicted places like the Forge, administrations have often granted bad cadets clemency in order to keep banking their parents' tuition dollars. At one point, this pot apparently included funds from notorious pedophile and sex trafficker Jeffrey Epstein. In an October 2010 email released by the Department of Justice, Epstein personally approved a $9,201 Forge tuition payment for the son of his bodyguard and driver, former UFC fighter Igor Zinoviev.

The school's pattern of abuse and impunity seemingly reached its zenith in the 2010s, when all manner of hell-raisers were kept on. One crew of cadets found guilty of sodomizing, or "tooth-pasting," younger cadets was allowed to stay, as was a kid who stabbed someone with scissors, and one who bashed his friend with a baseball bat. Two other attackers who left a sixteen-year-old boy with severe facial fractures were both permitted to graduate.

In another troubling case highlighted by Robert Wood, the Forge's Title IX officer from 2008 to 2015, four male college cadets conspired with a fifth to covertly film his sexual encounter with a drunk female cadet. A disciplinary board advised that all the perpetrators be dismissed, but the school's president ignored the recommendation and allowed three of the five to stay. As punishment, they were ordered to paint the commandant's house. One of the boys spoke at graduation. Wood said, "the young lady who had been assaulted had to sit there and listen." The school "doesn't want to deal with sexual harassment," said a female Forge cadet in a school survey around this time, adding that those guilty of sexual misconduct saw their behaviors "pushed under the rug."

In a 2015 complaint to the U.S. Department of Education, Wood alleged a "propensity" among TACs to cover up and interfere with serious allegations, with school officials once demanding he "cease" his investigation of a sexual assault. He resigned under pressure soon after. It wouldn't be until nearly a decade later, during the summer of 2024, that the Department of Education finally issued a heavily redacted determination letter finding that "evidence indicates that staff interfered with and impeded" Wood's work. In the years after Wood left, local police were called to campus hundreds of times. Between 2015 and 2020, the Forge logged more than thirty incidents of alleged sexual misconduct, from stalking and fondling to rape, as well as fistfights, assault with a knife, even arson. Additional police reports I obtained involve cadets as young as thirteen experiencing psychiatric crises, including suicidal behavior.

In May 2016, Forge cadet Carey Lecamp killed himself in his dorm room. He was eighteen. By all accounts, Carey was a model student with dreams of being a general. He memorized the Forge's rules and treated them as sacrosanct, maintaining a spotless room and perfectly pressing his clothes. "His shoes were like glass, you could literally see your reflection in them," his roommate told me. On his iPhone, Carey had saved a photo of

West Point cadets saluting then-president Barack Obama—a piece of visual inspiration he kept close and consulted often.

Carey could be aggressive and domineering. He liked shooting guns and playing Call of Duty. But when he felt most comfortable, he was prone to goofiness, often contorting his face or crossing his eyes to make friends and family laugh. "He had this side of him that got pushed down very early on that was open to expression, that was very sensitive," his brother, Bryce, recalled. "He created a thin exterior of badassery over something mushy and ill-formed and insecure."

Carey had wanted to serve since reading *The Odyssey* in middle school. In journal entries, he wrote admiringly of Odysseus, the great Greek warrior, who, through the Trojan War's brutal battles, was "broken down and re-birthed into a wise and resilient individual." He hoped the Forge would spur a similar metamorphosis. "Something more important in my life was missing and all I knew was that I had to change it all and start over again to find my own purpose," he wrote. "I had no idea how far I had to grind my-self down, how much pain I had to endure to find my limit. This was my odyssey."

But Carey soon discovered that he was operating in a flawed military meritocracy, one where terrible behavior was often tolerated. Cadets could skip a dozen classes a week and pass. "I swear to you, I didn't do a single math problem all year and got a 98 in calculus," one of his friends boasted. Another said the academic environment left him totally unprepared for college. "It felt like I was reading Greek when I got into my first college calculus class," he said. Carey sometimes took cell phone videos to prove to his mother how bad things had gotten. One shows a cadet snoring at his desk. Another features a couple of cadets punching each other.

Carey once brought a clip of a disruptive cadet to a senior administrator, hoping she would punish the miscreant. Instead, he was told to erase the video immediately. The order hit him particularly hard. In this quasi-military atmosphere, which supposedly prioritized accountability above all else, he'd been directed to suppress a problem. "I think Carey lost his faith in the military," one of his friends told me, echoing others. "I think that's what took him out."

A few months after his passing, police responded to reports of a Forge cadet having "thoughts of harming himself." That December, another cadet was hospitalized after expressing "depressed feelings." This same year, a father of two Valley Forge cadets received a call from one of his sons who was crying and suicidal. "I can't do this anymore," he said.

ATHLETES AT MILITARY ACADEMIES, much the same as their peers in civilian schools, have long enjoyed special status on campus. West Point's football players long operated from a particularly hallowed place, though they haven't always been untouchable. West Point's 1951 cheating scandal, for instance, ensnared a majority of team members, and the academy dismissed them all, even as they knew it would gravely hurt the season's success. During the years after the 9/11 Army-Navy game, however, their hard-partying, predatory antics grew out of control.

A particularly influential steward of this subculture was Bobby Ross, who led football teams at the Citadel, Virginia Military Institute, and in the NFL before becoming West Point's head coach in 2004. There, Ross commanded a $600,000 government salary—evidence of the power of the Pentagon budget and the academy's eagerness to rebound after a 0–13 season. As part of his recruitment tactics, Ross is reported to have treated prospects to nights of underage binge drinking and womanizing on a party bus often escorted by military police. These affairs included school cheerleaders and female athletes, some of whom made out with teenage recruits, and kissed each other. Lieutenant Colonel Chad Davis, then the director of football operations, privately described the hedonistic ventures as critical to showing potential players that "there are not just masculine women that attend West Point," but also "pretty girls."

Players developed bad drinking and drug habits, some of which were birthed out of athletic injuries. After a frigid morning practice in March 2014, defensive back Jared Rodger secured an opioid prescription after suffering severe frostbite. He got hooked. Before long, he and other players nursed routine bumps and bruises with narcotics, which were available to the team for a few bucks a pill. As Jared's addiction intensified, a teammate connected him to a prominent cadet dealer on campus. He sold cocaine, Xanax, and opiates, all substances with quick metabolic schedules that make it easier to pass drug tests.

After hiding his addiction for a while, Jared came up dirty, and West Point pounced. While drug abuse among footballers was then apparently rampant, West Point chose to depict and prosecute a small ring that cast Jared as kingpin. He claims that six of the seven cadets they ultimately targeted, including himself, were Black. "They didn't want to open that can of worms," he told me. "It would have looked so bad for West Point."

At the same time, one of Jared's teammates, star quarterback Ahmad Ali Bradshaw, was accused of raping a female West Point cadet named Madeline Lewis. Madeline's grandfather had attended West Point and played football. She loved the team so much that, during many Halloweens as a child, she dressed up as a West Point cheerleader. When she sought accountability for Bradshaw's action, however, she said she was treated by fellow cadets like "a vial of poison." Some taunted her online as "the whore of the corps," or even suggested she should be killed.

According to *The Daily Beast*, West Point's internal investigation of the incident concluded that the two had engaged in a consensual sexual affair. The conclusion fit a broader pattern. Of the seventy-eight restricted reports of sexual misconduct filed over the previous few years, only twenty-seven had been substantiated. Bradshaw, it turned out, had also been previously found guilty of cheating, received a minor punishment, and stayed on the team. During the 2017 season, he scored a game-winning touchdown against Navy, breaking the Black Knight's fourteen-game losing streak to its archrival.

After the Army expelled Jared, they ordered him to repay them $256,000—the assessed value of his education at West Point. This immediately destroyed his credit score, limited his career options, and spurred a self-destructive spiral. In 2019, Jared overdosed on opioids and nearly died, unresponsive even after three doses of Narcan. "I got into drugs even harder after I left," he told me. "So much of my identity was tied up in being a West Point cadet. A lot of my struggle was not knowing who I was." The same year as Jared's overdose, the captain of the football team at Alden Partridge's Norwich University was allowed to keep playing despite facing felony assault charges stemming from a random attack that left one student with stitches and a badly bruised eye, and two others with less serious pain but lasting fear.

Meanwhile, West Point did little to deal with the team's drug problem after expelling Jared and his fellow Black teammates. A few months after he was dismissed, star cornerback Brandon Jackson drove drunk into a guardrail near campus at ninety-seven miles an hour and died immediately. Sources later claimed that school officials had permitted his drinking, and, in violation of school rules, let him have a car and drive off base. Two months later, another player was arrested for drunk driving. Others were sent off to treatment programs. A few years after that, six more players overdosed on fentanyl-laced cocaine while on spring break in Florida.

IN LATE 2010, THE AIR FORCE ACADEMY LAUNCHED an internal inquiry into football team misconduct, code-named "Operation Gridiron." That November, an agent with the branch's Office of Special Investigations contacted a twenty-year-old cadet named Eric Thomas and enlisted him to go undercover.

Eric believed in the mission and told me he was friends with a female cadet who had allegedly suffered abuse. He was initially hesitant about his undercover tactics, which technically violated the honor cadet's edict against lying. But he had been selected after being caught by police at an off-campus party and had no other option. For roughly two years, Eric embedded in the academy's toxic underbelly, secretly recording cadets suspected of sexual misconduct and drug abuse, many of whom were football players. He briefed his handler covertly, behind the academy's static B-52 bomber, which is nicknamed "Diamond Lil" and features a painted pinup girl near its tip. Eric's intel led to the first three sexual assault convictions at the Air Force Academy in more than fifteen years. Another twenty drug investigations were also launched thanks to his findings.

Eric had juggled this secret mission with soccer and academics, hard work that paid off when he earned a coveted slot to be a fighter pilot. But top commanders, including then-superintendent Michael Gould, became increasingly frustrated by Operation Gridiron's targeting of football team members. After his work contributed to the expulsion of the team's star, senior brass decided to intervene, disavowing Eric's work and issuing him hundreds of demerits. Their rationale was that he had repeatedly sneaked off base and drank while underage, actions, Eric insisted, that had been directed by his handlers.

It didn't matter. Eric was forcefully punished and ordered to march endlessly in squares. He was also confined to an administrative room for more than four hundred hours. Then, six weeks before Eric was set to graduate, on April 8, 2013, the academy expelled him and discharged him from the military entirely. While the school had once hailed Eric as having the "highest level of character, diligence, honor, integrity and fortitude," now it vilified him as a "liar with low moral character, who was not fit for service."

"They gave me a worse rating than the guys who got convicted of sexual assault," Eric told me. "It has ruined my name." After his career was violently derailed, Eric moved to South Dakota, mostly in hopes that Mike Rounds, the state's powerful senator on the Armed Services Committee, might take up his case. He worked at a health supplement store during the day and cranked away on his case at night. When Rounds didn't pan out, Eric moved to Arizona, then Georgia, chasing other senators in hopes they would help him secure his diploma, and get back into military service.

When we spoke, Eric, now thirty-four, assured me that he is still physically fit to serve, thanks to his gig as a strength and conditioning coach just outside of Atlanta. Due to his discharge status, he is ineligible for the draft, has no access to benefits from the Department of Veterans Affairs, and has struggled at times with employment. "It's hard to build a life with anyone 'cause I have this gap in my life that I'm still trying to fix," he explained.

Eric is clear-eyed now about how the military protects itself. "The power isn't visible, but you can feel it," he explained. "It's not just about power, it's also about image." He argued that this mentality of suppression inhibits battlefield performance. "One of the pinnacles of tactical warfare is to recognize when something doesn't work, to bring that to the forefront, and to modify it," he said. "But we don't do that when it comes to sexual assault. We say victims are weak and we don't address it. As an institution you have to face those things to become stronger."

Though he left the academy more than a dozen years ago, Eric still speaks as if he is part of the Air Force brotherhood. "We have to find our perfection in our imperfections," he told me. "If we deny our imperfections, we will never be perfect." It's a fair critique, one grounded in Eric's abiding respect for Air Force values. "It's not the ideas that are wrong," he concluded. "It's the implementation of the ideas."

Chapter 18

The Enemy Within

On June 16, 2015, Donald J. Trump entered the Republican presidential primary as a brash underdog in a crowded field. During the early stages of his campaign, Trump ginned up attention, in part, by playing up his time at the New York Military Academy. He visited his alma mater on the trail, speaking before supporters alongside his harsh old mentor, Theodore "Maj'" Dobias, who, at ninety, was suffering from cancer, relying on a cane, and was weeks away from death. Still, Maj' mustered an energetic endorsement to the crowd. "[Donald will] make a damn good president, won't he?" Maj' asked rhetorically, to cheers.

The New York Times had recently surfaced comments that Trump had told a biographer that he "always felt that I was in the military." The presidential aspirant reasoned that, over the course of his five years as a cadet, he got "more training militarily than a lot of the guys." Others piled on. Trump's onetime roommate, Ted Levine, also conflated his time at the school to a legitimate service record. In a newspaper interview, Levine marveled at how Trump is "so mentally strong," estimating that what he stomached on campus was "harder basic training than the Marines."

Levine observed, too, that the "grandiose confidence and bulldog aggression" Trump developed on campus were proving to be strong assets on the campaign trail. While wrapping himself in the prestige of military service, Trump distinguished himself from his Republican foes by fiercely renouncing the Global War on Terror, along with foreign intervention more broadly. He also expressed a strongman's belligerence toward various foreign actors—and American citizens. Trump formulated and first delivered this message to the election's early front-runner, Jeb Bush, a Florida governor who was also the blood brother and son of the two chief architects of America's conflicts in the Middle East.

In one candidate forum, Trump charged point-blank that Jeb's brother, George W., had lied about weapons of mass destruction. Trump called this "the worst decision" in the history of the American presidency. "Frankly I think the son, being loyal to the father, I think he really wanted to go into Iraq, even if it wasn't the right thing to do," Trump said, perhaps thinking about his own warped dynamics with Daddy.

Trump's cutting diagnosis resulted in unprecedented support among military veterans. Vietnam War hero John McCain had won the veteran vote by 10 points during his 2008 presidential bid. Trump, who took direct shots at McCain's time as a POW, won this same constituency by a startling 26-point margin. A subsequent Cornell analysis of 2016 voting found exceptionally high support for Trump in American communities that had suffered the highest combat-casualty rates, which, the authors suggested, was crucial to his victories in three decisive swing states: Pennsylvania, Michigan, and Wisconsin. A few years later, two psychology professors at Penn State crunched 2016 and 2020 Trump voting data. They found that hegemonic masculinity—a worldview defined by potent sexism and prejudice but consistent with the foundational military requirement of masculine dominance—was the best predictor of whether people saw Trump as a good leader. This metric even surpassed party affiliation. An ultra-macho strain had by then indelibly tainted the political stage. It also infected American warfighting, led largely by the visage of the highly trained special operator, a masculine archetype that Trump showered with love.

THE FIRST MAJOR ACT OF BRAND-BUILDING for special operators came in 2007, when the Navy gave a bulked-up SEAL named Marcus Luttrell time off to write *Lone Survivor*, a bestselling memoir later adapted into a Mark Wahlberg movie about a violent clash with the Taliban. The Navy subsequently supported *Act of Valor*, an action film that cast active-duty SEALs. On premiere night, the Navy pulled out all the stops, enlisting their elite parachute team, the Leap Frogs, to land on a red carpet in Hollywood.

SEAL notoriety expanded in 2011, when President Obama publicly identified SEAL Team 6 as the force that killed Osama bin Laden. The White House later leaked details of the killing to the filmmakers of *Zero Dark Thirty*, which, with an initial release date just ahead of reelection day, was pegged to burnish Obama's reputation at a critical juncture. (While the film was ultimately delayed until November, a quick-and-dirty TV movie about the raid, produced by Harvey Weinstein, was broadcast two days before the election.) The bin Laden raid spurred a glut of SEAL memoirs and an imprint of St. Martin's Press focused exclusively on special operation stories.

Whereas Obama had passively endorsed the antics of the operator, Trump bear-hugged the most bloodthirsty in the bunch. He invited Marcus Luttrell and his twin brother, Morgan, also a special operator, to speak at the 2016 Republican National Convention, then spent the back half of his first term granting clemency to a bunch of troops credibly accused of gruesome war crimes, including Mathew Golsteyn, a West Point graduate and Green Beret charged with premeditated murder after allegedly freeing, then shooting, a prisoner he suspected of making bombs for the Taliban.

One major consequence of Trump's strict "Make America Great Again" focus on the home front was that it uncomfortably spotlighted, and often exacerbated, a litany of festering problems that were direct outgrowths of the GWOT. Many forget that war not only demolishes enemy territory; it also wreaks havoc on the invading society's soul. America had become jumpier in the decades since 9/11, more distrustful and divided and trigger-happy. Over this period, it became seized by the signature plagues of a war-torn country: poverty, addiction, polarization, oligarchy, and violence. America, it seemed, had caught a super-strain of Vietnam Syndrome, one borne by domestic underfunding and foreign over-fighting that again culminated in an embarrassing military defeat on the world stage.

With the Pentagon ailing, men sought alternative forms of masculine validation on the home front. They started militias, flocked to ICE, became security guards, or joined the ranks of the cops. Many funneled through a pipeline reinforced by the Obama administration, which put tens of millions of dollars into creating veteran police positions in cities and towns across the country. While former service members have long been hailed as prototypical cops, the available data suggests otherwise. In 2018, the Marshall Project found that veteran cops in Miami and Boston were more likely than non-serving officers to face use-of-force complaints. The nonprofit news site calculated that one-third of fatal police shootings in Albuquerque, New Mexico, between 2010 and 2014 involved military veterans. Another study of the Dallas Police Department found that veteran cops were more likely to fire their guns, regardless of their deployment history. Such urges for force were sated through the Pentagon's 1033 program, which has spread special operator culture across the country by outfitting police officers with billions in surplus military gear, including M16 rifles for campus police at the University of Louisiana and grenade launchers for cops with the LA school district.

IN 2018, MARJORY STONEMAN DOUGLAS HIGH SCHOOL, in South Florida, experienced the deadliest high school shooting in American history. Its student body included Nikolas Cruz, who, by the age of nineteen, felt deeply alone. He had little else to care about other than JROTC. The JROTC curriculum has a history of romanticizing weapons, with one programmatic text promoting the fact that the "Founding Fathers encouraged an armed citizenry." Materials also reasoned that "cooling-off periods" for gun purchases violated the Second Amendment, explaining the "popular argument" that "If guns were outlawed, only outlaws would have guns." Cruz became an expert marksman through a program funded by the National Rifle Association. Cruz's JROTC classmates said he dreamed of becoming a Green Beret. One said shooting "seemed almost therapeutic to him." At some point, they started calling him "Wolf."

On February 14, 2018, Cruz entered Marjory Stoneman armed with an AR-15 and sporting a maroon shirt with the logo for the school's JROTC program. Once Cruz found his classmates, he opened fire, killing seventeen students and wounding seventeen others. Investigators later found violent comments he had posted online, including his desire to "die fighting killing shit ton of people." This urge seemed to flourish in his isolation. He later told a psychologist that he committed the shooting on Valentine's Day because he believed that no one loved him.

When I contacted Peter Mahmood, Cruz's former JROTC instructor, he insisted that the program was strictly a "leadership citizenship course," not military education, and that it was unfair to connect Cruz's time in the air rifle program to his mass shooting. "I don't see how the two equate," Mahmood said bitterly, then ended the call. The basic truth, contrary to his assertion, is this: 45 percent of all cadets who complete JROTC enter some branch of the military—and also, according to a 2023 study from the University of Maryland, military service ranks as the single strongest predicator of violent extremism in America.

In the wake of Trump's 2016 election victory, thousands of children under eighteen flocked to JROTC programs, but also the Border Patrol Explorer Program, funded jointly by the Boy Scouts and the Department of Homeland Security. It provides children with paramilitary training at border postings. One participant, a twelve-year-old Latino boy, expressed his eagerness to "take down illegals." Around this time, at a sweltering summer program at the Marine Military Academy, in Texas, another child daydreamed about following in the footsteps of his uncle, who, he bragged, "killed Taliban in Afghanistan." At a survival school in north Florida, a nine-year-old confessed that "one time, I shot my dad's shotgun secretly."

Trump's rise inflamed these attitudes and cultivated a cult of personality among the most militant Americans. "I have the support of the police, the support of the military, the support of the 'Bikers for Trump'—I have the tough people," he told Breitbart News in 2019. "But they don't play it tough—until they go to a certain point, and then it would be very bad, very bad." Trump followed up these comments in a 2024 Fox News interview where he identified his domestic opponents broadly as "the enemy within" and mused that perhaps they should be "handled" via military force.

DURING THE CIVIL WAR, President Lincoln famously gathered a "Team of Rivals," including his dissidents, to debate and weigh in on all matters. Trump, on the other hand, convened a virtual clown car crew of different right-wing factions and power centers, including the so-called West Point Mafia. Its most powerful member was Secretary of State Mike Pompeo. In April 2019, as his tenure was winding down, Pompeo spoke before a large crowd at Texas A&M University. The first query in the question-and-answer portion concerned the secretary of state's alma mater and how it had shaped his "perceptions of diplomacy." Pompeo initially responded with platitudes, emphasizing the importance of listening and teamwork. A few minutes later, however, he momentarily let his diplomatic mask slip, copping to the honor code's incompatibility with the dirty work of American foreign policy. "What's the cadet motto at West Point? You will not lie, cheat or steal—or tolerate those who do," he said. "I was the CIA director. We lied, we cheated, we stole." Students laughed uproariously, and Pompeo flashed a devilish smile.

Untold numbers of military school graduates have violated the oath, but few other than Pompeo have publicly pled guilty. His admission was remarkable considering his status as one of the school's exemplars. Pompeo had graduated first in West Point's class of 1986, which picked a particularly idealistic creed as its class motto: "Courage Never Quits." After graduating, Pompeo had an unremarkable military career, serving his obligatory five years, mostly as an armor officer in Germany, before returning to civilian life and cashing in on his academic connections. In 1997, he and a few fellow West Point classmates acquired an aircraft parts contractor in Kansas they named "Thayer Aerospace." Its major venture funders included the Koch brothers, two billionaire industrialists from Kansas with arch libertarian views who subsequently formed the most powerful dark money political network in America—one that was crucial to Pompeo's own entrance into politics. After leaving his U.S. House seat for the State Department, Pompeo brought on as his two top aides a pair of West Point classmates turned partners at Thayer Aerospace: Ulrich Brechbuhl and Brian Bulatao.

Mark Esper, also from the Class of '86, served as Trump's Army and defense secretaries, and H.R. McMaster served as his national security adviser. The key conduit between Trump and the academy was David Urban, a lobbyist, CNN commentator, and Trump confidant, also from the class of '86.

Trump was himself intimately familiar with basic precepts of military life thanks to his time as a suffering cadet at New York Military Academy. He also knew what a high rank allowed. Having now been promoted to the apex role of the military—commander in chief—Trump could demand a lot from those lower on the chain. Many bristled when the president referred to these men as "my generals," though it was largely a truthful reflection of how the hierarchy worked.

Mainstream figures insisted that the West Point Mafia was an "axis of adults," one that would protect Americans from Trump's worst impulses. "West Point taught us all a very strong value system, having a moral compass, doing the harder right versus the easier wrong," explained Joe De-Pinto, the CEO of 7-Eleven and yet another member from the class of 1986. "I'm personally someone who sleeps better at night knowing that those guys are in the positions they're in."

Pompeo and Brechbuhl performatively stressed their moral superiority at the State Department, in part by drafting a "professional ethos" statement for all employees. It demanded, among other things, "uncompromising personal and professional integrity" and "unstinting respect." Many career officials viewed this knockoff of the honor code as a poorly disguised loyalty oath and struggled to see the mafia's integrity. Members seemed driven not by public service, some felt, but naked ambition.

During Trump's first term, Urban leveraged his White House connections to help triple his lobbying profits. In one especially notable case, he connected his client, Raytheon, with Pompeo, seeking to circumvent a congressional blockade on arms sales to the Middle East. Shortly after Pompeo met with the company, his State Department issued a waiver allowing the firm to sell billions of dollars' worth of missiles and bombs to Saudi Arabia and the United Arab Emirates.

Pompeo also leveraged his perch to advance his political ambitions. He used taxpayer dollars for lavish dinners with powerful political figures and conservative mega-donors during business trips, including his former investment partner, Charles Koch. Pompeo and his capos later spun their time working for Trump into lucrative book deals, board seats, and foundation fellowships.

WHEN TRUMP REMARKED that there were "very fine people on both sides" of the deadly 2017 white supremacist rally in Charlottesville, Virginia, McMaster—West Point class of 1984—defended him. McMaster also provided the president cover after Trump shared top secret intelligence with senior Russian officials on a phone call, calling the conversation "wholly appropriate."

Pompeo and Brechbuhl were themselves on another infamous Trump call two years later in which the president allegedly demanded Ukrainián president Volodymyr Zelenskyy dig up dirt on Hunter Biden's Ukrainian business exploits in exchange for foreign aid. The two men voiced no apparent concerns over the proposed quid pro quo, and may have, in fact, been complicit in the request, and helped push it forward.

In the waning days of his first term, Trump turned to more fringe military officers to help him hold on to power. They included Army colonel Douglas Macgregor, a West Pointer who was appointed by the president to his alma mater's Board of Visitors, alongside Navy reservist Sean Spicer and Kellyanne Conway. Macgregor had once served as a clear-eyed critic of the COINdinistas. Now he was trafficking in racist rhetoric and promoted the "great replacement" conspiracy theory, a belief that Democrats aim to replace white Americans with immigrants to lock in political majorities.

During the George Floyd protests in 2020, Macgregor informally advised the Trump administration about the use of the Insurrection Act. Esper, for his part, partook in Trump's authoritarian photo op that summer in front of a Washington, D.C., church. Soon after, he claimed that he and others had been duped into the exercise and clarified that he didn't support the deployment of troops to the streets. Esper also apologized for comments made days earlier describing the domestic D.C. environment as a "battlespace."

A few months later—specifically one day after Joe Biden was declared president-elect in November 2020—Macgregor was appointed to be a Pentagon adviser. He was joined by a new defense secretary, Christopher Miller, replacing Esper who, to his credit, was internally trying to hinder Trump's authoritarian urges, like for troops shooting protestors in the streets. These two late-term appointments had curious timing; the men had only about two months before the Biden administration, freshly activated and in power, would surely tell them to pack up their boxes. Both men had another timeline in mind. Each later admitted under questioning that they thought Trump might remain in office beyond inauguration day.

Once in charge of the Pentagon, Defense Secretary Miller instigated a worrying pause in the transition of power, abruptly canceling dozens of meetings with incoming Biden officials. It's still not entirely clear what, exactly, Miller, Macgregor, and other senior Trump military officials were doing in the short blackout period that followed. But three days before January 6, all ten living former defense secretaries penned a cryptic warning in *The Washington Post* of a coming military coup. Their op-ed name-checked Miller specifically, warning of grave consequences should he abrogate his constitutional duties. Around this time, Representative Mark Green, a Tennessee Republican who also hailed from West Point's class of 1986, was sending Trump's chief of staff, Mark Meadows, harebrained theories on how to decertify the election results and "declare Trump winner."

When, on January 6, the insurrectionists first arrived on Capitol Hill, they were greeted with a fist pump by Senator Josh Hawley of Missouri, who later penned a reactionary book on manhood that explicitly romanticized the warrior archetype. Scores of rioters fit that archetype exactly, including the swarm's most famous member, Jacob Chansley, a Navy veteran known as the "QAnon Shaman," who walked through the Capitol wearing a horned fur hat. Other military veterans there that day included Adam Newbold, a former Navy SEAL, who confessed that he was eager to leave lawmakers "shaking in their shoes." Donovan Crowl, a Marine veteran, said he served as "security" for an unnamed group of "VIPs." Emily Rainey, an Army psychological operations officer, had ferried roughly a hundred followers to Washington from North Carolina.

As they charged up the steps of the Capitol, rioters in battle gear formed a tactical line known as a Ranger File—a "chilling sign," according to the AP, that many who "stormed the seat of American democracy either had military training or were trained by those who did." Larry Rendall Brock Jr., a 1989 Air Force Academy graduate and retired fighter pilot, arrived on the Senate floor armed with zip-tie handcuffs. He and others appeared to be rifling through members' desks as part of what Brock described as an "information operation." On the other end of the Capitol, a police officer shot and killed Ashli Babbitt, an Air Force veteran turned Trump devotee and QAnon disciple, as she tried to enter the speaker's suite. Four others died in what appeared to be the first battle of a cold civil war. Other service academy alumni were in the crowd that day, including David Eastman, a West Point graduate, Oath Keeper, and far-right state legislator in Alaska, though he claims he never breached the Capitol.

The Pentagon ultimately suppressed the rioters, but only after a series of puzzling delays. Ryan McCarthy, then the Army secretary and a graduate of the Virginia Military Institute, became virtually impossible to find in the days leading up to the attack. Then, during the siege itself, a panicked subordinate was forced to run around the Pentagon looking for him.

Macgregor was also at the Pentagon that day. He later told investigators that he paid little attention to the riots, and "went home early." When asked if he thought January 6 constituted an insurrection, Macgregor replied, "I don't think it did."

William J. Walker, a Black major general who led the heroic D.C. National Guard response that day, had a far different assessment. "Somebody or somebodies were willfully, deliberately delaying making the decision" to deploy, he claimed in congressional testimony. "I think it would have been a vastly different response if those were African Americans trying to breach the Capitol."

Roughly 230 people arrested in connection with the January 6 insurrection were ultimately found to have had a military background, a stark reflection of the fact that military service most strongly predicts extremist violence in America. In the wake of January 6, the Joint Chiefs of Staff released a memo reminding service members that "any act to disrupt the constitutional process is not only against our traditions, values and oath, it is against the law." A Pentagon official later promised "we will not tolerate extremism." And yet the force was hopelessly divided at all levels. In addition to the military rioters, 124 retired generals and admirals signed a letter contesting the 2020 election results, while retired lieutenant general Michael Gould, a former superintendent of the Air Force Academy and CEO of the academy's alumni association, declined to condemn the actions on January 6.

As for Pompeo, the much-heralded West Point leader of the class whose "Courage Never Quits" . . . well, it did. Eager to stay in Trump's good graces, Pompeo did what was becoming a familiar one-two dodge-and-defend: refusing to accept the 2020 election results, then underplaying the violence on January 6. In Pompeo's case, that meant describing that day as a "peaceful transition of power."

AS IT HAPPENED, January 6 also marked the one-month anniversary of President-elect Joe Biden's nomination of the nation's first Black secretary of defense, West Pointer Lloyd Austin. Amid the chaotic authoritarian mania of the Trump administration, Austin's appointment appeared to be a welcome and long-overdue stabilizing force. In breaking the "brass ceiling" in the executive management of the armed forces, Austin was heralded, like former Joint Chiefs chairman Colin Powell before him, as the public face of a post-racial military, where stubborn divisions along racial and ethnic lines could at long last be put to rest.

The shock of the insurrection, however, made clear that the military's racist elements were alive and well. Austin responded by ordering American military units worldwide to "stand down" for a day and discuss extremism. He also promised a series of more far-reaching reforms, and, in April 2021, launched a Countering Extremism Working Group. Austin tapped as its leader Bishop Garrison, a fellow Black West Point graduate who served two combat tours in Iraq and earned two Bronze Stars. Garrison was tasked with exploring new and better ways to screen out problem recruits. He updated the Uniform Code of Military Justice to empower judge advocate generals to charge hate crimes. His working group sought to increase cooperation between military and civilian law enforcement authorities, while also commissioning an independent study on the extent of military extremism.

Garrison was given just ninety days to enact these ambitious plans. He quickly built a one-hundred-person team from across the Pentagon's five service branches composed of members of relevant offices, like personnel and readiness, the office of general counsel, and intelligence. The group seemed smart and motivated, but it immediately faced intense resistance, both inside and outside of the building.

The first whiff of public opposition set in a few days after the working group was formed, when two four-star commanders each claimed, under oath before the Senate Armed Services Committee, that there were "zero" extremists among the hundreds of thousands of service members under their purview—claims that Garrison publicly challenged. "There is a problem with extremist behavior in the military," he said. "That is to say that one extremist is one too many." Weeks later, thirty Republican lawmakers signed a letter singling out Garrison and complaining of "creeping left-wing extremism" in the military. Around this time, he started receiving death threats.

Some of the most powerful criticism came from Republican veterans in Congress, who for years had used the sheen of respectability conferred by their service to launder extremist ideas into the mainstream. Leading this fight were Senator Tom Cotton of Arkansas, a former Army officer, and Representative Dan Crenshaw of Texas, a former Navy SEAL, who invited "whistleblowers" to contact their offices with stories of anti-racist wokeism run amok. Representative Michael Waltz of Florida, the first Green Beret in Congress and a graduate of the Virginia Military Institute, vehemently criticized a West Point course focused on critical race theory.

While most Republicans masked their attacks as a "war on wokeness," Waltz went a step further, introducing legislation to explicitly prohibit federal funds from being used to investigate military extremists. Senator Tommy Tuberville, an Alabama Republican, was similarly transparent when asked by a Birmingham public radio station if he thought white nationalists should be allowed to serve in the military. "Well, they call them that," he said. "I call them Americans." Tuberville had, by then, spent weeks blocking all pending senior promotions due for Senate approval—an unprecedented move that he claimed was necessary to combat access to abortion within the military, along with other symptoms of reprobate wokeism. Others noted that his actions could also help ensure the rise of MAGA-aligned officers should Trump reclaim the title of commander in chief.

As the political attacks on the working group stretched into the summer, CNN reported that Austin's public support for Garrison "evaporated." One anonymous official told the network that he was "deemed to be a distraction," a harsh comment that undermined the brotherly instincts of West Point ring knockers. Months later, the appropriators drafting the final 2022 defense bill boosted spending while stripping out eight provisions meant to combat extremism.

While the Pentagon updated the screening questionnaire used by recruiters, it wasn't widely enforced. In August 2023, the military's inspector general found that only 40 percent of would-be recruits in a sample were asked about or responded to questions about extremist or gang ties. Only 9 percent were screened for tattoos that could indicate such affiliations. The Defense Department had also managed to develop a pathbreaking approach to mining data from a security clearance database to identify white supremacist and extremist incidents, potentially providing a massive tool to root out extremism. But according to an AP investigation, it never made its way to Garrison, and was thus never implemented. This was an especially deflating outcome considering the Pentagon was then presumably being overseen by President Biden, who claimed that his decision to enter the 2020 race was a direct result of the militant white supremacy he witnessed in Charlottesville, and who later made reckoning with January 6 a cornerstone objective.

A FEW MONTHS AFTER HE LAUNCHED his ill-fated reform efforts, Austin returned to West Point and addressed the graduating class of 2021. Despite the military's decidedly mixed record on racial progress, and West Point's persistently discriminatory subculture, the ceremony offered a bit of hope in the form of 148 Black graduates—an exponential increase from Austin's era.

Still, in his speech, Austin acknowledged the startling similarities between today's force and the Army he had entered. Now, as then, military officers served a nation in crisis: "a democracy under strain, economic fallout, painful issues of racism and discrimination, [and] social tensions at the end of a long and controversial war."

It was one of Austin's most candid moments in his highly private public life. Here he was hinting at an immutable truth, namely that every major military conflict in the United States has led to a domestic surge of white violence. "If you look at the surges in Klan activity throughout its life from the late 1800s forward, the best predictor for a major surge in that kind of action is not economic need, anti-immigration fervor, populism or any number of explanations that people have sort of pointed to," historian Kathleen Belew, author of *Bring the War Home*, explained to NPR in 2021. "The best predictor for rises in Klan activity is the aftermath of warfare."

There are no shortage of examples involving white power militarism, but Austin was right to spotlight the Cold War as a particularly disturbing era—both for its resurgent right-wing extremism and for the military's all-too-familiar unwillingness to grapple with the problem.

A major hotspot back then was Austin's old base in North Carolina: Fort Bragg, named after a slave-owning Confederate general. In 1986, *The New York Times* uncovered evidence that U.S. Marines and soldiers based at Bragg and Camp Lejeune, which sits 130 miles east, were involved in white power groups. That same year, a retired member of the Special Forces wrote to a North Carolina legislator that if leaders failed to support the needs of white citizens, "then we have no alternative but to resort to armed revolution to replace them."

Austin's time at Bragg overlapped with James Burmeister II and Malcolm Wright, two skinhead paratroopers who, in 1995, murdered a Black couple in nearby Fayetteville, North Carolina. Austin was a junior officer at the time, though he has declined to specify what role, if any, he had in the Army's reaction to the killings. In their wake, the brass investigated the base and identified twenty-two white supremacist skinheads—plus a smaller opposing force of anti-racist skinheads. The Army strained to note that this population represented less than one percent of the Airborne force. Some leaders defensively claimed that the skinheads had been impossible to spot.

Austin echoed this narrative during his Senate confirmation hearings in 2021, explaining that "we just didn't know what to look for" in the effort to root out extremism at Bragg. Yet Bragg had long been identified as a breeding ground for white hate. Indeed, the months leading up to the murders were marked by a slew of violent assaults in neighboring communities launched by skinheads with suspected military ties.

One of the murderers had previously made racially pointed remarks toward a Black soldier and fought him. His room had Nazi flags on the wall, and his personnel file showed he was counseled for wearing a Nazi medallion. West Pointer and retired Army major general Paul Eaton told me he found it hard, in general, to believe that military extremism goes easily undetected. "Squad leaders are expected to know their men absolutely, as well as their families and their extended families," he said. "You hear the term brotherhood, that's what it is. For a guy to survive as an extremist would take almost a conspiracy to allow it to occur and endure." And, indeed, some commanders quietly admitted later that they had been aware that toxic ideas had permeated the base. Some tolerated this ideology, they said, because they thought military values would ultimately stamp it out.

Austin's legacy on racial issues turned out to be largely fleeting, and almost entirely cosmetic. In 2019, West Point did away with the football team's slogan—"God Forgives, Brothers Don't"—after discovering its association with the Aryan Brotherhood of Texas. In 2022, the Point scrubbed its Confederate monuments and removed its plaque honoring the Klan. A bunch of military bases and one VA hospital named after Confederate leaders were also renamed, including Bragg, which was renamed Fort Liberty.

Shortly before this official 2022 rechristening, a member of the 82nd Airborne at Bragg was discharged after prosecutors uncovered his Nazi leanings, as well as social media posts in which he said he signed up for the Army so that he could become more proficient in killing Black people. Months later, prosecutors charged a twenty-three-year-old Airborne soldier named Noah Anthony for planning an "operation to physically remove as many [Black and brown people]" from the three counties surrounding the base.

Anthony's case was additionally noteworthy for the way his plot was uncovered. He was not rooted out by an in-depth military investigation, or due to a background check, or because a fellow soldier tipped off the brass. No, his hateful beliefs and agenda came to light via a completely random search of his car. As military police rustled around, they found a handgun, ammunition, and an American flag altered to show a swastika where the fifty white stars normally appear. A few days after Anthony was charged, Bragg was officially renamed, an occasion that spurred a patriotic statement from the base's garrison commander. "Liberty lives here," he said. "It is part of our ethos and it's part of who we are."

Chapter 19

My Generals

A few weeks after Trump's decisive 2024 reelection win, he celebrated with a few handpicked loyalists in a glassy VIP box at the Army-Navy game. Draped over Trump's seat was a customized Army football jersey embossed with his last name and "47," denoting his renewed membership in the ultra-exclusive fraternity of American presidents. During the game, Trump sipped Diet Coca-Cola and strategized over his second term with military and political leaders. At one point, his visage flashed on the Jumbotron, spurring excited cheers from a crowd composed mostly of cadets, midshipmen, military officers, and their families. "Thank you," Trump mouthed to them. "USA! USA!" they roared in response.

This moment of unbridled enthusiasm portended the unprecedented power Trump would soon exert over the Pentagon and, indeed, America writ large. The president had craved total military autonomy during his first term, but selected his senior military officials largely based on surface-level criteria, fretting over appearance and persona instead of pure ideological overlap, and loyalty. Early in his first term, he affectionately called these men "my generals," only to discover that their looks could be deceiving.

During his first term, Trump could generally rely on the loyalty of the West Point Mafia. Other military advisers stymied his most problematic orders, and some bitterly denounced him in retirement. Trump's first defense secretary, James "Mad Dog" Mattis, publicly called him a threat to the Constitution, while Trump's former Joint Chiefs chairman, Mark Milley labeled him "fascist to the core." Shortly thereafter, his former chief of staff, retired Marine general John Kelley, agreed with Milley. (None were West Point graduates.)

As Trump's first term drew to a close, he had become deeply distrustful of the military establishment, venting to close allies that he wished for "the kind of generals that Hitler had." Now, as his second term dawned, Trump was dead set on avoiding the mistakes of the past. He would build an officer class not unlike that of the Third Reich, one that was faithful, fervent, and willing to turn American firepower inward.

While many deemed Trump a pariah after January 6, the U.S. military was generally more forgiving. As Election Day 2024 approached, more than two hundred retired admirals and generals endorsed Trump. Days later, when Americans went to the polls, he improved on his already historic popularity with veteran voters. He also enjoyed a massive, 12-point shift among men eighteen to twenty-nine, a payoff for Trump after he drenched his reelection campaign in masculine symbology, making an explicit pitch promising men he would reassert gender norms around strength and submissiveness. "I want to protect the women of our country," Trump said in one Wisconsin rally. "I'm going to do it whether the women like it or not." The president followed this up by comparing his strength as commander in chief to the great gridiron hero Brett Favre, backing his comparison up with a favorite piece of military propaganda: "I defeated ISIS in four weeks instead of five years."

One of the great revisionists of January 6 was Princeton ROTC graduate Pete Hegseth, who, at the time of the insurrection, was a National Guard officer and telegenic weekend host on *Fox & Friends*. In one TV segment, he portrayed the crowd that day as pure patriots, saying they "love freedom" and had "been re-awoken to the reality of what the left has done" to their country. In all honesty, much of the American left itself felt similarly frustrated, even if their diagnosis differed. Many felt, like those on the right, that they were running out of legitimate options to spur long-overdue change.

Immediately after January 6, National Guard units were deployed to protect the Capitol—including Hegseth's brigade. Just ahead of this domestic deployment, a fellow soldier flagged Hegseth to his superiors as a potential "insider threat," citing military regulations that prohibit extremist ink.

On a subsequent podcast with Shawn Ryan, a former Navy SEAL now serving as the Joe Rogan of conservative military media, Hegseth flashed his right pectoral muscle and showed the tattoo that, he said, led to his extremist label: a large, inky Jerusalem cross associated with the Christian right.

"My orders were revoked to guard the Biden inauguration," Hegseth explained.

"What a punishment," Ryan responded sarcastically. Then the two men laughed.

The truth, however, was that a soldier had flagged another one of Hegseth's tattoos. This one, on his right tricep, read "Deus Vult," or "God Wills It"—a motto from the Crusades that has been invoked by white supremacists and was seen at Charlottesville.

Trump's box at the 2024 Army-Navy game included Hegseth, who had been recently nominated by the incoming president as defense secretary in a pick that shocked the Washington establishment. Also in attendance were members of Trump's roster of military loyalists. They were mostly men, but included Tulsi Gabbard, a lieutenant colonel in the Army National Guard poised to be his director of national intelligence. The men included Mike Waltz, a VMI graduate and former Green Beret who would serve as Trump's national security adviser, then U.N. ambassador, and David Urban, the West Pointer from the class of '86. Also, Wesley Hunt, a far-right West Pointer representing Texas's 38th congressional district. And J.D. Vance, Trump's newly minted vice president and a Marine Corps veteran.

Vance had invited as his special guest Daniel Penny, a fellow Marine who, days earlier, had been acquitted of homicide charges after choking to death an unarmed homeless Black man, Jordan Neely, in the New York City subway. Ahead of the game, Vance held Penny up as an exemplar of the American man, a "good guy," in his words, who had been targeted by the left simply for showing a "backbone."

IN ADDITION TO DRIVING THE MILITARY'S ESPRIT DE CORPS, football games at the service academies offer a visceral reminder of the military industrial complex's mammoth power and profitability. Major weapons contractors have sponsored these games for decades, with arms executives often sitting in VIP boxes. This forms a strange gladiatorial dynamic in which America's merchants of death observe the hulking strength of those who will one day operate their machines. One of the sponsors of the 2024 game was Palantir, the Peter Thiel–led Silicon Valley technology company that is being paid hundreds of millions of dollars to develop targeting systems and massive surveillance tools powered by data and AI.

The major sponsor of the Army–Air Force football game, known as the "Armed Forces Bowl," is Lockheed Martin, which, in 2020, snagged a glut of taxpayer-funded contracts that eclipsed the entire budget of the U.S. Department of Education. In an era of educational disinvestment and ballooning student debt, military contractors like Lockheed have used their largesse to overcome any moral qualms among potential recruits, offering lucrative salaries, plus loan assistance and tuition reimbursement. "A lot of people that I talk to aren't 100 percent comfortable working on defense contracts, working on things that are basically going to kill people," a Georgia Tech graduate named Cameron Davis told *In These Times* in 2022. But, he added, the money "drives a lot of your moral disagreements with defense away."

The firm's charm offensive has come to include "Lockheed Martin Day" at more than a dozen participating colleges, in which Black Hawk and Sikorsky helicopters filled with recruiters land on campus to trawl for students. As of this writing, the University of Maryland's board is chaired by a former Lockheed executive, while the president of the University of Texas at El Paso serves on the Lockheed board. The Board of Visitors at Howard University's engineering school includes a Lockheed vice president overseeing HR in the firm's "missiles and fire control" department. Meanwhile, the former CEO of Northrop Grumman sits on MIT's Board of Trustees.

On January 20, 2025, a few weeks after the Palantir-sponsored Army-Navy game, Trump's second inaugural took place in Washington. Its sponsors included Lockheed and Boeing, among other contractors. They each ponied up $1 million. During the festivities, dozens of cadets hailing from military schools across the country marched obediently in the inaugural parade, which had been cramped into the Capitol One Arena due to blisteringly cold weather conditions. As with Trump's first inaugural, the schools represented that day included the New York Military Academy, Trump's alma mater, where he had once marched in midtown Manhattan and, like Bonaparte, staked out a territory he aimed to conquer. As the new class of NYMA boys passed by the president's dais, he cracked a smile and saluted them.

Minutes after Trump was officially reinstated, he returned to the White House and signed an executive order releasing virtually all of those convicted for their activities on January 6. Those pardoned included more than two hundred military veterans, dozens of whom were affiliated with militia groups like the Oath Keepers and the Proud Boys. From here, Trump signed a flurry of actions to establish a more pliable Pentagon. One executive order aimed to restrict and reshape the composition of the military by pledging to overhaul the "leadership, curriculum, and instructors" at the military service academies. Trump's order prescribed a new kind of teaching, and a new kind of professor, someone who dispenses with knotty topics and uncomfortable facts in favor of a blinkered worldview: that "America and its founding documents remain the most powerful force for good in human history."

That same month, Hegseth ventured to Capitol Hill for his confirmation hearing. The Princeton-bred Army veteran donned a navy-blue suit and an American flag pocket square. Perhaps Hegseth hoped his patriotic wardrobe might inoculate him from a series of problematic and fast-proliferating allegations against him, among them: alcohol abuse, financial mismanagement, rank misogyny, Islamophobia, and rape. One memo from Hegseth's former employer, an Astro Turf veterans group founded by the Koch brothers, alleged he became so intoxicated during a 2014 Christmas party that he had to be carried up to his room. While drunk at a bar in Ohio, Hegseth had also allegedly chanted "Kill all Muslims!"

Dark as they were, the charges against Hegseth revealed him to be a tragic avatar of the GWOT generation. "There's a deep sense of sacrifice and loss for nothing," Adam Weinstein, a Marine Corps veteran who deployed to Afghanistan, told me. "And that can lead to fatalistic beliefs; it can lead to Islamophobia. In its healthier form, it can lead to questioning the principles of interventionism and the U.S. foreign policy establishment." Hegseth harbored deep animosity toward the military establishment. But his fix was to gut the place of caution and critical thinking in favor of a force that was cold-blooded and unquestioning. As in Vietnam, Hegseth adopted pseudo-historical narratives that blamed women and weak men for his war's failure, rather than the Pentagon's profound intelligence and tactical problems.

Midway through Hegseth's contentious hearing, it became Tommy Tuberville's time to talk. The former Auburn football coach and Alabama senator said his top issue was military recruitment, explaining that a constituent of his had worked like hell to get into West Point, only to back away. "I got him a nomination, I got him accepted, and he turned it down. He says 'Coach, I'm not getting involved in that mess.'" Tuberville groused that the service academies had become too woke, and that, as a result, he was encountering an increasing number of students reasoning, "Why would you fight for a country that you don't love?" He continued: "That's an excuse I get from a lot of our kids. We've gotta break that."

In the preceding years, military school recruitment had indeed dipped across the board, with applications dropping 10 percent at West Point, and

30 percent at the Air Force Academy. Tuberville couldn't or wouldn't acknowledge that this trend in any way stemmed from two decades of military failure, with President Biden's disastrous 2021 withdrawal from Afghanistan precipitating an especially dramatic 10-point drop in public confidence in the Pentagon. Instead, Tuberville claimed the Pentagon's problems could be pinned on the "woke universities" like the ones he used to coach at.

Hegseth was intimately familiar with a liberal arts environment. Between two college programs—West Point and Princeton—he had chosen the latter, opting to attend a school that not only conferred power but proximity to capital. He grew up middle class but dreamed of money, wishing in his yearbook biography to one day "roll in the dough."

Hegseth was once proud of his Princeton pedigree. As a student, he had become a leader in the Ivy's storied ROTC program, known as the "Tiger Battalion," which counts as an alumnus Mark Milley, whose official Defense Department portrait Trump had removed from the Pentagon within hours of his second inauguration.

In college, Hegseth distinguished himself as publisher of the hyperconservative *Princeton Tory*. He has since reflected on the connection between these pursuits, noting that ROTC taught him how to "channel nervous energy into physical confrontation," while the *Tory* built his ability to "stomach ideological warfare." In time, however, Hegseth became grossly disillusioned by higher education. In 2022, he scribbled in Sharpie on his Harvard graduate degree "Return to Sender," a bizarre PR stunt for his then-new book *The Battle for the American Mind: Uprooting a Century of Miseducation*, itself a polemic and call to arms for what Hegseth described as an "educational insurgency."

When Tuberville asked how to fix the recruiting crisis, Hegseth was well-armed with an answer. If confirmed as Trump's defense secretary, Hegseth pledged to "rip, root and branch the politics and divisive policies" out of service academies like West Point by ridding them of civilian faculty, some of whom, he wildly alleges in his 2024 book *The War on Warriors*, had responded in the weeks after 9/11 with a "'we deserved this' narrative."

"We need more uniformed members going back into West Point, the Air Force Academy, the Naval Academy as a tour to teach with their wisdom of what they've learned in uniform," Hegseth said to Tuberville. "Instead of just more civilian professors that came from the same left-wing, woke universities that they left, and then try to push that into service academies."

Despite much political handwringing over Hegseth's disqualifying history, thirty-two military veterans serving in the U.S. House of Representatives recognized Hegseth as one of their own, endorsing his nomination in a letter that deemed him "a critical connector to the force of tomorrow." This was not initially enough to clear up concerns among certain Senate Republicans. Hegseth's fate was, for a moment, in the hands of a woman: Republican senator Joni Ernst of Iowa, herself a combat veteran and sexual assault survivor who had conducted dangerous convoy security in Iraq. Ernst was clearly unenthusiastic about Hegseth's regressive views on women and his checkered personal history. But MAGA conservatives launched a pressure campaign against her, and she ultimately backed down, pledging to "work with Pete to create the most lethal fighting force." Ernst's rhetoric suggests a commitment to militarism is still capable of obscuring a multitude of sins.

TO GRAHAM PARSONS, the nomination of Hegseth as defense secretary at once offered a fascinating case study and an immediate threat to his career. Since 2012, Parsons had been a civilian professor at West Point, where he taught cadets military ethics and researched the knotty relationship between gender and warfare. Hegseth was an exemplar of Parsons's scholarship, a tattooed alpha male whose vision of military service is built on undermining and expelling female and transgender troops.

Unlike some civilian professors, Parsons could easily be mistaken for a colonel out of uniform. He is tall, bald, gravelly voiced, and to the point. Parsons comes from strong military stock, with his family roots reaching back to both sides of the Civil War. His father enthusiastically enlisted as a Marine to fight in Vietnam, while his childhood friends were a bunch of wild-eyed hooligans who organized into a loose gang. "There's a veneer of toughness on campus," Parsons told me. "I realized I could play that part."

During his junior year of high school, Parsons's crew got jumped by a far larger group, one of whom had a knife. "There was a level of violence in that moment that made me realize, 'I can't do this,'" he recalled. Years later, at CUNY graduate school, Parsons began untangling his childhood urges, thanks to mentorship from two prominent feminist philosophers: Virginia Held and Linda Martín Alcoff.

Days after his confirmation, Hegseth blasted out a memo to military school faculty prohibiting instruction that could be in any way construed as promoting "Critical Race Theory, Gender Ideology, and DEI." He then gathered service academy leaders on a teleconference. Beamed into each campus, Hegseth issued a clear order: focus on history, warfighting, and engineering and hobble much of the rest. Department heads moved quickly, telling faculty to review their syllabi for materials potentially in conflict with the defense secretary's dictate. This was the first action in a muscular campaign that appeared to double as a trial run on how to fundamentally reshape America's civilian colleges and universities.

The list of texts Parsons submitted focused on affirmative action, feminism, and political theory. One reckoned with the racist underpinnings of philosopher Emmanuel Kant's work. He expected they would survive because he believed that "the academy was preparing to fight back." It didn't. West Point ultimately banned Parsons's entire bibliography, part of a broader sweep across the service academies that scrubbed hundreds of books from courses and library catalogues, including work by James Baldwin and Toni Morrison, plus a slate of texts exploring aspects of masculinity. West Point also dissolved its sociology major and abolished at least a dozen student diversity clubs, including a chapter of the Society of Women Engineers and the Latin Cultural Club. They also removed history and English courses, including one called "Power and Difference."

Administrators capped this off with a new draconian policy requiring military approval for all "journal publications, conference presentations, media interviews, podcasts, opinion editorials, blog posts, [and] social media posts." According to three faculty members, West Point civilian law professor, Tim Bakken, protested the speech restrictions as unconstitutional during a faculty council meeting in March 2025. Before he could conclude his case, a fellow professor and colonel snapped at him hard. "You've said enough," he said.

During Trump's first term, Parsons had authored a piece critical of the president's transgender military ban. According to the professor, West Point's press office wasn't thrilled, but then-dean Cindy Jebb backed him up, asserting that he was exercising his academic freedom. But Jebb had since left, and others had been elevated, forming a new school hierarchy that saw things differently. Shortly before Trump's 2025 inauguration, West Point pleaded with Parsons to withdraw a piece he had written for *Lawfare* about the importance of nonpartisanship in the military, worried it might attract the incoming administration's ire. Parsons reluctantly complied, but as West Point's academic crackdown intensified throughout the spring, Parsons lost faith in leadership. He also worried that what was happening on campus portended bad and bigger things to come. In early May 2025, he articulated these concerns in *The New York Times*, writing that the school was now aiming to "indoctrinate, not educate" America's future military leaders.

Parsons stayed home on the day West Point was notified by the *Times* about his soon-to-be-published comments. His department head tried to contact Parsons that morning. By the afternoon, West Point had declared him AWOL. When the professor returned to campus the day after his piece was published, he was tense but heartened somewhat by quiet gestures of support from civilian and military staff and faculty.

In a meeting that morning in Jefferson Hall, Parsons said he was notified that he was under investigation for "allegations of misconduct," but that the inquiry would end if he formally resigned. Parsons was prepared for this, having secured a temporary appointment just down the Hudson River, at Vassar College. Ironically, an expert in military masculinity moved to a school that long served only women. While Parsons was sad to be leaving his post, Hegseth was giddy, writing on X, "You will not be missed Professor Parsons."

Other West Point academics left under pressure, too, as did dozens more at the Air Force and Naval Academies, plus the Naval and Army War Colleges. This was all part of Hegseth's broader plans to expel as many as sixty thousand civilians across the Pentagon. Among the topics these departing professors taught were military ethics, history, national security strategy, and engineering. One of these professors, Pauline Shanks Kaurin, wrote an entire book on the contrasting cultures of obedience in military and civilian environments. She lamented to me the fast snap of compliance among military school administrators, noting that troops are expected to reject illegal orders, which, she reasoned, these academic dictates may be. "Their legality is at least contested," she said.

Retired general Martin France, an Air Force Academy graduate and former chair of the academy's Department of Astronautics and Engineering, viewed this campus crackdown as a myopic effort to eliminate courses that encourage independence. "Our officers should be sentient beings who understand just war theory, the laws around conflict, the orders that they are morally obligated to disobey," France told me, arguing that the Trump administration, by contrast, wants to breed compliance rather than teach nuance. This, in turn, France alleged, forms an officer class of "flesh-and-bone drones."

In her 2025 retirement speech, Air Force Academy Dean Linelle Letendre argued that good teaching "doesn't make the fog of war go away, but it gives us the tools to see through it." It was, perhaps, a swiped veil at her boss, Superintendent Tony Bauernfeind, who floated plans to eliminate as many as a hundred civilian positions. He also dropped the word "educate" from the school's mission statement. Three faculty members at the Air Force Academy said that as part of Bauernfeind's inquiries into reducing civilian faculty, staff sought to understand how many PhD positions could be eliminated without threatening the school's accreditation status.

MANY FORMER CADETS RANK CIVILIANS among their favorite professors. One Naval Academy graduate from the late 1990s said military professors tended to focus on memorization and test taking, forcing midshipmen into a cycle of fleeting knowledge they called "pump and dump." "Civilian professors generally weren't that way," he added, echoing the sentiments of graduates across generations. "They were far better teachers of material."

Despite their popularity, civilian professors often felt like second-class citizens, barred from chairing academic departments, ineligible for well-appointed on-campus housing, and shut out of job protections contained within the system's Permanent Military Professor program. In the back half of President Joe Biden's term, civilian faculty, with support from military peers, secured basic tenure protections, but, under Hegseth, they were in jeopardy.

At the same time West Point enacted tenure, administrators kneecapped the humanities by shuttling them out of Lincoln Hall and into a funky multistory tent structure. It had classrooms, heat, and air-conditioning. According to Parsons, there was "supposed to be plumbing, but they never got the sewer attached." Amid their two-year deployment in this tent, humanities faculty were further notified, without any real rationale, that their department was to be broken up. English would move into the foreign languages department, while philosophy would be attached to law. Meanwhile, not far from the tent, work commenced on West Point's $138 million, 136,000-square-foot Cyber and Engineering Academic Center.

This series of unfortunate events was comical enough to be confused for a hazing ritual. Civilian professors had long been the subjects of military initiation rites, both formal trainings and off-the-books pranks. In 2013, as one example, a West Point economics professor wrote in *The New York Times* that, on her first day, someone apparently replaced her chalkboard eraser with an M16 magazine. To preempt those odd rites, many civilian faculty hoped to receive bits of military training alongside their academic work, with some invited on naval ships, sent to war zones, and trained in weaponry. Parsons, for his part, once participated in a videogame warfare simulator with his civilian peers.

In December 2018, as law professor Bakken was becoming an increasingly vocal critic of West Point orthodoxy, a military police officer at Thayer Gate scanned his employee I.D., then declared him the subject of a "random" search. Bakken, formerly a fellow at Columbia and Cambridge law schools, questioned the legal rationale behind the search, and requested to speak with a supervisor. He writes in his 2020 book *The Cost of Loyalty* that the officer cussed him out and directed him to the search zone. There, he ordered Bakken to spread his legs and put his hands against his car, then searched him aggressively. While Bakken complied with the search, he writes that the officer later claimed he had refused it, then said incorrectly, "You can't work at West Point anymore."

Ruth Ben-Ghiat, a leading scholar on fascism, told me that the Pentagon's fixation on the service academies is part and parcel of a broader effort to shore up military loyalty, a campaign, she argued, that is "at its root, a pedagogical project."

THE MILITARY BRASS'S REACTION to Hegseth's 2025 extreme reimaging of the military was unusually muted. This seemed to embolden the administration. Hegseth and Trump went on to fire the chairman of the Joint Chiefs of Staff, Charles Brown, a pioneering Black fighter pilot and only the second person of color to hold the job, and Admiral Lisa Franchetti, the first woman to lead the Navy. Laura Loomer, a MAGA conspiracy theorist and informal Trump adviser, also influenced Army Secretary Daniel Driscoll, an Iraq war veteran and Yale Law School classmate of Vice President Vance, to rescind a coveted West Point professorship for Jen Easterly, an alumna and former Rhodes Scholar whom Loomer baselessly accused of being a Democratic stooge.

At the same time, Trump and Hegseth ordered military funeral honors for Ashli Babbitt, the slain January 6er; signed a decree reverting Fort Liberty's name back to Fort Bragg; and renamed a Naval oil replenishment vessel originally honoring assassinated gay San Francisco city official and Navy veteran Harvey Milk to instead bear the name of Oscar Peterson, a Mormon Medal of Honor recipient who died in World War II. The Pentagon also reinstated at West Point the portrait of Robert E. Lee that depicts a slave in the background. Then Hegseth hung on his office wall a painting of General George Washington in prayer at Valley Forge.

Hegseth broadly branded his vision through yet another (unofficial) renaming: reverting the Defense Department to the title it held up until the end of World War II: the Department of War. The Trump administration made it exceptionally clear, though, that it had no tolerance for gauzy World War II nostalgia, abruptly canceling in late 2025 the annual ceremony for the Sylvanus Thayer Award, which was to be awarded to actor Tom Hanks, one of the most influential boosters of Greatest Generation hagiography, and an inoffensive symbol of pop culture anti-fascism.

"The core of fascism in Italy and Germany were combatants who followed their leader to bring the war home and turned their force against their own people," said Ben-Ghiat. She was slated to discuss historical examples of strongmen and the military at the Naval Academy's vaunted 2024 Bancroft lecture, scheduled to take place a few weeks before the 2024 election. Ben-Ghiat planned her talk to be explicitly apolitical, in keeping with the academy's regulations, focusing strictly on historical figures like Augusto Pinochet and Benito Mussolini.

But after conservative alumni groups caught wind of her forthcoming speech, they exerted intense pressure for it to be canceled. "They did not want those 500 midshipmen to hear about Pinochet," Ben-Ghiat said, "because one of my points was going to be that militaries under autocracy become ravaged by corruption, and that politicization undermines professionalization. Instead of loyalty to the nation, it becomes service to a leader."

After sustaining a days-long MAGA firestorm, Naval Academy Superintendent Yvette Davids called Ben-Ghiat while she waited for a plane in Ohio. Davids curtly canceled her talk. Before the line went dead, Ben-Ghiat tried to teach the superintendent a basic schoolyard lesson: "If you fold to a bully, they're going to keep bullying you." It turned out to be a prescient warning. In the summer of 2025, Hegseth sacked Yvette Davids.

"If you're planning a fundamental reorientation of the military—and you're going to go past the third rail of deploying against Americans—you have to really shift the whole mentality, shift the culture, permit radicalization," Ben-Ghiat told me. "Already, I think we're pretty far down the road."

A few months later, in September 2025, Hegseth issued a highly unusual order: requesting the presence of every general and flag officer at the one-star level and above at the Marine Corps base in Quantico, Virginia, for an unknown reason.

Around this time, Trump deployed immigration and border agents, the National Guard, and Marines to major American cities, over the objections of local leaders. Some ICE agents, poaching a grisly practice from Vietnam, left ace of spade—or "death cards"—in the vehicles of people they detained. The president mused again about designating citizens as "enemy" combatants, part of his rhetoric around the "invasion" from within. Trump paired his ramping up of domestic military with a clear charm offensive, first giving a set of commencement remarks at West Point where he fluffed up graduating cadets with a body beauty quip reminiscent of Bernarr Mac-Fadden. Looking out at the graduating cadets, he called the class "a bunch of male models—I can't stand it." Shortly thereafter, he held a major military parade in Washington, D.C., producing a factory line of sorts in which representatives from all the major Army divisions marched past Trump and saluted him.

At the ordered gathering of generals, Hegseth paced tensely before a tightly stretched American flag, a backdrop reminiscent of the infamous speech in the 1970 film *Patton*, giving a Ted-style talk for the military brass in which Hegseth aimed, to borrow a term from Ben-Ghiat, to "shift the whole mentality."

He failed to dedicate a single word to geopolitical affairs—that, he pledged, was "another speech for another day." Instead, he leveled a cultural firebombing against what he claimed was the left's grievous wounding of the strong culture of military manhood he held so dear. From here, he laid out his plans to bring standards back to a "male level."

Perhaps this was a mandate borne from Hegseth's own boyhood shame about his softness. "I didn't get in fights as a kid and shied from confrontation because, frankly, I was scared of it," he writes in his 2016 book *In the Arena*. He goes on to hail his father, Brian, for his "integrity" and "Scandinavian work ethic," while evincing regret that Brian failed to teach him the art of aggression. "My father was—and is—an incredible man," Hegseth insists. "But confrontation isn't necessarily his forte."

The military, he believed, would succeed where his father had failed. As a boy, Hegseth had stared admiringly at vets in local military parades. *In the Arena* tells of a mythic, unnamed Vietnam war veteran he met at nineteen. The vet's advice was simple: "Whatever you do, *don't miss your war*."

Many young men seek strength but ultimately confuse it for the Pentagon's brand of violence and domination. Hegseth, it seems, appears to be one such case. He showed up just in time for his wars, deploying to Iraq, Afghanistan, and Guantánamo Bay, before serving in various conservative Astro-Turf groups, and then at Fox News, as a fierce defender of the GWOT.

Once it became impossible to defend, Hegseth moved to pin many of its failures on those he deemed insufficiently "lethal"—an argument contravened by the copious kill count in the war on terror, in which American troops eliminated 700,000 opposition fighters and civilians in the service of still-uncertain aims. Now in charge, Hegseth was finally able to construct a strong, perfect vision of the American man in his own image, one where women were second-class citizens, hazing was encouraged, and dominance was expected.

This, Hegseth said in his speech, meant building a force composed of fit men, not "fat generals." Hegseth further insinuated that he wasn't interested in liberal or racially diverse officers, either. He was sick and tired, too, of what he saw as the military's light touch. He felt that the best way to forge militarism, and manhood, was through a strong hand, taking umbrage at how hazing was, in his mind, "weaponized and bastardized inside our formations."

"The definition of toxic has been turned upside down, and we're correcting that," Hegseth pledged. "That's why today, at my direction we're undertaking a full review of the department's definitions of so-called toxic leadership—bullying and hazing—to empower leaders to enforce standards without fear of retribution or second guessing."

If his conception of military masculinity "makes me toxic," Hegseth reasoned, "then so be it."

Conclusion
Rest in Peace

In an unpublished 1995 letter to a friend and former classmate, J.D.
Salinger—the reclusive author, World War II veteran, and Valley Forge
graduate—expressed some regret for the sunny three-stanza poem he had
written just before graduation, which was put on display in the school
chapel after the author got famous. It reads, in part:

> *Hide not thy tears on this last day*
> *Your sorrow has no shame;*
> *To march no more midst lines of gray;*
> *No longer play the game.*
> *Four years have passed in joyful ways—*
> *Wouldst stay those old times dear?*
> *Then cherish now these fleeting days,*
> *The few while you are here.*

Salinger, then seventy-six, seemed to think his assessment of his alma
mater had been too saccharine. "I've planned for years to stop by and either
tear the exhibit down or at the very least add a little obscene graffiti at the
bottom," he wrote to his friend. Salinger reflected, too, on the "interesting
collection of misfits" he had befriended at the Forge, and the memories
they shared, bad and good.

Still, it was leaving military school that brought Salinger the greatest joy:
"Though [the Forge], to me, was on the whole a thoroughly bad joke, its
pretenses and posturing irreversibly sham, contemptible," Salinger wrote, "I
wonder if I ever again felt as free, as gratefully on the loose, as I did on that
pretty walk to Wayne and the diner on a Sunday after signing out."

In another as yet unpublished piece of writing shared by his son, Matt, Salinger lamented the "profound handicap" produced in Americans at an early age. He called it an "unhealthy respect for nominal authority."

Speaking for himself, Salinger wrote: "The conditioning was variable and yet incessant in my childhood and youth. The absolute authority of my parents (who were ignorant people), the absolute authority of almost all public elementary teachers in the twenties and thirties (most of whom, or many of whom, were power-lovers, sour old maids, with rare and beautiful exceptions), and then, later, military school and the ruthless authority, absolute power of the faculty and cadet officers and non-coms (as terrible a bunch, on the whole, as the mind can imagine)." The flip side of Salinger's bleak depiction is a childhood full of free expression and natural development, unburdened by the power, rules, and discipline imposed by world-weary adults.

Twenty-five years after Salinger wrote his letter, on a crisp night in September 2020, a cadet leader at the Forge named Jordan Schumacher reached his wits' end. Like Holden Caulfield, he was ready to split from the campus for good. Weeks earlier, the school's top brass had elevated Jordan, a twenty-year-old college sophomore, to the highest rank available to cadets: first captain. A former Boy Scout who joined a junior ROTC program at eleven, he was proud of the promotion and ready to lead. But as he navigated the school's toxic environment in his new role, he felt increasingly helpless and depressed. A dearth of healthy adult oversight and accountability had put Jordan face-to-face with a culture replete with assaults, verbal abuse, and sexual violence, leading him and a handful of fellow cadets to shield students from bullies, break up fights, and rush injured or dangerously intoxicated kids to the hospital.

Out on patrol that night, Jordan was overwhelmed by all of it, later telling me that he felt on "the brink of darkness." As he paced along a brick pathway, he spotted something suspicious. Behind a toolshed, out of sight of campus surveillance cameras, a group of upperclassmen was tormenting a few shivering plebes. Jordan had stumbled upon an unsanctioned version of the capshield exam, an induction rite wherein new students are quizzed on the Forge's nearly one-hundred-year history. The exam is the culmination of the school's boot camp–style indoctrination. Those who pass are welcomed into the Corps of Cadets, which he now commanded, and received a capshield medal, a brass badge depicting the mythical moment when general George Washington, standing on the Pennsylvania battle-ground for which the school was named, prayed for the survival of the fledgling American republic.

The exam revolved around lofty principles, yet often culminated in a "capshield handshake," wherein plebes point the prick of the badge toward their palm and accept a vigorous handshake. A minor stabbing, but telling, to Jordan, of the far more extreme hazing that adult leaders seemed willing to tolerate, and sometimes participate in.

After breaking up the exam, Jordan cracked, storming past the chapel holding Salinger's poem, and into his dorm. There he gathered his belongings and threw everything into his truck, all the while yelling and banging doors as he vented his rage. As he sped off campus, he started to cry and contemplated his own death. "I was just mentally shattered," he said.

Sympathetic fellow cadets later found Jordan parked on the roadside, in shock, and urged him to come back inside the gates. Ten other cadets left the campus that weekend, some for a temporary taste of freedom, but others trying to escape permanently. Jordan returned that night but left the school for good soon after. "It brings out the best and the worst in people," he told me. "I don't want to say that's a goal of the school, but it's something that happens. It showed me who I didn't want to be."

MANY BOYS HARBOR DREAMS of what they want to be before the military swoops in. Salinger was a perfect example of this, a man who reviled fighting and loved writing, but was nonetheless conscripted to serve. When the military seems like the only viable path to masculine redemption or class mobility or acceptable public service, it can feel impossible to defect.

The military does its best to silence doubts and frustrate a troop's escape from their clutches, casting pacifism as unnatural and aberrant. The only way to formally leave the military on moral grounds is as a conscientious objector, or CO. To secure this status, one must navigate a fraught and frustrating bureaucratic process that often takes more than a year. Officers aggressively scrutinize one's background, records, and beliefs. All must submit to long interviews and a psychiatric evaluation.

After Joy Metzler, a 2023 Air Force Academy graduate, publicly outlined how the academy's screening of violent drone killings to cadets led her to seek CO status, a fellow academy graduate and retired lieutenant colonel named Ken Hamlin penned an angry rebuke demanding she pay back the military for all they had invested in her. He also insisted that "since the dawn of written history, man chose the most violent course of action."

Years earlier, Naval Academy Midshipman Michael Izbicki became similarly embittered with the military following a class in which "we calculated the extent of civilian casualties and whether these numbers were politically acceptable." As Izbicki fought his case, a Navy commander compared the Quakers assisting him to Reverend Jim Jones's infamous suicide cult.

The figures assisting COs represent the last vestige of the religiously imbued anti-war movement, one spearheaded by religious leaders and first organized under the Committee on Militarism in Education a century ago. These forces are today operating under the Center on Conscience & War, which was formed in 1940 by America's three peace churches: the Quakers, the Mennonites, and the Brethren. Their headquarters is located six miles due north of the Pentagon, inside a modest Episcopal church on Connecticut Avenue, in Washington, D.C.

The center's longtime director is Bill Galvin, a conscientious objector from the Vietnam era who has reviewed and supported hundreds of applications since the 1970s. He told me he's frequently seen troops hesitate over worries that their friends and family will "perceive them to be pussies." An Air Force officer he once worked with had been especially anxious about his parents, both of whom served—and rightly so. After his family learned about his CO status, they disowned him.

The center offers not only a hub of assistance, but also an alternative theory on man's penchant for peace. "Part of basic training is deliberately designed to override your conscience," Galvin argued. He pointed to the 1947 study *Men Against Fire*, penned by General S.L.A. Marshall. It claimed, among other things, that fewer than 25 percent of World War II combatants actually fired their weapons at the enemy. "The military changed their training after that," Galvin explained.

Metzler alleged that much of the Air Force Academy curriculum today is "designed to get you thinking about killing in your daily life." This included the disturbing screening of graphic drone footage, as well as more mundane practices, like shooting sports, history courses that focus on conflict, and violent marching chants, like "blood makes the grass grow," which falsely imbues killing with regenerative properties.

Refusing to support this ideology is not cowardly, but brave, and often personally reaffirming. Metzler felt her sense of humor come back, while

Izbicki said his discharge "opened the whole world up to me." During the Vietnam War, Cary Donham became the first-ever West Point cadet to apply for CO status. His application was rejected because the military deemed him "insincere," an assertion rejected by his life's work in the church, which was first motivated by an Old Testament passage, "blessed are the peacemakers."

MANY COS ASSISTED BY THE CENTER ON CONSCIENCE later give back to support pending applications, be it through volunteer work or donations. Galvin's unyielding dedication to this work stems from the assistance he received during Vietnam by Thurston Griggs, a World War II–era conscientious objector who belonged to Galvin's hometown church, in Maryland.

Galvin grew up on the borderline of Patapsco Park, a verdant, sixteen-thousand-acre forest with a river cutting through it. He spent much of his youth exploring this wondrous setting, camping with his Boy Scout troop, attending church picnics, and skating on the river in the winter. Little did he know then, but Patapsco had served as a shelter and staging ground during World War II for men who rejected the military.

In 1941, Patapsco hosted America's first civilian-directed, non-military alternative service camp for drafted conscientious objectors. It was overseen by the freshly formed (and short-lived) Civilian Public Service, which created camps for more than twelve thousand men during World War II. General Lewis B. Hershey, the director of the Selective Service System, acknowledged at the time that this program was an important feature in a democratic society, one that could "preserve minority rights in a time of national emergency."

The Patapsco locale was fittingly described by *The Washington Post* as "a peaceful Maryland valley" filled with "men willing to work, but not fight for their country." Dozens of COs flowed into the camp within days of its establishment. There, they followed a similar schedule to the Army, but with a few key exceptions. There was, for instance, no drilling or hazing. Breakfast was served at the crack of dawn, but it was followed by twenty minutes of meditation.

The draftees spent their days doing hard labor without pay. Over many weeks, they completely refurbished the park, repairing camp roofs and screens, reforesting the land, building roads, installing water systems, and growing a nursery.

Similar camps were placed in other rural settings, largely to keep out of the public light. Perhaps the military was afraid to showcase nonviolent forms of masculinity. Some were aggressively opposed by local American Legion posts. They aimed for camps to be relocated elsewhere, while some local businessmen put out disparaging signs with messages like "No conchies allowed," a derisive term for COs. One man in Illinois deemed the COs at a nearby camp a "gang of traitors."

At one point, some local Legionnaires near Patapsco tried to enlist the men in quasi-military work, namely to build an access road for an air-raid tower. It was a mission they successfully abstained from. When locals later objected to the Patapsco crew's one Black member, the white COs stuck up for him.

The park's superintendent initially harbored his own skepticism of the men, glumly predicting that his job would now involve "riding herd on an assortment of freaks and malcontents." And yet, as the *Post* reported, he found himself "rubbing his eyes over his protégés' habit of getting jobs done in about half the scheduled time—and without taking orders from anyone."

These men embodied core traits of manhood, like strength and bravery, without sacrificing themselves to military subjugation. The Patapsco crew also proved their athletic prowess by winning a baseball game against a crew of soldiers from nearby Fort Meade. Many pleaded to be shipped over to Europe to rebuild infrastructure and provide aid to war victims, a request the military denied.

Eventually, COs were given more serious assignments. Some served as smoke jumpers. Some helped build the Blue Ridge Parkway. Another three thousand fanned out to sixty-one mental health hospitals across the country, and treated patients with dignity, not hitting them, for example, which was standard practice at the time. Some snuck in cameras to document the terrible conditions and fed them to *Life* magazine, which published an exposé that precipitated a national outcry and meaningful reforms.

Five hundred more COs volunteered for dangerous medical experiments, including a study on human starvation. Others ingested irradiated foods or were injected with the hepatitis virus.

"I was willing to take risks on my own body," one of them reflected, "but I just did not want to kill someone else."

By the war's end, these men had performed 120 different types of work that resulted in 2.2 million cumulative days of public service, and many more millions of dollars' worth of contributions to state and federal governments. Many COs from World War II went on to become progressive movement leaders, including Bayard Rustin, who helped organize the Freedom Rides and mentored Martin Luther King Jr.; David Dellinger, the pacifist leader of the Chicago 7; and A.J. Muste, a tenacious labor organizer. All of them stared down the barrels of government guns as part of their organizing, and none of them flinched.

The men at Patapsco not only served their country, but they also confirmed and enriched each other's commitment to peace. "I believe that the power of human and divine love can overcome the problems that lead to war," one of the Patapsco men told a reporter. "I believe it is possible for men to devote the same energies wasted in war to the making of a better world. By constructive service to impoverished people everywhere, by the repairing of damage done in a world of violence, by a more unselfish way of living, men can serve a higher cause."

Acknowledgments

This book would not exist but for my agent, Caroline Eisenmann, and my editor, Alessandra Bastagli. It was Caroline, many moons ago, who brilliantly steered my magazine story on Valley Forge into an expansive book proposal on the history of military masculinity. Caroline also found me a perfect editor in Alessandra, who, via close edits and many wonderful conversations, imbued this book with her fearless politics, sharp wit, and sense of humor.

Thanks very much to Rola Harb for her vital behind-the-scenes hustling and thoughtful feedback, and to the entire team at Simon & Schuster: designers, proofreaders, publicists, copyeditors, marketers, and lawyers. I am eternally indebted to my ace fact-checkers, Sophie Hurwitz and Sarah Szilagy, two tenacious young journalists who stress-tested this book with aplomb. Thanks to the many hardworking librarians who assisted in book research, especially the staff at the New York Public Library and Dartmouth College's Rauner Collection. Thanks to Arlo Haskell and Katrin Schumann at the Key West Literary Seminar for providing me three blissful weeks of palm-shaded book time.

There are a few important figures who made my writing career in New York City possible. First is my longtime Crown Heights landlord, Brian Saunders, who gave me dirt-cheap rent and high-class living for seven wonderful years. Thanks also to my silly and supportive roommates at 617: Dan Chelemer, Michael Sciortino, Ibaad Kamal, Matt D'Amico, and Riley Rae Craven. (Thanks also to the Walpoles, who gave me a home away from home while I was reporting in Washington, D.C.)

I am immensely grateful to *The Nation* internship program and what is today the Type Media Center. During my first six months in Gotham, these invaluable journalistic institutions paid me a decent wage, taught me fact-checking, helped me build a beat, and connected me to many wonderful people. Thanks, in particular, to Katrina vanden Heuvel, Naomi Gordon-Loebl, Chris Shay, Jayati Vora, Esther Kaplan, Sarah Blustain, Taya McCormick-Grobow, Nina Zweig, and Maha Ahmed.

Other editors in New York, and elsewhere, have shaped my writing and thinking immeasurably. Thank you, Mark Johnson, Aaron Glantz, Lauren Katzenberg, Jess Bergman, Will Stephenson, Pat Caldwell, John Patrick Pullen, Reyhan Harmanci, Elena Saavedra Buckley, Minju Pak, Paul Szoldra, Adam Weinstein, Elizabeth Hewitt, Matthew Shen Goodman, Zach Webb, David Dayen, Colin Meyn, and John Thomason. Michael Mechanic at *Mother Jones* deserves special credit for marshalling my Valley Forge magazine piece into existence, and then for being exceptionally patient as I repeatedly missed deadlines on another piece while cranking away on this book. Kate Daloz provided me warmth and indispensable guidance in the early, uneasy stages of writing.

It can feel awkward, even sacrilegious, to aggressively cover the military as a civilian. My confidence to do so is owed to a cadre of military writers who, in their style, rigor, outlook, and, in many cases, personal counsel, showed me the way. Thanks to C.J. Chivers, David Philipps, Adam Linehan, Seth Harp, Anthony Swofford, Davis Winkie, Steve Beynon, Sarah Jones, Haley Britzky, Kelly Kennedy, Andrew Bacevich, Kayla Williams, Nick Turse, Quil Lawrence, Spencer Ackerman, Phil Klay, Danny Sjursen, Patricia Kime, Kris Goldsmith, Matt Gallagher, and Jasper Lo. Matt Farwell, the last true gonzo in America, deserves special recognition for being an essential influence on my work, and a really great friend.

Thanks to the hundreds of troops and veterans who have trusted me to tell their stories over my decade on this beat, especially those who, at great professional risk, divulged institutional secrets or, despite much personal pain, shared their darkest memories.

The work of Howard Zinn, George Saunders, J.D. Salinger, Richard Ford, Rick Perlstein, Kurt Vonnegut, Avery Trufelman, Dan Schwartz, Kathleen Belew, Tim Bakken, Garrett Graff, and John Ganz provided major inspiration for this book. So, too, did the artwork of Sunny Maher, Chris Maggio, Bill Evans, Jonny Greenwood, Cameron Winter, Trent Reznor, and Stanley Kubrick.

Thanks to the many wonderful teachers who developed my sense of writing at an early age, among them Jenny and John Mackenzie, Glenn Ehrean, Hank Eaton, Stephen Kinzer, Dick Lehr, David Carr, and Ta-Nehisi Coates. Thanks to the editorial staff at *The Caledonian-Record*, who gave me my first column, "A Teen's Time to Talk," at the ripe old age of fourteen.

Thanks to the dedicated folks at the Veterans Healthcare Policy Institute for teaching me so much and supporting me for years. I'm especially grateful to Suzanne Gordon, Russell Lemle, Bruce Carruthers, Essam Attia, and Paul Cox. In 2022, Steve Early, alongside Suzanne, generously invited me to collaborate on a book investigating the state of American veterans. This effort offered an illuminating crash course in how to wrestle a manuscript into existence.

Thanks to my grandpa George Dennis O'Brien for his early philosophical feedback on the book. Thanks to Gary Miller for the last-minute copyedits. Thanks to my dad, Jay Craven, whose writing style, worldview, and tenacious history fighting the "Pentagoons" suffuse this book's every page. Thanks to my mom, Bess O'Brien, for showing me how to exercise empathy, how to listen, and how to genuinely build intimacy with strangers.

While navigating the myriad career stressors associated with freelance journalism, I've been perennially soothed by the counsel, support, and friendship of Glyn and David Fox, Miguel Salazar, Jake Bittle, Alex Sammon, Ali Winston, Shawn Musgrave, Gaby Del Valle, and my beloved BU Boys. Also, Blake Schoolcraft, Alex Iacono, and Max Johnson, my three best friends from childhood. Thanks, more broadly, to the tightknit community in Vermont's Northeast Kingdom that nurtured my growth, including Susan Rankin, Brooksie Stanton, Barry Bernstein, Greg and Barb Schoolcraft, Erica Heilman, Alec Morgan, Patrick Kennedy, and my beloved brother, Sascha Stanton-Craven, who has exemplified manhood to me in many beautiful ways.

My last and most profound gratitude is to Lauren Bastian, my gorgeous, funny partner in crime. Thank you for helping me fall back in love with reading and for being patient in the moments where I lost myself in writing. I love you forever, LoLo.

A Note on Sources

In reporting this book, I relied on thousands of pages of official government and military documents, newspaper and magazine articles, legal records and police reports, plus various academic journals and dissertations as well as trade, history, and academic books. I also conducted scores of interviews, many of them on background or off the record, with figures now or once connected to military education, including cadets, teachers, parents, TAC officers, and administrators. Below, you will find a list of textual sources that I relied on most.

Ambrose, S. *Duty, Honor, Country.* Johns Hopkins University Press, 2000.

Armstrong, C. *The Boy Scouts in the Great War.* Pen & Sword Books, 2021.

Bakken, T. *The Cost of Loyalty: Dishonesty, Hubris, and Failure in the U.S. Military.* Bloomsbury, 2020.

Barkalow, C. *In the Men's House: An Inside Account of Life in the Army by One of West Point's First Female Graduates.* Poseidon Press, 1990.

Broadwell, P., and V. Loeb. *All In: The Education of General David Petraeus.* Penguin Press, 2012.

Buttner, R., and S. Craig. *Lucky Loser: How Donald Trump Squandered His Father's Fortune and Created the Illusion of Success.* Penguin Press, 2024.

Coll, S. *Ghost Wars: The Secret History of the CIA, Afghanistan, and bin Laden, from the Soviet Invasion to September 10, 2001.* Penguin Press, 2004.

Coulter, J.A. *Cadets on Campus: History of Military Schools of the United States.* Texas A&M University Press, 2017.

Edstrom, E. *Un-American: A Soldier's Reckoning of Our Longest War.* Bloomsbury, 2020.

Eliot, G.F. *Sylvanus Thayer of West Point.* Messner, 1959.

Ernst, R. *Weakness Is a Crime: The Life of Bernarr MacFadden.* Syracuse University Press, 1991.

Franke, V. *Preparing for Peace: Military Identity, Value Orientations, and Professional Military Education.* Praeger, 1999.

Galloway, K.B. *West Point: America's Power Fraternity.* Simon & Schuster, 1973.

Gearhart, J. "The Boy Scouts of America: The Cold Warriors of Tomorrow." *IU South Bend Undergraduate Research Journal* 16 (2016).

Giroux, H. *The University in Chains.* Paradigm Publishers, 2007.

Goldner Peterson, S. *Self-Defense for Women: The West Point Way.* Simon and Schuster, 1979.

Haberman, M. *Confidence Man: The Making of Donald Trump and the Breaking of America.* Penguin Press, 2022.

Harp, S. *The Fort Bragg Cartel: Drug Trafficking and Murder in the Special Forces.* Viking, 2025.

Janda, L. *Stronger than Custom: West Point and the Admission of Women.* Praeger, 2002.

Kershner S., S. Harding, and C. Howlett. *Breaking the War Habit: The Debate Over Militarism in American Education.* University of Georgia Press, 2022.

Kinnard, D. *The War Managers.* University of Vermont Press, 1977.

Lee, J.L., Jr. *A Century of Military Training at Iowa State University, 1870–1970.* Iowa State University Press, 1972.

Leon, P.W. *Bullies and Cowards: The West Point Hazing Scandal, 1898–1901.* Greenwood Publishing Group, 2000.

Lipsky, D. *Absolutely American: Four Years at West Point.* Houghton Mifflin Company, 2003.

Logel, J.S. *Designing Gotham: West Point Engineers and the Rise of Modern New York, 1817–1898.* Louisiana State University Press, 2016.

Masland, J., and G. Lyons. *Education and Military Leadership: A Study of the ROTC.* Princeton University Press, 1959.

Morris, J. *Crucibles of Virtue and Vice: The Acculturation of Transatlantic Army Officers.* Columbia University Press, 2020.

North, O.T. *Under Fire: An American Story.* HarperCollins, 1991.

Pollarine, J. *Children at War: Underage Americans Illegally Fighting the Second World War.* University of Montana Press, 2008.

Postman, N. *Technopoly: The Surrender of Culture to Technology*. Alfred A. Knopf, 1992.

Salinger, J.D. *The Catcher in the Rye*. Little, Brown and Company, 1951.

Timberg, R. *The Nightingale's Song*. Free Press, 1996.

Trump, M.L. *Too Much and Never Enough: How My Family Created the World's Most Dangerous Man*. Simon & Schuster, 2020.

Valsania, M. *First Among Men: George Washington and the Myth of American Masculinity*. Johns Hopkins University Press, 2022.

Wolinsky, M., and K. Sherill. *Gays and the Military*. Princeton University Press, 1993.

Zeeland, S. *Sailors and Sexual Identity*. Haworth Press, 1995.

Zeiger, S. "The Schoolhouse vs. The Armory: U.S. Teachers and the Campaign Against Militarism in the Schools, 1914–1918." *Journal of Women's History* 15 no. 2 (2003).

Other Sources by Chapter

Introduction

For the introduction, I interviewed Valley Forge Academy alumnus Scott Newell, the mother and brother of Carey Lecamp; New York Military Academy alumni Rich Terlach and Rich Pezzullo, West Point alumnus Kris Fuhr. Also, a half-dozen additional military school alumni, parents, and administrators whose identities I have agreed to protect. I further relied on these sources:

Associated Press. "Howe Military Academy Closing After 135 Years in Operation." *South Bend Tribune*, March 19, 2019.

Associated Press. "Former Student Alleges Abuse at Missouri Military Academy." FOX2Now, November 30, 2022.

Bases, D. "New York Military Academy Sold in Bidding War to Chinese Investors." Reuters, September 30, 2013.

Bennett, M. "'Public Service' Charter School Planned at Valley Forge Military Academy." *Radnor Patch* (Pennsylvania), October 15, 2025. https://patch.com/pennsylvania/radnor/public-service-charter-school-planned-valley-forge-military-academy.

Bull, E. "The Making of Masculinity: Hazing, Fighting, and Cadet Culture at West Point, 1897–1901." Honors Thesis, Rutgers University, 2021.

Butcher, E., and J. Rogers. "Innocence Under Fire: How Children Were Used in Warfare of the Past." HistoryExtra 2021. https://www.historyextra.com/period/first-world-war/how-children-used-warfare-fighting-child-soldiers/.

Craven, J. "Hazing, Fighting, Sexual Assaults: How Valley Forge Military Academy Devolved into 'Lord of the Flies.'" *Mother Jones*, May-June 2022.

Craven, J. "Inside Pete Hegseth's Civilian Purge at West Point." *Politico*, August 28, 2025.

Eisenhart, R.W. "You Can't Hack It Little Girl: A Discussion of the Covert Psychological Agenda of Modern Combat Training." *Journal of Social Issues* 31, no. 4 (1975). https://www.semanticscholar.org/paper/You-Can%27t-Hack-It-Little-Girl%3A-A-Discussion-of-the-Eisenhart/2a91f8964575ad9aa63314bb94da90f617b8f7ac.

Galaviz, B., J. Palafox, and E.R. Meiners, et al. Caucus of Rank and File Educators, National Network Opposing the Militarization of Youth, Northeastern Illinois University, & School of the Art Institute of Chicago. "The Militarization and the Privatization of Public Schools." *Berkeley Review of Education* 2, no. 1 (2011): 27–45. https://files.eric.ed.gov/fulltext/EJ1169719.pdf.

Geiger, A. "The Changing Profile of the U.S. Military: Smaller in Size, More Diverse, More Women in Leadership." Pew Research Center, 2019. https://www.pewresearch.org/short-reads/2019/09/10/the-changing-profile-of-the-u-s-military/.

"Georgia Teen Military Academy Shut Down After Massive Brawl." FOX 5 Atlanta, January 17, 2023. https://www.fox5atlanta.com/news/georgia-national-guard-youth-challenge-academy-fort-gordon-investigation-report.

Hinojosa, R. (2010). "Doing Hegemony: Military, Men, and Constructing a Hegemonic Masculinity." *Journal of Men's Studies* 18, no. 2 (2010): 179–94. https://doi.org/10.3149/jms.1802.179.

Knott, K. "What to Know About Trump's Compact for Higher Ed." *Inside Higher Ed | Higher Education News*, 2025. https://www.insidehighered.com/news/government/politics-elections/2025/10/20/5-things-know-about-trumps-higher-ed-compact.

Make, J. "Wyo. Military Academy Closure Draws Wide Concern." *Wyoming Tribune Eagle*, January 7, 2022.

Marin, M., W. Bender, and R. Briggs. "How Valley Forge Military Academy Fell Apart Nearly a Century After Its Founding." *The Inquirer*, September 19, 2025.

McGurk, D., D.I. Cotting, T.W. Britt, and A.B. Adler. "Joining the Ranks: The Role of Indoctrination in Transforming Civilians to Service Members." In A.B. Adler, C.A. Castro, and T.W. Britt (eds.), *Military Life: The Psychology of Serving in Peace and Combat: Operational Stress*. Praeger Security International, 2006, 13–31.

Micheletti, A.J.C., G.D. Ruxton, and A. Gardner. "Why War Is a Man's Game." *Proceedings of the Royal Society B Biological Sciences* 285, no. 1884 (2018):20180975. https://doi.org/10.1098/rspb.2018.0975.

Schogol, J. "Marine Corps May Replace 'The Few, The Proud' as Its Recruiting Slogan." *Marine Corps Times*, August 19, 2022.

"The Peninsula." *The Peninsula Qatar*, August 26, 2022.

"Two Black Cadets and the Struggle for Diversity at an Elite US Military Institution." Reuters/*US News & World Report*, March 30, 2024.

U.S. Department of Defense (DoD). Quarterly Suicide Report (QSR), 1st Quarter, CY 2022, Dr. Liz Clark, Acting Director, Defense Suicide Prevention Office (DSPO). https://www.dspo.mil/Portals/113/Documents/2022QSR/TAB%20A_20220630_OFR_Rpt_Q1%20CY22%20QSR.pdf?ver=MTb1QAwuRxan-Wo3FJ2XqA%3D%3D.

U.S. Department of Defense. Agency Financial Report, 2024. https://comptroller.war.gov/Portals/45/Documents/afr/fy2024/1-About_the_DoD_Agency_Financial_Report-DoD_At_A_Glance_Table_of_Contents.pdf.

U.S. Department of War. "Secretary of War Pete Hegseth Addresses General and Flag Officers at Quantico, Virginia" (transcript), September 20, 2025. https://www.war.gov/News/Transcripts/Transcript/article/4318689/secretary-of-war-pete-hegseth-addresses-general-and-flag-officers-at-quantico-v/.

Zehner, H. "The Gaza Protests Were a Mask-Off Moment for American Universities." *The Nation*, May 30, 2024. https://www.thenation.com/article/archive/university-war-machine-gaza-protest/.

Chapter 1

For chapter 1, I relied on these sources:

Chernow, R. *Washington: A Life*. Penguin Press, 2011.

Crane, J., and J.F. Kiely. *West Point*. McGraw-Hill Book Company, Inc., 1947.

Ferling, J. "Myths of the American Revolution." *Smithsonian Magazine*, November 15, 2013.

George Washington to Alexander Hamilton, December 12, 1799. https://founders.archives.gov/documents/Washington/06-04-02-0402.

George Washington to Robert Dinwiddie, May 18, 1754. Founders Online, University of Virginia Press, n.d. https://founders.archives.gov/documents/Washington/02-01-02-0050.

George Washington to the Society of Quakers, October 13, 1789. https://founders.archives.gov/documents/Washington/05-04-02-0188.

Hparkins. "Strategically Important: West Point." *Pieces of History*, June 10, 2015. https://prologue.blogs.archives.gov/2015/06/10/strategically-important-west-point/.

Hunter, L. "Both James Madison and the Anti-Federalists Were Right About Standing Armies." *Forbes*, July 29, 2012.

"Journal of Occurrences." *The News Media and the Making of America, 1730–1865*. https://collections.americanantiquarian.org/earlyamericannewsmedia/exhibits/show/age-of-revolution/item/130.

Mackowiak, P. "George Washington's Recurrent Health Problems and Fatal Infection Re-examined." *Clinical Infectious Diseases* 72, no. 10 (2021): 1850–1853. https://doi.org/10.1093/cid/ciaa1324.

Martin, J. "The Thankless Spirit of '77." *Washington Post*, November 21, 1993.

Nichols, J. "Will Civilians Control the Military?" *The Nation*, May 9, 2006.

Schiff, S. "Guess Who Else Sent Troops to Quell Protests in American Streets." *New York Times*, June 24, 2025.

The Federalist Papers, No. 8. (n.d.). The Avalon Project. https://avalon.law.yale.edu/18th_century/fed08.asp.

"The 9 Deadly Diseases That Plagued George Washington." PBS News, July 4, 2011.

"The Original Version of the Second Amendment: Religiously Scrupulous of Bearing Arms." Duke Center for Firearms Law, April 15, 2024. https://firearmslaw.duke.edu/2022/07/the-original-version-of-the-second-amendment-religiously-scrupulous-of-bearing-arms.

"What Happened at Valley Forge." Valley Forge National Historical Park (U.S. National Park Service). n.d. https://www.nps.gov/vafo/learn/historyculture/valley-forge-history-and-significance.htm.

Chapter 2

For chapter 2, I relied on these sources:

Abrams, R.M. "U.S. Military and Higher Education: A Brief History." *Annals of the American Academy of Political and Social Science* 502 (March 1989): 15–28.

"Armed Forces: What Price Honor?" *Time*, June 7, 1976.

"Army Inquiry Board Probing into the Hazing of Cadet Booz." *San Francisco Call* 87, no. 18 (1900).

"Bill for the Relief of Discharged Cadets." *Birmingham News*, April 22, 1910.

"Booz Not Fit to Take Part in Fight." January 18, 1901. https://www.macarthurmemorial.org/DocumentCenter/View/554/Episode-35-Booz-Not-Fit-to-Take-Part-in-Fight-January-18-1901?bidId=.

Boroff, D. "West Point: Ancient Incubator for a New Breed." *Harper's Magazine*, December 1962.

"Cadets Troubles Grieve Army Men." *Chicago Inter Ocean*, May 26, 1901.

Correll, D. "How Mutiny Aboard the USS *Somers* Helped Birth the U.S. Naval Academy." *Navy Times*, November 30, 2023.

Dickens, C. (1842). *American Notes for General Circulation, 1842*. https://charles-dickens.org/american -notes-for-general-circulation/ebook-page-120.php.

Fleming, T. "The Father of West Point." *Quarterly Journal of Military History* 20, no. 1 (Autumn 2007).

Fleming, T. "West Point Cadets Now Say, 'Why, Sir?'" *New York Times*, July 5, 1970. https://www.ny times.com/1970/07/05/archives/west-point-cadets-now-say-why-sir.html.

Francis H. Smith Secession Correspondence from Virginia Military Institute (1860-1861). VMI. http:// digitalcollections.vmi.edu/digital/collection/p15821coll14/id/479/rec/1.

GAO Report. "More Changes Needed to Eliminate Hazing," November 1992. https://www.gao.gov /assets/nsiad-93-36.pdf.

Geiling, N. "Eggnog: It's All Fun and Games Until Someone Starts a Holiday Riot." *Smithsonian Magazine*, December 19, 2013.

Graziano, M. "America's 'Peculiar Children': Authority and Christian Nationalism at Antebellum West Point." *Religions* 8, no. 1 (2017): 6. https://doi.org/10.3390/rel8010006.

Hadley, A. *AMCSUS and the Struggle for the Survival of Military Preparatory Schools in America*. University of Kentucky Press, 1999.

"He Was Waterboarded at the VMI. How Tormentors Got into the Military." *Washington Post*, December 30, 2021.

Heise, J.A. *The Brass Factories: A Frank Appraisal of West Point, Annapolis, and the Air Force Academy*. Public Affairs Press, 1969.

Hill, M. "West Point Orders About-Face on 108-Year Tradition of Hazing Cadets." *Los Angeles Times*, March 9, 2019.

Hsieh, W. "Antebellum Military Education of Civil War Leaders." *Essential Civil War Curriculum*. n.d.

Kavanagh, C. "How and Why Hazing Evolved Sapiens." *Human Nature*, June 15, 2017. https://www .sapiens.org/culture/why-hazing-evolved/.

Keller, K. "Shameless, Villainous, and Wicked: A Keller Family History." *The Appendix*, October 6, 2014. http://theappendix.net/issues/2014/10/shameless-villainous-and-wicked-a-keller-family-history.

King, E.L. "Who Needs West Point?" *New York Times*, April 29, 1972.

Locating Slavery's Legacies @ Virginia Military Institute (n.d.). https://locatinglegacies.org.locatin glegacies.reclaim.hosting/s/VMI/page/home.

Oeser, J. "A Tradition of Silence: The Antecedents of the Pelosi Affair." USMA Library, November 6, 1990. https://usmalibrary.contentdm.oclc.org/digital/collection/p16919coll1/id/54/.

O'Halloran, K. et al. "An Experiential Report on the Thayer Method of Teaching across College-Level Chemistry, Biology, Math, and Physics Courses." *Georgia Journal of Science* 78, no. 2 (December 31, 2019): 4.

Partridge aka "Americanus." "The Military Academy of West Point Unmasked: or Corruption and Military Despotism Exposed." *Norwich University Archives*, 1830.

Report of the Secretary of War, American Indian and Alaskan Native Documents in the Congressional Serial Set: 1817–1899 12-1-1861. University of Oklahoma College of Law. https://digitalcommons .law.ou.edu/cgi/viewcontent.cgi?article=9589&context=indianserialset.

Schambelan, E. "Special Journey to Our Bottom Line." *N+1*, February 16, 2024.

Shell, A.E. "The Thayer Method of Instruction at the United Stated Military Academy: A Modest History and a Modern Personal Account." *Primus* 12, no. 1 (2002): 27–38. https://doi.org/10.1080 /10511970208984015.

S.K. "Sylvanus Thayer: The Man Who Made West Point." *American Heritage* 29, no. 4 (June/July 1978).

Snyder, M.T. "Oscar Booz's Hazing at West Point." *The Reporter Online*, September 23, 2021.

The Civil War Defenses of Washington: Historic Resource Study (Appendix C). n.d. https://www.npshistory .com/publications/cwdw/hrs/appc.htm.

"The Civil War West Point Under Fire." Hudson River Valley Institute. n.d.https://www.hudsonriv ervalley.org/the-civil-war-west-point#:~:text=Many%20in%20Congress%20saw%20the,a%20 lack%20of%20democratic%20principles.

United Fraternity. Dartmouth College, Libraries Archives & Manuscripts. n.d. https://archives-manuscripts .dartmouth.edu/agents/corporate_entities/839.

"West Point Military Academy, Major Barnard Reviews the Opinion of Secretary Cameron." *New York Times*, July 19, 1861.

"West Point Revelations; More Testimony in Regard to the Booz and Breth Cases." *New York Times*, January 8, 1901.

"What Officers Think of the Hazing Question." *New York Times*, August 9, 1908.

Wiggins, P. *New England's Influence on Sylvanus Thayer's West Point Probity Doctrine*. Dartmouth College, Hanover, New Hampshire, May 2019.

Williams, H. "The Attack upon West Point during the Civil War." *Mississippi Valley Historical Review* 25, no. 4 (March 1939): 491–504.

Zanger, J. "Crime and Punishment in Early Massachusetts." *William and Mary Quarterly* 22, no. 3 (July 1965): 471–77, Omohundro Institute of Early American History and Culture. https://www.mountvernon.org/library/digitalhistory/digital-encyclopedia/article/first-in-war-first-in-peace-and-first-in-the-hearts-of-his-countrymen.

Chapter 3

For chapter 3, I relied on these sources:

Abrahamson, J. "David Starr Jordan and American Antimilitarism." *Pacific Northwest Quarterly* 67, no. 2 (April 1976).

Bartlett, L., and C. Lutz. "Disciplining Social Difference: Some Cultural Politics of Military Training in Public High Schools." *Urban Review* 30, no. 2 (1998).

"Boy Scouts at Work." *Daily Telegraph* (London), May 4, 1910.

DeRensis, H. "Merchants of Death." *The American Conservative*, June 20, 2022.

Kington, D.M. "The Plattsburg Movement and Its Legacy." *Relevance* 6, no. 4 (Autumn 1997).

Livermore, S.W. "The Sectional Issue in the 1918 Congressional Elections." *Mississippi Valley Historical Review* 35, no. 1 (June 1948).

Morgan, J.P. to President Wilson (August 21, 1914). https://history.state.gov/historicaldocuments/frus1914-20v01/d90.

Murphy, D.W. "Ideal Patriots: The Boy Scouts of America as Propaganda During the First World War." Master's thesis. 171. University of Missouri, St. Louis, 2016. http://irl.umsl.edu/thesis/171.

"1,000 N.Y. Schoolboys to Camp." *Harvard Crimson*, June 1916.

Snyder, A. "Learning from the Past, Facing the Future." *Of Souls & Silos*, May 25, 2019. https://annesnyder.org/2019/05/25/learning-from-the-past-facing-the-future/.

Ward, R. "The Origin and Activities of the National Security League, 1914–1919." *Mississippi Valley Historical Review* 47, no. 1 (1960).

Chapter 4

For chapter 4, I relied on these sources:

"Abolishment of Compulsory Military Training at Schools and Colleges." Hearings before the Committee on Military Affairs, House of Representatives, 69th Congress, First Session, on H.R. 8538, April 29, 30, and June 15, 1926. https://babel.hathitrust.org/cgi/pt?id=mdp.39015076644916&seq=5.

"Cardinal Raps ROTC List as Laughable." *Capital Times* (Madison, Wisconsin), February 23, 1928.

"Col. A.S. Burkett Installs Chapter Military Order." *Coe College Cosmos*, February 11, 1921.

DBK Admin. "The Era of Mandatory ROTC." *The Diamondback*, December 31, 1999.

George Albert Coe, Biola University. n.d. https://www.biola.edu/talbot/ce20/database/george-albert-coe.

"Move to Abolish Military Training: Group of Prominent Persons Urge Its Removal from Schools and Colleges." *New York Times*, December 7, 1925.

"Penn State ROTC Tactics Assailed." *Evening Sentinel* (Carlisle, Pennsylvania), March 27, 1936.

"Remarks to a Committee from the National Students Federation." *American Presidency Project*, n.d. https://www.presidency.ucsb.edu/documents/remarks-committee-from-the-national-students-federation.

"ROTC Brutality in Penn State Corps Occasions Protest." *Miscellany News* 20, no. 41 (April 15, 1936).

Setran, D.P. "Morality for the 'Democracy of God': George Albert Coe and the Liberal Protestant Critique of American Character Education, 1917–1940." *Religion and American Culture: A Journal of Interpretation* 15, no. 1 (2005): 107–44. https://doi.org/10.1525/rac.2005.15.1.107.

"Students' Peace Parading a Bit Noisy But Orderly." *Brooklyn Times Union* (Brooklyn, New York), April 22, 1926.

"The Nye-Kvale Bill: Colonel Lewis's Attack on Measure Held to Be Unwarranted." *New York Times*, February 10, 1936.

"Voice of the People." *Capital Times* (Madison, Wisconsin), February 22, 1928.

Chapter 5

For chapter 5, I relied on these sources:

DLA Brochure. https://www.dla.mil/Portals/104/Documents/DispositionServices/Library/HistoryBookWebOptimized.pdf.

East, W.B. *A Historical Review and Analysis of Army Physical Readiness Training and Assessment.* Combat Studies Institute Press, US Army Combined Arms Center, Fort Leavenworth, Kansas, March 2013.

"Faces Larceny Charge: Man Accused of Taking $5,000 to 'Fix' West Point Appointment." *New York Times*, May 12, 1945.

Foer, F. "Mussolini's team." *Slate Magazine*, September 11, 2001.

Folk, G.E. "The Harvard Fatigue Laboratory: Contributions to World War II." *American Journal of Physiology: Advances in Physiology Education* 34, no. 3 (2010): 119–27. https://doi.org/10.1152/advan.00041.2010.

Ganz, J. "The Jock/Creep Theory of Fascism." *Unpopular Front*, March 27, 2023.

"Georgia Congress Endorses School Victory Program." *Atlanta Journal*, February 7, 1943.

Gibson, J.W. *Warrior Dreams: Paramilitary Culture in Post-Vietnam America*. Farrar, Straus and Giroux, 1994.

"How Hollywood Became the Unofficial Propaganda Arm of the U.S. Military." CBC Radio, November 30, 2022.

Ireland, C. "Harvard Goes to War." *Harvard Gazette*, October 6, 2016.

"Let Prof. Do-It" advice column. *Newsday* (Suffolk, New York, Edition), February 8, 1945.

Murtha, R., C. Heffernan, and T. Hunt. "Building American Supermen? Bernarr MacFadden, Benito Mussolini and American fascism in the 1930s." *Sport in Society*, December 31, 2020. DOI: 10.1080/17430437.2020.1865313.

Original advertisement. Conscription Bill War Bernarr MacFadden Book, Period Paper Historic Art LLC, 1917. https://www.periodpaper.com/products/1917-ad-conscription-bill-war-bernarr-macfadden-book-original-advertising-073900-tin2-276.

Sicard, S. "How a 12-Year-Old Tricked the Navy into Letting Him Fight in WWII." *Military Times*, October 5, 2022.

"The Press: Just Babies." *Time*, July 25, 1932.

Wallis, W.A. "The Statistical Research Group, 1942–1945." *Journal of the American Statistical Association* 75, no. 370 (June 1980).

Watson, B. "The Strange Tale of a World-Changing Fitness and Sleaze Titan." *Esquire*, June 28, 2022.

Webb, J. "Jim Webb: Women Can't Fight." *Washingtonian*, January 3, 2019.

Wernicke, L. "Benito Mussolini and the Fascist Love Affair with Soccer." *Quillette*, April 27, 2025. https://quillette.com/2022/10/29/benito-mussolini-and-the-fascist-love-affair-with-soccer/.

Wesley, D.A. "The High School Victory Corps of World War II." *Peabody Journal of Education* 45, no. 4 (1968): 244–48. http://www.jstor.org/stable/1490474.

"West Point Hails 143rd Anniversary." *New York Times*, March 19, 1944.

World War II | Columbia University Libraries. n.d. https://library.columbia.edu/libraries/cuarchives/warmemorial/world-war-ii.html#:~:text=Beginning%20in%201942%2C%20Columbia%27s%20Morningside,for%20duty%20in%20the%20fleet.

Young, Dr. H.H. "Military Training Would Make Us a New Race." *New York Times*, January 7, 1917.

Chapter 6

For chapter 6, I interviewed former Air Force Academy chaplain Melinda Morton, former Air Force Academy professors Carlos Bertha and Martin France, Air Force Academy alumnus and religious freedom activist Mikey Weinstein, former Air Force Academy superintendent Mike Regni, retired Army colonel Lawrence Wilkerson, and various cadets and family members who endured aggressive or unwanted religious proselytizing. I further relied on these sources:

"Air Academy Cadets Start Two-Week Tour." *Colorado Springs Gazette-Telegraph*, June 11, 1960.

Brady, J. "Colorado Springs a mecca for evangelical Christians." NPR, January 17, 2005.

"Colorado Scientists to Examine Famed Shroud of Turin." *Daily Sentinel* (Grand Junction, Colorado), October 8, 1977.

Frkyholm, A.J. "Cadets for Christ." *Christian Century*, January 10, 2006.

"German Air Cadets Find Contrast in Academies." *Colorado Springs Gazette-Telegraph*, October 9, 1962.

Goodstein, L. "Evangelicals Are a Growing Force in the Military Chaplain Corps." *New York Times*, July 12, 2005.

"How a Dirty Trick and Charles Lindbergh Helped Bring Air Force Academy to Colorado Springs." Colorado Public Radio, June 29, 2019. https://www.cpr.org/2014/04/03/how-a-dirty-trick-and-charles-lindbergh-helped-bring-air-force-academy-to-colorado-springs/.

Kelley, D. "How Churches Helped Shape the City of Colorado Springs." *Colorado Springs Gazette*, July 25, 2025.

Kitchens, R. "Cadet Chapel Serves Cadets, Academy Staff, for 52 Years." *USAF Military News*, September 30, 2015.

Larner, J. "The Court-Martial of Captain Noyd." *Harper's Magazine*, June 1, 1968.

Leopold, J. "'Jesus Loves Nukes': Air Force Cites New Testament, Ex-Nazi, to Train Officers on Ethics of Launching Nuclear Weapons." *Truthout*, July 27, 2011.

Lindsay, M.D. "Evangelical Elites in the U.S. Military." *Journal of Political & Military Sociology* 35, no. 2 (Winter 2007).

Loveland, A.C. "American Evangelicals and the U.S. Military, 1942–1993." Internet archive, 1996. https://archive.org/details/americanevangeli0000love/page/2/mode/2up?q=Air+Force+academy.

Martin, D. "Dale Noyd, Vietnam Objector, Dies at 73." *New York Times*, January 28, 2007. https://www.nytimes.com/2007/01/28/us/28noyd.html.

Morton, M.S.I. "Arming the Hypermasculine Jesus: Salvific Form and General Works at the United States Air Force Academy." Thesis, Lutheran School of Theology at Chicago, April 2016.

"Most Americans Hunger for Religion." *Colorado Springs Gazette-Telegraph*, May 28, 1978.

Mulson, J. "Retracing Some of Colorado Springs' Earliest Churches." *Colorado Springs Gazette*, September 29, 2021.

Rodda, C. "The Officers' Christian Fellowship, Commissioning Military Officers as Government-Paid Missionaries." *Daily Kos*, November 14, 2019.

Schultz, W. "Making Jesus Springs: Colorado Springs and the New Geography of Evangelicalism." Business History Conference, 2017.

United States Airforce Academy Yearbook. https://www.e-yearbook.com/yearbooks/United_States _Air_Force_Academy_Colorado_Springs_Polaris_Yearbook/1962/Page_396.html.

"Vatican of the West—CSPM." Colorado Springs Pioneer Museum, February 26, 2021. https://www .cspm.org/cos-150-story/vatican-of-the-west/.

Walker, S. "'You Don't Brag About Wiping Out 60–70,000 People': The Men Who Dropped the Atomic Bombs on Hiroshima and Nagasaki." *Guardian*, June 22, 2025.

"Westmore Church Honors Military." *Colorado Springs Gazette-Telegraph*, October 23, 1971.

Chapter 7

For chapter 7, I interviewed Matt Salinger, West Point alumnus Rudy Ehrenberg, and New York Military Academy alumni Frank Chamandy, Jack Serafin, Rich Pezzullo, Rich Terlach, Sandy McIntosh, and Peter Ticktin. Further, I relied on these sources:

Alfaro, M. "Trump, Who Avoided Combat, Accepts Gift of Purple Heart from Veteran." *Washington Post*, October 24, 2024.

Bases, D. "Taps May Sound for New York Military Academy, Trump's Alma Mater." Reuters, September 23, 2015.

Borger, J. "Sins of the Father." *Guardian*, February 22, 2018.

Brantley, B. "Calder Willingham Is Dead; Novelist and Screenwriter." *New York Times*, February 21, 1995.

Breslow, J.M. "The FRONTLINE Interview: Sandy McIntosh." *Frontline*, PBS, September 28, 2016.

Chamandy, F. "The President, His Mentor, and Me: I Know What Makes Donald Trump Tick." *Globe and Mail*, October 16, 2020.

Connolly, K. "Historian Finds German Decree Banishing Trump's Grandfather." *Guardian*, February 9, 2018.

Dougherty, P.H. "'Discipline with a Capital D' Is Watchword for Cadets at New York Military Academy Military School, 75 Years Old, Strives to Improve Its Image." *New York Times*, March 3, 1964.

Eltanamly, H., P. Leijten, S. Jak, and G. Overbeek. "Parenting in Times of War: A Meta-Analysis and Qualitative Synthesis of War Exposure, Parenting, and Child Adjustment." *Trauma Violence Abuse* 22, no. 1 (January 2021): 147–60. https://pubmed.ncbi.nlm.nih.gov/30852950/.

"Head of Academy Resigns." *New York Times*, March 8, 1964.

Hendricks, M. "Military Strategy: Foreign Cadets Are Exposed to American Ideals at West Point." *Los Angeles Times*, March 11, 2019.

Hirsh, M. "Trump Has Mocked the U.S. Military His Whole Life." *Foreign Policy*, September 8, 2020.

"J.D. Salinger's Letter to Ernest Hemingway." *Huffington Post*, August 8, 2012.

McDuffie, B. "When Hemingway Met Salinger." *Kansas City Star*, March 16, 2014.

McIntosh, S. "Culture of Hazing: Donald Trump, Me, & the End of New York Military Academy." *Long Island Press*, October 5, 2015.

McIntosh, S. "How Young Donald Trump Was Slapped and Punched Until He Made His Bed." *Daily News* (New York), August 11, 2017.

Miller, M. "Decades Later Disagreement Over Young Trump's Military Academy Post." *Washington Post*, January 9, 2016.

"New Data Issued about Bay of Pigs." *New York Times*, April 17, 1984.

"NYMA Buried Trump's Academic Records." *Washington Post*, March 5, 2019.

O'Harrow, R. "Trump Swam in Mob-Infested Waters in Early Years as NYC Developer." *Washington Post*, October 16, 2015.

"Ring of Valor"—United States Naval Academy (1965) (Video). Naval History and Heritage, YouTube, March 26, 2012. https://www.youtube.com/watch?v=mBbZn8epT-Y.

Ruiz, S. "How JD Salinger's World War II Service Shaped His Writing." Military.com, November 6, 2023. https://www.military.com/history/how-jd-salingers-world-war-ii-service-shaped-his-writing .html.

Salinger, J.D. "The Magic Foxhole," Unpublished short story, Princeton University Library Archive, 1944. https://www.universityarchives.com/auction-lot/j.d.-salinger.-rare-signature-and-inscrip tion-in_2DB4B8899B.

Schaerlaeckens, L. "Was Donald Trump Good at Baseball?" *Slate Magazine*, May 5, 2020.

Slawenski, K. "He's No Phony: How Fighting in World War II Changed J.D. Salinger and *The Catcher in the Rye*'s Holden Caulfield." *Vanity Fair*, January 20, 2011.

Stilwell, B. "This Famous Son of a Mobster Was Also a West Point Grad." We Are the Mighty, December 6, 2022. https://www.wearethemighty.com/mighty-history/mobsters-son-attended-west-point/.

Stracqualursi, V. "New York Times: Daughters of Foot Doctor Say He Diagnosed Trump with Bone Spurs as 'Favor' to Fred Trump." CNN, December 26, 2018.

Tanenhaus, S., and R. Dress. "The Godfather Presidency: How Donald Trump's Governing Style Mimics the Mob." *Vanity Fair*, July 1, 2025.

Zecca, A. "Exiled King Cleans Boots." *Bristol Daily Courier*, October 30, 1958.

Chapter 8

For chapter 8, I interviewed West Point alumni Lucian Truscott IV and Andrew Bacevich, Valley Forge alumnus Scott Eberly, and Air Force Academy alumnus Michael Rose. Further, I relied on these sources:

"A Portrait of West Point's Ill-Starred Class of '66." *Philadelphia Inquirer*, October 15, 1989.

"Airforce Lawyer Attacks Honor Code." *Daily Times-News* (Burlington, North Carolina), May 15, 1974.

Beecher, W. "General, Ex-Aide Accused of Murdering Vietnamese." *New York Times*, June 3, 1971.

Benemann, H., H. McCartin, T. Russell, D. Cash, and A. King. "Sadistic Masculinity: Masculine Honor Ideology Mediates Sadism and Aggression." *Personality and Individual Differences* 206 (May 2023). https://www.sciencedirect.com/science/article/pii/S0191886923000417.

Borman, F. "Report to the Secretary of the Army by the Special Commission of the United States Military Academy." Antipodean Books, Maps & Prints, December 15, 1976.

Brzezinski, M. "Deviant Cohesion and Unauthorized Atrocities: Evidence from the American War in Vietnam." *Perspectives on Politics* 23, no. 1 (2024): 213–33. https://doi.org/10.1017/s15375927 24000963.

Carter, M.N. "Cheating by West Point Class Spurs Inquiry into Honor System." *Lima News* (Lima, Ohio), May 30, 1946.

Chady, R. "Army's West Point Is Alive and Well." *Tulare Advance-Register*, June 26, 1971.

Charlton, L. "West Point Graduate Seeking Discharge Over Vietnam Issue." *New York Times*, March 17, 1970.

DePastino, T. "Nixon Announces 'Peace with Honor' and the End of the Vietnam War." Veterans Breakfast Club, January 23, 1973. https://veteransbreakfastclub.org/nixon-announces-peace -with-honor-and-the-end-of-the-vietnam-war/.

Feron, J. "New Cheating Case Erupts at West Point." *New York Times*, April 7, 1976.

Feron, J. "Honor Code at West Point Focus of Renewed Turmoil." *New York Times*, April 16, 1976.

Feron, J. "West Point Easing Procedures in Administering Honor Code." *New York Times*, May 23, 1976.

Feron, J. "West Point Sued Over Honor Code." *New York Times*, June 2, 1976.

Feron, J. "Cadets at West Point Will Assume Full Responsibility for Honor Code." *New York Times*, November 11, 1976.

Hemphill, P. "Kris Kristofferson Is the New Nashville Sound." *New York Times*, December 6, 1970.

Hersh, S.M. "Two Ousted Teachers Say Air Force Stifles Academic Freedom." *New York Times*, July 16, 1974.

Hersh, S.M. "The Scene of the Crime." *The New Yorker*, March 23, 2015.

Kaiser, C. "Borman Son Denies Bribe at West Point." *New York Times*, September 10, 1976.

Kilgannon, C. "The Point, Front and Center." *New York Times*, November 25, 2001.

Macaulay, A. "'An Oasis of Order': The Citadel, the 1960s, and the Vietnam Antiwar Movement." *Southern Cultures* 11, no. 3 (2005): 35–61. http://www.jstor.org/stable/26390819.

McArthur, G. "'Screaming Eagles' 372 Days in Combat." *Springfield Leader and Press*, January 29, 1967.

Murphey, D.D. "Kent State Revisited." *Journal of Social, Political and Economic Studies* 18 (Summer 1993).

Novelly, T. "Air Force Academy Investigating Nearly 100 Cadets for Cheating, Honor Code Violations." Military.com, February 28, 2025. https://www.military.com/daily-news/2025/02/28 /nearly-100-air-force-academy-cadets-investigated-honor-code-violations-cheating-tests.html.

Pomerantz, A.L., S. Foster, and K. Bell. "Invincible Honor: Masculine Honor, Perceived Invulnerability, and Risky Decision-Making." *Current Psychology* 43, no. 6 (2023): 5282–90. https://doi.org /10.1007/s12144-023-04722-x.

Robinson, D. "Agnew Salutes West Point Class." *New York Times*, June 4, 1970.

Robinson, D. "Army Drops Charges Against General Accused of Killing 6 South Vietnamese Civilians." *New York Times*, December 10, 1971.

Ronan, T.P. "Downey Says West Point's Board of Visitors 'Operated in a Vacuum' in Cheating Scandal." *New York Times*, July 6, 1977.

Rose, M.T. "A Prayer for Relief: The Constitutional Infirmities of the Military Academies' Conduct, Honor and Ethics Systems." JD thesis, NYU Law School, 1973.

Rose, M.T., and D.A. Peppers. "Military Cover-Ups Extend to Academies." *Columbian* (Vancouver, Washington), June 27, 1974.

Salpukas, A. "Judge Acquits Guardsmen in Slayings at Kent State." *New York Times*, November 9, 1974.

Sheehan, N. "Lieutenant Accuses Two Generals of War Crimes." *New York Times*, February 22, 1971.

Sterba, J.P. "Air Force Academy Concedes Injuries at Mock P.O.W. Camp." *New York Times*, July 1, 1973.

"Students: Scandal in Colorado Springs." *Time*, March 3, 1967.

Turse, N. "The Vietnam War Is Still Killing People, 50 Years Later." *The Intercept*, April 30, 2025.

"Was My Lai Just One of Many Massacres in Vietnam War?" BBC News, August 28, 2013. https://www.bbc.com/news/world-asia-23427726.

"West Point Cheating Informer Among 98 Invited to Return." *Independent* (Long Beach, California), May 14, 1977.

Chapter 9

For chapter 9, I interviewed West Point alumni Percy Squire and David Brice, plus other pioneering Black cadets on background. Further, I relied on these sources:

Bryson, D. "Special Report—Two Black Cadets and the Struggle for Diversity at an Elite US Military Institution." Reuters / *US News & World Report*, March 30, 2024. https://www.usnews.com/news/world/articles/2024-03-30/special-report-two-black-cadets-and-the-struggle-for-diversity-at-an-elite-us-military-institution.

Carola, C. "2 NY lawmakers: Strip Robert E. Lee's Name from West Point." Associated Press / *Army Times*, August 17, 2017.

"Cooperate and Live Great." Columbia Surgery, in *West Point Magazine*, Summer 2025.

"Defenders of the West Point Oath" (Video). USMA History & War Studies Department, February 9, 2021. YouTube. https://www.youtube.com/watch?v=2zDTtC7G4WI.

Delaney, P. "U.S. to Study Race Issues Among Troops in Europe." *New York Times*, August 31, 1970.

Downs, D.A. *Cornell '69: Liberalism and the Crisis of the American University.* Cornell University Press, 1999.

Fraser, C.G. "N.A.A.C.P. to Open German Branch." *New York Times*, July 11, 1971.

Grant, T. "Former Cadet Is Indicted in 1992 Citadel Shooting." *Tampa Bay Times*, January 5, 2020.

Hansen, S.D. "The Racial History of the US Military Academies." *Journal of Blacks in Higher Education* 26 (Winter 1999–2000).

Haygood, W. "Citadel of Silence." *Boston Globe*, October 13, 1996.

"Henry Flipper Grave Ceremony with Secretary Lloyd Austin 2017." City of Thomasville, Georgia. (Video). YouTube, February 21, 2025. https://www.youtube.com/watch?v=6woInir0OYM.

Hunt, T. "Black Officer Dismissed in 1882 to Get Pardon." *Herald-Sun* (Durham, North Carolina), February 19, 1999.

"'I'll Bleed for Myself,' Says Black U.S. Soldier in Europe." *New York Times*, October 11, 1970.

Johnson, T.A. "N.A.A.C.P. Plans Inquiry in Germany." *New York Times*, December 19, 1970.

Levin, K. M. "West Point's Robert E. Lee Problem." Civil War Memory, June 5, 2022. https://kevinmlevin.substack.com/p/west-points-robert-e-lee-problem.

McAllister, B. "FBI Solves '92 Shooting at Citadel." *Washington Post*, August 27, 1996.

McManus, R. "Harassment of Women Charged at West Point." *Daily Item* (Port Chester, New York), November 10, 1979.

Meaney, T. "White Power." *London Review of Books*, November 6, 2019.

Oral History: Priscilla "Pat" Locke. n.d. https://westpointcoh.org/interviews/army-strong-exemplified-breaking-barriers-with-the-usma-class-of-1980.

Oral History: Lloyd J. Austin III. n.d. https://www.westpointcoh.org/interviews/perfect-people-living-the-west-point-ideal.

"Remarks at the United States Military Academy Commencement Ceremony in West Point, New York." *The American Presidency Project*, June 1, 1991. https://www.presidency.ucsb.edu/documents/remarks-the-united-states-military-academy-commencement-ceremony-west-point-new-york.

Richard Nixon Foundation. "President Nixon Addresses West Point's Graduating Class of 1971." Richard Nixon Foundation Blog, December 19, 2019. https://www.nixonfoundation.org/2014/05/president-nixon-addresses-west-points-graduating-class-1971/.

Seidule, T. "Black Power Cadets: How African American Students Defeated President Nixon's Confederate Monument and Changed West Point, 1971–1976." *Hudson River Valley Review*, Autumn 2019.

"SLED Enters Probe of Cadet's Shooting at The Citadel." *Greenville News* (Greenville, South Carolina), January 7, 1993.

Tritten, T. "Austin Recounts Childhood Struggles with Racism in University Address Focused on Military Inclusion." Military.com, May 15, 2023. https://www.military.com/daily-news/2023/05/13/austin-recounts-childhood-struggles-racism-university-address-focused-military-inclusion.html.

"West Point Cadets All Under Arrest." *New York Times*, September 26, 1910.

Chapter 10

For chapter 10, I interviewed West Point alumni Pat Locke, Sue Fulton, John Ferrari, Cathy Wells, Cathy Long, Luci Fitzgerald, Susan Spieth, Valerie Coffey, and Kris Fuhr, plus other early female cadets and military school staff whose identities I have pledged to protect. Further, I relied on these sources:

Baker, D.P. "By One Vote VMI Decides to Go Coed." *Washington Post*, September 22, 1996.

"Dead Rats Welcome VMI Women." Associated Press / *Pensacola News Journal*, August 21, 1997.

"ERA Opposed by Rehnquist." Associated Press / *Wisconsin State Journal*, September 10, 1986.

"Former Kempter Cadet Pleads Guilty in Killing." Associated Press / *Springfield News-Leader* (Missouri), July 14, 1987.

Grant, T. "Valley Forge No Longer a Males-Only Military College." *Pittsburgh Post-Gazette*, November 7, 2025.

Hornblower, M. "Draft Signup Proposed." *Washington Post*, February 9, 1980.

Howlett, C. "Westmoreland: West Point's Controversial Graduate." *New York Almanack*, March 17, 2020.

Ismay, J. "The True Story of the First Woman to Finish Special Forces Training." *New York Times*, February 28, 2020.

Kornahrens, K.U. *"Bring Me Men . . ." Brought Women: Marching with the First Female Cadets at the U.S. Air Force Academy*. McFarland, 2023.

McCord, J., and P. Jensen. "Reports of Hazing Leaves Cloud Over Naval Academy." *Baltimore Sun / Seattle Times*, June 3, 1990. https://archive.seattletimes.com/archive/19900603/1075118/reports-of-hazing-leaves-cloud-over-naval-academy.

McCormack, P. "West Point's First Female Cadets Encounter Hostility," *Brownsville Herald* (Texas), May 24, 1977.

"Military Academy Urged for Women." *New York Times*, October 1, 1944.

Oral History: Priscilla "Pat" Locke. n.d. https://www.westpointcoh.org/interviews/army-strong-exemplified-breaking-barriers-with-the-usma-class-of-1980.

"Pride and Excellence: The First Class of Women at West Point." National Museum of the United States Army. n.d. https://www.thenmusa.org/articles/first-class-of-women-at-west-point/.

Reed, D. "Now ACLU Blast VMI Coeducation Proposal." *Anderson Independent Mail* (North Carolina), September 24, 1996.

Schemo, D.J. "Rate of Rape at Academy Is Put at 12% in Survey." *New York Times*, August 29, 2003.

Schmitt, E. "Friends See Secretary as Honorable but Ill-Served." *New York Times*, June 27, 1992.

Shapira, I. "VMI's Male Cadets Were Berating Her: The 1997 Hell Week Photo Went Viral." *Washington Post*, August 18, 2022.

Temp, M., and M. Monteagudo. "Reporting the Tailhook Scandal 30 Years Ago Led to Changes in Military." *San Diego Union-Tribune*, October 29, 2021.

Tolley, L. "Reaction Mixed to Recent Allegation Against A&M Corps." *Standard-Star* (New Rochelle, New York), October 11, 1991.

"West Point Prepares for Women Plebes." *Daily Journal* (Flat River, Missouri), January 16, 1976.

"Westmoreland, William Childs." *South Carolina Encyclopedia*, August 26, 2022. https://www.scencyclopedia.org/sce/entries/westmoreland-william-childs/.

Chapter 11

For chapter 11, I relied on these sources:

Ahern, D., and R. Shenk. *Literature in the Education of the Military Professional*. U.S. Air Force Academy, 1982.

Boog, J. "The Military Toy Industrial Complex." *The Believer* 57 (October 1, 2008).

"Cadets." *The Morning Call* (Allentown, Pennsylvania), January 8, 1982.

Carll, K. "How Tom Cruise Replaced Uncle Sam." *Harvard Political Review*, October 19, 2022. https://harvardpolitics.com/cruise-replaced-sam/#google_vignette.

"Class of 1968 Continues to Rally Around Oliver North." *Baltimore Times*, January 22, 1989.

Dolan, M., and R.E. Meyer. "Friends Recall Fired Aide: North Tended from Start to Go Too Far." *Los Angeles Times*, March 1, 1987.

Farber, M.A. "The Westmoreland and Case: A Broken West Point Tie." *New York Times*, February 24, 1985.

Harris, A. "The Abiding Riddle of Oliver North." *Washington Post*, December 23, 1986.

Hiam, M. "The Uncounted Enemy: A Vietnam Deception (part 1 of 3)" (Video), January 4, 2016. YouTube. https://www.youtube.com/watch?v=PFXTCfY5qME.

Johnston, D. "North Is Angered by Fierce Attack on His Integrity Lead." *New York Times*, April 12, 1989.

Jones, F. "Post-War Truth Telling: The War Managers." War Room—U.S. Army War College, August 2, 2024. https://warroom.armywarcollege.edu/articles/the-war-managers/.

Leonard, J. "A Dropout's Account of Life at West Point." *New York Times*, September 3, 1976.

McCormack, J. "Playing War: Caleb Brennan." *The Baffler*, February 3, 2025.

"MSG Max J. Beilke, USA, retired." 9/11 Pentagon Memorial, October 22, 2024. https://www.pentagon memorial.org/biographies/msg-max-j-beilke-usa-retired/.

"Oliver North Seen as 'a Tremendously Complex Man.'" *Roanoke Times*, October 26, 1994.

Perlstein, R. "The Story Behind the POW/MIA Flag." *Newsweek*, April 13, 2016.

Provan, A. "Interview with Lt. Col. Robert K. Brown, Founder, Editor, and Publisher of Soldier of Fortune." *Magazine Bazaar* 21 (Summer 2010). https://www.bidoun.org/articles/magazine-bazaar -interview-with-lt-col-robert-k-brown-founder-editor-and-publisher-of-soldier-of-fortune.

Scanlan, C. "The Liberation of Tam Minh Pham." *Washington Post*, July 4, 1992.

Schneck, D. "Timothy Hutton: He's Afraid of Those Kids Who Salute Instead of Smile." *The Morning Call* (Allentown, Pennsylvania), December 18, 1981.

"Scout Post Learns Guerrilla Warfare." Associated Press / *San Bernardino County Sun*, November 24, 1980.

Smith, H. "Bui Tin: Soldier Who Fought the French and Americans in Vietnam But Was Exiled by Its Communist Rulers." *Independent*, April 16, 2019.

Stilwell, B. "The Last Combat Soldier to Leave Vietnam Was Killed in the 9/11 Attacks." Military.com, March 28, 2022. https://www.military.com/history/2021/08/31/last-combat-soldier-leave-vietnam -was-killed-9-11-attacks.html#:~:text=On%20March%2029%2C%201973%2C%20Master ,Nhut%20Airport%20left%20as%20agree.

Stilwell, B. "The Tailhook Scandal: How a 'Top Gun Mentality' Led to a Disastrous Navy Conference." Military.com, August 11, 2022. https://www.military.com/history/tailhook-scandal-how-top-gun -mentality-led-disastrous-navy-conference.html.

"Two Planeloads of Flag-Waving POWs Head Home." *Daily Freeman* (Kingston, New York), March 30, 1973.

Urben, H.A. "Civil-Military Relations in a Time of War." PhD in Government dissertation, Georgetown University, Washington, D.C., April 14, 2010.

Webb, J. "Jim Webb: Women Can't Fight." *Washingtonian*, January 3, 2019.

Weinraub, B. "Generals in Survey Assail Vietnam War." *New York Times*, September 25, 1977.

Weinraub, B. "West Point Found Deficient by Study." *New York Times*, September 28, 1977.

Chapter 12

For chapter 12, I interviewed Valley Forge cadet Jesse Holland and former West Point cadet Mark Jones, plus, on background, other cadets who have endured abuse. Further, I relied on these sources:

"Assault Charges Stand Against NJ Cadets." Associated Press / *Daily Journal* (Vineland, New Jersey), October 13, 1993.

"Congress Has No Business Lecturing Others on Ethics." *Baltimore Sun*, September 30, 2021.

Dewar, H. "Frustrated Byrd Hits Back at Reagan." *Washington Post*, July 30, 1987.

Edwards, J. "Many Cadets Enjoy Hazing the Plebes." *Corpus Christi Caller-Times*, April 1, 1988.

Feron, J. "Head of West Point Acts to Stress Academics and End Plebe Abuse." *New York Times*, October 26, 1977.

"Florida's 'Two-Strikes' Law Put Him in Prison for Life. Even His Victim Said It Was Too Harsh." *Frontline*, PBS, April 24, 2025.

Henry, C. "A Firm Stand Against Hazing." *Philadelphia Inquirer*, September 13, 1990.

Henry, C. "Valley Forge Students Accused of Harassment." *Philadelphia Inquirer*, May 3, 1990.

Hill, M. "West Point Orders About-Face on 108-Year Tradition of Hazing Cadets." *Los Angeles Times*, March 9, 2019.

Leff, L. "Panel Wants Military to Study Ethics." *Washington Post*, July 23, 1990.

McCord, J., and P. Jensen. "Reports of Hazing Leaves Cloud Over Naval Academy." *Baltimore Sun*, June 3, 1990. https://archive.seattletimes.com/archive/19900603/1075118/reports-of-hazing-leaves -cloud-over-naval-academy.

"Middies." *News Tribune* (Tacoma, Washington), June 17, 1990.

Miller, L. "Expelled Cadet Tackles Army." *Houston Chronicle*, April 4, 1988.

Murphy, D. "Army Football Program Dropped Motto of White Supremacist Origin." ESPN.com, December 5, 2019.

"Naval Academy Lacked Zeal in Probe of Scandal, Inspector General Says." *Baltimore Sun*, September 29, 2021.

"Officials Knew of Overcharging on Arms to Iran." *Baltimore Evening Sun*, May 5, 1989.

"Report Condemns Hazing at Military Academies." Associated Press / *Fort Worth Star-Telegram*, November 24, 1992. https://www.gao.gov/assets/nsiad-93-36.pdf.

"S.C. Lawmakers Seeking to Amend '87 Hazing Law." Associated Press / *Charlotte Observer*, October 14, 1993.

Schmitt, E. "A Mean Season at Military Colleges." *New York Times*, April 6, 1997.

Sullivan, K. "Good Bad and Ugly." *Washington Post*, December 17, 1991.

Taylor, M., et al. "Stressful Military Training: Endocrine Reactivity, Performance, and Psychological Impact." *Aviation Space and Environmental Medicine* 78, no. 12 (December 2007): 1143–49.

"Valley Forge Cadets Arrested in Hazing." *Times Leader Sun* (Wilkes-Barre, Pennsylvania), April 1, 1990.
Wilson, M. "Navy Plebe." *News Tribune* (Tacoma, Washington), June 17, 1990.
Wilson O'Reilly, M. "Senator Robert Byrd's Legacy." *Commonweal*, June 28, 2010.

Chapter 13

For chapter 13, I interviewed cadets who endured sexualized abuse, including former Valley Forge cadet Ryan Niessner. I also interviewed Naval Academy alumnus Anthony Chiffolo, as well as other queer military school graduates whose identities I have pledged to protect. Further, I relied on these sources:

"A Few Bad Men." *Time*, February 15, 1993.
Baker, K.J. "Butt Plugs and Bitches: The Emails West Point Doesn't Want You to See." *Jezebel*, June 12, 2013.
"Battle Lines Form on Gay Ban." *Miami Herald*, January 29, 1993.
"Bill Clinton's Draft Letter | The Clinton Years." *Frontline*, PBS, November 18, 2015.
Brooks, D. "Huah." *New York Times Book Review*, July 13, 2003.
Buchanan, P. "Culture War Speech: Address to the Republican National Convention." Voices of Democracy, March 23, 2016. https://voicesofdemocracy.umd.edu/buchanan-culture-war-speech-speech-text/.
Christensen, M. "Nunn Takes Gay Hearings Shipboard Today." *Atlanta Constitution*, May 10, 1993.
"Clinton Friend Mixner Among 28 Arrested at White House Protest." Associated Press / *Los Angeles Times*, July 31, 1993.
Davenport C. "Gay Alumni Open a New Chapter." *Washington Post*, November 28, 2004.
Davenport C. "Naval Academy Group Denies Chapter for Gay Alumni." *Washington Post*, December 2, 2004.
Elving, R. "'Don't Ask' Repeal Fulfills Another Clinton Promise." NPR, December 18, 2010.
Fiske, W. "Robb a 'Cheerleader' on Gays-in-Military Policy." *Roanoke Times*, July 18, 1994.
Gabriel, T. "David Mixner, Fierce Fighter for Gay Rights, Is Dead at 77." *New York Times*, March 12, 2024.
"Gay Rights Groups Denounce Nunn." Associated Press / *Quad-City Times* (Davenport, Iowa), December 7, 1992.
Gellman, B. "Clinton Says He'll Consult on Allowing Gays In Military." *Washington Post*, November 13, 1992.
"Goldwater Backs Gay Troops," Associated Press / *New York Times*, June 11, 1993.
Healy, M. "Clinton to Stress Conduct as Key for Gays in Military." *Los Angeles Times*, March 7, 2019.
"History and Traditions of the Herndon Monument Climb." n.d. https://www.usna.edu/PAO/faq_pages/herndon.php.
Isikoff, M. "Gays Mobilizing for Clinton as Rights Become an Issue." *Washington Post*, September 28, 1992.
Karpinski, K.R. "The Iconography of an All-American Icon: Sailors, Homoeroticism, and Mid-Century Queer Cultural Politics." New York City College of Technology, *Journal of American Culture* 45, no. 4 (December 2022).
Kelly, M. "Undeclared Candidate; Perot Shifts on Homosexuals in Military." *New York Times*, July 10, 1992.
"Lifting Gay Ban Hits Emotional Chord." *Los Angeles Times*, November 19, 1992.
Lopez, C.T. "Male Hazing Most Common Type of Sexual Assault, Expert Reveals." U.S. Army, April 18, 2016. https://www.army.mil/article/166188/male_hazing_most_common_type_of_sexual_assault_expert_reveals.
Lowrey, N.S., and Joint History and Research Office. "Repealing Don't Ask, Don't Tell: A Historical Perspective from the Joint Chiefs of Staff." *Special Historical Study 15* (2021). https://www.govinfo.gov/content/pkg/GOVPUB-D5-PURL-gpo223759/pdf/GOVPUB-D5-PURL-gpo223759.pdf.
Meadows, S.O., C. Engel, C. Collins, et al. *2015 Health Related Behaviors Survey: Sexual Orientation, Transgender Identity, and Health Among U.S. Active-Duty Service Members*. RAND, June 21, 2018. https://www.rand.org/pubs/research_briefs/RB9955z6.html.
Miller, A.C. "Gays Are New Willie Horton, Activists Say." *Los Angeles Times*, March 7, 2019.
Mixner, D. *Stranger Among Friends*. Random House, 1997.
"Most Gays Voted for Clinton, Polls Show." *Chicago Tribune*, November 6, 1992.
Newsweek Staff. "Gays and the Military." *Newsweek*, March 13, 2010.
Newsweek Staff. "Homoeroticism in the Ranks." *Newsweek*, March 13, 2010.
"Nunn Opens Hearing on Gays in Military." Associated Press / *Casper Star-Tribune* (Wyoming), July 21, 1993.
Pimentel, F. "The Constitution as Chaperon: President Clinton's Flirtation with Gays in the Military." *Journal of Legislation*, 1994. https://scholarship.law.nd.edu/cgi/viewcontent.cgi?article=1256&context=jleg.

Reidy, D.E., J.P. Smith-Darden, K.S. Cortina, R.M. Kernsmith, and P.D. Kernsmith. "Masculine Discrepancy Stress, Teen Dating Violence, and Sexual Violence Perpetration Among Adolescent Boys." *Journal of Adolescent Health* 56, no. 6 (June 2015): 619–24. doi:10.1016/j.jadohealth.2015.02.009. PMID: 26003576; PMCID: PMC5859556.

Rivera, R. "Naval Academy Warns Off Gay Protest." *Washington Post*, October 19, 2005.

Schmalz, J. "Gay Areas Are Jubilant Over Clinton." *New York Times*, November 5, 1992.

Schmalz, J. "Gay Politics Goes Mainstream." *New York Times Magazine*, October 11, 1992.

Schneider, H. "The Case of the Gay Midshipman." *Washington Post*, November 25, 1989.

Schuyler, A., C. Klemmer, M.R. Mamey, S. Schrager, et al. "Experiences of Sexual Harassment, Stalking, and Sexual Assault During Military Service Among LGBT and Non-LGBT Service Members." *Journal of Traumatic Stress* 33 (June 2020): 257–66.

Shogan, R. "Perot Draws Line on Posts for Gays and Adulterers." *Los Angeles Times*, July 16, 2019.

Sinclair, G.D. "Homosexuality and the Military: A Review of the Literature." *Journal of Homosexuality* 56, no. 6 (2009): 701–18. https://doi.org/10.1080/00918360903054137.

Steelman, Ben. "Crae Pridgen Dead; Made News in Mickey Ratz Case." *Wilmington Star-News*, April 6, 2018.

Steffan, S. *Honor Bound: A Gay American Fights for the Right to Serve His Country.* Villard, 1992.

Strasser, M. "West Point Class of '80 Grad Reflects on First Class of Female Cadets." U.S. Army News Service, May 26, 2010. https://www.army.mil/article/39838/west_point_class_of_80_grad_reflects _on_first_class_of_female_cadets.

Thomma, S. "Undecided and Dissatisfied." *Grand Forks Herald* (North Dakota), August 29, 2004.

"Volunteer Army'll Make It." Associated Press / *Ithaca Journal* (New York), June 6, 1974.

Waters, M. "We Finally Have Data about the Number of LGBT People in the Military." *The Outline*, August 2, 2018.

Webb, J. "Jim Webb: Women Can't Fight." *Washingtonian*, January 3, 2019.

Chapter 14

For chapter 14, I interviewed West Point graduates Erik Edstrom, Dwight Mears, and David Escobar; former West Point TAC officer Riz Shah; former West Point professors John Schmitt and Tim Bakken; and former Defense Secretary Bob Gates, plus other sources whose identities I have pledged to protect. Further, I relied on these sources:

"AAU Announces National Defense Education, Innovation Initiative." Association of American Universities (AAU), January 26, 2006. https://www.aau.edu/newsroom/press-releases/aau-announces -national-defense-education-innovation-initiative.

Abnos, A. "FBI Turns to Colleges." *The GW Hatchet*, September 29, 2005.

Abramowitz, M. "Bush Says U.S. Is Learning from Iraq." Spokesman.com, May 29, 2008.

Air Force Academy High School. n.d. https://www.afahs.org/.

Alvarez, L. "U.S. Army Granting More Waivers for Criminal Backgrounds." *International Herald Tribune*, February 14, 2007.

"Army Recruiting Falls Short for 2nd Month." NBC News, April 5, 2005.

Bicksler, B.A., and L.G. Nolan. "Recruiting and All-Volunteer Force." U.S. Department of Defense (report), December 2009.

Bumiller, E. "Bush Evokes Cold War Fight." *Miami Herald*, May 28, 2006.

"Bush Gives Locker Room Pep Talk for Annual Army-Navy Game" (Video). Associated Press Archive, YouTube, July 21, 2015. https://www.youtube.com/watch?v=t7WRMPTYIkk.

"Cadet Suicides Prompt Change at West Point." CBS News, February 12, 2009.

Cannon, G. "Prison Sentences to End Ex-Cadets' Military Careers." *Times Herald-Record* (Middletown, New York), July 29, 2004.

Chow, K. "Cartoon on Bush Recalls Yale Frat Hazing." *Yale Daily News*, November 10, 2012.

Copp, T. "Recruiting a Generation with No Memory of Sept. 11." *Military Times*, August 19, 2022.

Craven, J. "Hazing, Fighting, Sexual Assaults: How Valley Forge Military Academy Devolved into 'Lord of the Flies.'" *Mother Jones*, April 2022.

Drake, R. "The Crisis of University Research." *The American Scholar*, April 30, 2021.

"Even More Importance on Army-Navy Game Today." Associated Press / *Daily News* (Lebanon, Pennsylvania), December 1, 2001.

Foderaro, L.W. "A Series of Suicides Unnerves West Point." *New York Times*, February 21, 2009.

Foderaro, L.W. "A Village Near West Point Looks for a Break, and a Little Land." *New York Times*, May 31, 2004.

Foderaro, L.W. "For a Bastion of Tradition, A New World; Events of Sept. 11 Altered West Point, Too." *New York Times*, March 16, 2002.

Gibbs, N. "Person of the Year 2003: The American Soldier." *Time*, December 29, 2003.

Golden, D. "After Sept. 11, CIA Becomes a Growing Force on Campus." *Wall Street Journal*, October 4, 2002.

"Harvard Law School Bows to U.S. and Allows Military Recruiters." *New York Times*, August 28, 2002.

Harwood, M. "Air Force Academy Whistleblower Alleges Dog Poisoned in Retaliation." *Truthout*, March 12, 2012.

Hassler, B. "Dr. Henry A. Kissinger Receives Thayer Award." West Point Association of Graduates, January 20, 2023. https://www.westpointaog.org/news/dr-henry-a-kissinger-receives-thayer-award/.

Hedges, C. "Mourning the Warrior, and Questioning the War." *New York Times*, September 22, 2004.

Jacobs, D.T. "A Little-Known Clause Can Be a Killer." *High Country News*, January 24, 2024. https://www.hcn.org/wotr/a-little-known-clause-can-be-a-killer/.

Kifner, J. "After the Attacks: American Airlines Flight 11." *New York Times*, September 13, 2001.

Kilgannon, C. "The Point, Front and Center." *New York Times*, November 25, 2001.

Kissinger, H. "Destroy the Network." *Washington Post*, September 11, 2011.

Left, S. "Iraq War 'Waged on False Intelligence.'" *Guardian*, July 15, 2017.

Lipsky: Absolutely American: Four Years at West Point. AV Club, August 11, 2003. https://www.avclub.com/david-lipsky-absolutely-american-four-years-at-west-p-1798198774.

Maadi, R. "For the Players, It's about Winning." *Morning Sentinel* (Waterville, Maine), December 1, 2001.

McFadden, R.D. "Gen. H. Norman Schwarzkopf, U.S. Commander in Gulf War, Dies at 78." *New York Times*, December 27, 2012.

Merritt, J. "Concern Mounts Over Cadet Suicide Attempts." 5280, January 4, 2005. https:/5280.com/concern-mounts-over-cadet-suicide-attempts/.

"Military Education: Student and Faculty Perceptions of Student Life at the Military Academies." In *Report to the Subcommittee on Defense, Committee on Appropriations, House of Representatives.* U.S. General Accounting Office, 2003. https://apps.dtic.mil/sti/pdfs/AD1176409.pdf.

Mrozowski, J. "Public Military Schools in Plan." *Cincinnati Enquirer*, April 23, 2002.

Munn, M. "Grads Take a Pass on Military." *Los Angeles Times*, March 2, 2019.

Phillips, K. "National Service Corps Bill Clears Senate." *New York Times*, March 23, 2009.

President Bush delivers graduation speech at West Point, June 20, 2002. https://georgewbush-whitehouse.archives.gov/news/releases/2002/06/20020601-3.html.

Revkin, A.C. "After the Attacks: West Point; New Enemy Challenges the Academy's Old Curriculum." *New York Times*, September 15, 2001.

Ricks, T.E. "Best Defense: Picking Fights with West Point." *Foreign Policy Magazine*, April 20, 2009.

"Rumsfeld Extols Lessons of West Point." Associated Press / *Washington Post*, May 29, 2004.

Schmitt, E. "Guard Reports Serious Drop in Enlistment." *New York Times*, December 17, 2004.

Schmitt, E. "U.S. Army Lowers Recruit Standards." *Deseret News*, January 14, 2024.

Stange, J. "Kissinger: War on Terrorism Unlikely to Have a Clear Ending." *Daily Journal* (Flat River, Missouri), December 7, 2001.

"The Campaign to Demilitarize Public Schools." Vietnam Veterans Against the War, n.d. https://www.vvaw.org/veteran/article/?id=3442&print=yes.

Turse, N. "The Military-Academic Complex." TomDispatch.com, April 29, 2004.

U.S. Military Academy Commencement, May 29, 2004. C-SPAN.org.

Van Epps, M. "As a Cadet at West Point During 9/11, Here Is How We Prepared to Defend America." *The Tennessean*, September 15, 2021.

Weidener, S. "Academy Has Molded Men for 75 Years." *Philadelphia Inquirer*, April 6, 2003.

Wendell, B. "At U.S. Military Academies, Eagle Scouts and Former Scouts Are Everywhere." Aaron on Scouting, April 24, 2017. https://blog.scoutingmagazine.org/2017/04/20/scouting-participation-military-academies-unsurprisingly-high/.

"West Point: the Gibraltar of the Hudson." American Battlefield Trust, n.d. https://www.battlefields.org/learn/articles/west-point.

Woodall, M. "Battle Lines Drawn at Elite Academy." Inquirer.com, October 18, 2007.

Wright, S.A. "US Military Academies Make Comeback After a Long Decline." *Boston Globe*, May 12, 2002.

Zehner, H. "The Gaza Protests Were a Mask-Off Moment for American Universities." *The Nation*, May 29, 2024.

Chapter 15

For chapter 15, I interviewed West Point alumnus Noor Merchant and other Muslim former military cadets whose identification I have agreed to protect. Also, former staff at the Afghanistan Military Academy including Scott Hamilton, John Nelson, Bill Schustrom, Nasima Omari, Khan Shinwaray, and Ahmad Shahpoor Askarzada. Further, I relied on these sources:

"Academy Schedules Cadet Training on Saturday Sabbath." Associated Press / *Daily Sentinel* (Grand Junction, Colorado), July 3, 2005.

Ackerman, S. "U.S. Military Taught Officers: Use 'Hiroshima' Tactics for 'Total War' on Islam." *Wired*, May 10, 2012.

Ackerman, S. "West Point Law Professor Who Called for Attacks on 'Islamic Holy Sites' Resigns." *Guardian*, July 14, 2017.

"AFA Superintendent Under Fire for Speaker Choice." CBS News, January 23, 2011.

"Air Force Academy Leader Admits Religious Intolerance at School." Associated Press / *New York Times*, June 4, 2005.

"Air Force Cadets Cite Christian Proselytizing." CBS News, October 29, 2010.

Brady, J. "Air Force Academy Embroiled in Religious Controversy." NPR, June 2, 2005.

Cohen, P. "Pentagon to Consult Academics on Security." *New York Times*, June 18, 2008.

Cooperman, A. "Air Force Eases Rules on Religion: New Guidelines Reflect Evangelicals' Criticism." *Washington Post*, February 9, 2006.

Cooperman, A. "Group Trains Air Force Cadets to Proselytize." *New York Times*, November 11, 2005.

"DoD Now Says It Is Not Funding Yale Special-Ops Center." This Just in | *Yale Alumni Magazine*, February 22, 2013.

Eakin, H. "Iraqi Files in U.S.: Plunder or Rescue?" *New York Times*, July 1, 2008.

Filkins, D. "Regrets Only?" *New York Times*, October 7, 2007.

Fitzgerald, M. "Religious Bias at the Academy." *Colorado Springs Independent*, August 4, 2021.

"Generals Erred by Taking Part in Christian Video: Fund-Raising Video for the Christian Embassy." *The Christian Century*. n.d. https://www.christiancentury.org/article/2007-09/generals-erred-taking -part-christian-video.

Glain, S. "Backward, Christian Soldiers." *The Nation*, February 28, 2011.

Gusterson, H. "Project Minerva and the Militarization of Anthropology." *Radical Teacher* 86 (Winter 2009).

Harwood, M. "Air Force Academy Whistleblower Alleges Dog Poisoned in Retaliation." Truthout.org, March 12, 2012.

Horowitz, I.L. "The Life and Death of Project Camelot." *American Psychologist* 21, no. 5 (1966): 445– 54. https://doi.org/10.1037/h0021152.

"Interviews: Kanan Makiya | Faith and Doubt at Ground Zero." Frontline, PBS, November 18, 2015.

Kilgannon, C. "Muslim Cadets Blend in with a Diverse Corps, but Their Profile Rises." *New York Times*, December 2, 2001.

"Lieutenant General John W. Rosa, USAF, Ret." The Citadel History, July 21, 2022. https://www .citadel.edu/citadel-history/presidents/lieutenant-general-john-w-rosa-usaf-ret/.

Lisee, C. "Debate Reignites Over Religion at Air Force Academy." *Sojourners*, July 17, 2012. https: //sojo.net/articles/debate-reignites-over-religion-air-force-academy.

Loveland, A.C. "The God Squadron." *Religion in the News* 8, no. 2 (Fall 2005).

Maass, P. "A Bulletproof Mind." *New York Times*, November 10, 2002.

MacFarquhar, N. "Speakers at Academy Said to Make False Claims." *New York Times*, February 7, 2008.

Metzler, J. "Air Force Academy Grad Deconstructs a Military Mindset." *Counterpunch*, October 14, 2024.

Price, B. "Project Camelot." In *The SAGE Encyclopedia of War: Social Science Perspectives*, vol. 4. SAGE Publications, 2017, 1395–97.

"Protestant Makeup Could Complicate Reform at Academy." Associated Press / *Fort Collins Coloradoan*, June 27, 2005.

Prupis, N. "Family's Fight Against Air Force Academy Intensifies Over 'Baa Baa Sisterhood Cook- book.'" Truthout.org, December 15, 2010.

Raum, T. "Bush Promises Crusade to Beat World Terrorism." *Berkshire Eagle* (Pittsfield, Massachu- setts), September 17, 2001.

Rodda, C. "A Holiday Letter from the Family of an Air Force Academy Graduate." HuffPost, May 25, 2011.

"Rumsfeld Praises Army General Who Ridicules Islam as 'Satan.'" Reuters / *New York Times*, Octo- ber 17, 2003.

"Skepticism Expressed over AFA Report, Citing Yale Divinity School's Previous Study." The Pluralism Project, June 24, 2005. https://pluralism.org/news/skepticism-expressed-over-afa-report-citing -yale-divinity-schools-previous-study.

Weller, R. "Religious Slurs Rise at Airforce Academy." *The Record* (Hackensack, New Jersey), April 20, 2005.

Chapter 16

For chapter 16, I interviewed former West Point superintendent Robert Caslen and other sources whose identities I have pledged to protect. I further relied on these sources:

Berry, K. "The Symbolic Use of Afghan Women in the War on Terror." *Humboldt Journal of Social Re- lations* 27, no. 2 (2003): 137–60. http://www.jstor.org/stable/23524156.

Bowman, T. "As the Iraq War Ends, Reassessing the U.S. Surge." NPR, December 16, 2011.

Caslen, R.L., Jr., and B.S. Loudon. "Forging a Comprehensive Approach to Counterinsurgency Operations." *PRISM* 2, no. 3 (n.d.).

Chotiner, I. "David Petraeus on American Mistakes in Afghanistan." *The New Yorker*, August 20, 2021.

"COIN Doctrine Under Fire." Military.com, November 28, 2017.

Coll, S. "The General's Dilemma." *The New Yorker*, August 31, 2008.

Cooper, H., D.E. Sanger, and T. Shanker. "Once Wary, Obama Now Relies on Petraeus." *New York Times*, September 16, 2010.

Fisher, C.T. "The Illusion of Progress: CORDS and the Crisis of Modernization in South Vietnam, 1965–1968." *Pacific Historical Review* 75, no. 1 (2006).

"Gen. Petraeus, Mosul's 'King David,' Being Considered for Top US Diplomat Role." Rudaw, November 29, 2016.

Hastings, M. "The Runaway General: The Profile That Brought Down McChrystal." *Rolling Stone*, July 1, 2021.

Hastings, M. "The Sins of General David Petraeus." BuzzFeed News, November 12, 2012.

Hsia, T. "Counterinsurgency—All Things to All Men." *New York Times*, May 21, 2010.

Kaplan, F. "Army to Petraeus: Fix Us!" *Slate*, November 21, 2007.

Knowlton, William A., Jr. "The Surge: General Petraeus and the Turnaround in Iraq." Case Studies, National Defense University, December 1, 2010.

Laub, Z. "The Iraq War." Council on Foreign Relations, December 1, 2022.

Lindsay, J.R. "Irregular Problems and Biased Solutions: Special Operations in Iraq." *Information Technology and Military Power* (Ithaca, NY, Cornell University Press), 2020.

Maass, P. "Professor Nagl's War." *New York Times*, January 11, 2004.

Mastin, L. "Last West Point Mentor at Afghan Academy Flies U.S. Flag." *U.S. Military Academy Public Affairs*, October 11, 2012.

"NY Times Book Review: FM 3-24." *Small Wars Journal* (Arizona State University), September 18, 2024. https://smallwarsjournal.com/2007/07/26/ny-times-book-review-fm-3-24/.

Packer, G. "The Lesson of Tal Afar." *The New Yorker*, April 3, 2006.

Payne, L. "Petraeus Echoes Westmoreland." *Newsday* (Nassau, New York, Edition), September 16, 2007.

Perlez, J. "Petraeus, in Pakistan, Hears Complaints about Missile Strikes." *New York Times*, November 3, 2008.

Philipps, D. "At West Point, Annual Pillow Fight Becomes Weaponized." *New York Times*, September 4, 2015.

"Selling the War, Through Advertising." ABC News, January 8, 2009.

Shanker, T. "The Time Has Come, the General's Here: Petraeus Preps for Testimony on Iraq." *New York Times*, September 8, 2007.

Shorrock, T. "Making COIN." *The Baffler*, May 10, 2017.

Shultz, R.H., Jr., and A.J. Dew. "Counterinsurgency, by the Book." *New York Times*, August 7, 2006.

Stout, D. "Slow Progress Being Made in Iraq, Petraeus Tells Congress." *New York Times*, September 10, 2007.

Swain, J., and J. Watson. "West Point Lieutenants Lack Self-Awareness." The Center for Junior Officers, West Point, June 2, 2021.

Tiernan, T. "Airmen, Soldiers Help Establish Military Academy." AirForce.com, November 2, 2007.

Van Natta, D., Jr. "Big Coffers and a Rising Voice Lift a New Conservative Group." *New York Times*, September 30, 2007.

Vitello, P. "Worried Town Recalls a Young Petraeus." *New York Times*, September 12, 2007.

Vizzard, J.W., and T.A. Capron. "Exporting General Petraeus's Counterinsurgency Doctrine: An Assessment of the Adequacy of Field Manual 3-24 and the U.S. Government's Implementation." *Public Administration Review* 70, no. 3 (2010).

"Westmoreland Urges Support of Vietnam War." *Tampa Tribune*, April 29, 1967.

"West Point Class Told of Importance of Volunteer Army." *New York Times*, June 6, 1974.

Whitlock, C. "McMaster Rebuked by Army in 2015 for His Handling of Sexual Assault Case." *Washington Post*, March 2, 2017.

Chapter 17

For chapter 17, I interviewed Silver Star recipient Leigh Ann Hester, West Point alumnus Sarah Locke, and other female graduates of various military schools, including Valley Forge, whose identities I have pledged to protect. Also, sources close to Defense Secretary Pete Hegseth. Further, I relied on these sources:

Anderson, A., and E. Deutsch. "Stop Assaults on Military Campuses." *New York Times*, May 12, 2015.

Bella, T. "West Point Cadets Overdose on Fentanyl While on Spring Break in South Florida, Police Say." *Washington Post*, March 12, 2022.

Berry, K. "The Symbolic Use of Afghan Women in the War on Terror." *Humboldt Journal of Social Relations* 27, no. 2 (2003).

Bush, G.W. "The President's Address to West Point Graduates." *Richmond Times-Dispatch*, September 13, 2002.

Caldwell, M. "Profiles of Valor: 1SG Leigh Ann Hester (USA)." *Chattanoogan*, April 4, 2025.

Chia, J. "Former West Point Cadet Who Accused Star Football Player of Rape Dropped Out After School's Response: Report." *Daily News* (New York), December 8, 2017.

Ellis, B., and A. Ash. "Academy Revealed Years of Sexual Assault Cover-Ups, But Findings Were Kept Secret." CNN.com, June 30, 2023.

"First Woman Since WWII to Receive Silver Star." Associated Press / *Daily Herald* (Everett, Washington), June 17, 2005.

"Former Air Force Academy Official Alleges Sexual Assault Cover-Ups." CBS News, December 12, 2017.

French, E., and C. Meyn. "Facing Burglary and Assault Charges, Norwich University Football Captain Plays On." VTDigger, November 17, 2019.

Gleeson, S. "Report: Army Used Alcohol, Women to Recruit Football Players." *USA Today*, October 26, 2014.

Hegseth, P. *The War on Warriors: Behind the Betrayal of the Men Who Keep Us Free.* Broadside Books, June 2024.

Horton, A. "Bronze Stars, Like Those Hegseth Earned, Are Common Among Military Officers." *Washington Post*, December 5, 2024.

Jenkins, D.M. "A Life Sentence for a Former Air Force Academy Cadet Who Helped Expose Sexual Assaults at the Academy? We Can't Let That Happen!" HuffPost, December 7, 2017.

Kheel, R. "60 Junior ROTC Instructors Accused of Sexual Misconduct in Past Five Years, Investigation Finds." Military.com, November 16, 2022.

Lamothe, D. "Pete Hegseth's Army Unit in Iraq Was Rocked by a War-Crimes Case." MSN.com, n.d.

Martin, R. "Silver Star Recipient a Reluctant Hero." NPR, February 22, 2011.

Monitz, D., and A. Stone. "Republicans Replace Women-in-Combat Plan." *USA Today*, May 19, 2005.

"Naval Academy Students Charged with Rape." *Fort Collins Coloradoan*, July 11, 2003.

Peralta, E. "Air Force Sexual Assault Prevention Chief Charged with Sexual Battery." NPR, May 6, 2013.

Philipps, D. "Informant Debate Renewed as Air Force Revisits Cadet Misconduct." *New York Times*, August 9, 2014.

Roeder, T. "Report: West Point Football Team Recruited High School Athletes with Booze, Women." *Colorado Springs Gazette*, October 25, 2014.

Schrader, E. "Pentagon Overhauls System for Sexual Assault Reports." *Chicago Tribune*, January 5, 2005.

Sullivan, J. "Woman Breaks Barriers at Valley Forge." *Times Herald-Record* (Middletown, New York), January 8, 2007.

Taylor, D.B. "West Point Cadet's Rape Conviction Is Overturned, Drawing Criticism." *New York Times*, June 9, 2019.

Weller, R. "Air Force Cadets Say Rapes Were Followed by Reprimands." *Courier-Journal* (Louisville, Kentucky), February 17, 2003.

"West Point: Cadet Guilty of Rape." Associated Press / *New York Times*, September 29, 2006.

"Women of Afghanistan." *Time*, December 3, 2001.

"Women Fighting and Dying in War, Despite Combat Exclusion Policy." ABC News, May 30, 2011.

Zadrozny, B., and J. LaPorta. "Cadet Run Out of West Point After Accusing Army's Star Quarterback of Rape." *Daily Beast*, December 8, 2017.

Zadrozny, B., and J. LaPorta. "West Point Let Football Star Break Rules Before Drunk Driving Death, Investigation Found." *Daily Beast*, September 20, 2024.

Chapter 18

For chapter 18, I interviewed former JROTC instructor Peter Mahmood, former West Point cadet Jared Rogers, former Air Force Academy cadet Eric Thomas, retired general Paul Eaton, and other military officials whose identities I have pledged to protect. Further, I relied on these sources:

"A West Point Football Player Got Hooked on Pain Pills. Now He Owes the U.S. $300K." NBC News, November 11, 2020.

Abadi, M. "Trump Won't Stop Saying 'My Generals'—and the Military Community Isn't Happy." *Business Insider*, October 25, 2017.

Aikins, M. "A Green Beret's Confession Outraged the Military. Then He Found an Ally in Trump." *New York Times*, September 30, 2025.

Baez, G., M. Joyner, and J. L. Glusco. "Fort Bragg Soldier's Alleged Plot to 'Physically Remove' Racial Minorities Offers Echoes of Race-Motivated Murders from 1995." WRAL.com, April 27, 2023.

Baker, M., N. Bogel-Burroughs, and I. Marcus. "Thousands of Teens Are Being Pushed into Military's Junior R.O.T.C." *New York Times*, December 11, 2022.

Bender, B., W. Morgan, and D. Lippman. "Trump's 'West Point Mafia' Faces a Loyalty Test." *Politico*, November 17, 2019.

Biesecker, M., J. Bleiberg, and J. LaPorta. "Capitol Rioters Included Highly Trained Ex-Military and Cops." Associated Press, January 15, 2021.

Bleiberg, J., S. B. Morgan, and J. LaPorta. "Army Investigating Officer Who Led Group to Washington Rally." Associated Press, January 11, 2021.

Broadwater, L., M. Haberman, C. Edmondson, and S. Lai. "Jan. 6 Transcripts Detail Failures in Surveillance and National Guard Response." *New York Times*, December 29, 2022.

Carless, W. "Youth Camps Shape New Generations with Patriotism, Push-Ups and Prayer." *Reveal*, June 30, 2021.

Carter, A., D. Cheney, W. Cohen, M. Esper, et al. "All 10 Living Former Defense Secretaries: Involving the Military in Election Disputes Would Cross into Dangerous Territory." *Washington Post*, January 3, 2021.

Cohen, Z., O. Liebermann, and H. Britzky. "Pentagon to Abandon Its Effort to Combat Extremism in the Military." CNN.com, May 20, 2023.

Copp, T. "Austin Carries Close Ties to Fort Bragg with Him as He Rises to Pentagon's Top Post." *McClatchy DC*, January 19, 2021.

Craven, J. "Democrats Are Ignoring One Key Voting Group: Veterans." *New York Times*, October 10, 2018.

Craven, J. "How the Military Turns Troops into Extremists." *The New Republic*, May 11, 2021.

Craven, J. "The Pentagon's Flailing Campaign Against Hate." *The Nation*, November 13, 2020.

Craven, J. "The Police's 'Sheepdog' Problem." *The New Republic*, November 28, 2023.

Dearen, J., M.R. Smith, and A. Kessler. "Takeaways from the Associated Press' Reporting on Extremism in the Military." Associated Press, October 17, 2024.

Demby, G. "When White Extremism Seeps into the Mainstream." NPR, January 15, 2021.

Diaz, J. "West Point Strips Racist Motto from Its Football Team Flag." *New York Times*, December 8, 2019.

"Donald Trump and Theodore Dobias at New York Military Academy (NYMA)." NYMA Videos. YouTube, June 10, 2016.

Donnelly, J. M. "Final NDAA Removes Most House Provisions on Hate Groups." *Roll Call*, December 14, 2022.

Garamone, J. "Austin Orders Immediate Changes to Combat Extremism in Military." *DOD News*, April 9, 2021.

Garamone, J. "Joint Chiefs Stress Service Members' Commitment to Constitution." *DOD News*, January 13, 2021.

Gibbons-Neff, T. "Army Charges Special Forces Soldier in 2010 Killing of Afghan." *New York Times*, December 14, 2018.

Glasser, S.B. "Mike Pompeo, the Secretary of Trump." *The New Yorker*, August 19, 2019.

Groves, S. "If Elected, Trump Plans to Further Test Limits of Military Power at Home." AP News, October 14, 2024.

Grunewald, W., S.S. Kinkel-Ram, and A.R. Smith. "Conformity to Masculine Norms, Masculine Discrepancy Stress, and Changes on Muscle Dysmorphia Symptoms." *Body Image* 40 (2022).

Guyer, J. "The Lucrative Afterlife of a Trump Official." *The American Prospect*, December 1, 2020.

Hertz, N. "You Should Not Be Allowed to Run the Government You Tried to Overthrow." *Politico*, February 21, 2023.

Horowitz, J., and R. Richard Pérez-Peña. "Pompeo Confirms He Listened to Trump's Call to Ukraine President." *New York Times*, October 2, 2019.

Johnson, B. "Trump Was Schooled in the Passion to Lead." *South Jersey Times*, September 13, 2015.

Lutz, E. "Defense Secretary Supposedly Didn't Know He Was Joining Trump's Authoritarian Photo Op." *Vanity Fair*, June 3, 2020.

Martin, M. "Former Pentagon Chief Esper Says Trump Asked about Shooting Protesters." NPR, May 9, 2022.

McCall, H.J. "Rep. Mark Green, the West Point Officer Who Opposed Certifying the Results of a U.S. Election." *Tennessee Lookout*, December 15, 2022.

McKenney, C. "Retired Navy Seal Is Questioned by FBI After Bragging in Video about Involvement in Capitol Riot." *Stars and Stripes*, January 13, 2021.

Musgrave, S., T. Meagher, and G. Dance. "The Pentagon Finally Details Its Weapons-for-Cops Giveaway." The Marshall Project, December 4, 2014.

Musick, M. "Meet the Boy Scouts of the Border Patrol." *The Nation*, January 21, 2020.

Nelson, L. "McMaster Calls Trump's Conversation with Russian Officials 'Wholly Appropriate.'" *Politico*, May 16, 2017.

"Pete Hegseth Had Been Flagged by Fellow Service Member as Possible 'Insider Threat.'" *Politico*, November 15, 2024.

Ryan, M., and D. Lamothe. "Trump Administration to Significantly Expand Military Response in Washington Amid Unrest." *Washington Post*, June 1, 2020.

Schmidt, W.E. "Soldiers Said to Attend Klan-Related Activities." *New York Times*, April 15, 1986.

Schwarz, J. "Josh Hawley Won't Let Go of His Manhood." *The Intercept*, May 14, 2023.

Shapero, J. "Pompeo Says There Was a 'Peaceful Transition of Power' on Jan. 6." *The Hill*, February 2, 2023.

"Shooting Suspect Was on School Rifle Team That Got NRA Grant." Associated Press / *New York Times*, February 16, 2018.

Sonne, P., and M. Ryan. "As He Tackles Extremism, Lloyd Austin Draws on Military's Experience Dealing with 1995 Racially Motivated Murders." *Washington Post*, January 31, 2021.

Spencer, T. "School Shooter Chose Valentine's Day to Ruin It Forever." AP News, October 6, 2022.

Stahl, J. "Trump Just Said His Friends in the Military, Police, and a Biker Group Might Get 'Tough' on Democrats." *Slate*, March 14, 2019.

Starr, B. "Pentagon Extremism Adviser Lays Out Challenge Facing Military After Two Commanders Deny a Problem Exists." CNN.com, April 21, 2021.

Toropin, K. "Researchers Say Military Service Is the 'Single Strongest' Predictor of Violent Extremism." Military.com, June 7, 2023.

Tritten, T. "Oath Keepers Claimed to Be a Veteran Support Group But Is a Dangerous Militia, Former Member Tells Jan. 6 Panel." Military.com, July 12, 2022.

Weichselbaum, S. "Dallas Cops with Military Experience More Likely to Shoot, Study Says." The Marshall Project, October 15, 2018.

Wong, E., and L. Jakes. "Pompeo Quietly Visits Conservative Donors and Political Figures on State Dept. Trips." *New York Times*, May 21, 2020.

Chapter 19

For chapter 19, I interviewed former West Point professor Graham Parsons, former Naval War College professor Pauline Shanks Kaurin, former Air Force Academy professor Brian Johns, and fascism scholar Ruth Ben-Ghiat, plus other military school staff whose identities I have pledged to protect. Further, I relied on these sources:

Babcock-Lumish, T. "The Magic of West Point." *New York Times*, December 4, 2013.

Bologna, G., and L.O. Sanderlin. "Campus Protesters Want Johns Hopkins to Divest. This Lab Is What They Mean." *The Banner*, May 13, 2024.

Bradner, E., and K. Sullivan. "Trump's Former Chief of Staff Says He Fits 'Fascist' Definition and Prefers 'Dictator Approach.'" CNN.com, October 23, 2024.

Cramer, R. "Trump Is 'Fascist to the Core,' Milley Says In Woodward Book." *Washington Post*, October 12, 2024.

Craven, J. "Inside Pete Hegseth's Civilian Purge at West Point." *Politico*, August 28, 2025. https://www.politico.com/news/magazine/2025/08/28/pete-hegseth-civilians-west-point-00523613.

Dunbar, M. "Pete Hegseth Replaces First Woman to Lead US Naval Academy with Marine Corps General." *Guardian*, July 19, 2025.

Forrest, B. "Former Air Force Academy Instructors, Staff Speak Out Against Proposed Civilian Cuts." KOAA News5, May 4, 2025.

Forrest, B. "Sources: Over 50 Civilian Instructors Have Already Left Air Force Academy with No Replacements." KOAA News5, July 1, 2025.

Gedeon, J. "Daniel Penny Will Be JD Vance's Guest at Army-Navy Football Game in Maryland." *Guardian*, June 24, 2025.

Goldberg, J. "James Mattis Denounces Trump as Threat to Constitution." *The Atlantic*, July 18, 2025.

Goldberg, J. "Trump: 'I Need the Kind of Generals That Hitler Had.'" *The Atlantic*, July 16, 2025.

Greenwood, S. "Military Veterans Remain a Republican Group, Backing Trump Over Harris by Wide Margin." Pew Research Center, November 11, 2025.

"Human Cost of Post-9/11 Wars: Direct War Deaths in Major War Zones." Costs of War, Brown University, September 1, 2021.

"Inside Lockheed Martin's Sweeping Recruitment on College Campuses." *In These Times*, August 11, 2022.

Jaffe, G. "A Fight Over a West Point Job Reveals Two Visions of America Under Trump." *New York Times*, August 3, 2025.

Kesling, B. "The Military Recruiting Crisis: Even Veterans Don't Want Their Families to Join." *Wall Street Journal*, June 30, 2023.

Kittle, M. "More Than 200 Retired Admirals and Generals Endorse Trump." *The Federalist*, September 30, 2024.

LaFraniere, S. "Police Report Offers Graphic Details of Sexual Assault Claim Against Hegseth." *New York Times*, November 20, 2024.

Matheson, J. "Naval Academy History Chair Resigns Over Ordered Removal of Symposium Paper." *Baltimore Sun*, June 11, 2025.

Mayer, J. "Pete Hegseth's Secret History." *The New Yorker*, December 2, 2024.

Miron, M. "Fox Commentator Pete Hegseth: 'If You Want Something, Go After It.'" *Press Publications*, March 24, 2015.

Moore, E. "Young Men Swung for Trump in 2024. Democrats Are Working on a Plan to Win Them Back." Oregon Public Broadcasting, June 13, 2025.

Myers, M. "Confidence in Military Continues to Fall After Afghanistan Withdrawal: Survey." *Military Times*, August 18, 2022.

Nichols, T. "A Military-Ethics Professor Resigns in Protest." Yahoo News, June 25, 2025.

Novelly, T. "Applications to Service Academies Plummet Amid Recruitment and Pandemic Woes." Military.com, August 19, 2022.

Parsons, G. "How the Pentagon Made Transgender Rights Disappear." Just Security, April 12, 2019.

Parsons, G. "West Point Is Supposed to Educate, Not Indoctrinate." *New York Times*, May 8, 2025.

Philipps, D. "Meet the Trans Troops the Trump Administration Is Barring." *New York Times*, February 27, 2025.

Sabes, A. "Pete Hegseth Vows to Send Back Harvard University Degree, Writes 'Return to Sender' On Diploma." Fox News, June 20, 2022.

Sadler, B. "Naval Academy's Choice of Anti-Trump Speaker Clearly Violates the Hatch Act." *Heritage Foundation*, n.d.

Ulaby, N. "Scholars Say White Supremacists Chanting 'Deus Vult' Got History Wrong." NPR, September 4, 2017.

Wentling, N. "Convicted Veterans Among Jan. 6 Rioters Granted Pardons, Commutations." *Military Times*, January 21, 2025.

Wolf, Z.B. "24 Former Trump Allies and Aides Who Turned Against Him." CNN.com, October 3, 2023.

Conclusion

For the conclusion, I interviewed former Valley Forge cadet Jordan Schumacher, former Air Force Academy cadet Joy Metzler, and Bill Galvin, the counseling director at the Center on Conscience & War. Also various conscientious objectors and former military school cadets whose identities I have pledged to protect. Further, I relied on these sources:

Cavanaugh, D. "During World War II, America Experimented on Conscientious Objectors." *National Interest Magazine*, December 29, 2020.

"Meet the First (and Only) Conscientious Objector from West Point." Metta Center for Nonviolence, September 7, 2023.

Vitello, P. "Midshipman, Then Pacifist: Rare Victory to Leave Navy." *New York Times*, February 22, 2011.

Wood, S., and E. Arvedlund. "Valley Forge Military Academy Faces Battle for Its Soul Between Entrenched Board and Upstart Alums." Inquirer.com, July 26, 2020.

Index

About the Author

JASPER CRAVEN is a freelance reporter covering the military and veterans' issues. His work has appeared in *The New York Times*, *Harper's Magazine*, *Politico*, and *The Baffler*, among other publications. He is the author of *God Forgives, Brothers Don't*, and he is also the coauthor, with Suzanne Gordon and Steve Early, of the academic book *Our Veterans*. Follow him on X @Jasper_Craven.